THE MYTHIC MIND

BibleWorld
Series Editor: Philip R. Davies, University of Sheffield

BibleWorld shares the fruits of modern (and postmodern) biblical scholarship not only among practitioners and students, but also with anyone interested in what academic study of the Bible means in the twenty-first century. It explores our ever-increasing knowledge and understanding of the social world that produced the biblical texts, but also analyses aspects of the bible's role in the history of our civilization and the many perspectives – not just religious and theological, but also cultural, political and aesthetic – which drive modern biblical scholarship.

Recent and Forthcoming books in the series:
Sodomy: A History of a Christian Biblical Myth
Michael Carden

Yours Faithfully: Virtual Letters from the Bible
Edited by: Philip R. Davies

Israel's History and the History of Israel
Mario Liverani

The Apostle Paul and His Letters
Edwin D. Freed

The Origins of the 'Second' Temple:
Persian Imperial Policy and the Rebuilding of Jerusalem
Diana Edelman

An Introduction to the Bible (Revised edition)
John Rogerson

The Morality of Paul's Converts
Edwin D. Freed

THE MYTHIC MIND

ESSAYS ON COSMOLOGY AND RELIGION IN UGARITIC AND OLD TESTAMENT LITERATURE

NICK WYATT

Routledge
Taylor & Francis Group
LONDON AND NEW YORK

First published 2005 by Equinox, an imprint of Acumen

Published 2014 by Routledge
2 Park Square, Milton Park, Abingdon, Oxon OX14 4RN
711 Third Avenue, New York, NY 10017, USA

Routledge is an imprint of the Taylor & Francis Group, an informa business

British Library Cataloguing-in-Publication Data
A catalogue record for this book is available from the British Library.

Library of Congress Cataloging-in-Publication Data

Wyatt, N. (Nick)
The mythic mind : essays on cosmology and religion in Ugaritic and Old Testament literature / N. Wyatt.
p. cm. -- (BibleWorld)
Includes bibliographical references (p.) and index.
ISBN 1-84553-042-X (hb) -- ISBN 1-84553-043-8 (pb) 1. Bible. O.T.--Criticism, interpretation, etc. 2. Myth in the Old Testament. 3. Biblical cosmology. 4. Ugaritic literature--Relation to the Old Testament. 5. Mythology, Ugaritic. I. Title. II. Bible world (London, England)
BS1183.W93 2005
221.6--dc22
2004021008

ISBN 13: 978-1-84553-042-6 (hbk)
ISBN 13: 978-1-84553-043-3 (pbk)

Typeset by CA Typesetting,

CONTENTS

Preface vii
Acknowledgments ix
Abbreviations x

Chapter 1
THE PROBLEM OF THE 'GOD OF THE FATHERS' 1

Chapter 2
THE DEVELOPMENT OF THE TRADITION IN EXODUS 3 6

Chapter 3
THE SIGNIFICANCE OF THE BURNING BUSH 13

Chapter 4
WHO KILLED THE DRAGON? 18

Chapter 5
SEA AND DESERT: SYMBOLIC GEOGRAPHY
IN WEST SEMITIC RELIGIOUS THOUGHT 38

Chapter 6
SYMBOLS OF EXILE 55

Chapter 7
OF CALVES AND KINGS:
THE CANAANITE DIMENSION IN THE RELIGION OF ISRAEL 72

Chapter 8
THE DARKNESS OF GENESIS 1.2 92

Chapter 9
THE SIGNIFICANCE OF *ṢPN* IN WEST SEMITIC THOUGHT:
A CONTRIBUTION TO THE HISTORY OF A MYTHOLOGICAL MOTIF 102

Chapter 10
THE VOCABULARY AND NEUROLOGY OF ORIENTATION:
THE UGARITIC AND HEBREW EVIDENCE 125

Chapter 11
THE MYTHIC MIND 151

Chapter 12
'WATER, WATER EVERYWHERE...':
MUSINGS ON THE AQUEOUS MYTHS OF THE NEAR EAST 189

Chapter 13
ANDROGYNY IN THE LEVANTINE WORLD 238

Bibliography 256
Index of References 286
Index of Names and Places 295

Preface

The essays reprinted here, with minor adjustments and standardization in presentation, with regard to spelling, the system of reference and a common bibliography, and occasional references to more recent discussion, range from 1978 to 2004.

My first teaching post, in the University of Glasgow, held from 1970 to 1988, with intervals in the Universities of Stirling and Ibadan, required me to teach Israelite Religion and Indian Religion(s). Colleagues working in Religious Studies will be familiar with the required spread. At times these seemed to be two quite distinct and largely unconnected worlds, a perception encouraged by colleagues jealous of encroachments on their territory by others with ideas from outside, and unhappily still all too rife in a political climate which should be encouraging interdisciplinarity, if for no better reason than to demonstrate to our paymasters that it is academic and not financial considerations which should shape the modern university.

Fortunately, I became increasingly convinced that the themes common to both areas indicated that there was room for comparative work, and encouraged a recognition of the deeper cultural ties which already in early historical times connected different parts of the world. So the description of Pangloss' discipline as Métaphysico-théologo-cosmolo-nigo-logie (Voltaire, *Candide*, chapter 1) is not to be taken *here* as a satirical label, but rather as recognition of connections that really do exist. My comparative papers are not reprinted here, but are mentioned in the bibliography as Wyatt 1985c, 1986b, 1988a, 1989 and 1990a. In addition to these, I have also written '*Aśvamedha* and *Puruṣamedha* in Ancient India', *Religion* 19 (1989): 1-11, and 'David's Census and the Tripartite Theory', *VT* 40 (1990): 352-60. The former attests a ritual tradition practised from Ireland to India, while the latter suggests another instance of Indo-European thinking abroad in the ancient Near Eastern world. I have seen no reason to change my views radically with regard to a westward drift of cultural influence, notwithstanding the somewhat inadequate critique by Professor Becking in the pages of *DDD* (first edition, cols. 1631-4 see 1633, 2nd edn, pp. 866-67). The main exception is 1988a, discussed in Wyatt 1998a and superseded in Chapter 12 below.

Acknowledgments

The author acknowledges with gratitude the generosity of the editors of the following periodicals and publishing houses for permission to reprint various chapters, as follows:

Aula Orientalis, Chapter 4;
Scandinavian Journal of the Old Testament, Chapters 7 and 11;
Svensk Exegetisk Årsbok, Chapter 6;
Ugarit-Forschungen, Chapter 5;
Vetus Testamentum, Chapters 3 and 8;
Zeitschrift für die Alttestamentliche Wissenschaft, Chapters 1 and 2;
CSIC, Madrid, Chapter 12.
Ugarit-Verlag, Münster, Chapters 9 and 10.

ABBREVIATIONS: PERIODICALS, SERIES AND REFERENCE BOOKS

AA	*American Anthropologist*
AASOR	Annual of the American Schools of Oriental Research
ÄAT	Ägypten und Altes Testament
AB	Anchor Bible
AB	*Animal Behaviour*
ABD	David Noel Freedman (ed.), *The Anchor Bible Dictionary* (New York: Doubleday, 1992)
AJBA	*Australian Journal of Biblical Archaeology*
AION	*Annali dell'istituto orientale di Napoli*
AJSL	*American Journal of Semitic Languages and Literatures*
AKM	*Abhandlungen für die Kunde des Morgenlandes*
AL	*Anthropological Linguistics*
ALASP	Abhandlungen zur Literatur Alt-Syrien-Palästinas
ALUOS	*Annual of the Leeds University Oriental Society*
AnBib	Analecta Biblica
ANEP	James B. Pritchard (ed.), *Ancient Near East in Pictures Relating to the Old Testament* (Princeton: Princeton University Press, 1954)
ANET	James B. Pritchard (ed.), *Ancient Near Eastern Texts Relating to the Old Testament* (Princeton: Princeton University Press, 1950)
AnOr	Analecta Orientalia
AOAT	Alter Orient und Altes Testament
AP	*Archaeologia Polski*
ArOr	*Archiv Orientálni*
ARW	*Archiv für Religionswissenschaft*
ATD	Das Alte Testament Deutsch
AUS	American University Studies
BA	*Biblical Archaeologist*
BAH	Bibliothèque Archéologique et Historique
BAR	*Biblical Archaeology Review*
BASOR	*Bulletin of the American Schools of Oriental Research*
BBS	*Behavioral and Brain Sciences*
BDB	Brown, Driver and Briggs
BH^3	R. Kittel (ed.), *Biblia Hebraica* (3rd edn)
BHS	*Biblia Hebraica Stuttgartensia*
BiOr	*Bibliotheca Orientalia*
BKAT	Biblische Kommentar zum Alten Testament
BRA	Beiträge zur Religionsgeschichte des Altertums

BVSAWL	Berichte über die Verhandlung der Sächsischen Akademie der Wissenschaften zu Leipzig
BWANT	Beiträge zur Wissenschaft vom Alten und Neuen Testament
BO	Biblica et Orientalia
BS	The Biblical Seminar
BZAW	Beihefte zur *Zeitschrift für die Alttestamentliche Wissenschaft*
BZNW	Beihefte zur *ZNW*
CA	*Current Anthropology*
CAD	*The Assyrian Dictionary of the Oriental Institute of the University of Chicago* (ed. I.J. Gelb *et al.*; Chicago: Oriental Institute, 1964–)
CAH	*Cambridge Ancient History (*vols. I.1, I.2, II.1 and II.2; ed. I.E.S Edwards *et al.*; London: Cambridge University Press, 3rd edn, 1970-75).
CBQ	*Catholic Biblical Quarterly*
CIS	Copenhagen International Seminar
CS	*The Context of Scripture* (3 vols.; ed. W.W. Hallo; Leiden: Brill, 1996-2002)
CSRT	Cambridge Studies in Religious Traditions
CTA	A. Herdner (ed.), *Corpus des tablettes en cunéiformes alphabétiques découvertes à Ras Shamra–Ugarit de 1929 à 1939* (2 vols.; BAH, 79; MRS, 10; Paris: Imprimerie nationale Geuthner, 1963)
CW	*Christentum und Wissenschaft*
DDD	*Dictionary Deities and Demons in the Bible* (ed. K. van der Toorn *et al.*, Leiden: E.J. Brill 1995, 2nd edn, 1999)
EI	*Eretz Israel*
EJ	*Encyclopaedia Judaica*
ERTR/SWC	*Edinburgh Review of Theology and Religion/Studies in World Christianity*
FAT	Forschungen zum Alten Testament
FuF	*Forschungen und Fortschritte*
GK	Gesenius Kautsch
HALOT	*Hebrew and Aramaic Lexicon of the Old Testament* (5 vols.; ed. L. Koehler and W. Baumgartner; Leiden: E.J. Brill, 1994-2000; ET by M.E.J. Richardson)
HAR	*Hebrew Annual Review*
HdO	Handbuch der Orientalistik
HR	*History of Religions*
HSM	Harvard Semitic Monographs
HTR	*Harvard Theological Review*
HUCA	*Hebrew Union College Annual*
ICC	International Critical Commentary
IEJ	*Israel Exploration Journal*
JANES	*Journal of Ancient Near Eastern Studies*
JAOS	*Journal of the American Oriental Society*
JB	*Jerusalem Bible*

JBL	*Journal of Biblical Literature*
JBR	*Journal of Bible and Religion*
JCS	*Journal of Cuneiform Studies*
JEA	*Journal of Egyptian Archaeology*
JJS	*Journal of Jewish Studies*
JNES	*Journal of Near Eastern Studies*
JNSL	*Journal of Northwest Semitic Languages*
JPOS	*Journal of the Palestine Oriental Society*
JQR	*Jewish Quarterly Review*
JRAI	*Journal of the Royal Anthropological Institute*
JSOTSup	*Journal for the Study of the Old Testament*, Supplement Series
JSS	*Journal of Semitic Studies*
JSSMS	*Journal of Semitic Studies,* Monograph Series
KTU	Keilalphabetische Texte aus Ugarit
LAPO	*Littératures de l'Ancien Proche Orient*
LCL	Loeb Classical Library
LSJ	H.G. Liddell, Robert Scott and H. Stuart Jones, *Greek–English Lexicon* (Oxford: Clarendon Press, 9th edn, 1968)
LUÅ	Lunds Universitets Årsskrift
MARI	*Mari: Annales des Recherches Interdisciplinaires*
MCAAS	Memoirs of the Connecticut Academy of Arts and Sciences
MRS	Mission de Ras Shamra
NCB	New Century Bible
NEB	*New English Bible*
NW	*New World*
OBO	Orbis Biblicus Et Orientalis
OECT	*Oxford Editions of Cuneiform Texts*
OLP	*Orientalia Lovaniensia Periodica*
OTL	Old Testament Library
OTP	*Old Testament Pseudepigrapha* (Charlesworth)
OTS	*Oudtestamentische Studiën*
QD	Quaestiones Disputatae
PEQ	*Palestine Exploration Quarterly*
PGM	K. Preisendanz (ed.), *Papyri Graecae Magicae*
PJ	*Preussische Jahrbücher*
RB	*Revue biblique*
RHR	*Revue de l'histoire des religions*
RP	*Revue Philiosophique*
RSF	*Revista dei Studi Fenici*
RSPT	*Revue des Sciences Philosophiques et Théologiques*
RSR	*Revue des Sciences Religieuses*
RTU	Wyatt 1998c, 2002a
SAACT	State Archives of Assyria Cuneiform Texts
SBLDS	Society of Biblical Literature Dissertation Series
SBE	Sacred Books of the East
SBT	Studies in biblical theology

SEÅ	*Svensk exegetisk årsbok*
SEL	*Studi Epigrafici e Luinguistici*
SFSHJ	South Florida Studies in the History of Judaism
SJOT	*Scandinavian Journal of the Old Testament*
SJRS	*Scottish Journal of Religious Studies*
SLBWAW	Society of Biblical Literature, Writings from the Ancient World
SMSR	*Studi e Materiali di Storia delle Religioni*
SR	*Studies in Religion/Sciences religieuses*
SS	Studi Semitici
ST	*Studia Theologica*
STS	Semitic Texts and Studies
SVT	Supplements to *Vetus Testamentum*
TGUOS	*Transactions of the Glasgow University Oriental Society*
TLS	*Times Literary Supplement*
TS	*Theological Studies*
UBL	Ugaritisch-Biblische Literatur
UCOP	University of Cambridge Oriental Publications
UF	*Ugarit-Forschungen*
UUÅ	*Uppsala Universitets Årskrift*
VKAWA	Verhandelingen der Koniklijke Akademie van Wetenschappen te Amsterdam, Afdeeling Letterkunde
VT	*Vetus Testamentum*
WA	*World Archaeology*
WBC	Word Biblical Commentary
WMANT	Wissenschaftliche Monographien zum Alten und Neuen Testament
ZÄS	*Zeitschrift für die Ägyptische Sprache*
ZAW	*Zeitschrift für die Alttestamentliche Wissenschaft*
ZDMG	*Zeitschrift für die Morgenländische Gesellschaft*
ZDPV	*Zeitschrift des deutschen Palästina-Vereins*
ZNW	*Zeitschrift für die Neutestamentliche Wissenschaft*
ZTK	*Zeitschrift für Theologie und Kirche*

Abbreviations: General

BCE	Before the Common Era
BD	Book of the Dead
BM	British Museum (catalogue entry prefix)
BP	Before Present (baseline 1950)
CE	Common Era
D	Pentateuchal source associated primarily with the book of Deuteronomy. Odd phrases throughout the rest of the Pentateuch supposedly betray its influence.
E	'Elohist': Pentateuchal source, distinguished from P (q.v.), associated primarily with the use of the term *'elōhîm* ('God') of the deity, particularly in Genesis.

EA	El Amarna (siglum for texts)
EV(V)	English version(s) (this is where English and Hebrew verse numberings do not match)
J	'Yahwist': Pentateuchal source, distinguished from E and P (q.v.), associated primarily with the use fo the term *yhwh* ('Yahweh', German 'Jahwe') of the deity, particularly in Genesis.
LXX	Septuagint
MT	Masoretic Text
OB	Old Babylonian
P	'Priestly (writer)': Pentateuchal source, distinguished from E and J (q.v.), and by its predominantly priestly concerns and formal style.
P.	Papyrus
RS	Ras Shamra (siglum for texts)
Sam.	Samaritan Pentateuch
Syr.	Syriac
TN	Toponym
Vg.	Vulgate
WS	West Semitic

Chapter 1

THE PROBLEM OF THE 'GOD OF THE FATHERS'*

The significance of the formula 'the god of my father(s)' and variants, which was the subject of A. Alt's important monograph,[1] has been discussed intermittently since, but without the problems involved having been resolved entirely satisfactorily. In what follows, I wish to offer a new explanation for the problems, which is consistent with current scholarly estimates of the other evidence in Genesis concerning 'patriarchal religion'.

A. Alt was writing before the discovery of the Ugaritic texts had led to a complete reappraisal of the nature of the god El, and was able, in the fashion of the time, to dismiss the various El-forms found in Genesis as local *numina*.[2] The 'god of the fathers', however, was felt to point to the distinctive feature in patriarchal religion, the cult of a god revealing himself to the cult-founder and being worshipped by subsequent generations conscious of their historical link with the founder.

J. Lewy suggested that the apparently anonymous 'god of the fathers' could be identified with El Shaddai, on the basis of Genesis 49.25, where *'ēl 'ᵃbîkâ* and *šadday* are parallel.[3] However, his interpretation involved understanding the *'ēl* in the former phrase as a generic in the construct (i.e. the equivalent of the prose form *'ᵉlōhê*), and required the alteration of the *'et* preceding *šadday* into *'ēl*.[4] The former suggestion begs the question concerning the generic use of *'ēl*, while the latter seems unnecessary. If the two particles *m* and *'et* are understood to have an instrumental force, then the text of MT yields a perfectly good sense:

> By (*m*) El your father, may he assist you!
> and by (*'et*) Shaddai, may he bless you![5]

There is no reason not to take *'ēl* here as being the divine name El, and the two forms *'ēl* and *šadday* seem to be a good example of a divided binomial form, such as is found in Job 15.25, 21.14-15 and so on.[6] If this interpretation of Genesis 49.25 can be sustained there is no reference here after all to the 'god of your fathers', and the consequent identification of this deity with El Shaddai cannot be demonstrated on this evidence.

H.G. May drew attention to the distinction between the singular expression 'the god of my (your etc.) father' (*'ābî-*, *'ªbî-*) and the plural 'the god of my (your etc.) fathers' (*'ªbôtê*).[7] The latter expression was, he argued, a later formulation, and he pointed out that it was used predominantly in exilic or post-exilic passages (by the Deuteronomist, 11 times; by the Chronicler, 29 times; in Daniel, once). It is clear from the usage in these passages, where the name Yahweh is usually also present, that it is the ancestral faith of Israel that is in question: in 21 out of 28 cases it is a matter of faithfulness to or apostasy from the traditions of the covenant people. So there is no question of an allusion to the patriarchs. There are four passages which are apparently early where the formula is found – in Exodus 3.13 (E), 15 (E), 16 (J), and 4.5 (J). H.G. May suggested that there may be late editing here, and certainly the formula is suspicious.[8] In the E passages it is a deliberate use, intended to indicate the continuity between past and present[9] despite the change in the divine name. It reflects the theological presuppositions of the writer(s) of E, rather than those of Moses and his time. In the J tradition of course we already have the presupposed continuity in the use of the divine name, and here Yahweh comes to rescue 'his' people (Exodus 3.7, cf. 'the sons of Israel', 3.9 E), so that the 'fathers' of the formula need not be the three patriarchs Abraham, Isaac, and Jacob, but simply the ancestors in general of the enslaved Hebrews. The addition of the three patriarchal names in both passages is artificial and clearly secondary.[10]

It is the singular expression, 'the god of your father', which H.G. May argued is much more significant for our present purposes. It occurs only infrequently in passages normally ascribed to J. It is found at Genesis 26.24 and 28.13, where the name 'Abraham' has been added;[11] 31.53a is allocated by A. Alt to J,[12] but in any case *'ᵉlōhê 'ªbîhem* is patently a gloss designed to solve the problem of the implied polytheism; 43.23 presents a textual problem – two manuscripts, supported by Sam. and LXX, read *'ªbôtêkem* for *'ªbîkem*,[13] and apart from the more awkward (plural) reading being preferable, the entire phrase should be treated as a gloss on the preceding *'ᵉlōhêkem*. The last example is in Genesis 49.25, taken by A. Alt to be J,[14] but apart from the literary complexity of the chapter anyway, we have seen that the formula does not in fact occur here.

Contrasting with the rarity of its use in J, in each case not without suspicion, the formula occurs several times in E. Its use is straightforward in 31.5. 29 (*'ªbîkem* MT, *'ªbîkâ* Sam., LXX). 31.42, 32.10 (*bis*), 46.1, 50.17, Exodus 3.6. In Genesis 31.53a (if E), we have seen it to be secondary, and in 31.53b it may be abbreviated or mutilated in the reading *bᵉpaḥad 'ābîw yiṣḥaq*. We have seen that in 49.25, if the verse is to be assigned to E (see n. 14) there is in fact no case to be made. Now this passage does not stand alone and may give a clue to the significance of the curious usage to be found in 46.3, the clarification of which may provide an explanation for the whole construction. In 46.3 we read *'ānōkî hā'ēl 'elōhê 'ābîkā*. This is an unusual expression, and it looks as though there may have been at some stage an expansion of the text. The term which E uses fairly consistently for God is *'elōhîm*. There is an artificial, literary flavour to its use. Frequently it occurs where we would expect a divine name to appear. It is as though an editor of the tradition has at some stage deliberately tried to suppress all references to a particular divine name. Occasionally this leads to a rather forced situation. In the snatch of poetry quoted in Genesis 27.28, for example, we have the exhortation:

> May Elohim give you dew from heaven...

A specific divine name would appear so much more natural here than the colourless *'elōhîm*. Also, in 28.17, 22, where the narrative clearly locates Jacob at Bethel (cf. J, and 35.21ff., E) we have the curious expression *bêt-'elōhîm*, where *bêt-'ēl* would have been so much more plausible, and I suspect was originally the term used.

This example gives us our clue – *'elōhîm* has apparently, with a greater or lesser rigour, displaced *'ēl* in the E source of Genesis. Further evidence can be adduced to support this conjecture. In 32.31, for example, we read that Jacob named the place Peniel (*penî'ēl*) 'because I have seen God face to face' (*kî-rā'îtî 'elōhîm pānîm 'el-pānîm*). Why has the writer not simply used *'ēl*, as the whole explanation being offered for the name really demanded? Somehow or other, he appears to have a strong aversion to the term. At other times he is confronted with theophanies of the deity at Bethel, and here we have the formula *hā'ēl bêt-'ēl* (31.13, cf. 35.1, 3 *lā'ēl* – note the pointing). In view of the normal usage of E, we would expect *'elōhê* (or *hā'elōhîm* if one wishes to take *bêt-'ēl* as a divine name). In any case, *'ēl* is not a normal prose usage for the generic sense of the term. It seems possible, therefore, that the article has been added in an attempt to destroy the titular use of the term here, altering its sense from 'El' to 'the god (of)...'

If we now turn to 46.3 we find this use of the article again: *'ānōkî hā'ēl*. This time however, because the context allows it, which it does not in the other cases, the writer has made quite sure that there will be no misunderstanding by adding *'elōhê 'ābîkā*. Some commentators have argued that the *hā'ēl* here is a secondary insertion. But if my reading of the situation is correct, this is hardly likely. Did the tradition which I am arguing has been deliberately modified read originally just 'I am El' or something more? I suggest that the construct form *'elōhê* is also a part of the editorial expansion, so that the underlying formula before modification would have read *'ānōkî 'ēl 'ābîka* – 'I am El your father'. This is the formula which we have found to be present in Genesis 49.25, and we have in such language an ancient expression of the intimate relationship felt to exist between El and his worshippers, and in particular of course between El and a tribal eponym.

The development of the tradition may be argued to have been roughly as follows: an archaic phrase, by which was indicated the relationship of physical paternity, or at any rate of intimacy, between the deity El and tribal eponyms, was felt to be offensive by the tradents of the B material. They therefore neutralized the phrase and all the references to El, by reading *'elōhîm*, or by putting an article before *'ēl*. This also led – perhaps quite incidentally – to the emphasizing of the theme of continuity, so that * *'elōhîm 'ābî...* became fixed as *'elōhê 'ābî...* The J writer, for whom it was clearly not a standard expression, adopted it (Rje, or 'late J') and in the long run it came to be understood as no more than an archaizing equivalent of the late expression *'elōhê 'ābôtê...* Its continued use in the singular was justified by the individual character of the patriarchal narratives: national 'prehistory' is presented in terms of individual 'biographies'.

It seems to me that if the material is analysed on the lines suggested, then a certain amount of confirmation may be found on internal grounds. For example, there is no consistency in the use of the expression 'the god of my father'. In 31.4-9, Jacob speaks firstly of 'the god of my father' (v. 5) but subsequently of 'God' (*'elōhîm*) in vv. 8-9. On any view which insists that there is something distinctive about the former usage, how is the change to be explained? If my interpretation is followed, then El is referred to in all three cases, in the first case with the additional statement of his relationship to Jacob ('my father'). There is no inconsistency, however, in the omission of this word from vv. 8-9.

It may be objected that the external evidence cited by scholars proves the existence of 'gods of the father(s)' of various identities, and that therefore it is probable, or at least possible, that they were found among the patriarchal forebears of Israel and Judah. The first part of this is reasonable, but not the inference which follows. The historical nature of the patriarchal traditions would be required to be established firstly, and recent studies on the problems involved in this matter would seem to point to the monarchy and even in some cases the time of the exile as the most likely background to and point of reference of the traditions.[15] If this is the case, then the religious context of the traditions is also most reasonably to be seen as that of the monarchy and later, rather than being any kind of authentic historical memory of an earlier period.

There remains the question of the reason for the apparent antipathy to the cult of El in the E tradition, since both J and P are not at all averse to identifying Yahweh with various hypostases of El. That is a problem for a further study.

Endnotes

* First published in *ZAW* 90 (1978): 101-104.

1. Alt 1929; ET 1966. References are to the ET.

2. Alt 1966: 8-9. Cf. Oesterley and Robinson 1930: 118; Lods 1932: 124-25; Loehr 1936: 20ff.; Meek 1950[2]: 85.

3. Lewy 1934: 55.

4. Also suggested in BH[3] appar.

5. On the rendering 'El your father' rather than 'the god of your father', see below. The jussives suit the context better than the imperfects of most interpretations.

6. Cf. Dahood 1965-70: iii, xxxix-xli.

7. May 1941.

8. See Chapter 2 for further reasons for a late date for these verses.

9. Cf. the priestly treatment of the same question, Exodus 6.2-3.

10. Cf. May 1941: 155; Lewy 1934: 54; Dougherty 1955: 151.

11. See K.T. Anderson 1962.

12. Alt 1966: 17, nn. 43, 44.

13. BH[3] appar.

14. Alt 1966: 20. See also Skinner 1910: 512. Contrast von Rad 1963: 447; Hooke 1962: 176.

15. See for example the following studies: Winnett 1965; Tucker 1966; Mazar 1969; van Seters 1972a; *idem*, 1972b; *idem*, 1975; Thompson 1974.

Chapter 2

THE DEVELOPMENT OF THE TRADITION IN EXODUS 3*

The narrative in Exodus 3 is normally divided by scholars among the sources J and E, with the allocation of the verses as follows: to E, vv. 1, 4b, 6, 9-15, 19-22; to J, vv. 2, 3, 4ac, 5, 7, 8, 16-18. I see no reason to quarrel with this basic division, though I hope to show in the following pages that there is every reason to reject the commonly held assumption that we have in the text thus divided a ninth or eighth century version of the tradition (E), and a tenth century version (J) respectively. Since the passage is clearly a central one in the matter of the origins of the Israelite cult of Yahweh, our conclusions, if they can be sustained, will be seen to have far-reaching conclusions for Old Testament studies.

1. *The E Tradition*

The lack of homogeneity in the E version has been widely acknowledged. M. Noth drew attention to the reference to Horeb in v. 1, and to 'the middle of the bush' in v. 4b, and suggested that these were added by Rje.[1] Most attention has been paid however to vv. 13-15, where it has been noted that there must have been a succession of expansions to an older form of the tradition, since Moses' question in v. 13 elicits no less than three responses (vv. 14a, 14b, 15), each of which could stand on its own. But there is no unanimity regarding the explanation of the process of expansion that is supposed to have occurred. D.M.G. Stalker, for example, takes vv. 13, 14 to be part of the original E tradition, with v. 15 a later expansion by Rje.[2] According to this interpretation the problematic v. 14 is part of the original tradition concerning the revelation and meaning of the divine name. This is not, of course, impossible, and accords with the view that takes Moses to be the 'founder' in some sense at least of the cult of Yahweh in Israel. Thus, for those who subscribe to the hiphil explanation of the tetragrammaton, this verse, a key to the theory, is to be regarded as being as old as the first revelation of the name. But even taking the verse as original, it can be argued that it is already dependent upon generations if not centuries of reflection upon both the role of Moses and the revelation and significance of the name.

Other scholars take a different line. Noting that there are three answers to Moses' question, v. 15 is taken to be the original, straightforward answer to the question. Within v. 15 the expression 'the god of your fathers, the god of Abraham, the god of Isaac and the god of Jacob' is recognized to be a later expansion. More importantly, v. 14 is regarded as secondary, being perhaps incorporated in two stages, first 14a, and later 14b.[3] J. Morgenstern thinks that while the verse is secondary, it is still due to the Elohist writer; G. Fohrer says that it is impossible to tell whether the addition (in two stages) goes back to E or is to be attributed to a later hand, while J.P. Hyatt dates v. 14a to the seventh or sixth century, with 14b a little later.

J.P. Hyatt's rather late dating could be defended on the grounds that the kind of theological idea underlying v. 14a is unparalleled in any pre-exilic literature, and yet admirably fits the period of the exile, when the message of the statement would be both particularly relevant and also consonant with the teaching of Deutero-Isaiah.[4] Certainly, if the passage is to be understood as having any kind of monotheistic sense, it would be hard to defend an earlier date.[5] If this is reasonable, then not only can the verse hardly be used as evidence for the original meaning of the name or character of Yahweh, but it also ceases to have any serious historical value as evidence of such new ideas as Moses may have contributed to the cult of Yahweh.[6]

But these pruning activities of various kinds, however valuable they may be for the practice of biblical topiary, seem to me to fail to get to the heart of the historical problem involved – that is, what is the oldest form of the tradition before us? An answer to this question is a prerequisite for any serious study of the development of the tradition within the history of Israel.

In the light of recent discussion of the patriarchal problem, it is not unreasonable to take the view that not only the formula in v. 15, but also that in v. 6, is a secondary addition to the text, to be dated to the exilic period, when the diverse strands of the patriarchal traditions were woven together into a genealogical framework.[7] This leaves v. 6 reading as follows:

> 'I am the god of your father' he said. At this Moses covered his face, afraid to look at God.

The expression 'the god of your father' is suspicious here, and particularly when the patriarchal formula is excised. I have argued recently, however, that this expression is itself a deliberate expansion and disguise of the form 'I am El your father'.[8] The use of the term *'elōhîm* in E throughout Genesis and the early part of Exodus can be argued to be a consistent glossing of *'ēl* to read *’^{e}lōhîm*. The reason for this becomes plain in the present chapter of Exodus.

There is a *non-sequitur* in v. 12 as it stands, which does not appear to have been adequately explained. In the verse as we have it, the sign which is promised appears to be the coming of the Israelites to worship at the mountain after their departure from Egypt. This can hardly constitute the sign, but is rather an appropriate conclusion to the whole episode. The sign required is mentioned in v. 20, however, and v. 20 should probably be regarded as having been displaced from following v. 12a. This sequence is supported by Exodus 10.1-2:

> Go to Pharaoh, for it is I who have made his heart and his courtiers stubborn, so that I could work these signs of mine among them; so that you can tell your sons and your grandsons how I made fools of the Egyptians and what signs I performed among them, to let you know that I am Yahweh (JB).

It is evident from this passage that the authenticating sign is Yahweh's mighty acts in Egypt.

If my explanation of v. 6 is tenable, then the whole block of vv. 13-15 becomes superfluous to an original tradition in which El, rather than Yahweh, was involved, and may be regarded as secondary.[9] This appears to be corroborated by the sequence v. 12a, 20 (with 12b probably following, and 19, 21-22 being regarded as part of the final narrative expansion), which leaves no room for Moses' question.

The early form of the E tradition, then, which has been modified by a later writer or writers, may be reconstructed as follows:

1 Moses was looking after the flock of Jethro, his father-in-law, priest of Midian. He led his flock to the far side of the wilderness and came to...[10] the mountain of El.
4b And El called to him from...[11] the mountain.[12]
6 'I am El your father', he said... At this Moses covered his face, afraid to look at El.
9 'And now the cry of the Sons of Israel has come to me, and I have witnessed the way in which the Egyptians oppress them.
10 So come, I send you to Pharaoh to bring the sons of Israel...[13] out of Egypt.'
11 Moses said to El, 'Who am I go to Pharaoh and bring the sons of Israel out of Egypt?'
12a 'I shall be with you' was the answer, 'and this is the sign by which you shall know that it is I who have sent you:
20 I shall show my power and strike Egypt with all the wonders I am going to work there. After this he will let you go.
12b After you have led the people out of Egypt you are to offer worship to El on this mountain.' (JB, modified).

This account presents what was, I suggest, the original kerygma of Israelite religion. K.T. Anderson and M. Noth have both expressed doubts that the original refugees from Egypt were worshippers of Yahweh, and that only later was the god of the exodus identified with or as Yahweh, but unfortunately without elaboration.[14]

Some justification for the identification of the god in question may be felt to be in order. Without wishing to elaborate on this at present, we may note simply that there is a tradition of El as the god of the exodus. It survives explicitly in such passages as Numbers 23.22, 24.8, and Psalm 106.19-22, where to regard *'ēl* as nothing more than a poetic or archaizing allusion to *'ᵉlōhîm* or Yahweh begs the question, and there are other passages too where a case can be made for the tradition being present.

2. *The J Tradition*

The problem I wish to consider briefly here is the matter of dating. On the conventional view of the documentary hypothesis, the J account of the events in Midian antedates the E account, at least in the present state of both accounts. However, while we may conclude in the light of our discussion above that the present form of the E narrative (apart of course from harmonizing glosses) is substantially late, we have been able to recover an older form of E which is quite clearly independent from the J account as we now have it.

There are also features in the J account which point to a late dating. These are as follows: first, the list of the nations in vv. 8, 17, which J. van Seters has argued belongs to a late stage in literary compilation.[15] Second, the plural expression 'the god of your fathers' in v. 16 is a late development from the older formula 'the god of your father'.[16] Third, the list of the three patriarchs in v. 16 is a late formulation, as we have seen above, and fourth, the phraseology of the description of the land in vv. 8, 17 is thoroughly deuteronomistic, that is, belonging to the later strata of Deuteronomy. All of these 'late' features are most satisfactorily to be dated in the exilic period, and the presence of so many 'late' features in this short story, the excision of which would really leave nothing substantial behind, points to the exilic period as the time of composition of the story, as a literary unit.

The J story appears to be in fact a free composition in the time of the exile, inspired by the E tradition but in no way bound by it. This raises an important question of principle in the relation of the pentateuchal sources. If a southern source such as J contains a tradition which is most probably to be seen as originating in the north (such as the exodus and conquest traditions) then it should be taken that all things being equal, northern versions of the tradition antedate rather than postdate the southern versions. Even if no 'local' version of a localized tradition appears to have survived, but we find only an E account of a southern tradition, or a J account of a northern tradition, it should be apparent that the conventional allocation of material to the sources is at least questionable, or at any rate that the process of transmission needs re-examination, with a possible modification of the dating. In the case of the patriarchal narratives, my preliminary enquiries have led me to consider the possibility that Isaac was originally a northern patriarch, in fact the eponym Israel, a name later appropriated by the southern patriarchal figure Jacob, while Abraham is essentially a symbolic invention of the exilic age, presented as the forefather of the other two in the literary structure of Genesis which is intended to present a pan-Israelite synthesis of all the major themes of election, land-tenure and so on, which had suddenly become such vital matters in the sixth century,[17] though elements in this synthesis had hitherto been operative only in certain areas.

If my reconstruction of the E tradition in Exodus 3 is tenable, then it naturally throws into the melting-pot again the question of the origins of Yahwism. There have been those who never took the biblical tradition at its face-value, such as T.J. Meek, and in recent years the theory of the amphictyony has come under severe attack from A.D.H. Mayes and C.H.J. de Geus, leaving little secure basis for a serious belief in any ordered political or cultic life until very shortly before the rise of the monarchy.

The so-called Kenite hypothesis can hardly be regarded as certain either, and with regard to its attempt to explain the rise of Mosaic Yahwism, it must be regarded as being very flimsy, quite apart from the implicit objections raised by what I have said above.

The non-Mosaic aspect of the Kenite tradition, that is the possibility that Genesis 4 hints at an ancient cult of Yahweh among the Kenites, together with the settlement of the Kenites in Judah and the existence of the Judahite traditions of Yahweh's coming from the south, suggests that we should look to the reign of David for the first rise to national importance of the cult of Yahweh, never of course exclusive in the early monarchy. It may be that David imposed the cult of Yahweh upon his northern subjects who were hitherto, and no doubt remained afterwards at heart, devoted to El as their chief god. Only with the rise of the deuteronomic school in the north would the 'kerygma' of Israelite El-worship – that El had rescued his people from Egypt – be seized upon by Yahwists in the north who would naturally insist that it was *their* god Yahweh, and not El, who had performed the mighty acts of the exodus and conquest.

Endnotes

* First published in *ZAW* 91 (1979): 437-42.

1. Noth 1962: 28, 38.

2. Stalker 1962: 211, §178a.

3. See Arnold 1905: 133ff., 162; Morgenstern 1920–21: 256; Bowman 1944: 3; Noth 1962: 43; de Vaux 1971: i, 330; Fohrer 1973: 67; Hyatt 1967: 375.

4. Cf. such passages as Isaiah 40.25-26, 41.4, 42.8, 43.11, 44.6, etc., and the use of the exodus motif as a symbol for the restoration of Israel to the Land of Canaan.

5. For discussion of the problem of the origins of Israelite monotheism, see the useful compendium of E.J. Christen and H.E. Hazelton 1969. See also Barr 1957–58; Snaith 1963–65.

6. The matter of the exegesis of v. 14a does not concern us here. For the range of views see, e.g., Irwin 1939; Dubarle 1951; Schild 1954; Allard 1957; Bourke 1958; Eissfeldt 1965b; Albrektson 1968.

7. The recent studies of Thompson 1974, and van Seters 1975 must at least be acknowledged to have completely opened up the problem of the book of Genesis again. On the dating of the stories, I am inclined to accept late rather than early datings of the stories in their present forms, with none of those involving Abraham in their present form antedating the exile. However, in several cases our final stories show all the signs of extensive reworking of much older traditions. On the artificiality of the patriarchal genealogy, see K.T. Anderson 1962, 177; cf. Holt 1964: 28.

8. Surviving at Genesis 49.25, to be assigned to E. See Chapter 1.

9. On an exilic dating for vv. 13-15 on independent grounds, see van Seters 1972b: 456-57.

10. On the exclusion of Horeb, see above. It should be taken as a deuteronomistic identification of the mountain rather than as Rje.

11. Omitting *tôk* as a harmonizing gloss by Rje; cf. v. 2.

12. See above. An original 'mountain' has been altered to 'bush' to harmonize with the J narrative.

13. Omitting 'my people' as a further gloss by Rje. 'My people' is the phrase characteristic of J (v. 7), since the relationship of Yahweh and his people in J has been long established. In E the relationship is only now being inaugurated.

14. K.T. Anderson 1962: 185; Noth 1960: 136-37. (See also, now, M.S. Smith 2001: 146-48).

15. See van Seters 1972a.

16. See May 1941.

17. A further example of the kind of reassessment that appears to be necessary is found in the narrative of Exodus 7.14-25. In the account of the first plague, in Egypt, the narrative divides fairly readily into three self-contained versions:

(a) vv. 14, 16, 17a, 18, 21a, 24, 25;
(b) vv. 15, 17b, 20b, 28;
(c) vv. 19, 20a, 21b, 22.

There is a progressive heightening of the miraculous element here; in (a), the Nile is befouled; in (b) it turns to blood; in (c) every drop of water in Egypt turns to blood.

Also in (a) Yahweh speaks in order to effect the sign; in (b) Moses uses his magic wand; while in (c) Aaron the aide-de-camp of Moses uses the magic rod. Now on the conventional allocation of the sources here, the stories are respectively J, E, and P. This is in keeping with the usual dating of the sources in descending chronological order.

But this begs the whole question of the nature of the transmission. If the exodus tradition originated as I believe among the northern tribes, how are we to account for its initial recording in the southern document? To say that this must have happened during the united monarchy is not sufficient, for all the cultic allusions to the exodus events give little support to the idea of any ideological cross-fertilization before the exilic period, and certainly not before 721. However, if we reassign (a) to E and (b) to J, then the process of adaptation of the tradition in the light of historical likelihood immediately makes sense, though it requires a reassessment of the dating of J. The northern tradition (a), which in its present form clearly antedates the derivative (b) can confidently be assigned to E, while (b) can be readily explained as a late J adaptation of it, comparable to the late J adaptation of the Exodus 3 narrative. Whether this can be dated with any greater precision than in the period 721 to c. 550 is a matter that will require more detailed analysis. I am inclined to think of a low rather than a high date, since an ever-increasing number of J narratives appear to make more sense when read against an exilic background.

Chapter 3

The Significance of the Burning Bush*

The meaning given to a story when it is handed down over successive generations, in written or oral form, will often change imperceptibly. This is particularly true of stories which have a specifically ideological or religious content, for it is then in the interest of the preserving community to continue to relate the story, if it is believed to have continuing value, to their circumstances and developing understanding of themselves. A direct result of such a process is often the loss of the original meaning. It seems to me that the original significance of the curious episode of the burning bush in Exodus 3 has been lost in this way.

The recovery of an original meaning will to a large extent depend on our ability to recover the original circumstances in which the story took shape, and indeed to ascertain precisely the literary type to which the story belongs. So long as the present story is regarded as being rooted, however obscurely, in the history of the pre-settlement era, then its true meaning, both theologically and in the history of religious thought, can only remain hidden. In this brief discussion I shall suggest a different historical context from the one normally accepted, in order to obtain a better understanding of the story.

The burning bush episode falls within the block of material usually isolated within Exodus 3 as J. In an earlier discussion of the E material,[1] with which we are not here concerned, I suggested that the J parts of the story do not simply constitute an alternative tradition to the E source, but instead presuppose E in its final form. E shows evidence of progressive reworking over a considerable period. J therefore must be given a later date than the final form of E. I suggested that J is in fact exilic. Now if this is a tenable position, then it follows that we should look to the conditions and concerns of the exile for an explanation of the significant features of the story.

The relevant part of the J story is told very succinctly in Exodus 3.2, 3, 4ac, 5 (continuing in vv. 7-8, 16-18).[2] It contains two striking features: first the mysterious bush which burns and yet is not consumed – a seeming contradiction in terms – and secondly its location on 'holy ground'. These two elements require some explanation. The first may be regarded simply as an expression of the miraculous, though this hardly contributes to a serious discussion,[3] and we should rather seek a more substantial explanation which recognizes the symbolic dimension of the image, and explains it in terms of what we know of the symbolic thinking of the ancient Near East at large, and of ancient Judah in particular. The second is the more startling when we consider that the J passage undoubtedly presumes, though it does not state, that the episode takes place in the wilderness. We may conclude this without reference to Exodus 2,[4] but rather on the basis of J's derivative status with regard to the E material in Exodus 3 (it being therefore controlled by 3.1). It might be argued that the holiness of the place is due to its proximity to, or even identification with, the 'mountain of God'. But the specific mountain location is not made explicit in J. However, to turn an old argument on its head, it is possible that the J writer, far from designating the mysterious plant (on which the botanists are still hard at work)[5] by a conscious paronomasia on the name of Mt Sinai, which of course is the sacred mountain in the J tradition but is not named in the present context,[6] names the plant in anticipation of its association in the reader's ear with the mountain name. He thus gives the coded message that this place, though in the wilderness, nevertheless does not partake of the normal symbolism of the desert, but rather of that of the sacred mountain.[7] The wilderness location of itself would in any event strike the reader as an incongruous place for the deity to reveal himself. It represented the very antithesis of holiness, and even of reality. It was a 'non-place'.[8]

In the arid climate of the Near East, any green plant is a vivid sign of life etched sharply against the dry terrain. It would be futile to try to identify with any certainty the precise area in Midian the writer had in mind, to ascertain whether trees grew there with any frequency, if at all; if we are to think of a writer living in exile, he probably had little idea of the whereabouts of Midian, and none at all of its real conditions. He was concerned rather with the image of a sterile land, in which grew this miraculous plant, the locus of a hierophany. A widespread motif throughout the artistic and religious expressions of Near Eastern culture was the tree of life – the epitome of the tenacity and regenerative power of nature in unprepossessing conditions – commonly represented as the medium of theophanies.[9] In temple symbolism the tree is particularly important, representing the centre, the *axis mundi,* from which flows all vitality. It is clear from numerous Old Testament passages from the pre-exilic era that the Judahite mind was saturated with this symbolism. Obvious examples are the tree of life in

Eden, itself a mythical conceptualization of the sanctuary,[10] and the *'ᵃšērâ* constantly alluded to in the cult, and perhaps simply to be identified with the tree of life in the sanctuary.[11] In the present story, this paramount image of the centre is used to transform the desert, paramount image of the boundaries of the cosmos, into something which it is not perceived to be.

An exilic writer could hardly fail to be aware of this tradition, and to recognize that, shorn of syncretistic associations, the tree of life growing in the wilderness was a striking image with which to convey an important theological message to his contemporaries and fellow-exiles. It represented a message of hope in the midst of despair, and the promise of life in an environment of sterility and death. But the burning bush combines two images: that of the tree of life, and that of light shining, its burning nature suggesting a torch or a candelabrum. Now since the very notion of a theophany implies cultic ideas and the associations of the sanctuary, such a double image almost inescapably evokes the cultic lampstands—the *mᵉnôrôt* – of the temple. No representations of the *mᵉnôrâ* are known before the Roman period, but a possible prototypical form has been discerned by E.R. Goodenough as early as the thirteenth century BCE,[12] and though our information in 1 Kings 7.49 comes from the exilic Deuteronomist, there is no reason to doubt the presence of *mᵉnôrôt* in the Solomonic temple. The detailed instructions for the (post-exilic re-) construction of the lampstand – now apparently only one is envisaged – in Exodus 25.31-40, and its manufacture in 37.17-24 is undoubtedly based on ancient tradition. Its arboreal form is clear from these passages (cf. Numbers 8.1-4), and is confirmed when iconographic representations appear later, because the tripedal base has the form of tree roots. Its divine significance – as the 'light of the world' – is also borne out by the description of Zechariah's vision (Zechariah 4.1-14), for the two olive trees which flank it (and incidentally provide it with an uninterrupted supply of oil, so that it is, as all sacred fires should be, a perpetual fire – it burns, as it were, and is not consumed) represent the two anointed ones (here Zerubbabel and Joshua) who stand before 'the Lord of the whole world'. The temple *mᵉnôrâ* then represents a 'perpetual theophany', and this surely is the meaning of the unconsumed bush in Exodus.[13]

Let me now offer a hypothesis for our understanding of the burning bush. Moses, an archetypal figure whose stature grew enormously during the exilic period (in Deuteronomy 1.37, 3.26, 9.18-20, 10.10, for instance, he is presented in the latest recension as a redeeming, almost christological figure, and in the Pentateuch at large he is presented in transparently royal terms),[14] here represents exilic man – his treatment in Deuteronomy, just mentioned, reinforcing the idea of his solidarity with sinners. He is in the wilderness – at the edge of the world, at the furthest remove from the centre – conceived of course by the exiles as the sanctuary in Jerusalem. Suddenly, to his amazement, in the darkness and sterility of his condition, he discerns a tree or bush – symbol of life and divine grace – and it burns and is not consumed, just like the temple *m*ᵉ*nôrâ*. As if to confirm his intuition, which he dare not articulate, a voice from the very heart of the vision confirms that this is indeed holy ground, just like the *temenos* of the temple, and instructs him to remove his shoes. The wilderness is a symbol of Babylon, and even here Yahweh brings the exiles hope in despair: he reveals himself, paradoxically and against all traditional expectation, in the very place which seems formally to deny his presence. Such a story was drawing out for the exiles the most important theoretical principle of the recently developed monotheism of the period: that Yahweh was no longer to be conceived in territorially limited terms; his rule and power were universal. Such a message must have been of great comfort to people whose traditional beliefs could not seriously accommodate the misery of deportation and the destruction of Jerusalem.

Endnotes

* First published in *VT* 36 (1986): 361-65.

1. See Chapter 2.

2. On the division cf. Noth 1962: 34; cf. Childs 1974: 52; and Habel 1965: 301-302, for a different view.

3. Cf. the naturalistic explanation offered by W.R. Smith 1927: 193, and the more sober assessment of Hyatt 1971: 72.

4. If Exodus 2.1-23a is allocated to J, then the burning bush episode is set in Midian, since it presupposes 2.15, 22.

5. Cf. Tournay 1957: 410-13.

6. The bush is called *s*ᵉ*neh,* the mountain *sînay.* The association is generally rejected in modern discussions: Hyatt 1971: 71, Noth 1962: 39-40. (See further, Wyatt 1995c.)

7. On the negative symbolism of the desert see Pedersen 1926: 454ff.; Haldar 1950; Talmon 1966. (For further discussion see Chapter 5.)

8. Cf. the significance attached to the wilderness in the treatment of the second scapegoat on Yom Kippur: D. Davies 1977: 394.

9. See Ward 1910: 219-38; Mayani 1935; Perrot 1937; Danthine 1937; Frankfort 1939: 204ff.; Widengren 1951. For more general treatments see Eliade 1958: 265-330, and Cook 1974.

10. See Wyatt 1981.

11. Cf. for instance Judges 6.25-28 (where it is adjacent to an altar), and 2 Kings 23.6 (where it is in the temple: the parallel passage in 2 Chronicles 34.3-4 omits the allusion).

12. Goodenough 1954: 73 and fig. 6.

13. Cf. Wirgin 1962: 141, who observes that we have in the imagery (of Zechariah) an intentional transfer of the symbolism of the olive tree that 'never dies' and therefore represents the tree of life to the lamp which never goes out. We need not see a transfer of symbolism, which is already there, but rather an intensification of it, by the highlighting of its royal and hieratic connotations.

14. Cf. Widengren 1950: 22ff.

Chapter 4

WHO KILLED THE DRAGON?*

The Ugaritic Baal cycle appears to be familiar with no less than three accounts of the killing of the Sea god, who is to be construed as a dragon. Such variety in mythological tradition should occasion no surprise, but clearly it does raise questions of consistency within the space of one literary work. In the present article I shall examine the various forms that occur, and attempt to reconcile them with one another, in the sense of seeking an appropriate explanation of the variety in terms of Ugaritian theology.

The three accounts attribute the victory over Yam to three different deities, and it is here that inconsistency arises, because the first two, by Athirat and Anat respectively, superficially at least detract from the literary force of the third, by Baal. We shall deal with these in turn.

1. *Athirat*

Ugaritic mythology gives no account of this myth, but we may infer its existence from the goddess' chief title, *rbt aṯrt ym*, as proposed by Albright.[1] He interprets the formula as 'the Lady who treads on the Sea [-dragon]', and understands this to be an allusion to a myth in which Athirat overcomes Yam. While this may be regarded as no more than a conjecture, it is a very plausible one. No obvious significance in the more conventional form ('the Lady who walks on the sea') presents itself: we know of no good reason for a general maritime connection for Athirat, and the existence of a fisherman assistant (KTU 1.4 ii 31) or the Tyrian and Sidonian connections (KTU 1.14 iv 38-39 etc.) require explanation themselves rather than provide it for the broader context. The alternative, that *ym* be construed as 'day', so that the title alludes to the goddess crossing the heavens by day in her solar capacity,[2] has not generally found favour among Ugaritic scholars.

The theme of conflict between goddess and Sea god is quite in keeping with the solar character of the goddess, for we have two parallels to the supposed Ugaritic myth; these are the conflict of Marduk and Ti'amat in the Babylonian *Enuma Elish*,[3] and of Ra and Apepi in Egyptian tradition.[4] I do not propose to try and sort out the question of primacy here, in view of its endless ramifications in terms of ethnic movements in prehistory, the problem of the Semitic element in Egyptian, and so forth.[5] Suffice to say that there is undoubtedly contact between the Egyptian and Sumero-Akkadian traditions, and with the Canaanite world lying between the two cultural matrices, it should occasion no surprise to find traces of the same tradition. Its faintness, surviving in no more than a divine title, points both to its antiquity within the tradition and to the complexity of the subsequent development of Ugaritian mythology, which saw the rise of the other versions to be treated below. It may be true to say that it is a myth appropriate to riverine cultures, dependent on irrigation and sunshine for the maintenance of the economic order, where the sea (or the sudden flash flood and wild storm) are seen as potentially disruptive and baneful influences, rather than a maritime city such as Ugarit, for which the sea was an important economic lifeline. In this case the Ugaritic version is certainly to be seen as derivative, whatever its actual origin.[6]

Now both the Mesopotamian and the Egyptian versions of the myth are cosmogonic in character. The daily character of the Egyptian myth in no way detracts from this, for each new dawn, marking the triumph of Ra, is in effect a renewal of the world and the reassertion of the cohesive power of sun-god and the monarchy symbolized in it. Albright suggests a similar cosmogonic dimension in the Ugaritic allusion,[7] and this will be seen to be the point of contact between the different versions.

While the myth in which Athirat plays the primary role is in no passage actually narrated, we may have a more extensive allusion to it in KTU 1.6 vi 45-52. Although there are unfortunate gaps in the column, it appears that the conflict between Baal and Mot is finally resolved by the intervention of Shapsh. She warns Mot to desist from fighting, for fear of enraging El, and he appears to concede victory to Baal (lines 22-35). The gap in the text which then ensues makes it impossible to be certain who is being addressed when the narrative resumes. Either Shapsh herself is apostrophized, as an underworld deity who presides over the dead and the gods of the region, or Mot is told that Shapsh will subject him to the chthonian powers. On purely grammatical grounds either is possible. The following may be compared:

i. Shapsh is addressed[8]

Shapsh, the spirits[9] are beneath you,
  below you, Shapsh, are the ghosts!
The gods are around you, lo!
  the dead are round about you!
Kothar is your companion
  and Hasis your familiar.
On the sea of the monster and the dragon
  Kothar-and-Hasis navigates you,
  Kothar-and-Hasis propels you.

ii. Mot is addressed[10]

Shapsh will subject you to the spirits,[9]
  Shapsh will subject you to the ghosts!
The gods will be around you,
  lo! the dead will be round about you!
Kothar will be your companion
  and Hasis your familiar.
On the sea of the monster and the dragon
  Kothar-and-Hasis navigates you,
  Kothar-and-Hasis propels you.

(The final three lines in particular are susceptible to different translations, but the gist seems to be either a journey as above or perhaps a banishing of monster and dragon – and Sea too?[11] – to be construed as a metaphor for a journey.) The sea-journey appears to be of a subterranean nature, and suggests the use of the same motif found in Egyptian thought, where Ra travels through the night and the underworld on a solar bark in an image complementary to his daytime journey across the heavens.

The problem concerning the two versions given above is, which is the more plausible not in grammatical but in mythological terms? Just as the various chthonian forms of Ra (Horus, Khepri, Ra himself) serve both a macrocosmic and microcosmic purpose in mortuary theory, so that on the first level we have the theme of cosmic renewal, and on the second that of individual regeneration, so the two versions here would seem to belong to the first and second level respectively. So in the second case we should understand Mot's subterranean journey – signifying presumably his own death, but also his possible regeneration. This seems an unlikely purpose here, since the whole point of the text is presumably his final defeat and the triumph of Baal. Accordingly, the first translation – or something on the same lines – seems preferable: that is, Shapsh is addressed, and her own chthonian role is described in terms of her having power over the inhabitants of the underworld. That Kothar should be her companion is not surprising: Eusebius tells us on the authority of Philo that Kothar was the inventor of navigation[12] and his connection with Ptah may be regarded as fairly certain, the latter in his mouth-opening function and mummiform iconography having obvious underworld associations.[13] Now if we are to see here an analogue of Ra's nightly subterranean journey, as Kothar's derivation and indeed implicit identification with Ptah seem to suggest, then it is not unreasonable to see in the allusions to 'monster and dragon' (and even to sea itself – see n. 10) a reference to a serpent-vanquishing myth. This would provide the explanation of Athirat's title on the supposition of the equivalence of the two goddesses (see n. 2).

2. *Anat*

In KTU 1.3 iii 32ff. Anat sees the messengers of Baal who have come to bid her celebrate his victory over Yam with a *hieros gamos*, and breaking into a cold sweat, bursts out:

> What enemy has risen against Baal,
> what foe against the Charioteer of the clouds?
> Did I not smite the Beloved of El, Sea?
> Did I not kill River, the great god?
> Did I not muzzle the dragon?
> I closed his [mouth]![14]
> I smote the writhing serpent,
> Tyrant[15] with seven heads!
> I smote the Beloved of El, the monster![16]
> I destroyed the bull-calf of El, Atik!
> I smote the Bitch of El, Fire,[17]
> I killed Flame, the daughter of El![18]

The primary question of interpretation here is the form of the verbs. Kapelrud takes them to be second person singular, so that Anat expresses surprise that there should be enemies risen against Baal, since he has killed Yam and his confederates.[19] But this fails to account for the prefixed conjugation forms in line 40.[20] The majority of other translators have taken all the verbs to be first person forms, so that Anat claims the victory herself, as above.[21] This then raises the problem that we have already had an account of Baal's victory over Yam (KTU 1.2 iv 27-28) and that Mot's words to Baal in KTU 1.5 i 1-3 – which are formally similar to the passage just cited – clearly understand him (Baal) to be Yam's destroyer:

> When you smote Litan the twisting serpent,
> destroyed the writhing serpent,
> Tyrant with seven heads...

(The passage appears to be repeated in the damaged section in lines 27-30). In a curious way, which we shall consider below, this further seeming confusion points to a possible solution to the whole issue of multiple authorship of the dragon-slaying. We need not therefore resort to any emendation of the text by way of attempt to solve the present apparent contradiction. Our discussion will also explain what appears to be a case of a myth transferred from one goddess to another.

3. *Baal*

There is no immediate problem concerning Baal's killing of Yam in KTU 1.2 iv 27-28: it is the climax of the narrative in the first two tablets of the Baal cycle, and the resolution of the conflict inherent in the competing claims of Yam and Baal for kingship among the gods. It also anticipates the second victory by Baal, over Mot, and confirms his rule over the world of men.

But a problem clearly does arise when we consider the presence of these three variants of the same myth, firstly within one fairly coherent and geographically concentrated community, and secondly – and all the more acutely – within the one corpus, on the assumption that the *Baal* cycle belongs together as one relatively homogeneous composition. Now the divine name Litan appearing in KTU 1.5 i 1 just cited provides us with a clue. For this is surely the equivalent of the form Leviathan appearing in biblical tradition.[22] Now the biblical passages alluding to the motif are of particular interest insofar as they introduce a *fourth* candidate as dragon-slayer, that is, Yahweh. A number of scholars have supposed that a certain amount of the imagery associated with Baal in the Ugaritic tradition has been attributed to Yahweh in the Old Testament,[23] but it is altogether more plausible to suppose – though the supposition can only be presented as a conjecture for the sake of argument – that as Yahweh is derived from El,[24] so the attribution of the dragon-slaying to the former actually points to an original myth in which it was El who performed the deed.

It may be countered at this point that our discussion has left reality behind by departing from the evidence. But the alleged presence of Baal (here the Canaanite storm-god, Hadad) in the Old Testament is hardly established by the use of the epithet *bʿl*, which points to a god, but never once clearly identifies him. Indeed, such evidence as there is suggests that 'the Baal' is rather El himself, who is the object of Hosea's vituperation, for example.[25] The reasons for El being at once the bitter rival of Yahweh and the deity from whom Yahweh himself was derived are complex, and would require a survey of a large amount of biblical evidence, but it lies in brief in the religious divisions which as much as ethnic, political and historical divisions, separated Israel and Judah. In Israel El was reinstated as the object of the state cultus by Jeroboam, in direct rejection of the Yahweh-cult imposed by David, while in Judah Yahweh's pedigree is attested in frequent references.[26]

If we may take it, for the sake of argument, that the Canaanites were familiar with a myth in which El had originally destroyed the primordial dragon, then a different complexion is put upon the problem facing us. For a fourth candidate does not further complicate the issue, but rather resolves it. A diagram may clarify the question of the relationships of the various deities.

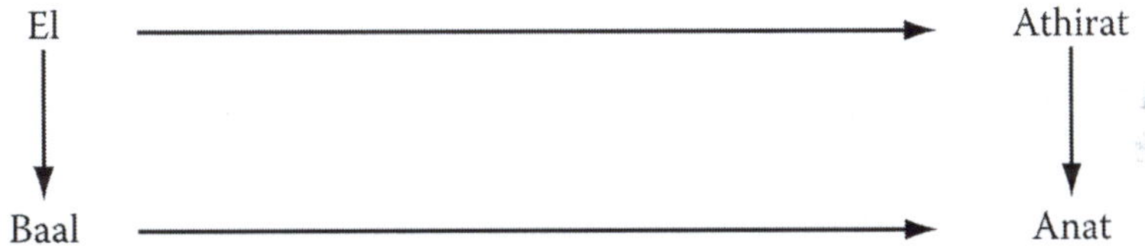

Diagram 1.

In the case of the horizontal relationships, we have in each case a god and his consort. Now for purposes of the narrative of mythology, husband and wife are commonly presented as quite independent persons, each with a well-developed personality. But this should not blind us to the theological reality lying behind them, for they are two facets of the same transcendent power, expressed in the imagination in terms of the poles which are reconciled at the 'ontological level' of the *coincidentia oppositorum.* There is thus much wisdom in Albright's view of Anat as the 'Wrath of Baal',[27] whatever one thinks of his particular argument. The transfer of a mythical motif from one to another is eminently logical in such a theological milieu, and is even more to be expected if there is any worth in my suggestion that the goddess is in effect the *śakti*, or active power, of her consort.[28]

So far as the vertical relationships are concerned, we have in the lower figures, Baal and Anat, *alter egos* of the primary divine couple. There may of course be a matter of historical differentiation here, in which the former belong to an immigrant society in Ugarit, but simply to state that would be to miss the point, for they have been formally incorporated into the theological system as microcosmic counterparts to the macrocosmic deities whose stature is if anything enhanced by the advent of younger deities.[29] The actual absence of any reference to El killing the dragon, and the shadowiness of Athirat's role in the matter, are only to be expected in the developed system in which Baal and his consort are charged with the actual task. There is no question of El becoming a *deus otiosus* (or of his consort undergoing the same fate), but rather his transcendence is increased by raising him above the concerns of the world. Baal on the other hand might be in danger of no more glorious a role than a demiurge, and his formal raising to kingly status among the gods serves to grant him a relative transcendence too.

One purpose in the seeming overloading of the tradition – a kind of mythical overkill! – is undoubtedly to reinforce the message contained in the myth: to express in as comprehensive a manner as possible the triumph of the divine realm. But a triumph over what? In analysing the biblical evidence, N.K. Kiessling characterizes the various dragons as 'horrible but vague incarnations of evil, darkly outlined opponents of both God and man'.[30] Is this a fair picture of the biblical scene, and is it of any value in assessing the Ugaritic evidence? I think it contains a half-truth with regard to the latter, because Yam and his associates (including Mot) represent the forces of chaos over against those of cosmos, and such an opposition naturally finds expression in the polarity good and evil. But the situation is rather more complex than this. In some of the biblical passages the world is actually constructed from the corpse of the dragon, a motif also occurring in the Mesopotamian tradition.[31] We may infer that the same thinking lies behind the Canaanite tradition,[32] and this transformation of chaos into cosmos shows the ultimate inadequacy of the absolute opposition of good and evil. In the real world, good and evil are relative principles. In the transcendent world they are subsumed within a higher reality: a *transcendentia oppositorum.* The fact that the world can be actually constructed out of the dragon, which is ultimately of 'divine' origin,[33] not only expresses the resolution of the tension between the opposed forces in the universe, but effectively both divinizes the world in a pantheistic sense and transforms the potential for evil into good.

We can discern this process at work in another fashion by recognizing that the expression of familial relationships between the various protagonists on either side in the struggle, El and Athirat as husband and wife, Baal and Anat as their children and as brother and sister as well as husband and wife on the one hand, and Yam (and also his *alter ego* Mot) as 'Beloved of El' —a title which confers legitimacy and implies sonship[34] – on the other, is a traditional narrative vehicle for speculation regarding the processes of transformation and evolution which an ultimately unitary cosmic principle undergoes. It may seem overbold to propose such a motivation behind the telling of Canaanite mythology of which we know relatively little, but on the analogy of those cultures where such processes *can* clearly be discerned it is a reasonable proposition.[35]

Two analyses of the Baal cycle which have proved useful for our understanding of the cosmic and cosmogonic processes to which the Baal cycle refers are those by M.K. Wakeman[36] and by D.L. Petersen and M. Woodward.[37] These different approaches are complementary rather than antagonistic, and I hope that in what follows I may further complement what they have to say. No single interpretation of a myth is likely to exhaust its potential, and the last word is certainly not being offered here.

If for the sake of argument at least we accept that there are indeed four candidates for the killing of Yam, then we may develop the diagrammatic relationship of the various participants in accordance with the structural patterns established by Petersen and Woodward, assisted by M.K. Wakeman's view that the killings of Yam and Mot are not ultimately to be differentiated, being 'wet' and 'dry' versions of the same theme. Let us consider the following set of relationships.

Diagram 2.

The 'shadowy' killing of Yam by El and by Athirat – 'shadowy' in the sense that the events have left only vague traces and are clearly no longer dominant themes in the mythology of the Baal cycle (though that is far from saying that their roles have been forgotten) – belong to a primordial situation, both in the historical sense that it is an older mythology than that in which Baal and Anat participate, and also in the thematic sense that it is logically prior to the main events of the Baal cycle. This is actually suggested in diagrams $R_{0,1,2}$ in Petersen and Woodward's study[38] though perhaps it was only half guessed at by the authors. These diagrams indicate the macrocosmic status of the situation, and implicitly have El (and I suggest, by extension, Athirat as well) as the chief protagonist in the overcoming of Yam. The structure almost forces us to recognize the full awareness by Ilumilku the scribe, or at least the tradition he preserves, of El's original active role in the drama, even though it does not find an explicit reference in the Baal cycle.

Diagrams $S_{0,1,2}$ in Petersen and Woodward's study by their structural similarity with $R_{0,1,2}$ reinforced by the isomorphic patterns later established,[39] are seen indeed to deal with an analogous situation, but in this instance it is Baal and Anat who appear as the opponents of Yam's 'dry' counterpart Mot. Significantly, while the resolution of the Yam conflict is the establishment of the macrocosm, the outcome of the Mot conflict is that of the microcosm. If then we imagine Yam, Mot and Athtar, to whose role we shall refer in a moment, as middle, or focal figures, as their position in diagram 2 suggests, it is striking how the divine pairs El and Athirat, Baal and Anat, appear mirror-fashion on either side, the microcosm and the resolution of its conflicts reflecting the macrocosm and the resolution of *its* conflicts.

My linking of the three middle figures of Yam, Mot and Athtar may be felt to require some justification, being far from self-evident. I have alluded to the matter elsewhere, but may briefly recapitulate. The titles used of the first two are more than statements of El's affection for them,[40] but represent their ideological role as potential cosmic kings.[41] The same is true of Athtar, chosen to be king after Baal's death (it is a matter for remark not only that he is called *aḥd bbnk* – to be construed as an ordinal rather than as a cardinal[42] – but that he also becomes king instead of Mot, whom we might expect to benefit from Baal's death, and moreover rules from the underworld, the very domain of Mot)[43]. It is difficult to avoid seeing some kind of equivalence between Athtar and Mot; since one has already been implied in the structurally identical roles of Yam and Mot, it seems that we have here in the three deities three hypostases of the same fundamental principle. We have just suggested that Yam and Mot are 'potential cosmic kings'. It is precisely their potentiality that is important, and we may alternatively describe them, with Athtar, as precosmic royal figures. The three are in opposition to Baal's actual(ized) cosmic kingship, and the tensions between the three and the one constitute a perfect example of Jung's quaternity theory[44] – the fourth element, Baal, representing the fulfilment of all the promise, or potentiality, contained in the three. All four are equally important in the overall economy, which is the working out of the macrocosmic purpose of El. This is why it is certainly wrong in the Ugaritic context to characterize Baal's opponent(s) as the embodiment of evil, whatever a later age may have made of these mythical themes.[45]

Comparative evidence suggests that Athtar, far from being the apparently minor god – even something of a comic figure – that his somewhat undignified rebuff in KTU 1.2 iii 12-25, and his rather gawkish 'enthronement' in 1.6 i 56-65 suggest, was in origin the apotheosis of kingship (and thus a central figure in cosmology) and was a member of the original Semitic triad whose existence may be inferred from its ubiquity in Semitic culture.[46] Originally (in a mythology which we can no longer reconstruct) he was undoubtedly the key figure in the initiation of the microcosm. It would have been as a result, we may conjecture, of Semitic settlement in Ugarit that he became associated with the prototypes of Yam and Mot. A later settlement of Amorites bringing with them the deities Baal and Anat, a complete reappraisal of cosmogonic and cosmological ideas must have taken place, which is reflected in the Baal cycle (though this may well be a version centuries younger than its earliest form). Gods once belonging to the cosmic order took on a new 'pre-cosmic' or even 'anti-cosmic' role: a phenomenon in religious history paralleled elsewhere. We shall consider below an interesting Indian analogy to the present context.

A further diagram may clarify the way in which Yam, Mot and Athtar do not simply operate as a pivot in the relationships outlined above, but play a dynamic role in the process of cosmicization. The events or states appear in the order in which they appear in a sequential reading of KTU 1.1-6.

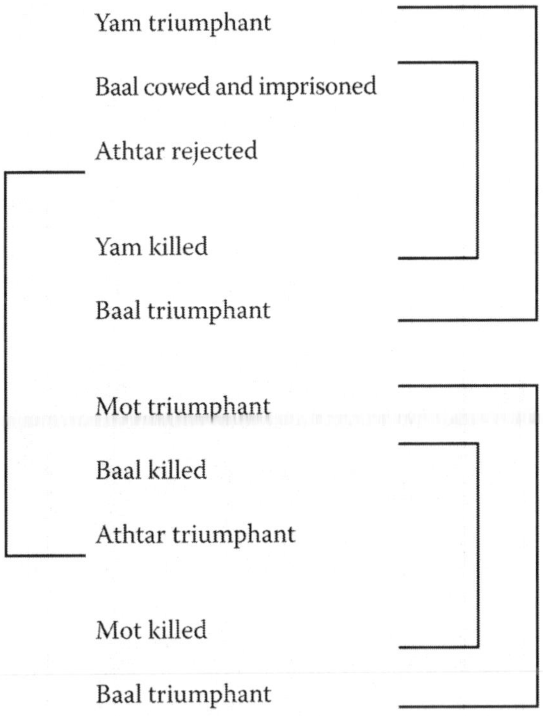

Diagram 3.

In that alone of all these gods Baal actually acquires a temple (and the plaintive cry of Athtar that he has none operates in the long term as a disqualifier of both Yam and Mot as well)[47] the 'triumphs' of his rivals are ephemeral. Indeed, it is the hollowness of their victories, unreinforced by the 'territorial power' of a temple, which highlights the construction of Baal's temple as a main theme of the Baal cycle – a concrete image of his victory in battle and of the microcosm he establishes.

Athtar is not, of course, a combatant, and his distinct role is indicated by his appearance as a foil to Baal's fortunes in each main block of the cycle (an echo of his ancient role?), so that his two conditions and those of Baal are a reverse image of those of Yam and Mot. While triumph and death are the fates of the latter two, it is rejection or imprisonment (rather less drastic than death) and triumph which are the fates of the former. At the same time, Athtar somehow has to be eclipsed in favour of Baal in the second part of the cycle, and this is done by no more sophisticated a technique than simply ignoring him after his enthronement.

Diagram 3 also makes clear another structural feature of the Baal cycle. Each block of material is in the form of a chiasmus. As Watson has noted, chiasmus has a distinctive character in Ugaritic poetry, 'to show two or more individuals acting as one'.[48] Within each block there is perhaps no such unifying process here, but the repetition of the entire structure may be regarded as reinforcing the view expressed above that Yam and Mot are two aspects of one reality.

In our discussion so far we have sought to show that the seeming overloading of the mythology of the Baal cycle is an integral part of its construction, in which the various individual deities act as representatives of different orders of reality. This is in part a serendipitous outcome of the slow process of mythological modification which is bound to occur in a culture as it passes through its history, and in part the unconscious working of both the collective and the individual mind of the people handling the tradition.

Having tried to answer the question 'Who killed the dragon?' we must now address ourselves to the obvious corollary: 'Why was the dragon killed?'

I have already alluded to cosmogonic motifs in the Baal cycle, but it is by no means obvious, at least to judge from the academic literature, that this is the theme, or a theme, of the cycle. There is no need to review the considerable variety of interpretations that have been proposed, and while I believe that some are manifestly improbable, notably the so-called 'seasonal interpretation',[49] it is entirely possible that a myth, particularly one as complex as our present concern, has a variety of meanings, so that each exegetical enterprise throws increasing light on the subject. I am a fervent advocate of eclecticism![50] What I want to attempt here is a further consideration of the Baal cycle in the light of some discussion which has taken place on the theme of Vedic cosmogony.[51] There is always danger in undertakings of this sort, because we are talking of two quite different cultures and even language families, with their inevitable diversity of experience and cosmological tradition. Yet there is a striking similarity, noted by a number of commentators, between the Vedic myth of Indra and his conflict with Vṛtra, and the conflict between Baal and Yam.[52] However, I am here concerned not with narrative similarities, but with underlying cosmological problems.

We may consider these in two aspects: firstly in terms of the cosmogonic process, and the relationship of different stages within this process, and secondly in terms of different orders of divine reality and power.

There is of course no one single model of cosmogony in the *Ṛgveda*. Nor is there any serious attempt to reconcile and coordinate the diverse images that are used. The nearest approach to such a rationalization occurs in the proto-philosophical hymns of the late period, which already anticipate (and even participate in?) the cosmological revolution of the *Upaniṣads*: *Ṛgveda* 10.81-82, 90, 121 and 129. These overlay the different motifs, of cosmogony by combat, sexual generation and sacrifice, asceticism and divine *fiat* in a manner we tend to consider simply confusing (or confused!), but which nicely exemplifies the Indian, or we may generalize and say the mythological, propensity for what W.D. O'Flaherty felicitously called 'the toolbox approach'.[53] There may be a caution here for our tendency to try and over-rationalize Ugaritic mythology. Reading between the lines of the different Ṛgvedic allusions to cosmogony, we may reconstruct the following broad scenario. In primordial times, the one reality was water. It was swathed in twilight, but contained within it the germ of life, imagined variously as the sun, the earth, or an unspecified 'One'. Its chief characteristic was lack of differentiation.[54] However, it was in a condition of potentiality, and from the waters emerged Tvaṣṭṛ, primordial deity and creator of all, perhaps to be identified with the 'One' of 10.129.3(?). He produced Dyaus and Pṛthivi (Heaven and Earth) and they bore the gods. Now in the *Ṛgveda* there are two distinct orders of gods, the Asuras and the Devas (spiritual, divine ones and bright ones respectively). W.N. Brown suggested that in the two orders we may have evidence of non-Indo-European and Indo-European gods;[55] were that proven to be the case, we might compare it with the pre-Amorite and Amorite levels at Ugarit mentioned above, and see in the later cosmogony of the *Ṛgveda* an even more interesting and closer analogue of the Baal cycle than I am seriously proposing.

The surprising feature that emerges when we examine the use of the term *asura* in the *Ṛgveda* is that, far from a neat differentiation being recognized by the tradition between deities so designated and the Devas, virtually all the major gods (many of whom are clearly *Deva* in post-Vedic cosmology) are actually referred to as *Asura.* This curious feature[56] led F.B.J. Kuiper to refer to the Asuras as 'the central problem of Vedic religion'[57] and to reconstruct a process which looks promising as an analogue of the Ugaritic problem. He proposed that collectively the Asuras were the gods of the primordial order we have described above. Their relative *status quo* was interrupted by the arrival of Indra. As Kuiper noted, he is of indeterminate origin.[58] This seems to place him in some indeterminate way outside the older pantheon, although he too is called an Asura.[59] He is a demiurge rather than a creator, and Kuiper understood his arrival to initiate a transformation of the primordial, undifferentiated pre-cosmos into the differentiated cosmos. Indra is also the first of the Devas, and in view of his light-bringing, establishment of the world-axis, and other cosmicizing acts, other Asuras become his allies, so that a dual order of gods develops, reflecting the dual cosmos.

The process of distinction is expressed mythologically in the conflict between Indra and Vṛtra. The latter, whose name is susceptible to different explanations,[60] was identified by Kuiper as a force resisting Indra's attempt to break open the primordial mountain, which is the raw earth contained within the waters – though the two remain undifferentiated – in order to organize the cosmos.[61] Later Hindu tradition preserves the elements of this rather more clearly than the Ṛgvedic allusions, because it has the battle take place on the seashore, where it is neither land nor sea, at twilight, when it is neither night nor day, with the weapon hidden in or made of the sea-foam, which is neither wet nor dry.[62] These figures of non-differentiation are pointers to the prevailing conditions: it is only as a result of Indra's victory that differentiation, that is cosmicization, can take place.

But there is more to the Vedic tradition than this, which is of interest to us. While Indra later becomes king of the gods, he is in origin merely an agent of a higher power. As the warrior-god (which is his role before he also develops into a storm-god) he represents the second function in the Indo-European tripartite cosmic and social structure. Sovereignty belongs to others.[63] In a differentiated world, the divine dyad Mitravaruṇau are the gods of sovereignty, the first function. Varuṇa is himself also the god of the waters and chief among the ancient Asuras. Following the cosmogony, he is the guardian of *ṛta*, cosmic law. But while he becomes foremost of the Devas, he continues to have a relationship with the Asuras, and has an ambivalent status. Brown noted the distinction of the Asuras into two groups, the Dānavas ('binders' – a metronymic from *dānu*— √*dā* 'to bind': Vṛtra is their chief) and the Adityas ('unbound, free' – a metronymic from *aditi* – √*dā* + *a* privative —Varuṇa is their chief). The latter became the first-function group among the Devas. While Brown insisted on the contrast between the two types,[64] he failed to note Varuṇa's ambivalent position, because he is associated with the *pāśa*, the noose with which he binds enemies and strangles first-function sacrificial victims. In other words, unbound, he is nevertheless a binder.[65] This curious role is brought out rather nicely in Kuiper's diagrammatic representation of the cosmogony.[66] Varuṇa remains a bridge between the two realms of Asuras and Devas, and within the cosmos (a microcosm) he is associated with the underworld, a dangerous place which itself partakes of the two orders, cosmos and chaos.[67]

It would be erroneous to insist on one-for-one relationships between the Vedic and the Ugaritic cosmogonies. But I imagine that a certain number of similarities will already be apparent. Yam, for instance, the sea and river god, conceptualized like Vṛtra in the form of a dragon,[68] is best construed not in seasonal or strictly environmental (here the environment of Ugarit, on the coast) terms, but rather in terms of a precosmic reality, akin to Ti'amat in the Babylonian tradition. Indra appears to share both warrior and weather roles with Baal, and Varuṇa's ambivalence is perhaps echoed in El's, since the latter, the ultimate figure of sovereignty, is not simply a supporter of Baal's cause, but initially offers Yam a palace, and both Yam and Mot are referred to as 'beloved of El', the language of royal ideology.

More important than these elements, however, is the structural similarity between the Vedic and Ugaritic traditions, even allowing for the element of differentiation in the Ugaritic case, where Yam and Mot together correspond to Vṛtra. They represent the danger chaos presents to cosmos from either end, so to speak, preventing its arrangement at the beginning (Yam) and threatening its destruction at the end (Mot). Like Vṛtra as representative of the pre-cosmic gods, they belong to a unitary, undifferentiated reality which we may, adapting Kuiper's figure 1, stage I, picture thus.

Primordial World	Pre-cosmic gods (El, Athirat, Yam, Mot)

Diagram 4.

Because of the distinctive presentation of events in the Baal cycle, we cannot adequately adapt Kuiper's other figures, but may represent the altered situation at the conclusion thus.

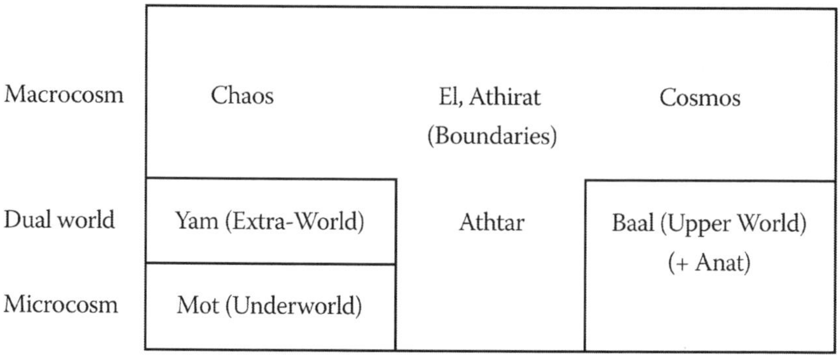
Macrocosm
Chaos
El, Athirat
(Boundaries)
Cosmos
Dual world
Yam (Extra-World)
Athtar
Baal (Upper World)
(+ Anat)
Microcosm
Mot (Underworld)

Diagram 5.

Athtar appears not to fit very easily into such a scheme. Indeed Petersen and Woodward simply exclude him from their discussion. If he is to be seen as of any significance at all, he must surely be seen as serving two mythological purposes. Firstly, as Athirat's choice for the substitute king, he reflects his old role in the triad, as mentioned above; secondly, as a deity who is both *alter ego* of Yam and Mot *and* substitute for Baal, he lies along the boundary between the worlds they represent, and come to rule (under the overall kingship of El), and represents the uneasy and delicate balance between the two. If we go further, and suggest that Ugaritic royal ideology looked, as we might expect, to Athtar as the apotheosis of terrestrial kingship,[69] then perhaps for all the reticence of the Baal cycle concerning his role, we should see him as a type of the king, who in his cultic office is charged precisely with the management and preservation of the cosmos. I offer this view with due diffidence, without wishing thereby to propose a strictly cultic interpretation of the cycle. But no satisfactory explanation for his presence in the cycle has so far been offered.[70]

El's position may at first seem uncomfortably ambivalent within this model. That is precisely what it is. As overall cosmic lord, his concern is for a broader perspective than that of society's self-interest. The making of a stable microcosm is all very well, but cannot take account of all kinds of necessary tensions resulting in and from its production: it is in a sense too good to be true, and mythology is well aware of the laws of entropy. The macrocosm is as it were a safety net into which the microcosm can fall as it periodically bursts asunder under its internal stresses. While I think a cosmogonic explanation of the Baal cycle makes better overall sense than alternative theories – except of course where different explanations may legitimately be held concurrently – it seems to me that it has a prospective quality: that is, it looks beyond the cosmogony *in illo tempore* towards the present world of mundane reality, and states in the language of symbols that it is fraught with tension and danger, and man must acclimatize himself to this uncomfortable fact. But he may take some comfort in the ultimate, if inscrutable, benevolence of El.[71]

I believe that further analysis of the Baal cycle is possible from the premises of the conclusions I have reached here. Unfortunately, due to our very scanty knowledge of certain aspects of Ugaritic thought in particular, progress is likely to be slow. But one aspect that could be explored might be the significance of the realism the gods represent in terms of elements (earth, air, fire and water) or the various symbolic overtones (especially sexual) of water in its different manifestations here. These are the themes of some very fruitful discussions in Indian and African mythology, and while we *know* virtually nothing of their significance in ancient Canaanite thought, we may be sure that they were replete with cosmological significance.

Endnotes

* First published in *AuOr* 5 (1987): 185-98.

1. Albright 1968: 105; *idem*, *EJ* III: 704 (art. Ašerah). For the more usual rendering ('the Lady who walks on the sea') see *idem*, 1965: 76. In support of the view expressed in the first two references, we may cite M.C. Astour's discussion in Astour 1967: 206, though without endorsing his etymology of Atargatis.

2. Nielsen 1936. See discussion of Nielsen in Gray 1949: 73-74. On the solar associations and character of Athirat see also Wyatt 1983: 273. On the etymology of *aṯrt* in ESA, see Jamme 1947: 109, n. 467; Höfner 1965: 497; see also Lipiński 1972. (The solar idea has been resurrected independently by Watson 1993 and Binger 1997.)

3. *ANET* 66-67. (tablet IV).

4. *ANET* 6-7. See also Faulkner 1937; *idem*, 1938. The late Edfu tradition appears to identify Apepi with Seth (a roaring serpent called Be): cf. Fairman 1935: 32. If this is anything more than a purely casual thematic link (i.e. if there is some ancient substance to the identification) then we may further cite the Horus and Seth conflict as an example of the same solar myth. Seth is after all the storm-god, who in Egypt represents not beneficence and fertility – provided by Osiris, the Nile – but rather the wild destructiveness and chaos brought about by tropical storms. See Zandee 1963; te Velde 1977: 25. The latter also notes the opposition of Seth and Apepi; te Velde 1977: 71, 99ff.

5. For the most recent discussion see Trigger 1983: 11ff., 36ff. On the particular problem see J. Day 1985.

6. On the other hand it may be argued that it is precisely a myth of the sea, with the riverine cultures of Mesopotamia (and Egypt?) actually borrowing it from Canaan. The same goes for the Indian analogue of the conflict between Indra and Vṛtra, since here too we have a myth concerning primaeval waters arising in a land-locked milieu. A psychological rather than an environmental origin would of course make such discussion superfluous. (See now further discussion in Wyatt 1988a, and revision in Chapter 12 below.)

7. Albright 1968: 105.

8. Cf. Gibson 1978: 81; Astour 1967: 287-88. See also Wyatt 2002a: 144-45, where I construe the text as follows:

> Shapsh, you rule the saviours;
>   Shapsh, you rule the chthonian gods.
> Your company are the gods;
>   lo, mortals are your company.
> Kothar is your associate,
>   and Hasis is your companion.
> In the sea of Arsh and the dragon,
>   Kothar-and-Hasis, steer (the bark)!
>   Pilot (the ship), Kothar-and-Hasis!

9. The *rpum* are (legendary) dead kings (cf. KTU 1.161). (See Wyatt 2002a: 434, n. 19.)

10. Cf. del Olmo 1981: 234-35, who appears to regard Baal as the addressee.

11. Del Olmo 1981: 235.

12. Eusebius, *Praeparatio Evangelica* 1.10.11.

13. On the equivalence of Kothar and Ptah cf. KTU 1.3 vi 4-5, where we are told that 'Caphtor (Crete?) is the seat of his dwelling/enthroning, Memphis the land of his inheritance'. *hkpt* is commonly construed as Egyptian *ḥt k3 ptḥ*: see, e.g., Gaster 1950: 155; Albright 1968: 119, 120, n. 69; del Olmo 1981: 547; Gibson 1978: 146. Cf. also KTU 1.3 vi 8-9: *iht np šmm* – which Gibson translates as 'the islands of Noph (Memphis) of the heavens'. Cf. Oldenburg 1969: 80; Sanmartín 1978: 352-53, n. 26; de Moor 1971: 51, n. 52. On Kothar in Egypt, see Leibovitch 1948.

14. Cf. del Olmo 1981: 185, 634, and restoring *p* in the lacuna.

15. Gibson 1978: 50; Watson 1977: 274-75; del Olmo 1981: 629.

16. Reading *arš*, taking it as the same term that appears in KTU 1.6 vi 51 above, and construing accordingly, with *m* of the preceding *ilm* taken to be an old mimation of the genitive or as an enclitic – in either case for euphony in declamation. However, the final letter of *arš* is in doubt, and some scholars have taken it to be *ṣ*. On this reading, I like Cassuto's (1971: 135) rendering of the line: 'I smote the Beloved of the denizens of the underworld'. Cf. Astour 1967: 292. Albright's (1941: 16) translation is a hybrid. On the first translation the question of why the monster should be 'beloved of El' is resolved if we recognize it as Yam and see in this his ideological title, for the significance of which see Wyatt 1985a: 120-25.

17. Or: 'the divine bitch'. It would seem that here we have the West Semitic prototype of the Greek Cerberos (Κερβερος) in spite of the need for a sex-change. Cf. West Semitic *balbal* > βαρβαρος (*l* > *r* with case-ending). On its ultimate Mesopotamian origin cf. Cassuto 1971: 135.

18. See now Wyatt 2002a: 79-80:

What manner of enemy has arisen against Baal,
  of foe against the Charioteer of the Clouds?
Surely I smote the Beloved of El, Yam?
  Surely I exterminated Nahar, the mighty god?
Surely I lifted up the dragon,
  I overpowered him?
I smote the writhing serpent,
  Encircler-with-seven-heads!
I smote the Beloved of El, Arsh,
  I finished off El's calf, Atik,
I smote El's bitch, Fire,
  I exterminated El's daughter, Flame.

19. Kapelrud 1969: 54ff.

20. H.L. Ginsberg, who clearly liked this view, recognized the problem: Ginsberg 1941: 13. Cf. *ANET* 137.

21. Virolleaud 1938: 51; Gordon 1949: 19-20; Driver 1956: 87; Gibson 1978: 50; Gaster 1950: 214; Ginsberg, *ANET*: 137; Jirku 1962: 30-31; Caquot *et al.* 1974: 167-68; Gray 1965: 39; Astour 1967: 292; del Olmo 1981: 185.

22. The closely parallel vocabulary of KTU 1.5 i 1ff., and Isaiah 27.1 make the identification inescapable. Cf. del Olmo 1981: 573; Cassuto 1971: 50; Caquot *et al.* 1974: 239, n. b; Gray 1965: 30; Dahood 1965–70: ii (1973[2]), 205-206; Kaiser 1974: 221, n. d; Emerton 1972; *idem*, 1982. Other biblical allusions to the motif occur in Psalms 74.13-17 (cosmogonic); 89.11-13 (EVV 10-12, cosmogonic); 104.26; Job 3.8 (read *yam* rather than *yôm* in parallel to *lwytn*); 7.12, 40.25ff.; Isaiah 27.1 is eschatological (= a new cosmogony); cf. Isaiah 51.9-10 (cosmogonic: cf. Stuhlmueller 1970: 86-91).

23. For the most recent discussion see J. Day 1985. For a review article, see Wyatt 1985b.

24. Cf. Cross 1973: 71-73.

25. Cf. Hosea 8.5-6, and H. Tur-Sinai's proposal, 1964: i, col. 31. See also Pope 1955: 35; Cassuto 1971: 57 n. See also Chapter 7 below.

26. Cf. the frequent paralleling of El and Yahweh in the Psalms and Job (the epithetal elements *ᶜᵉlyôn* or *Šadday* in no way invalidate the point). (See further Chapter 7.)

27. Albright 1968: 117.

28. Wyatt 1984: 329. (This stela is not in fact from Ugarit, but of unknown provenance; once in the Michaelides collection, it is now apparently lost).

29. See discussion in Petersen and Woodward 1977. For treatment see below.

30. Kiessling 1970: 167; Gordon 1966.

31. *ANET* 66-67.

32. On the Baal cycle as cosmogonic see below. On the idea of the scattering of Yam and Mot as transformational see Wyatt 1985a: 125, n. 28.

33. Our thinking in terms of the opposition of gods and demons (or God and Devil) is inappropriate to the era in which our texts were written. All supernatural principles were 'divine', whether benevolent, malevolent, or neutral. That this 'holistic' view still held true of Jewish thought in the sixth century BCE is clear from Isaiah 41.23; 45.7.

34. Cf. Wyatt 1985a: 120-25.

35. Cf. the cosmogonic traditions of Egypt – particularly the rationalizing 'theology of Memphis' in the Shabaka stone inscription (*ANET* 4-6), of India – particularly late Ṛgvedic hymns such as 10.81-82, 10.90, 10.121, 10.129 and their derivative material in the *Brāhmaṇas* and *Upaniṣads*, and of Greece – particularly in Hesiod's *Theogony*. This last of course invites comparison with the Sanchuniathon-Philo Byblius traditions preserved in Eusebius as quasi-speculative theology in a Phoenician milieu.

36. Wakeman 1973.

37. See n. 28.

38. Petersen and Woodward 1977: 238-39.

39. Petersen and Woodward 1977: 240-42.

40. So Gibson 1984: 208, 219.

41. Wyatt 1985a: 120.

42. Wyatt 1973–74: 87; *idem*, 2002a: 131, n. 70.

43. KTU 1.6 i 65.

44. Jung 1969: 164-87.

45. Cf. Kiessling 1970: 167; Gordon 1966. (An important contribution to the understanding of the monstrous, and is theological significance, has now been offered by Beal 2002. See also my review, Wyatt 2004b.)

46. Cf. Nielsen 1927: 213ff. His general theory is summarized and criticized by Jamme 1948, but he hardly demolishes it. Cf. *idem*, 1947: 11ff.; Ryckmans 1947: 327; Brillant and Aigrain 1953–57: iv, 256ff.

47. KTU 1.2 iii 19-20.

48. Watson 1983: 164.

49. See de Moor 1971. He discusses earlier seasonal assessments at length. For assessments, see now M.S. Smith 1994b: 60-75; Wyatt 1996b: 144-55.

50. See the very apposite discussion in O'Flaherty 1980: 3-12.

51. See Brown 1942; Kuiper 1975–76.

52. E.g. Gaster 1950: 142; Wakeman 1973: 9ff.; Fontenrose 1980: 194 ff. See also Wyatt 1988a, though I have subsequently abandoned this analysis: cf. Chapter 12.

53. O'Flaherty 1980: 5-7.

54. Kuiper 1975-76: 108: 'None of the contrasts which constitute our phenomenal world yet existed. There was no heaven or earth, no day or night, no light, or, properly speaking, darkness.' This explains my use of 'twilight' here, which will become clear(!) below.

55. Brown 1942: 88. We may compare similar dual orders (whatever their origins, they become differentiated powers in a developing cosmos): the Mesopotamian Igigi and Anunaki, the Norse Aesir and Vanir, the Greek Titans and Olympians. The Asuras later become the demons of Hindu mythology. *Ṛgveda* 10.82.5 appears to regard the two divine orders as originating at the same time, but this may be a later rationalization. The equivalence of the Sanskrit and Avestan terms *asura* : *ahura* and *deva*: *daeva* shows that the distinction predates the Aryan descent into India, and thus disproves any original connection between the Asuras and the gods of the Indus culture, though some of the latter undoubtedly later became Asuras.

56. Some examples: Dyaus: *Ṛgveda* 1.54.3, 8.20.17, 10.31.6; Varuṇa: 1.24.14, 8.42.1, 10.10.2; Agni: 5.10.2, 7.2.3, 10.11.6; Soma: 9.73.1, 9.99.1, etc. Those from maṇḍala 10 are the more interesting because of their relative lateness. Cf. Wyatt 1986b.

57. Kuiper 1975–76: 112.

58. Kuiper 1975–76: 109, citing *Ṛgveda* 2.12.5, 10.73.10; Brown 1942: 92, refers to allusions to his origins such as 4.17.4, 10.120.1, but these are not very precise, and in any case must postdate a tradition of his unknown origin.

59. *Ṛgveda* 1.174.1, 3.38.4, 6.20.2, 6.36.1, etc.

60. 'Obstruction', 'resistance', Kuiper 1975–76: 110; 'encloser, investor, imprisoner', Macdonell 1974: 296C; cf. Monier-Williams 1899: 1007b. Cf. the Indo-European √**ver* in n. 62; *Śathapata Brāhmaṇa* 1.6.3.9 offers a paronomasia on the term *vṛt* 'to roll' – no doubt suggested as much by Vṛtra's serpentine form as by alliteration (SBE 12: 166).

61. Kuiper 1975–76: 109-10; cf. Wakeman 1973.

62. *Mahābhārata* 5.9.3-22: *myth* §25 in O'Flaherty 1975: 77-85, esp. 84. Cf. *Ṛgveda* 10.129.2.

63. Cf. the extensive writings of G. Dumézil *et al.* For up-to-date bibliography and appraisal of Dumézil's theory see Littleton 1982. I have explored possible connections between this thought-world and that of Ugarit in Wyatt 1985c.

64. Brown 1942: 88.

65. On *pāśa* see for instance the imagery of *Ṛgveda* 1.24.15, 1.25.21, 7.88.7, 10.70.10. The etymology of Varuṇa has always caused problems. The forms Οὐρανος, Varuṇa and Varana have been equated (the latter meaning 'heaven'. Boyce 1975: 33-34, rejects this and endorses H. Peterson's explanation (*Studier tillegnade E. Tegner*, Lund 1918, 231ff.) linking Varana and Varuṇa to Indo-European **Vorueno* *√*ver*, 'to bind' (this fits the noose, so to speak!). Cf. Dumézil 1934: 49. But this is rejected in turn by Littleton 1982: 53. While Indo-European philology is hardly my *forte*, how about the Avestan term *Xvarənah* ('sovereignty') as a cognate? On the ritual strangulation motif, see *Śathapata Brāhmaṇa* 3.7.4.1-3 (SBE 26: 181), 3.8.1.15-6 (*ibid.*: 189-90).

66. Kuiper 1975–76: 113 (fig. 1), 119 (fig. 2). The latter represents the later Hindu cosmology in which Viṣṇu has become supreme deity.

67. See Brown 1942: 85.

68. Vṛtra is commonly called *ahi* – 'dragon'.

69. Cf., e.g., my analysis of the king in Wyatt 1983: 277.

70. Gaster's view, for instance, that he represents irrigation water during the summer drought (Gaster 1950: 126, 196) requires the prior demonstration of the seasonal interpretation. I find it profoundly unsatisfactory. (See further Wyatt 2002b.)

71. Cf. Gibson's remarks, (Gibson 1984: 218-19). That even El's position is not beyond question is implied in his reaction to Baal's death in KTU 1.5 vi 11ff., and also in the ultimately provisional nature of the resolution of the Baal-Mot conflict. Though he is at first killed, Mot re-emerges after seven years, and is only pacified by Shapsh.

Chapter 5

SEA AND DESERT: SYMBOLIC GEOGRAPHY IN WEST SEMITIC RELIGIOUS THOUGHT*

In recent discussion of the biblical expression *yam sûp* it has been proposed that instead of the usual rationalizing exegetical tradition, which seeks to locate the sea-crossing in Exodus 14–15 within the real geographical area between Egypt and Palestine, we should read an original *yam sôp* or *yam sûp* in Exodus 15.4, and understand the water traversed to be 'the sea of extinction'.[1] This has two obvious advantages over the conventional view: it solves the problem of the relationship between *yam sûp* as somewhere along the course of the Suez Canal or one of the lakes or lagoons of the region, and the same usage in Hebrew to denote either the Gulf of Suez (as perhaps in Exodus 10.19) or the Gulf of Aqaba (as in 1 Kings 9.26), or even the assimilation of the two to the Red Sea itself, as was presumably understood by the time of LXX (*Erythra Thalassa*, see now Chapter 12). It also opens up the exegetical possibilities raised by the idea that Egypt is a symbolic 'Land of Death' in biblical thought. This may not be the idea behind, but is certainly enhanced by, the usage in Genesis in particular, where the common terminology of movement to and from Egypt is the verbs *yārad* and *ʿālâ*. Particularly striking are the following associations of verses, where a reference to Joseph's descent into Egypt is followed by Jacob's response: Genesis 37.25 and 35, Benjamin's descent, with Jacob's response: 44.23, 26 and 31, and the latter two together in 42.38. The reiterated horror of a return to Egypt which runs as a *Leitmotif* through biblical thought (see Genesis 24.5-8, Exodus 13.17, Numbers 14.2-3, Deuteronomy 17.16, Hosea 9.3, 11.5, Isaiah 30.2, Jeremiah 42.19 [MT]) would be rather banal if it were simply a disagreeable memory in history or legend. That there is an implicit symbolism is suggested by Exodus 14.11, where the people indignantly ask Moses: 'Was it for lack of graves in Egypt that you brought us out to die in the desert?' Going down to Egypt is like going down into the underworld; being in Egypt is like being in the tomb. The point about *yam sôp/sûp* is that it divides this dead land from the land of the living, which becomes, as one moves further from the littoral, the Holy Land. I mean this not in the conventional Judaeo-Christian sense, but rather in the cosmological sense underlying this designation.

An understanding of the significance of the exodus within this conceptual framework explains why the language of cosmogonic conflict can be so readily applied to it in biblical poetry. The various expressions of the conflict between Yahweh and the sea dragon which occur in the Old Testament[2] are not so much the application to a historical memory of a convenient or evocative mytheme, but rather the formal cosmological explication of the real significance of that event, or even, for those who are sceptical concerning the historicity of the exodus, the ultimate source of the entire tradition. The essentially parabolic and even typological nature of the material is most evident in its use in Deutero-Isaiah, where the old exodus provides the paradigm for and promise of the new one, from Babylon. And as several scholars have noted,[3] the redemption which is anticipated by the exilic poet can be articulated in terms of the primordial, because creation and redemption are in effect synonymous. In so far as the motif of cosmogonic conflict is applied to Babylon (Isaiah 51.9-11, to which cf. 43.1-2, 16-21; 44.27; 50.2) a further element is present which is perhaps of some importance, in view of its incidence both in certain royal ideological contexts in the Old Testament, and in Ugaritic mythological usage. This may be termed the symbolism of the boundary. Perhaps the most explicit allusion to the motif in Deutero-Isaiah is Isaiah 43.5b-7:

> From the sunrise (m.) I shall bring your seed
> and from the sunset (m.) I shall gather you.
> I shall say to the north (f.): 'Yield!'
> and to the south (f.): 'Do not withhold!'
> Bring back my sons (m.) from a distance (m.)
> and my daughters (f.) from the end[4] of the earth (f.).
> All those called by[5] my name,
> for my glory I have created them,[6]
> I have formed them,[7]
> yea, I have made them.

These lines concentrate a wealth of cosmological thought, assisted in its expression by the poetic techniques employed. The genders used enhance the oppositions occurring.[8] Thus east and west, both referred to by masculine terms and in natural opposition to one another, are also in opposition to north and south logically, and this is emphasized by the use of feminine terms. Finally, in the third bicolon, this opposition is expressed once more by the internal gender change. It is almost a verbal ballet on different coordinates, with the cardinal points expressing the totality of the dispersion which is to end with the divine ingathering. Further mythical nuances are contained in the vocabulary. Thus sunrise and sunset (*mizrāḥ, ma'ᵃrāb*) probably contain something of their radical sense, the shining forth of the sun at dawn and its entering in at dusk evoking the diurnal crisis as the sun undertakes its subterranean journey.[9] The other opposition, of north and south, is without doubt more pregnant. This is indicated by the syntactic shift from imperfects in the first bicolon to imperatives in the following two. The terms used (*ṣāpôn, têmān*) implicitly carry the sense of enormous distance taken up in the third bicolon, but also have specific cosmological senses. *Ṣāpôn* echoes the cosmic mountain imagery of Ugaritic thought, which is also applied to Jerusalem in Psalm 48.3 (EVV 2) and very probably in Isaiah 14.13, where its identity with the mountain of assembly is explicit.[10] Thus while in one manner of speaking the remoteness of the north is evoked, in another we have here a paradoxical figure for the centre, to be identified with the temple mount.[11] With *têmān* the opposite is the case. It is a designation of the far south, remote from the Holy Land, and in spite of this – or, paradoxically because of it, as we shall see – is the locus of theophany traditions, and therefore partakes of holiness in spite of its emphatic removal from the centre.[12] There is another point about the present verses which anticipates our further discussion. This is the implication that the children of the deity (the image evoking royal ideological motifs) are born in these remote parts, far removed from the centre. While this is inevitably the case in that they are the offspring of deportees in Babylon, there is also an important echo of a persistent theogonic motif, again with royal connections. The bringing up of these children, that is, an expression of redemption, is characteristically expressed in the formal language of creation which is again found in royal contexts.[13]

The calling of the exiles from the four corners of the earth clearly makes no sense in real geographical terms. However confused the biblical writers may appear by our standards, they certainly had a basic working knowledge of the real geography of their environment. The point about the new explanation for *yam sôp/sûp* is that it transfers the issue from a real to what we may term a symbolic geography. The same is the case with Deutero-Isaiah, who can readily equate Babylon with Egypt, and redemption from the one with release from the other. We are in the presence of a mode of thinking which saturates the royal psalms in particular, and which determines the choice of much theological language in general in the West Semitic world. We have two models at work for space: a vertical one, which sees the gods as dwelling above, with man on the earth, and the dead beneath the earth. The mythical expression for this is most commonly the sacred mountain, often if not invariably construed as an omphalos, the point of intersection between the three realms.[14] And also a horizontal one, which sees 'reality' as the central point of a plateau, which diminishes in significance and value the further removed from the centre, until it becomes the amorphous and featureless desert, bounded by the cosmic ocean (sea, river or abyss are all terms applied to it), beyond which lies the realm of the dead and chaos. At times the seemingly two-dimensional models are combined into a three-dimensional one, as in the notion of the supra-firmamental waters *(mabbûl)* of the biblical flood story. The ultimate source of this spatial imagery of the cosmos, and in particular the horizontal one, which is undoubtedly the more archaic as being the more purely 'biological', lies in the biological awareness of space found in man, and shared with many other species, which commonly finds expression in the experience and use of territoriality (later rationalized as a concept). More precisely, it lies in the notion of personal space, in which every degree of social relationship from total intimacy to public distance is set out in culturally determined gradations of distance from the subject. These range from virtual identification (sexual intimacy is a total union: an annihilation of distance; one's children and closest friends are virtually extensions of oneself) to 'distance' (the term used affectively in English to refer to lack of intimacy – 'closeness' – between people) and 'alienation'. People outside the immediate emotional environment are of less consequence to us.[15]

The application of these psychological realities to cosmology and in particular to its religious and ritual aspects is beyond question. The idea of ultimate reality being found in the sanctuary of a temple, in the image of a deity, which is commonly set at the midmost point of the sanctuary (such thinking may lie behind the very precise measurements of the *debîr* in the Jerusalem temple, for instance)[16] is probably widespread. Not only is a sanctuary a microcosm, and thus an ideal model of the world, but it is also closely related to anthropocentric experience, and is in effect a model of man himself,[17] so that its construction is an objectification of man's own inner reality.[18] The four grades of proximity analysed by Hall, for instance (n. 15), may correspond precisely with the four grades of holiness in a courtyard temple (*d^{e}bîr, hêkāl, 'ûlām* and the *temenos* or the wider world beyond). Social stratification can work in analogous ways, both in hierarchical societies, and also for instance in theories of cult and its implications, as elucidated by D. Davies.[19] Indeed these diverse structures are to be seen as extrapolations of the fundamental psycho-biological principles. I have spoken of the curious relationship between the centre and the periphery as paradoxical. But this is to be seen not so much in the sense of contradictory, or flying in the face of reason, as complementary. It is so in two senses. First there is the figure of merismus, in which a total structure is described in terms of its (opposing) constituent parts. Thus 'reality' lies not so much in one extreme or the other as in a dimension which reconciles or transcends them. This mode of thinking is perhaps not so thoroughly developed in ancient Near Eastern thought as it is in Indian tradition, where it is the key to much of the symbolic thought of the Veda,[20] but it *is* found (as in such biblical passages as Genesis 1.1, Isaiah 41.23c, or 45.7),[21] and we may describe the present polarity as an implicit form of it. Secondly, if religious thinking (I use the term loosely!) is indeed bound up in the reification and objectification of inner processes (n. 18) then the periphery is formally an extension of the centre. Thus it can be a formal denial of the reality of the centre.[22] In such a guise its mention serves to enhance the vitality of the centre. Or it can be seen to be an analogue of the centre against the whole weight of emotional expectation. This is, I think, the point about the desert locale of Moses' encounter with the deity in Midian.[23] This story makes an important contribution to the exiles' perception of their peripheral location in the 'wilderness' of Babylon: even here, against the grain of centuries of liturgical thought concentrating reality in the sanctuary of Jerusalem, the formerly territorial god Yahweh is experienced as universal, having boundless sway. This is strictly the case, in that even the encircling ocean, the ultimate boundary between reality and non-existence, no longer denies his lordship of even the underworld.[24] In the case of the exilic Jews, we may perhaps detect the beginning of a break-down of the purely spatial conception of these issues, so that they become a metaphor for a relational structure (such as is expressed, for instance, in the polarity of being 'in covenant' with the deity, or 'cut off').

The problem which initiated this train of thought, however, is the more archaic thinking that probably underlies a number of interesting allusions in Ugaritic literature, and the matter of its significance. If the cosmological interpretation of *yam sôp* referred to above is tenable, then presumably it drew on generally received ideas, and since it has been shown that the background to the dragon-killing mythology used to describe the exodus is Canaanite,[25] so the general cosmological context is also to be taken as Canaanite, and the passages to be treated now are the oldest we have at present dealing with the issues.

The passages that concern us are the following:
KTU 1.12 i 14-29, 34-37:

Get you out, OTalishu, handmaid of Yarihu,
  O Dimgayu, handmaid of Athirat!
Take your stool,
  your litter,
  your swaddling clothes,

and go out into the Vale of Takamu,
    into the midst of the awful desert of Sa'iyu.
With your elbows dig the dust,
    with your hands the soil:
labour, and give birth to the Eaters;
    kneel, and bear the Devourers.
The gods will pronounce their names...
Baal wanders to and fro hunting.
    he comes to the edge of the desert
and comes upon the Eaters,
    and finds the Devourers.

KTU 1.23.4, 30, 33-35, 60-68:[26]

In the wilderness of the dunes [ ]...
[Now El goes out to] the sea shore,
    and strides along the shore of the deep...
May El's penis grow long as the sea,
    and the penis of El as the tide![27]
El's penis grows long as the sea
    the penis of El as the tide...
The two wives of El have given birth.
What have they borne?
    Gracious gods, gluttonous from birth,
    sucking at the nipples of the Ladies' breasts.
A lip to the underworld,
    a lip to the heavens,
and there enter into their mouths the birds of the air
    and the fishes from the sea.
And wandering about, piece by piece
    they stuff things into their mouths from right and left,
    and are not sated.
O wives whom I have married,
    O sons whom I have begotten,
    take up, prepare (offerings?) in the midst of the holy desert.
There you shall dwell among the stones and the trees
    for seven entire years,
    for eight revolutions of time.
The gracious gods go to and fro in the steppe;
    they roam on the edge of the desert.[28]

These are the primary passages, though certain of their allusions are also taken up in the Baal cycle, which supplies us with further details, which will be treated later. There are various difficulties in translation, but none which are critical to the present discussion.

The first point to make about the two texts KTU 1.12 (col. i) and 1.23 is that they are full of royal ideological motifs, which do not appear to have been noticed,[29] but which are clearly integral to the texts as a whole. In spite of detail differences, both texts are versions of a common tradition, also found in other recensions. Taken as a class of myths, not all examples are by any means to be construed as having a royal dimension. The underlying motif may be designated as socio-sexual, concerned with the ritualization of sex (that is, in marriage) and then perhaps its extension into economic (livestock) and cosmological spheres. But these matters must have early become linked with developing political 'theory' – that is, the concentration in the ruling family of the diverse psychological, environmental, economic and cosmological concerns of society, so that the royal marriage becomes as it were the paradigm of the sacred marriage. This is nowhere more apparent in the present context than in the West Semitic material. The myths before us are the apotheosis of the ritual performance. This is particularly clear in the case of KTU 1.23, with its stage directions in the form of marked-off rubrics (ll. 6-7, 12, 14-15, 19-20, 26-27, 54, 57) and the sevenfold repetition of the rite. The latter suggests, if only on the basis of human endurance, that we are to envisage a symbolic drama rather than an act of copulation in this case.[30] It is also quite clear in this instance that the primary rite has been applied out of context to some other point of reference.[31] Similarly KTU 1.12 has been applied to a rite of atonement, and perhaps KTU 1.24 has become a liturgy for use in marriage services. None of these secondary applications however disproves the royal element in the first two texts. We may compare this general application of a dominant motif with the ubiquitous allusions in Egyptian ritual to the Horus and Seth conflict. The ideological elements are the following.

Firstly, we are dealing in both texts with El's offspring. The king in Ugaritic thought is represented as the son of El. This is expressed both in terms of El's title *ab adm,* which I have argued is to be construed as Father of Man (that is, Primal Man, the king) rather than simply a general allusion to the divine paternity of mankind,[32] and in terms of what is probably a coronation formula underlying El's declaration *šm bny yw il*[*m*].[33] Secondly, the children in KTU 1.23, Shahar and Shalem, are to be taken as the morning and evening forms of Venus, so that they are twin hypostases of Athtar. He has a royal function, as is suggested by the formula *dmlk* used of him in KTU 1.2 iii 12, 18,[34] and may be inferred from his broader role in the Baal cycle.[35] While the forms *aklm, ʿqqm* in KTU 1.12 may be construed as plural, in the light of the analogy of Shahar and Shalem, we may conjecture that they are two in number, and this supposition is reinforced by the similar pairing of the mothers (that is, the gemination of one mother). This emphasis on pairing and twinning, echoed in the biblical recension (Isaac and lshmael, cf. Esau and Jacob, though the mother is not here geminated) is in part a reflection of the celestial phenomena – the two manifestations of Venus – but in part an allusion to the double nature of kingship. One of the important but hitherto unexplored implications of the Baal cycle is the 'functional twinning' of Baal and Athtar, the latter being substitute king during the period of Baal's demise. There is insufficient evidence in the extant literature from Ugarit to develop any clear theory on this matter, although its presence is, I believe, unquestionable. Perhaps the Egyptian models of king and ka (Horus and Khonsu) or of institution (Osiris) and incumbent (Horus) had their West Semitic analogues. The third ideological element is the term *amt* ('handmaid') used of the wives in KTU 1.12 i 15-16. It appears elsewhere in specifically royal contexts: KTU 1.14 ii 3, iii 25 allude to the king as *bn amt* – son of a/the handmaid[36] – that is, born of the sacred marriage; Psalms 86.16, 116.16 use the formula *bn 'mtk* as the equivalent of *ʿebed*, another term with specific royal connotations.[37] That this meaning for *amt* is correct in the context is borne out by the suckling of the children, a fourth ideological element, which is not stated, but may be inferred in KTU 1.12 (see l. 11, where they devour their mothers' breasts while still embryos!), and is stated in KTU 1.23, 59, 61. This is to be construed in accordance with the idiom in KTU 1.15 ii 26-27, where Keret's heir is to be one who

> shall drink the milk of Athirat;
> he shall suck the breast of the Virgin [ ].[38]

This is a way of referring to the supernatural (and implicitly divine) nature of the king. His real mother who suckles him is to be ritually identified as the goddess Athirat, which is also the general implication of any correlation drawn between the mythical texts and sacred marriage rites.[39] A fifth element which is without doubt to be understood ideologically is the statement in KTU 1.12 i 28-29 that the gods will pronounce the names of the Devourers, that is, will give them their names. Behind this allusion we should probably discern a coronation formula, such as may be preserved in KTU 1.1 iv 15ff., where the same verb (*pʿr*) occurs four times. In view of the fact that a specific deity is always the subject of the verb (in KTU 1.1 iv 15, 19, 29 it is El, in 17 the passive has Yam as subject and, probably, El as agent, in 1.2 iv 11, 18 it is Kothar – naming the clubs, in 1.13.32 it is passive of children born to Baal and Anat),[40] it is possible to read the *m* of *ilm* as an enclitic or old mimation, so that it is specifically El who pronounces their names.[41] Yasibu's name is given him by El (KTU 1.15 ii 25) and we may compare the divine authority for royal names or titles in 2 Samuel 12.25, Isaiah 7.14 (= Matthew 1.23!), Matthew 1.21.[42]

It is important to recognize these ideological features in the tradition, because they have implications for the geographical location of the conception and birth of the offspring. This appears to draw on the persistent symbolism of the desert, or as I put it above, of the boundary. In the Ugaritic example of KTU 1.23, this must be taken as symbolic, if only on the commonsense ground that the Syrian desert lies over a hundred miles from the sea. So the picture of El strolling on the shore (where the parallel *ym* || *thm* have cosmological overtones[43]) which is apparently adjacent to the desert, points to the notion of the end of the world. It appears, then, that the setting of the Canaanite tradition is the same as that envisaged in the passage in Deutero-Isaiah discussed above. There the children were formed (that is, begotten)[44] at the end of the world. Here their begetting takes place on the edge of the sea, in the desert. This is to be understood as the equivalent of the place described in slightly different detail in the Baal cycle. This is the boundary between the world and the underworld (also, on the horizontal model, to be seen as an 'outer world' – that is, a non-world beyond the cosmic ocean). There are two main versions:
a. KTU 1.4 viii 1ff. (= 1.5 v 12ff.):[45]

> So then set your face towards the rock of *trgzz*,
> towards the rock of *šrmg*,
> towards the two hills[46] bounding the earth.
> Lift up a rock on your hands,
> a massif on your palms,
> and go down into the house of freedom of the earth;
> be numbered among those who go down to the underworld.[47]

b. KTU 1.5 vi 4ff. (cf. 1.5 v 19, 1.6 ii 19ff., 1.16 iii 3-4):

> We went around the edges of the earth,
> to the edges of the watery region.
> We came to 'Pleasure', the land of pasture,
> 'Delight', the steppe by the shore of death.[48]

These are best understood as complementary: the tradition evidently sees no contradiction. The latter passage does not really contain an idyllic picture, as may appear to be implied by the translation. Rather are the names euphemistic.[49] But it is striking that the boundary should receive names analogous to that of the centre in the biblical tradition (*ʿēden*: 'delight').[50] Herein is a further example of the paradoxical relationship of the two locations noted above. The pasture/steppe of the final bicolon, which runs down to the ocean, is not to be distinguished from the desert of KTU 1.23: it is the amorphous, 'unterritorialized' land of the nomads which stretches away from the farmlands of settled people, although of course it refers to no specific geographical area, having instead a symbolic sense. It may be significant that it is in the environment described in passage b) that a sacred marriage between Baal and Anat takes place, KTU 1.5 v 17-23, resulting in the birth of progeny called *mṯ*. This term has been construed by some as 'twin',[51] which suggests that the episode in question has a thematic link with the sacred marriage of KTU 1.12 and 1.23. It is a microcosmic counterpart of the primary theogony, recapitulating it as an apotropaic episode to counterbalance the imminent death of Baal. While Baal is in no sense the father of Athtar, there must also be a thematic link between this provision for Baal's descent into the underworld and the ensuing substitution of Athtar as king, which is perhaps supported by the locus of the latter's reign (*arṣ*).[52] The vertical imagery would then be a metaphor for hierarchy, reflecting the microcosmic status of these events.[53]

We have still not solved the general question of the symbolism of the boundary. It must in some way relate to the symbolism of the desert, which has been treated fairly extensively with regard to the Old Testament, but not perhaps very usefully from our present point of view.[54] The best discussion is to be found in the article by S. Talmon.[55] He rejects the view that there is a so-called 'nomadic ideal' or nostalgia for the desert as commonly proposed in earlier discussions. His specific objections are the following: there is no genuine nomadism even in 'Israel's' past: the patriarchs, even if historical characters, were still not nomads;[56] the wilderness period could be the source of the image, but its concentration into a 40-year period makes it incredible that it would make such an impact upon the entire social ethos. (This point may be reinforced by two observations: firstly, the whole point of the wilderness imagery of the so-called wilderness period is, by and large, its negative character.[57] The 40-year period of wandering is a punishment for disobedience, and there is even reason to suppose that the conception has been extended from one generation [that is, 40 years] to up to four generations, according to the period in which a pentateuchal passage was composed. This supports the second observation, that in fact the whole complex of ideas derives not from any historical experience, but from a mythical account of the exile and the gradual passage of time spent in Babylon.) To resume Talmon's objections: he notes that the conception of the desert reflected in biblical allusions bears 'witness to a deep-seated aversion to and a great fear of such conditions (we shall revert to the matter of fear), not a longing for them'.[58] The biblical figures who are most closely associated with the desert (that is, Ishmael and Esau) are, he remarks, not 'by any stretch of imagination...the Biblical writers' ideal type'.[59] The Rechabites, on the other hand, are not an ideal but a real people, and the historical reality of their social and environmental conditions cannot be taken as the source of the biblical motif.[60] Talmon himself takes the desert to have two primary references. These he deals with under the categories of spatial-geophysical and temporal-historical modes.[61] In the former, analysis of the term *midbār* indicates a wide range of meanings, covered broadly by the English 'drift', in the sense of pasturage which ranges from the edge of agricultural land to the desert properly speaking. As the fringe of settled regions and the amorphous space beyond, inhabited by wild men and wilder animals, the image is basically a negative one, though it can give rise to more positive features, such as the imagery of the shepherd[62] or that of the tent.[63] These however remain secondary characteristics.[64] In the latter, the distinction is drawn between historical reminiscence and the use of *midbār* as a motif. (I am not sure that this distinction can be maintained, especially if the 'historical' experiences are either influenced by or actually constructed out of the application of the motif). The motif is used mainly in pre-exilic literature.[65] It is dominated by two constituent themes: the Sinai theophany and the period of punishment. The latter, Talmon insists, is the more important.[66] But I cannot take seriously the latter of these categories as *pre-exilic.* It seems to me that the punishment in question is retrojected as paradigmatic from the real (that is historical) time of punishment, which is the exile itself. The notion of the wilderness period as punishment is in fact a metaphor for the concept of the pariah people, which itself emerged in exile.[67] When he turns to Hosea's use of the desert motif, Talmon sees a combination of two elements: a transition aspect which is 'obviously derived from the account of the historical desert trek', and a 'marital love image', which he links with the Song of Songs (3.6) and ultimately with KTU 1.5 v 18-23, the account of Baal's sacred marriage with Anat.[68] He insists on the separation of these, and sees the first as deriving from 'the account of the historical desert trek'. But the relationship may be reversed: that is, the whole notion of the desert trek may owe its ultimate origin to Hosea's metaphorical usage, which relates (I am suggesting) not to any memory of past events, but specifically to the sacred marriage motif, which refers in an extended and adapted sense to the nation's current predicament, and in an ideological sense to the notion of the nation as child of the deity (that is, the extension to the people at large of the royal ideological motif). We may even conjecture that behind the bicolon in Hosea 11.1 we have an original form reading somewhat as follows:

> For Israel was a prince and I loved him,
> and from the desert I called to him (or: called my son).

This involves only minimal alteration of MT, and is justified. As it stands the final colon reads 'and from Egypt I called to my son', which is hard to credit. BHS suggests *lô*, following LXX. In view of the strong possibility that we have an allusion to the sacred marriage, 'my son' seems equally plausible, and seems to have been in one recension, now combined with the other in MT.[69] For *mimmiṣrayim* I propose *mimmidbār*, as translated above, or even *mimmidbar yām* (the alteration of *db* to *ṣ* not being accountable in terms of a simple textual corruption, *miṣrayim* may be explained as an exilic gloss on *midbār*, or even an alteration from it, once the equation of Egypt and Babylon had developed in exilic thought.) The formula **midbar yām* would be conceptually identical with the locale of the sacred marriage in KTU 1.23. However, while this conjecture fits very nicely into the view I am taking here, it is not essential to it. I see the allegedly historical allusion here as a secondary historicizing of an originally mythical allusion. Thus the sacred marriage motif is the original theme being dealt with by Hosea, and it is significant that he treats it in accordance with the boundary symbolism we have detected in other versions.

But none of this answers the basic question: what is the relationship between the centre and the boundary? The problem is compounded by the lack of any clear rational links in the evidence so far considered. We do however have two passages which hint at just the nexus for which we are seeking. The first is Isaiah 21.1-10. There is no need to treat the entire oracle here. It is concerned with the destruction of Babylon (vv. 9-10). It begins with the formula *midbar-yām* which I have suggested may lie behind Hosea 11.1. If that be rejected, it appears here as a *hapax*, but has precisely the dimension which I suggested underlay the change in Hosea to *miṣrayim*, that is, the thematic identification of Egypt and Babylon. A southerly or southwesterly wind from the Negev, implicitly coming up from the sea (and therefore from the general direction of Egypt) heralds the doom of the eastern fringe of the world. The first verse reads:

> Oracle of the desert by the sea:
> As whirlwinds sweep from the Negev,
> from the desert they come,
> from the fearful underworld.[70]

This evokes the boundary image we have been exploring. In a sense, the whirlwind is a quality of the desert (and indeed echoes the term *sûp* or *sôp* applied to the sea: *sûpôt*) which as it were proceeds inwards from the boundary. The idea which I believe may be implicit here is explicit in Joel 2.3:

Before them fire devours
and behind them flame consumes.
Like the Garden of Eden is the land before them
and behind them is a wasteland *(midbar)* of devastation.

This is part of a description of swarm of locusts like an avenging army approaching Jerusalem on the Day of Yahweh. The second bicolon is the more important. It suggests that the army's (that is, the locusts') advance transforms Paradise (that is, the Holy Land) into a desert. Therefore, it undoes creation. The differentiation of Paradise and the desert is reversed: cosmos reverts to chaos. The two become one, which is another expression of cosmic destruction, since creation began with the separation of a primordial oneness (conceptualized as the sea-dragon) into its different constituents.[71]

We may say that the first principle of creation is a binary division. This is commonly expressed in terms of a primordial couple locked in close embrace. They separate, and the offspring of their coupling is the first of the lesser gods. This imagery of the archetypal marriage is to be understood on a number of levels. On the cosmological level it represents a sexual metaphor for the initial differentiation of primary substances. On a spatial level it represents the distinction of human space (that is, the home – city, town, village, tent – and the surrounding economically useful territory) from the amorphous and hostile wild country beyond. On a theological level it represents the myth of origin of a people's gods, and this in turn is a figure for and legitimization of the hierarchical and structural norms of a society, with its monarch at the head. The point about the contrast between centre and boundary is therefore not so much an ontological contrast, though as it develops into a dead metaphor it is understandable that such a distinction should arise, as an intuition of the first existential differentiation in the world at the time of its creation. The elements belong in the same relationship to each other as do *Apsu* and *Ti'amat* in *Enuma Eliš,* or heaven and earth (underworld?) in Genesis 1.1. In the latter instance, the moment before the differentiation takes place is *tōhû wābōhû,* that is a chaotic commingling of the raw materials of the cosmos.

Now while all peoples construct worlds after this fashion, with infinite variations on the common theme, there is also a common nostalgia for the precosmic condition. Life is separation and pain. Couples yearn to become one. While it has become somewhat distant from the purely sexual dimension, to which however it remains attached in the sacred marriage tradition, I suggest that the similar imagery used of the centre and the boundary, gods appearing in both, the remote divine dwelling place being comparable with the holy of holies in the city temple, the archetypal sacred marriage on the boundary being reenacted in rites within the temple, indicate an ultimate desire to reunite that which has been put asunder. Cult may be defined as 'the ritual structuring of space and time'. In the present context we may go further, and suggest that cult is also the ritual abolition of space and time. To the *illud tempus* corresponds the *ille locus*. Centre and boundary are its two aspects.

Endnotes

* First published in *UF* 19 (1987): 375-89.

1. See Montgomery 1938; Snaith 1965; Luysten 1978 (derived from Mesopotamian myth: against this view see Day 1985: 49ff.); Towers 1959; Wifall 1980 (both see Egyptian elements in the mythology); Hay 1964 (historical substratum influenced by cosmogonic traditions); Batto 1983. The reading *sôp* or *sûp* is immaterial – either a noun or an infinitive. A cosmological understanding has been rejected by Kloos 1986: 153-57.

2. Usefully collated and discussed by Day 1985. I have criticized some aspects of this study in Wyatt 1985b. See also the important discussion in Kloos 1986.

3. Rendtorff 1954; Stuhlmueller 1970. See also von Rad 1962–66: II, 241, and B.W. Anderson 1962.

4. *qaṣê* is masculine. It is arguable that to preserve the feminine value of the line we should read *miqṣat* (from the feminine *qaṣâ*).

5. Or: 'in'. In view of the significance of divine naming discussed below, this should perhaps to be understood to mean 'named by me'.

6. Omitting the *w* (BHS).

7. This may be intrusive (BHS). The line is certainly inelegant, but the three successive verbs, create, form, make, do give an emphatic conclusion to the section.

8. See Watson 1986: 123-27.

9. While we cannot be sure that a fully-developed myth on the analogy of Ra and Apepi was part of the West Semitic cosmological tradition, the hymn to Shapsh in the closing lines of the Baal cycle (KTU 1.6 vi 43-53) may be tentatively construed in this fashion. (See now, however, Husser 1997.)

10. Thus making nonsense of attempts to distinguish Baal's and El's abodes. Cf. my remarks, Wyatt 1985b: 380-81.

11. The same ambivalence is no doubt present in Ugaritic usage. While in one sense Mt Saphon is to be identified with Mt Ḫazzi/Kasios = Jebel El Aqra to the north of the city, in another sense there was undoubtedly a 'mystical identity' of it with the city acropolis and its temples. (On Saphon see now Chapter 9, and for the significance of spatial vocabulary, Chapter 10, and Wyatt 2001a *passim*.)

12. For Teman as connected with theophanies see Habakkuk 3.3.

13. Cf. Brueggemann 1972.

14. Cf. G.R.H. Wright 1970; Terrien 1970; Keel 1978.

15. Hall 1966.

16. See Hayman 1986. See also *PGM* XIII 335: Betz 1986: 181.

17. Cf. Marc 1977.

18. See Berger and Luckmann 1971 and Berger 1973.

19. D. Davies 1977.

20. See the illuminating comments of Staal 1975: 53 on *dvandva*. The *Upaniṣads* in particular are saturated with this way of thought.

21. For further discussion see Watson 1986: 321-24, with bibliography, 324.

22. Cf. Pedersen 1926: 474.

23. See Chapter 3.

24. For the early limited territorial conception see 1 Samuel 26.19 and 2 Kings 5.17. For Yahweh as absent from the underworld (and thus implicitly not in control of it) see Psalm 6.6 (EVV 5). Contrast the view of Psalm 139.7, 8.

25. Day 1985: 50. For Luysten 1978, following Pedersen 1940: 728-37, it is the myth which has given rise to the exodus tradition, and in particular the miracle at the sea.

26. I have omitted the following lines: 2: sons of the du[nes] (?)
My (former) student John Love has suggested that we should read here *bn .šp*[*š*] – 'sons of Shapsh': this is quite plausible in the context. (See also Wyatt 2002a: 325, n. 2.) In view of the matter of *yam sûp/sôp* we may conjecture that the surviving words are complete (i.e. *šp* = Hebrew *sûp/sôp*), reading 'sons of the end' (sc. reference to *yam sûp/sôp*). However, while Ugaritic *š* especially in initial position often = Hebrew *ś* (*sin*), it does not = *s* (*samek*), so we should require there to be a scribal error, an unnecessary accumulation of conjectures!

> 13 (cf. 28): Yea, divine are the breasts,
> the breasts of Athirat and Raḥma[y].

I have taken *šd* here to stand for *ṯd*. Alternatively we have a reference to *šd* = 'steppe'.

27. *mdb:* tide. See Albright 1934: 135, n. 181.

28. For slightly modified translations of both texts, with commentary, see Wyatt 2002a: 163-64, 325, 330, 334-35.

29. I can find no references to the issue in any of the literature on either text.

30. This interpretation is now to be regarded as superseded by the analysis of Tsumura and Watson, discussed and implemented in my translation in Wyatt 2002a: 332 and n. 45.

31. Cf. the view of Cutler and Macdonald 1982, that the rite is intended to counteract famine.

32. See Wyatt 1986a: 422.

33. KTU 1.1 iv 14. See Wyatt 1985a: 121, and now 2002a: 48, n. 51.

34. Gibson 1978: 37-38. Cf. del Olmo Lete 1981: 166-67.

35. Cf. my discussion in Wyatt 1986a, and in Chapter 4 above. I have taken these two discussions further in Wyatt 1986d.

36. The lines read *btrbṣ bn amt* – 'from the stable of the son of a/the handmaid'. The son is hardly El himself (Gibson 1978: 83, n. 8) but the king. As Gibson notes, 'the words are conventional', and are probably drawn from the bovine milieu of some of the versions of the sacred marriage. This suggests that we should construe the stable tradition in Luke 2.7, 12 not in its usual sense, implying the rejection of Christ, but rather in an ideological sense. (If 'stable' sounds too equine, perhaps render 'stall'.) See further Wyatt 1990b.

37. On the multiple levels of meaning of this term (general service, cult, and cultivation) see Wyatt 1988b. There may be a fourth sense: cf. the English 'serve' as a sexual term.

38. See Wyatt 1983: 273, and also 2002a: 209.

39. Cf. Ahlström 1963: 76.

40. This fragmentary passage also contains all the formulae being discussed here: birth from sacred marriage, divine parentage, suckling and naming, and even the legitimization formula 'beloved' (Wyatt 1985a). See del Olmo's version (1981: 494).

41. As is recognized by del Olmo 1981: 482.

42. Cf. n. 5 above. For an Egyptian example of divine naming see Beyerlin 1978: 30.

43. See Tromp 1969: 59-66; Keel 1978: 73-75. Cf. the imagery of cosmic kingship (i.e. of rule over the entire cosmos) in Psalms 72.8, 89.26 (EVV 25) (Keel 1978: 21-22, Wyatt 1998a). Yam's designation *zbl ym* || *ṯpṭ nhr* ('Prince Sea, Lord River) denotes not his control of the waters of Ugarit's immediate environment (sc. the Mediterranean and local streams) but his cosmic (or anti-cosmic) sway. His realm is comparable and ultimately identical with Mot's.

44. See n. 7. If 'formed' is retained, it has overtones of begetting. Cf. the Egyptian motif of the god Khnum making the king and his ka on the wheel, which is a constructional metaphor equivalent to his divine begetting.

45. The only innovation in the latter passage is that it reads 'towards the rock of my grave (or: libation pipe)'. (On the impossibility of the latter sense see now Pitard 1994.)

46. Lit. 'tells'. Though plural In form, *tlm* is to be taken as dual and identified with the two named rocks In the previous cola. C.H. Gordon construes *tlm* as 'furrow' – Gordon 1977: 101.

47. 'Earth...earth...underworld': *arṣ* in all three cases. At times the precise nuance is impossible to determine. The translation in Wyatt 2002a: 112-13, is slightly modified.

48. The translation in Wyatt 2002a: 126 (cf. 134, 231) is slightly modified.

49. So Gibson 1978: 73, n. 4. For *dbr* ('pasture') del Olmo (1981: 535) understands 'plague'. But see now Wyatt 2002a: 126, n. 51.

50. See Millard 1984. While it would be very convenient(!) in the present discussion to be able to show a link between *ʿeden* (of the centre) and Sumerian EDIN ('steppe'), Millard has shown that such a link is impossible. On the use of the morpheme *ʿdn* in Ugaritic see Millard 1984: 106, nn. 9, 10.

51. See de Moor 1969a: 106-107; *idem*, 1971: 187.

52. KTU 1.6 i 65.

53. As represented by Petersen and Woodward 1977.

54. See Budde 1895; Flight 1923; Haldar 1950.

55. Talmon 1966.

56. Talmon 1966: 34.

57. Talmon 1966: 37.

58. Talmon 1966: 38.

59. Talmon 1966: 36.

60. Talmon 1966: 37.

61. Talmon 1966: 39-46 and 46-55 respectively.

62. The shepherd is a primary image of royal leadership found widely in ancient Near Eastern thought, and is not specific to any Palestinian experience.

63. An important cosmological and cosmogonic motif, and again not specific to the context.

64. Talmon 1966: 46.

65. Talmon 1966: 47.

66. Talmon 1966, 48.

67. See Weber 1952: 3; Mol 1976: 37-38.

68. Talmon 1966: 50-51.

69. MT's *libnî* combines *lô* with *b*^{e}*nî*.

70. The final phrase (*mê'ereṣ nôrā'â*) may be translated 'from the land of fear', but the usage *midbār* || *'ereṣ* appears to bear the cosmological overtones suggested by my translation.

71. Kloos 1986, *passim*, rejects the idea of the killing of Yam as cosmogonic in not only the Ugaritic but also the Old Testament mythology.

Chapter 6

SYMBOLS OF EXILE*

The deportation of a small but articulate group of the citizens of Judah to Babylon during the early years of the sixth century BCE may be regarded as an essential element in the birth of Judaism, in distinction from the ethnic religion of previous generations, for the traditional parameters of religious experience were suddenly removed. The state cult of Yahweh found itself bereft of those institutional supports of which it was itself the legitimization. Indeed, the destruction of the state might itself have been regarded as precisely evidence that the real condition of the nation was no longer legitimate, as was recognized by at least one redactional strand within the *Deuteronomistic History*. The power of Yahweh was not in question: what was open to doubt was his continued interest in his people. This is how the situation might be assessed from a theological perspective. From an anthropological one, both propositions might be regarded as true, since the effect was that the deportees must have undergone an identity crisis, the national deity being the natural focus of the society's symbolic structures of national and individual identity. R.W. Klein observed that 'almost all the old symbol systems had been rendered useless (by the exile). Almost all the old institutions no longer functioned' (Klein 1979: 5). The point Klein is making here is worth elaborating, as it provides an explanation of some of the innovations or transformations in ritual and social behaviour in the exilic age.

If we begin with a characterization of the *status quo ante* under the monarchy we may without too great an over-simplification think of the ideological structuring of society in these terms: the king, as son of God, mediated divine reality to his people. That is, he was believed to actualize for the nation the cosmic symbolism which was contained in the language of royal ideology, with its mythical and theological allusions to royal divinity, the idealism of the Primal Man as cosmocrator and so on. Such language was a projection into the divine realm of human concerns and aspirations, and indeed at a more fundamental level of his biological needs as a species. These have been defined by ethologists as reproductive and territorial (e.g. Ardrey 1969), while H. Mol has emphasized that both are subsumed under the over-arching need for a sense of identity (Mol 1976: 1-15). We can see the applicability of sociological and ethological analysis to royal ideology, with its emphasis precisely on the two issues of fecundity and territoriality. It may come as a surprise to consider these aspects as extensions of the prior need for identity (in Mol's sense), but this does lend considerable support to the view that the motif of the Primal Man is the locus of just such an intuition within the context of royal ideology: that is, demonstrating that the Adam figure (or his counterparts elsewhere, *Anthropos*, *Puruṣa*, and so forth) really does belong within this pattern of thought, despite views expressed to the contrary.

If we put these matters into a theoretical form which can be useful in the analysis of some exilic phenomena, we may say that the themes of fecundity and territoriality are essential as biological and social facts in the well-being of a society, that as well as being needs in their own right they can serve as metaphors for the more fundamental need for identity, and that such imagery was focused in ancient Judah in the person of the king.

We can now imagine the scale or the trauma experienced by the deportees to Babylon who lost everything of significance, material and emotional, at a stroke. The entire framework of life in terms of the metaphysical structures which gave legitimacy and meaning to it was destroyed. In such circumstances we might expect a variety of responses, and no doubt these occurred. Some less resilient personalities would no doubt go into severe depression and pine away, life no longer having any meaning or purpose. Others would ask the age-old question which arises in moments of distress: 'Why me?' And this response gave rise to the self-justifying proverb about the sour grapes criticized by Jeremiah and Ezekiel. Indeed the overall response of the exilic Deuteronomist was hardly more adequate (or perhaps its relative adequacy lay precisely in its echoing of a widespread prejudice), even if it was dressed up in more seemingly profound theological platitudes: he still effectively exonerated his own generation by blaming all the royal figures of the past, the most egregious case being that of Manasseh, who is made to bear the whole burden of the nation's sin since even Josiah's piety could not deflect the divine wrath incurred by his predecessor's iniquities, real or imagined. Others still would acknowledge an overwhelming sense of guilt and would take upon themselves the blame for all the nation's sins past and present: such a response may be seen in the suffering servant figure; although his sense of guilt is of course specifically denied in the image of vicarious suffering, this may be a rationalizing of the poet's own sense of guilt. And guilt certainly comes to shape the entire priestly theory of sacrifice (Davies 1977).

Just as important as these varied responses was the exilic community's intuitive construction of new symbolic forms as vehicles for the ancient needs. The main innovations of the period in ritual and social observances begin to make sense only when it is recognized that they are adaptations to the new circumstances. These innovations cover every aspect of life, being either transformations of ancient practices, now filled with entirely new meaning, or entirely new departures in spite of superficial connections with past practices or attitudes. I shall deal with a selection of these; there are no doubt other instances which might be explored, but the following more than establish the point I wish to make.

1. *Sabbath Observance*

The Sabbath had undoubtedly been observed before the exile. But its origin and early significance are equally obscure. It may be conceptually related to the seven-year pattern attested both in the biblical and in the Ugaritic literature, but there is no compelling reason to think so. It may also be connected with cosmological theories engendered by the existence of seven known planets in the ancient world. These certainly had a considerable impact on traditional thought, including the spatial conception of the world and its constituent parts. The idea of a spatial equivalent for a temporal observance raises no problem – see further on this below – but again we have no hard evidence in favour of such a view. Given the importance of lunar cycles in the ancient calendars of Israel and Judah, it is possible that sabbaths began as quarter-days. But a 28-day month would very quickly become incompatible with actual lunations unless intercalary days were inserted. Another candidate for influence on the Sabbath system is the institution of the so-called *šapattu* days of the Babylonian calendar. This term seems to have been used for the fifteenth day of the lunar month, and then more generally for days of ill omen within the month. Modern writers are generally unconvinced by the arguments of earlier philologists in favour of a link (Fohrer 1973: 117; Kraus 1966: 81-82).

Although there is pre-exilic evidence for the Sabbath, none of it gives a clear picture of why it was observed. The passages alluding to it are the following. Exodus 23.12 legislates for rest on the seventh day (the term *šabbāt* not occurring). If original to its context, this passage belongs to perhaps one of the oldest parts of the Bible. The motive for cessation of work is purely humanitarian (or perhaps utilitarian!), without specific or intrinsic religious meaning, and indeed is probably independent of the cult of Yahweh, into which it was only later incorporated (Alt 1934 = 1966: 97ff.). There is no further reference to the observance until the mid-eighth century, when Hosea lists it along with other times of festival, for the first time indicating a religious aspect: Hosea 2.13 (MT). The juxtaposition with new moons suggests, but does not prove, some association with the full moon, and NEB offers this as an alternative translation. The same linking of new moon and Sabbath is found in the roughly contemporaneous Amos 8.5, which supports the connection with the full moon indirectly, by indicating that new moons, like Sabbaths, were the occasion for a rest from work: the complaint is that money-making is interrupted by these untimely observances. Further possible pre-exilic allusions, now incorporated into the exilic *Deuteronomistic History*, are 2 Kings 4.23 and 11.5, which add nothing to our information.

Other allusions to the Sabbath all belong to the exile or later. Three important passages have widely been taken to be early, but in every case an exilic date is more likely, even though they no doubt have a literary prehistory. These are Exodus 34.21 (J/E), 20.8-11 (E) and Deuteronomy 5.12-15 (D). The first of these purports to be the second *verbatim* account of the version in Exodus 20, but is in fact quite different. Far from being primitive, as its designation as a 'ritual' decalogue (actually a dodecalogue) may imply, the context in which it is written already presupposes Exodus 20; while this is in part the result of redactional activity, as Whitley has noted (Whitley 1963: 41), the whole vocabulary, style and presuppositions of Exodus 34 are derived from deuteronomistic (mid-exilic) thought, and it cannot in its present form be earlier. The case of the other passages is also complex. It has often been argued that of all the legal traditions the decalogue at least should be traced back to Moses. There is no objective reason for this. It is also widely assumed that the decalogue in Deuteronomy 5 is derived from that in Exodus 20. The reverse is more likely, because of the distinctive second person singular mode of address common to both. This is quite anomalous within Exodus, but is normative for older parts in Deuteronomy (Minette de Tillesse 1962). It makes better sense to argue that the Deuteronomy decalogue has been lifted wholesale, with minor adaptations but with the preservation of the form of address, than to argue that the Exodus decalogue has been taken as the model, since it is its singular form which is problematic, and it is clearly intrusive in its present context.

The original form and relationship of the two decalogues is not central to our argument, however. Even allowing a pre-exilic background, the significant feature for present purposes is the different motivation in each decalogue for Sabbath-observance. In Deuteronomy the motivation here, as for all piety, is loving gratitude for Yahweh's saving act in bringing Israel out of Egypt. In Exodus the Sabbath is to be observed as a memorial of the six days of creation, followed by Yahweh's rest on the seventh. Both contrast with Exodus 34.21, which in this respect at least is archaic, in that no reason for the observance is given: even in Exodus 23.12 we have seen that a rationale is offered. The allusion to the six days of creation also points to the exilic period as the milieu for Exodus 20, since it either presupposes Genesis 2.2-3, or is at least familiar with the cosmological background to the P creation tradition.

While the motivation for Sabbath-observance in Deuteronomy may be regarded as no more than the bringing of this, among other prescriptions, within the purview of the kerygma of Yahweh's saving acts, itself quite consistent with the exilic period which evidently saw a resurgence in interest in the old tradition, the reason in Exodus takes it back to its unconscious roots in cosmology: the very foundation of the world is established on a divine regard for the structure of time, and this is now prescriptive for man as well. Something of the genius of the connection made here will become clear in our discussion below. The complementary nature of the two motivations offered can be seen by their skilful amalgamation in the preaching of Deutero-Isaiah, for whom cosmogony and redemption become synonymous (Rendtorff 1954; Stuhlmuller 1970). So far as the Sabbath is concerned, each seventh day becomes a figure for world-renewal; this is not only a paradigm for the total reappraisal of their position which was forced on the exiles if they were to survive, but also served as an anamnesis of redemption, thus promising that out of the darkness of their present experience a new dawn was about to break.

Other important features of the Sabbath were brought out by Kraus and de Vaux. The former noted that 'the observance of the Sabbath became a confessional act of great importance in a land where different time systems prevailed' (Kraus 1966: 87). De Vaux pointed out that the exiles were prevented from continuing their regular sacrificial cult, and that the Sabbath grew in importance as a way of delineating 'sacred time', which was always a primary motive in the structuring of any cult (de Vaux 1965: 482). We may even define cult as the ritual structuring of space and time. The former can be observed in the theoretical and symbolic features of any temple (Keel 1978: 112ff.); here we see its temporal counterpart, or as de Vaux put it, a substitute for it. Exodus 35.1-2 prohibits fires on the Sabbath, while Numbers 15.32-36 gives an account of the fate of a man who ignored the prohibition. While purporting to deal with an ancient event, this has all the marks of a cautionary tale addressed to the exilic community. What strikes us as an extreme sanction is to be construed as a desperate remedy for what was understood to be a serious threat to cosmic equilibrium. Exodus

31.12-17 belongs to P, and serves as a fine peroration to the P material delivered on Sinai, suggesting that like creation in Genesis 1.1–2.4a, the cultic instructions preceding it are all to be understood as operative within a 'sabbatically conceived universe', that is, one structured within an order of reality represented and symbolized by the Sabbath. We shall take up this point below. Verses 12 and 13 may owe something to Ezekiel 20.12-13, or at any rate have some connection with it, both passages seeing the Sabbath as a sign (*'ôt*) – the term may here be defined as a 'perpetual theophany' – sealing the relationship of deity and people. The passage then continues, evidently with a history of some literary complexity (Noth 1962: 240-41), reiterating the idea of the sign and coupling it with that of the covenant (*berît ᶜôlām* || *'ôt ᶜôlām*, vv. 16-17). De Vaux remarked of the motives given in the two decalogues (Exodus 20 and Deuteronomy 5) for Sabbath observance that both are connected with the covenant (de Vaux 1965: 481-82). In neither case is this stated or even indicated in the text, but in so far as covenantal theory became a central motif of exilic theology, de Vaux's view is unobjectionable. But here the theme is explicitly stated: Sabbath observance is an indication of membership of the covenant community. The apparent lack of interest in a Sinaitic covenant in P has been noted (Ackroyd 1968: 95; van Seters 1975: 291); instead he gives in Genesis 17 his equivalent to J's patriarchal covenant of Genesis 15. The Sinai (Horeb) covenant has as it were been broken – a powerful metaphor for the disaster of 587 – and is now replaced by an unconditional offer to the patriarchs (Ackroyd 1968: 96-97; van Seters 1975: 265). It is evident that the issue is not quite so clear-cut as this suggests, for not only is the important image of the covenant renewed in Exodus 34 ultimately the responsibility of P, if only in his redactional capacity, but the present sabbatical covenant is set in the context of P's own Sinaitic material. It is also to be seen as a particular covenant, while having an obvious link with the universal application of Genesis 1. Furthermore, it is untrue to describe P's conception of the covenant as 'unconditional', since the very prescriptive language of Exodus 31.13ff. implies the conditional nature of the relationship that the sabbatical covenant is supposed to preserve, and the sanction of death for its breaking given in v. 15b ultimately applies to the whole nation. This may be compared with the sanction of excommunication in Genesis 17.14.

2. *Circumcision*

It is clear that circumcision, like Sabbath observance, has antecedents in the prehistory of Judahite and Israelite culture. It was probably practised among peoples with whom they had contact in the early period, since only the Philistines (1 Samuel 18.25 etc.) and the Hurrians (Genesis 34: see Wyatt 1990a) were remarkable for not observing the rite. Joshua 5.2ff. describes a rite of mass-circumcision to which Joshua subjected the tribes after they had crossed the Jordan. In v. 9 Yahweh says to Joshua: 'Today I have taken away (*gālôtî*) the shame of Egypt from you'. One point in the story is the aetiology of the name Gilgal, explained here in terms of 'rolling away' (*gll*) the shame – that is, the ritual pollution – caused by the people's sojourn in a foreign land. As we shall see below, the idea of residence in a foreign land causing pollution was a dominant one in the minds of the exilic community. Another important feature of this curious story is the fact that it is concerned with a second generation of people: those who had left Egypt had died off; these were their sons. This again points to the conditions of exile for its historical reference: the wilderness setting is parabolic. If the possibility of an exilic date for the narrative is accepted, then the paronomasia *gilgal, gālal, gālâ* makes excellent sense as an allusion also to *gālâ, gālût* referring to exile. The institution of circumcision – not a rolling, but a cutting away! – removes the pollution of exile. The story in Joshua 5 is not intended as an explanation of the origins of circumcision, since it specifically states (v. 5) that those who came out of Egypt had been circumcised.

When we start searching for the oldest Israelite, Judahite or earlier usage, it is surprising to find very little hard evidence for it. It is pointless looking for ancient legal prescriptions on the matter: there are none. Such information as there is deals primarily with other matters (as Exodus 12.48) or presupposes the historical process I want to examine here (Leviticus 12.3). The practice as attested elsewhere appears to have two alternative purposes: either it is a puberty rite or it is a marriage rite. In each case it is a *rite de passage*, ritualizing the transition from one condition to another. Since all the great transitions, these together with birth and death, are universally ritualized according to forms of great antiquity, we would hardly expect any ancient law-code to deal with them. Their practices are just taken for granted, and have no forensic connection.

The only evidence apparently from an early period which is relevant to our discussion is the curious story in Exodus 4.24-26. This passage may be attesting a change in the significance of the rite and in its manner of observance. If this is so, we may suspect an archaizing rather than archaic character, and perhaps see it as evidence of its exilic date. An alteration in a traditional ritual procedure requires a substantial reason, and while we can do no more than conjecture, the trauma and convulsions of the exile offer a far more plausible context than any other for this. In its present form the narrative appears to tell how Yahweh tried to kill Moses by night, and Zipporah quickly circumcised her son, touched his (the son's? Moses'?) genitals with the foreskin and declared 'Indeed you are a bridegroom of blood to me!' While the inclusion of Moses in the text is an unwarranted liberty in some versions, the touching of her son's genitals with the foreskin hardly squares with her words, and since Zipporah's action must be connected in some way both with Moses' immediate danger and with his status as her husband, it is not unreasonable to infer that the suffix to *raglāyw* does indeed refer to Moses. There is no other candidate (Kaplan 1981). Now while this tale bristles with difficulties, we may attempt an explanation. On the supposition that adult circumcision had been the norm, for which there are reasons as we shall see, it being a marriage rite, the story is saying that the new norm of infant circumcision is the more powerful in warding off the threat to Moses, who here represents the exilic community. Yahweh threatening Moses by night is a figure for the threat of death which hangs over the whole community during its 'night' – that is, its present experience of exile. There is also an undoubted symbolic dimension to the fact that Moses is *returning* to Egypt. Indeed, we may propose that the story originally stood outside its present context, and saw Moses' return to Egypt as something to be avoided at all costs (on this motif and related language in the Pentateuch, see Wyatt 1990c). This sense has however been partially obscured by its inclusion in the larger narrative framework.

In favour of seeing adult circumcision as the old norm, now replaced by infant circumcision, are the following points:

i. the story in Genesis 34, whether or not it has any direct historical reference, deals with an apparently early period in Shechem, and has Simeon and Levi impose premarital circumcision on Shechem and his fellow citizens. This can only represent an Israelite norm, since the Hivites (that is, Hurrians) were clearly not already circumcised. (See further, Wyatt 1990a.)

ii. The late circumcision of those coming from Egypt in Joshua 5 would make nonsense if infant circumcision were already the norm. As an adult rite, it adds greater piquancy to the crossing of the Jordan which precedes it: Israel has now crossed over from the land of death (Egypt and the wilderness) into the land of life (Palestine), and the image of the unleashing of new fertility is most appropriately represented by the relevant *rite de passage*. It is as though a national *hieros gamos* is about to be consummated.

iii. The terms *ḥōtēn* and *ḥātān*, which mean respectively wife's father and daughter's husband, or bridegroom (as in Exodus 4.25-26) are derived from a term meaning 'to circumcise', the former meaning literally 'the circumciser' and the latter 'the circumcised'. In other words, the terms are related to rites of circumcision in the context of marriage. (For evidence from Ugarit supporting this marital context, see now Wyatt 2002; Allan 1999.)

iv. The Passover rules in Exodus 12.43-49 – which incidentally reflect the exilic period in that they think of a confessing community – require that slaves who wish to participate in the Passover rites be circumcised. While this might conceivably include children, it presumably refers directly to adults who are not only bought for their present rather than their future capacity for work, but are also of an age to ask to participate.

The connecting of circumcision with the Passover marks this passage as transitional between the old social practice and the new confessional one, at a point before the changeover to infant circumcision. The transition may be explained on the analogy of baptism in the early Christian Church. Once it became a matter of community-allegiance, to the point where being uncircumcised 'cut one off' from the religious life of the community, there would be considerable pressure to bring males of whatever age within the community. Within perhaps no more than a generation, the changeover to universal infant circumcision would be complete, in that only adult proselytes would be uncircumcised, all males brought up within the community having undergone the rite before reaching maturity. A sanction would be required for this, and we have suggested that the narrative in Exodus 4.24-26 serves this purpose. It is however opaque to say the least, and Genesis 17 is an altogether more systematic presentation of the same point. Abraham is a useful ideological figure in exilic thought. Isaac represents the northern kingdom of Israel and Jacob the southern one of Judah; as their parent Abraham represents the broader concept incorporated into the term Israel once the destruction of the northern kingdom emancipated it from a purely political significance. The covenant made here between God and Abram, whose change of name to Abraham is itself a mark of the change of status, is to be marked (puns seem inescapable here) by circumcision. The rule given is eighth day circumcision of infant males, though Abraham himself is now circumcised only in his ninety-ninth year (v. 24), Ishmael at 13 years (v. 25) and Isaac only at Genesis 21.4 on the eighth day after his birth. The scaling down of the ages is almost a schematic account of the progressive reduction in age of candidates for circumcision. The allusion in Genesis 21.2 to Isaac's birth fulfilling a divine promise in Abraham's old age is a further pointer to the new significance now invested in the rite. Rather like the circumcision at the Jordan crossing, its specific reference to regeneration is stressed.

The significance of the entire story is perhaps also made clearer when it is recognized that the theme of the aged and childless patriarch who miraculously begets a son is a direct echo of the hierogamic tradition of the Ugaritic text KTU 1.23. J.R. Porter has shown how the story of Lot and his daughters in Genesis 19.30-38 is related to the Canaanite tradition (Porter 1978). The present context and its variant in the Ishmael cycle (Genesis 16.1ff., 21.8ff.) is also derived from the same milieu (KTU 1.12: Astour 1967: 86; on this material see also Wyatt 1996b: 219-91). The youthfulness of the child circumcised, so soon after birth, relates directly to his birth as the renewal of the community, and at the same time, being removed from the more overtly sexual context of marriage, makes the *passage* one of spiritual transformation, from the profane and natural world into the sacred, hieratic one of the confessing people of God.

3. *Dietary Laws*

The observance of dietary restrictions may have been of very early origin in ancient Israelite and Judahite society, just as Sabbath observance and circumcision had antecedents going back for centuries before the exile, although in both cases we have seen a new significance given to them in the exile. An examination of the texts dealing with dietary matters does not however give any secure sense of an adaptation of ancient practices. Deuteronomy 14.4-21a appears to be the only passage of pre-exilic date. But the section is couched in the plural, and is a later insertion into the singular material now surrounding it. It is this that provides a useful starting point to discussion, because before the incorporation of vv. 4-20, Deuteronomy 14.3, 21 would have read continuously (v. 21 all originally in the singular), and attest a type of dietary restriction which predates the development of the more elaborate, and indeed quite different, kind that concerns us here.

The original passage, in the second person singular, reads:

> You shall not eat any abomination (*tôʿēbâ*). You (read sg.) shall eat no carcase. To the resident alien (*gēr*) who is within your gates you may give it that he may eat it, or sell it to a foreigner. For you are a people separated (*ʿam qādōš*) to Yahweh your god.

The exact reference of the term 'abomination' is not immediately clear here, and it can easily be seen how a later generation has sought to give examples in order to clarify its meaning: it is a perfect example of a legal principle and its practical application. It is entirely possible that *tôʿēbâ* actually denoted so-called 'unclean animals', of course, but we cannot assume this as a principle of interpretation, especially since a distinct terminology (*ṭāhōr*: clean, *ṭāmê*: unclean) is used in the list of animals. While *tôᶜēbâ* denotes something that is offensive, we should not automatically suppose it to have a moral sense, though it may have, as in Deuteronomy 25.13-16, concerned with double dealing in weights and measures (and even here the moral sense may be secondary). Remarrying a divorced wife who in the meantime married someone else is *tôᶜēbâ*, as is the combination of incompatible religious practices (Deuteronomy 24.1-4, 1 Kings 14.24, etc.). G. von Rad suggested that the term originally denoted something disqualified from cultic use (von Rad 1966a: 101), and cited further examples of this and extended senses. The feature common to them all is that they are categorically unacceptable (in the strictest sense of the term) in Israel. That is, the question is one of a threat posed by the mixing of different categories, or of the same ones, when custom made this inappropriate.

The term *ṭāmê* corresponds in some respects to *tôᶜēbâ*, and any moral sense is again absent at least in its primary application. It covers, for instance, all kinds of sexual conditions (discharges, menstruation, childbirth) which are perfectly natural, as well as any kind of situation or contact which pollutes a person, even inadvertently. So far as animals are concerned, the following are significant: Leviticus 17.15 states that anyone eating an animal that has died other than by slaughter is made unclean, and must undergo ritual purification. Leviticus 7.21 refers to pollution caused by any contact with something unclean – including implicitly both the animals covered above and bodily conditions of the type mentioned – which makes subsequent participation in a communion sacrifice a capital offence. Leviticus 5.2, while betraying the influence of the dietary laws of Leviticus 11, refers again to such contacts and stresses a person's responsibility for his condition. All three passages refer to defilement by physical contact, and illustrate the general principle. It is immaterial whether an animal is classified as clean or unclean – that being a later development; what defiles is contact with a dead thing in the first and third examples, where the unclean status of the animal probably arises in the first instance because it is dead. (So far as bodily discharges are concerned, though the situation is probably more complex, it is perhaps in part because they are also 'dead', 'cut off' from the living body.) Indeed Leviticus 11.24-25, part of the summary of the dietary laws in the chapter, betrays its original independence of these laws, since the issue of uncleanness is specifically touching the animal's carcase. A similar concern lies behind the law of the nazirite in Numbers 6.6-11, and the general rule on defilement in Numbers 19.11-16.

Two pre-exilic passages are of interest to us. In Judges 13.2-7 the conception of Samson is announced to Manoah's wife in a theophany. Since his nazirite status obtains from that moment, she is to abstain from foods which would break his vow. She is to forgo any alcohol and to eat nothing unclean (*ṭāmê*). The double prohibition implies a double freedom, to consume both under normal circumstances: the prohibition on eating unclean food when under a vow presupposes that at other times it may be eaten. Deuteronomy 14.3, 21, discussed above, was presumably composed (during the eighth century) at a time when the rule on consuming such food was being tightened up for the Yahweh-worshipping community in the northern kingdom, perhaps due to a self-consciousness developing along lines not dissimilar to those obtaining during the exile. The other passage, in Hosea 9.3-4, is even more instructive because it alludes to deportations envisaged from the northern kingdom:

> They will not live in Yahweh's land,
> and Ephraim will return to Egypt,
> and in Assyria they will eat unclean food.
> They will not pour libations of wine to Yahweh,
> nor will their sacrifices be pleasing to him.
> As mourning bread to them will be all that they eat:
> they shall become unclean.
> For their food is for themselves (alone):
> it will not come into the house of Yahweh.

The parallelism of Egypt and Assyria is startling, and is dealt with by Wolff (Wolff 1974b: 14-15). The broad reference of the rest of the passage is to funeral feasting. There is no reason to think that this was frowned upon as a custom in early times, but since it involved contact however indirect with the dead, it inevitably caused pollution, which would then need to be expiated by ritual means. Hosea then goes on to compare this ritually impure condition, in which any participant would temporarily find himself, with the permanent condition in which the exiles to Assyria would find themselves. Exile, removal from the sacred territory of the national deity sanctified by his cult, was tantamount to a spiritual death: the exile would be as it were at a permanent funeral, everything eaten being polluting without any recourse to purification.

In none of the pre-exilic passages noted is there any evidence of familiarity with the lists of clean and unclean animals of Deuteronomy 14 and Leviticus 11. Even within the exile, a passage such as Ezekiel 4.9ff. betrays no such knowledge. Ezekiel's disclaimer in 4.14 indicates that for him 'polluted flesh' (*bᵉsar piggūl*) is not a certain species of animal but, in accordance with the ancient tradition, meat from an animal that has died naturally or been killed by a predator. The two lists must therefore post-date Ezekiel, and presumably belong to the later exilic period. This is because the distinction between clean and unclean animals in the J part of the flood story can hardly be later than the exile. The whole point of the flood story is as a parable of the destruction of Jerusalem (Clines 1978: 98) and presupposes the formal distinction made in the lists.

The relationship of the two lists of animals in Deuteronomy 14 and Leviticus 11 is not immediately obvious. The list of clean animals that may be eaten in Deuteronomy 14.4b, 5, which does not occur in Leviticus 11, could be argued to show that the sources are independently derived from a third. However, the priority of Leviticus 11 may be argued on grounds of probability. Noth has drawn attention to 'the lack, conspicuous everywhere, even in 1 Kings 8, of all positive interest in cult practices' in the *Deuteronomistic History* (Noth 1981: 6). This point can be made of Deuteronomy itself, taken as a whole, and we may speak of the 'lay' nature of its teaching. The list of clean animals betrays a concern for the practical concerns of ordinary people. The detailed distinctions that follow (Deuteronomy 14.6-8, Leviticus 11.3-8) are surprising in Deuteronomy, on account of their careful classification, which is more in keeping with the priestly concerns of Leviticus. Since the Deuteronomic list is manifestly secondary in context, but is based on a principle which became of enormous importance and occurs in Leviticus 11, this arguably is its only plausible source. There is also one small matter of vocabulary which clinches the argument, which we shall treat below.

There have been numerous and largely unsatisfactory attempts to give a serious account of the dietary laws. One which is generally reckoned to have been more successful is Mary Douglas' delightful chapter on 'The Abominations of Leviticus' (Douglas 1970). After surveying previous scholarship, she proposed that the dietary rules, as so many other rules in Leviticus, should be interpreted in accordance with the oft-repeated injunction to be holy (*qādôš*, Leviticus 11.45; cf. Deuteronomy 14.21c – part of the second person singular framework to the laws in Deuteronomy). The term *qādôš* involves two principles, of separation and wholeness. The applicability of the former to the dietary laws is explicitly stated in Leviticus 11.46-47. 'Holiness', said M. Douglas, 'means keeping distinct the categories of creation. It therefore involves correct definition, discrimination and order.' (Douglas 1970: 67). The principles of differentiation are based on common experience. The economy depended on cloven-footed ruminants, so these were taken to be the norm for animals to conform to, and those which did not, because they were deficient in one or other respect, were regarded as contravening the natural order. This simple taxonomy, when applied to fish or insects, regarded scaled and finned fish as the norm (with I suspect a tradition of gastronomy behind the reasoning) and therefore other marine creatures as anomalous, or treated locusts – part of a traditional diet – as normative, and therefore other insects and small creatures of different design as anomalous. At the same time, the principle of wholeness is maintained by seeing the unclean animals as in some way half-finished or incomplete. A further study (Douglas 1972) established a wide range of analogies between the animal and human worlds, showing similarities in structure between the two worlds, and thus validating animal categories as symbols of human ones.

M. Douglas confessed that the birds in the dietary laws are difficult to incorporate in a comprehensive interpretation, and took refuge in the problems involved in translating them (Douglas 1970: 69). It is possible to argue that the unclean birds (Leviticus 11.13-19, Deuteronomy 14.12-18) have been added after the main list was drawn up, but we may suppose that even so, this was done in accordance with some perceived significance in the list, even if this has escaped attention. Now while the translation of some of the ornithological terms may be open to doubt, enough of them can at least be identified as birds of carrion or prey to suggest that this is their common factor (Driver 1955). On this basis two explanations for their inclusion are possible. Firstly, they may be regarded as analogous to mammalian predators which are conspicuous by their absence, but would of course be implicitly unclean by the criterion of the cloven-hoofed ruminant. Whether or not this be the issue, they fall foul of the principle of holiness in that they deal in death directly or otherwise, and eat meat that has not been slaughtered according to the usual procedures: they eat it 'with the blood'. The confusion they symbolize is thus one not of species so much as of the more basic categories of life and death. They blur the careful ritual distinction that must be maintained between the two orders.

Another feature of M. Douglas' analysis which invites further comment is its ahistorical nature. The question which obviously arises is not simply the general one: in what social context did these rules take shape? but the more specific one: in what historical context did they do so? If my discussion above is sound, we have established that it was during the exilic period that they were composed, after Ezekiel 4.14 and before the J flood story (or at least the incorporation of clean and unclean animals as distinct groups in it). This brings us back to the situation which may be imagined as the background to the passages from Hosea and Ezekiel discussed. The new conditions of life for the exiles in Babylon would have been extremely harsh when viewed from the perspective of cultural traditions and emotional reaction. But simply in order to survive, adaptation would begin immediately. A problem would arise immediately from the commodities on sale in the markets of Babylon. Strange foodstuffs, meats never before seen, would be on open sale, perhaps along with more familiar kinds. By way of necessary compromise, we may suppose that the latter were soon accepted, while the unfamiliar kinds were looked on with revulsion, which gradually became rationalized according to the system in the lists. As well as the matter of species, it is also entirely possible that the susceptibility of the early Church evidenced in Acts 15.20, 29 was in the mind of the writer, though it found a convenient shape in the division we have. If this were so, since a weakness in the argument is that clean as well as unclean animals would have been sacrificed in Babylon, and that it would hardly account for many unclean ones, we may conjecture that all meat in the Babylonian markets was in fact eschewed, the exiles using such of their own flocks and herds as might be with them, together with such wild things as they had been accustomed to eat in Palestine.

A curious feature in some verses in the list is the matter of redundancy. In Leviticus 11.8b (= Deuteronomy 14.8c), 11c, 24b, 25, 31b and 39b, the fact that the unclean animals are dead is surely superfluous, since they are unclean while alive. This may be interpreted as support for the proposition that the lists take their origin from the foodstuffs actually encountered. Initially the list may have warned of contact with carcasses on sale, which was simply in accordance with pre-exilic susceptibilities about dead bodies; but then the problem arose of the exiles actually buying them for food.

One final feature of the list which establishes the priority of Leviticus 11 is the occurrence of the term *mîn*, meaning 'species'. The incidence of this word in the Bible is as follows:

> Genesis 1.11, 12 × 2, 21, 24 × 2, 25 × 3; 6.20 × 3; 7.14 × 4;
> Leviticus 11.14, 15, 16, 19, 22 × 4, 29;
> Ezekiel 47.10;
> Deuteronomy 14.13, 14, 15, 18.

This word is precisely in character with the concerns of the priesthood for systematic accounts of all aspects of human life, strict classification of acceptable and unacceptable cultic, social and sexual aspects of life, and here, dietary matters. Its usage also supports M. Douglas' view that the categories in the dietary laws are based ultimately on the divisions of life forms in Genesis 1 (Douglas 1970: 70). We may go further and suggest that so restricted is the use of the word that all the instances with the exception of Ezekiel 47.10 are arguably by one hand. Whether or not this be the case, the predominance of the incidence of the term in three distinctive contexts, in the creation story, the flood story and the exilic dietary laws, is of considerable significance.

In enlarging on this matter, it is also time to take up the various points made in the foregoing discussion on which further treatment was anticipated. We began with reference to central cultic motifs associated with kingship and the stability of the nation, namely identity. Now in the priestly account of creation in Genesis 1.1–2.4a, we have the double motif of the differentiation and extension of the world from its primordial, chaotic oneness into the ordered cosmos. Differentiation and spatial extent go together; they are inseparable. At the same time(!) a function of this newly created space is time, measured spatially by the placing of the greater and lesser lights in the firmament. And the interaction of the two modes of being – space and time – is to be characterized by fertility of the various species. The careful distinction of the animals according to species in the flood story shows that while indeed the deluge is the end of the world – cosmogony reversed – the survival of a redeemed community of animals prefigures the new cosmos which is about to be created. There are two interesting aspects to this. Firstly, it reinforces the theme that creation and redemption are functions of one another, as in Deutero-Isaiah; for present purposes this means that the use of the distinctive term *mîn* in both contexts points to the dietary laws, with their concern for differentiation of various species, as the ritual working out of the creative and redemptive implications of these two narratives: now, in the exile, a new creation is in process, and the Jew can participate in it, reaffirming his identity from out of the ashes of the old life, in his observance of the dietary laws. Similarly, Sabbath observance reiterates and celebrates the primordial sabbatical structure of creation, with the same thematic echoes. The rite of circumcision at first sight appears to have little connection with these broad cosmological themes, but it is the only one of the three observances discussed, which as a *rite de passage* can actually be understood to bring about the renewal of the state which the others presuppose. They do not themselves renew: they maintain that which has hitherto been renewed. Circumcision removes the pollution of exile (above): Sabbath observance and dietary restrictions maintain a pollution-free existence for the exiles. But this implies a further symbolic dimension. All the spatial and temporal imagery is far more than a nostalgia for the past: it means that a new space and time is now created in exile. This is not perhaps to be territorially located in Babylon, so much as to be interiorized within the collective identity of the exilic community. So these rites renew old space and time on a new, non-physical level. Having lost their nationhood, their history, their land, the exiles have in their newly-structured disciplines constructed symbolic substitutes for them. It is possible, and even probable, in spite of the dearth of evidence, that the institution of the synagogue, itself a substitute for the defunct temple cult, was the milieu in which this transformation of older behavioural patterns took place.

The dietary restrictions deal with animals which because of anomalies in design are not considered perfect examples of divine order. They 'break the rules'. It may be significant that in circumcision man is deliberately mutilated, and is thus changed from his original, natural state into a new unnatural one. We should perhaps see in this a figure of his alienation from the world (we are talking here of an exilic intuition on the matter) and at the same time a sign of his cultural formation. That is, circumcision separates man from the animals, as does culture, and is a sign of it. In contrast, uncircumcised man does not participate in (Jewish) culture and by his very naturalness belongs rather with other orders of living beings in opposition to (Jewish) man. Sabbath observance is also an interruption of natural time, and serves as a figure of the distinctive Jewish culture of the exiles. The classification of animals does not at first glance fit very easily into such a mode of thinking, but we may take the clean animals, which had always participated in (proto-Jewish) culture and cult as the type of all clean beings, as figures for the propriety and holiness (itself a kind of alienation) of the Jews, and in a sense by their very taxonomic propriety in opposition from the wild, uncultured animals which remained outside normal contact and therefore unclean. These in turn would become figures of man outside the covenant. Their 'naturalness' became an image of disorder, while the classification of clean animals, like the other observances, became an image of cosmos, a world renewed in the exilic community.

Endnote

* First published in *SEÅ* 55 (1990): 39-58.

Chapter 7

Of Calves and Kings: The Canaanite Dimension in the Religion of Israel*

At the beginning of his study on the book of Hosea, G. Östborn remarked that the relation between Yahweh and Baal is 'the main problem of the history of the Old Testament religion'.[1] This is true in so far as scholars attempt to trace the links between the Canaanite religious tradition and the forms of religion occurring in Israel and Judah. It may appear that a solution to this problem has now been found, since recent studies have argued forcefully for the derivation of Yahweh's conflict with the sea from the Ugaritic myth of Baal's combat with Yam. While in terms of a literary debt there is a strong case for this, the corollary that seems to be drawn, that Yahweh is a form of Baal,[2] is perhaps more questionable. How are we then to account for the apparently persistent rivalry between the two deities envisaged for example in Deuteronomistic thought? What are we to make of the fact that on the Ugaritic evidence Baal is a dying and rising god, whatever that means, while there is no such attribution given to Yahweh? And above all, what of the Old Testament's own evidence to the effect that Yahweh has a close relation with El? Clearly these and other questions remain to be answered. It is difficult to know where to start an enquiry into these matters. To the obvious retort that we should start at the beginning, one can only reply that it is difficult to know just where the beginning is, since traditions purporting to deal with the remote past often turn out on further enquiry to be dealing with a later period. I shall begin with what appears to be a historical episode, which has its antecedents, to be sure, and indeed appears at first glance to repeat an earlier event.

The episode is Jeroboam's reform, and the narrative of this in 1 Kings 12.26-33 has literary links with the story of the golden calf in Exodus 32.[3] Which of the two is the older? Did an event take place before the Israelites settled in Palestine, which then provided the narrator's model for a lampoon on whatever Jeroboam was attempting to achieve? Or has an account of his activities formed the basis of a midrash set in the wilderness period?

In a number of ways the treatment of these issues provides a valuable introduction to the characteristics of Palestinian religion. It also provides a fairly secure base, I believe, to the discussion of both the antecedents and the subsequent history of the cult, in both of which areas there seems a need to revise current views.

Let us begin our discussion with a brief résumé of the establishment of the monarchy. The author of Judges 17.6, writing of the time before the rise of the charismatic Saul to power in Israel, observes that:

> In those days there was no king in Israel, and every man did as he pleased.

Even allowing for whatever point he was trying to make, this affords us an important insight into the period before the rise of the state: before such a time, there could be no state cult. The idea that Yahweh was a 'national god' during the period before it is possible to speak of the 'nation' – that is a coherent and organized community of the size imagined, and usually envisaged as a collectivity of the 12 tribes of Israel – cannot be seriously entertained. His cult may well have been in existence, and indeed may have been popular, but he could not have been a national god. Indeed I think that it is unlikely that any of the tribes, northern or southern, worshipped Yahweh to any numerically significant degree before the time of David.

The point that concerns us here is the limited extent of Saul's kingdom. Several passages in 1 and 2 Samuel indicate that it did not include Judah. Thus in 1 Samuel 11.12-15, after the victory of Saul over the Ammonites, it is 'all the men of Israel' who proclaim him king. Judah is conspicuous by its absence. Similarly, the small standing army Saul built up according to 1 Samuel 13.1 was drawn exclusively from Israel. During his campaign against the Amalekites in the Negev, south of Judah, we read that Saul's army consisted of 200,000 infantry – the number is greatly exaggerated – and 10,000 men of Judah. The reference to Judahite troops appears to be additional, or at any rate to be distinguished from the Israelites. Perhaps they are mercenaries. The same impression is given by 1 Samuel 11.8. In the confrontation with the Philistines and Goliath in 1 Samuel 17.1-54, the location, Socoh, is stated to be a town in Judah, as though the reader (a putative Israelite) might not be expected to be familiar with it. The presence of David's brothers at the front, in an Israelite army, is cause for remark, v. 19, in addition to being a part of the plot of the narrative. Finally, after Saul's death, when an embassy is sent by David to the men of Jabesh Gilead, his message is delivered in these words (2 Samuel 2.7):

> Your Lord, Saul is dead, but the House of Judah have appointed me king over them.

There is no hint here of a secession by Judah from Saul's kingdom. The following verse states that Abner took Saul's son Ishbaal to Mahanaim in Transjordan, where he had him crowned over Gilead, the Ashurites (or Geshurites),[4] Jezreel, Ephraim and Benjamin, and over all Israel.[5] It is evident from this that from its inception the monarchy was not unitary, so that the schism which followed Solomon's death was a reversion to a pre-Davidic norm rather than a scandalous innovation. The historian is too honest for his own good, since this is in part the impression he wishes to convey.

David was able to benefit from the troubles that beset the small northern kingdom. When Ishbaal was murdered (1 Samuel 4.5-8), it was to him that the representatives of Israel came at Hebron to ask him to be king over Israel in addition to Judah (1 Samuel 5.1-3). He may already have had a claim to the Israelite throne by virtue of his marriage to Michal (1 Samuel 18.27).[6] So David became ruler over a double kingdom, each throne held independently of the other. Hebron remained his capital at first, but he captured Jerusalem, which with its territory had remained hitherto an independent enclave. This event, narrated in 2 Samuel 5.6-12, was to have significant consequences in the religious sphere, as we shall see later. Jerusalem became the new 'federal' capital of the united kingdom. David not only consolidated his kingdom by the resolution of the continuing Philistine threat (2 Samuel 5.17-25), but by a series of conquests he considerably enlarged it. Successful campaigns were waged against Moab, Edom, Ammon, and even Aram was contained (2 Samuel 8.1-14; 10.1-11.27; 12.26-31).[7] One of the immediate results of this dramatic territorial expansion must have been a severe strain on the administrative structure. This, together with evident favouritism of the government towards Judah, marked under Solomon, but perhaps reflecting the drift of policy in the time of his father, no doubt contributed to such intrinsically centrifugal forces to be discerned in Palestinian society. Absalom's bid for power, for instance, while taking place in Jerusalem and its environs, seems to have appealed primarily to, and perhaps to have responded to the mood of, the northern people. His supporters are consistently referred to as 'the men of Israel' in the account given in 2 Samuel 15–18. That is to say, they were Israelites as distinct from Judahites. There was also a rebellion by Sheba, from Benjamin, which of all the northern tribes appears to have accepted its common destiny with Judah, so that he must have appealed to a dissatisfied minority within the tribe; again the people gathered into two polarized camps, as is explicitly stated in 2 Samuel 20.1-2:

> There is no share for us in David,
> nor inheritance for us in the son of Jesse!
> Each man to his tents, Israel!
>
> So all the men of Israel forsook David for Sheba son of Bichri. But the men of Judah remained with their king from the Jordan as far as Jerusalem.

The verse Sheba quotes here is almost the same as that with which the Israelites retorted upon receiving Rehoboam's terms (1 Kings 12.16), at which juncture the final rebellion took place.

Solomon had a more elaborate civil service, within which there appears to have been a tendency to regard the northern people as somewhat inferior to Judah. In organizing the provisioning and maintenance of the government, he chose administrators in all the main parts of the north, but left Judah exempt (1 Kings 4.7–5.3: while Judah had a governor, he was not charged with a month's subsistence like his colleagues). For his building programme, Solomon imposed forced labour on the Israelites (1 Kings 5.27 [v. 13 RSV]; 11.28). To be sure, we have an account of forced labour under Solomon in which it is explicity stated that the men of Israel were exempt (1 Kings 9.15-24 [see v. 22]), but this is in contradiction with the verses cited previously. These are more in keeping with the account of the assembly at Shechem following Solomon's death, when the Israelites were negotiating with Rehoboam and stated the terms on which they would accept him as king, to be met with a haughty rebuff, as the new king followed the advice of his hangers-on (1 Kings 12.1-15).

One of the first acts of Jeroboam as the new king of Israel, elected by the assembly at Shechem (1 Kings 12.20) was to institute a religious reform. The implications of this for the significance of the cult in Jerusalem are interesting, though they are unspoken. Although the formal requirements of the law of Deuteronomy 12 lay far in the future, they are related directly to Jeroboam's concern, as we shall see. Evidently the people went up to the capital periodically as an integral part of the cult of Yahweh. Jeroboam sought to stop this practice, ostensibly because regular contact with the now separate state of Judah would undermine his own position, no doubt because it would implicitly challenge his legitimacy. This could have unfortunate consequences for him (1 Kings 12.26-27).

The circumstances of the reform emerge clearly enough from the narrative in 1 Kings 12.26-33. The significance of what occurred is perhaps less obvious, and the wide range of interpretations offered for its details indicate the difficulties faced by the historian. The first thing to strike the percipient reader is the similarity between the account of Jeroboam's reform and the narrative of the golden calf in Exodus 32. The number of points of contact is so considerable – Aberbach and Smolar list 13 specific equivalences between the two[8] – that some kind of literary dependence is demanded.

The tendency in recent scholarship has been to regard the event described in 1 Kings 12 as primary, in both the historical and literary senses.[9] The golden calf episode of Exodus 32 is thus to be seen as a later narrative, however complex its own inner history, which takes 'the sin of Jeroboam', by which the entire history of (northern) Israel had been damned, and presents it as an archetypal fault in the whole people, which justifies the exile to come. Indeed the narrative of Exodus 32–34, in which the covenant is remade after such an inauspicious beginning, seems to me to be a transparent parable of the theological revolution forced on exilic Jewry by its circumstances. The simplest argument in favour of treating Jeroboam's reform as primary is that it is the only one of the two for which we have a historical context with regard to the event, as distinct from the literary form. No such verifiable context is available for Exodus 32. Another reason is that Exodus 32 makes sense only as a story of apostasy, in the context of the narrative of the covenant making. In so far as this is late in its present form[10] the story is also late. The story of Jeroboam, on the contrary, must have begun not as a tale of apostasy, which it now appears to have become, but rather as an account of his good works, in which the king had the full support of his people. As we shall see, it is an account not of cultic innovations, but of a deliberate rejection of cultic innovations from without – that is, the monarchy in Jerusalem as an imperial power – in favour of a reversion to ancient norms which had been neglected.

The significance of Jeroboam's reform really depends on one issue: the identity of the deity represented by the calves. As may be expected, a wide range of opinions has been expressed on this matter. Perhaps the most widespread view is that the calves represented Yahweh, not as images of the deity, but as vehicles for the invisible presence of the god.[11] So Jeroboam was doing no more than providing an alternative focal point to replace the ark, which was now in the Jerusalem temple. Given the general cast of all the historical and legendary materials in the Old Testament, which take it for granted that Yahweh was always historically the god of both Israel and Judah, this may initially be felt to be in accordance with an overwhelming amount of evidence. However, as I hope to show, this is in fact far from being the case. For the moment we may simply note that if Yahweh were indeed Jeroboam's god, we may wonder why such an extraordinary fuss was made, for instance, by the Deuteronomist, who presents the very existence of the northern kingdom, let alone all the cultic and ideological paraphernalia that went with it, as an affront to Yahweh. It seems to me that scholars have been fooled by the propagandistic skill of the Old Testament writers. Following W.F. Albright's comments, many have been at pains to indicate that there was not even a question here of idolatry, and they have drawn attention to the supposed nature of image-worship in the ancient Near East at large, in which gods are not worshipped theriomorphically, and their associated animals are simply symbols of the gods.[12] Such enthusiastic apologies for Jeroboam imply that the southern historian frankly misrepresented or misunderstood his material, which may be so, but needs more than assumptions to this effect.

G. Östborn suggested that the calves of Jeroboam represented Baal, the Canaanite storm-god.[13] This important deity was certainly associated with bulls, and in his Assyrian form Adad is shown standing on a bull as vehicle in reliefs.[14] Fragments of such a free-standing vehicle, with the feet of an anthropomorphic deity on its back, have been found at Hazor and associated with Baal.[15] Baal copulates with Anat in the form of a heifer, and we may suppose that he adopts the form of a bull for this purpose, rather than assume that bestiality is implied.[16] However, he is by no means the only near eastern deity with such associations. The term *b*ᶜ*l* is indeed used in many passages in the Old Testament to designate a deity whose cult offended a given writer, but the fact that the plural *b*ᶜ*lym* is also found indicates that no one specific deity is necessarily intended. It appears to refer to all other gods. In the singular use it always appears with the article so that the term is simply epithetal, and does not allow us to assume that the storm-god is meant in every instance. The fact that even Yahweh may be so designated, as is suggested by Hosea 2.18, warns us against simple and convenient identifications. Perhaps we may say that *hb*ᶜ*l* generally means something like 'the (pagan) god', when it has pejorative overtones. The identity is to be left open, or deduced from the context where possible.

According to J.A. Montgomery,[17] the inauguration of the cult of Jeroboam was a deliberate rejection of Yahweh (we detect the sense: monotheistic cult of Yahweh) in favour of polytheism. 'With only one calf', he wrote, 'there was danger of confusion with the image of Yahweh; with the introduction of a second one the worship of the northern kingdom is represented as clearly polytheistic.' This is simply too vague to be useful. And apart from implying that Yahweh too had a bull or calf image – whence the confusion might arise – it shows a lack of appreciation of the iconographic tradition. Two similar images (we may indeed suppose them to be substantially identical in form) are simply two manifestations of one god. The confusion of which Montgomery was afraid would be compounded by his own theory, if we are to suppose that the Israelites took one iconogram to represent different deities! This solution has nothing to commend it.

In view of the kerygmatic statement that accompanies the installation of the images, to the effect that this god (or these gods) brought Israel out of Egypt, the two suggestions that follow imply a singular perversity in the worshippers. H. Graetz, followed by R. Pfeiffer,[18] proposed that the (bull-) calves were images of the Apis bull, the sacred animal of Osiris, and personification of the Nile (*ḫapi*). W.O.E. Oesterley and E. Danelius were of the view that the goddess Hathor was intended to be represented.[19] The latter pointed to the regular translation of *ʿgl* by δαμαλις in LXX, and attempts to make a case for Jeroboam having had a personal devotion to Hathor during his exile in Egypt. She argued that MT uses abbreviated forms (that is, for *ʿglh*) which have been missed by commentators, but were faithfully reproduced by LXX and Josephus. Apart from the sense of special pleading her argument gives, she overlooked the use of *šny* in 1 Kings 12.28, which on her argument ought to be the feminine form *šty*. Any error must be as old as the text. The apparent shift to the feminine forms in texts of the Hellenistic period may indeed reflect the influence of the cults of the time (such as Isis in Alexandria, and Atargatis in Syria, both of whom had cow associations), but scarcely provides sure grounds for a conjecture about Jeroboam's private religion. Her further argument that the final element in the name Jeroboam *ben Nebat* was a transcription of the Egyptian *nbt* ('Mistress'), a title of Hathor, as of other Egyptian goddesses, overlooks the problem of reconciling Egyptian *t* with Hebrew *ṭ*.[20]

In what appears so far to be a progression in improbability, J.M. Sasson argued that the calf of the episode in Exodus 32 was a theriomorphic symbol for Moses.[21] Hardly plausible in the context of Exodus, the proposal is even more unlikely if priority be given to Jeroboam's reform.

Besides, opposition to all that Jeroboam's policy represented was commonly enshrined in a tradition of loyalty to the teaching of Moses in Israel, as evidenced by the early growth of the book of Deuteronomy.[22]

A further suggestion at least brings us back into the realms of possibility. The golden calf in Exodus 32 has been suggested by some to be an image of the Babylonian moon-god Sin. J. Lewy argued that this divine name underlies the mountain name Sinai, and it is a short step from this premise to the supposition that the wandering Israelites encountered the moon-god at his sacred place.[23] The link between Sinai and Sin is in my view quite a reasonable hypothesis, preserved in the archaic divine titles *Zê Sinay* ('Lord of Sinai') and El Shaddai,[24] but the difficulties to be faced in linking a prehistoric encounter in Sinai with a strictly historical account of the exodus, since the two traditions appear to belong to the different territorial groupings in Palestine,[25] make the connection the more difficult to accept. If Sin is to be understood in Exodus 32, this would constitute a reason for the late dating of the narrative and further remove it from direct contact with the northern tradition of 1 Kings 12. It would involve an exilic revaluation of the nature of Jeroboam's cult. I think there is in fact a lunar dimension to the calf-cult, in both instances, and indeed more widely than is generally recognized throughout West Semitic religion, but we must recognize distinct cults of this type, each particular to its own place and time, and not simply lump them together, even if there is the possibility of tenuous or even substantial historical links.

Let us turn now to a final possibility concerning the identity of Jeroboam's god. C.F.A. Schaeffer suggested *en passant* that it was El,[26] without elaboration. I think this is worth pursuing. Let us consider the following passages:

i. *hinnê ʾelōhêkā yiśrā ʾēl ʾašer heʿelûkā mêʾereṣ miṣrayim*
Behold (or: here is/are) your god (or: gods) who brought you up out of the land of Egypt. (1 Kings 12.28);

ii. *ʾēlê ʾelōhêkā yiśrāʾēl ʾašer heʿelûkā mêʾereṣ miṣrayim*
These are your gods, Israel, who brought you up out of the land of Egypt. (Exodus 32.4 = 32.8);

iii. *zê ʾelōhêkā ʾašer heʿelkā mimmiṣrayim*
This is your god who brought you up from Egypt. (Nehemiah 9.18).

These raise a number of grammatical points. Firstly, *ʾelōhîm*, plural in form, can be singular or plural in meaning. When it is singular, it can take a singular or plural verb or epithet.[27] In 1 Kings 12.28 then a plural meaning is grammatically possible, while not necessary. We can see various senses being drawn from it. Regardless of whether he was a polytheist, we should envisage Jeroboam pointing to the duplicated image and saying 'Here is your god...', identifying the image as the saviour. Without even needing to alter the text, the deuteronomist can allow his readers to treat it as a plural if they want to. Certainly this is what was done by the author of Exodus 32. Since *hinnê* (consonantal *hnh*) was neutral and left open the question of number, he could have altered the first word of what is otherwise an identical text to read *ʾēlê* (consonantal *ʾlh*) 'these'. This factor alone would be evidence of the derivative nature of the Exodus passage. For in his haste to spell out what was possible in the Kings passage as the true meaning, the author introduced the *non-sequitur* that the plural demonstrative refers in the Exodus narrative to a single calf! We may further note that the reference to the calf in Nehemiah clearly understands it as a single divine image, since the demonstrative has been changed to the singular.[28]

But things are not perhaps quite so simple as this. I think we are to envisage this as a question of the history of interpretation following the composition of the text, particularly in the case of Exodus 32.4 and 8. In the oldest forms of the Hebrew text there would have been few, if any, *matres lectionis*, that is, consonants serving as vowel indicators. Let us then rewrite Exodus 32.4 (and 8), simply omitting the *matres*: the consonantal text would be

> *'l 'lhk ysr'l 'šr hʿlk m'rṣ mṣrym*

instead of the present form

> *'lh 'lhyk ysr'l 'šr hʿlwk m'rṣ mṣrym*

This can still be construed in the usual way, that is, supplying the necessary vowels. But it can also be construed quite differently:

> El is your god, Israel, who brought you up out of the land of Egypt.

As we shall see, there is some evidence to support this reading. But let us first see if it can be justified on orthographic grounds. Two explanations are possible. First, we would see a case of dittography, the *h* of the following *'lhk* being brought into the first word because of the similarity of the consonantal cluster *'l*. This is the less likely in that dittography would normally be expected to be progressive rather than regressive. Second, we may envisage a southern scribe handling the text, and coming across *'l* (naturally to be construed as El), wondering why this should be a scandal, since in the cult in Jerusalem El and Yahweh had always been identified without hesitation. There was never any question of Yahweh being associated with a bull, nor of El being so construed in the Jerusalem cult. The golden calf must surely refer to some abomination (apart from the simple fact of being an image). So he would supply the alternative vowels that *'lh* could bear, that is *ē, e*, giving the plural demonstrative, later to be standardized with the *mater* as *'lh*. By the time of this putative scribe, monotheism being the norm, the worst possible offence would have been for Israel to be polytheistic. There are in fact several examples of the demonstrative plural being written with only two consonants, as *'l*,[29] so that the proposal is in accordance with biblical usage. The change in the form of the verb (from *hʿlk* to *hʿlwk*) can be similarly explained: the *l* would have originally borne a *qibbuṣ* which has become a *hureq* with the addition of the *waw*. This suggests that phonetically the two vowels were probably indistinguishable.

I think that originally this interpretation of the formula must have been Jeroboam's intention too. There is no need to alter the text of 1 Kings 12.28 to make it conform to Exodus 32.4 and 8. In pointing to the image, to which *hnh* is the obvious verbal accompaniment, he would expect those assembled before him immediately to recognize which deity the image represented. To be sure, there are two Canaanite candidates for such a role, Baal and El. In my view, the evidence we have of bull images from the Levant points to two quite different forms, which would not have been confused by the ancients. The stocky shorthorn of the type found in Ugarit and at Hazor[30] corresponds to the Assyrian form which serves as vehicle to Adad,[31] and is to be seen as the animal of Baal. The much larger longhorn of the type found at Tyre,[32] corresponding not like the former to the common domestic animal of the time but to the now extinct aurochs, would have been the animal of El. Proof on such an issue is not possible, because the evidence is so scant and its interpretation so problematic. But the Tyre bull has some very distinctive features, which certainly differentiate it from those which have normally been associated confidently with Baal. Its male nature is clear from its ithyphallic form, although apart from this its general inspiration even to the curiously curved tail is derived directly from Egyptian representations of Hathor as the cow of heaven, as seen for example in the bed from Tutankhamun's tomb.[33] Like the cow, the Tyre bull has a sun-disc between the horns, inscribed with the *ʿanḫ* hieroglyph for 'life': The Egyptian cows have distinctive trefoil shapes all over their backs,[34] while the bull has instead tiny incised stars. Let us now attempt a brief interpretation of the iconography. It seems to be a clear example of the form rather than the content being borrowed. Hathor (or Isis, who also wears the sun-disc and horns – the two goddesses are commonly, though not invariably, identified, particularly in royal contexts, as they are both 'mother' of the king) is a sky goddess – Isis the deified throne – and the sun-disc that is carried between the horns is the sun-god Ra or his earthly representative the king (Horus, also the sky-god and son of Ra) borne aloft by the heavens in its daily epiphany. The trefoil patterns on the cows are hard to elucidate. It is tempting to interpret them as stars, but the Egyptians had a common five-pointed representation of stars which was in general use. As for the bull, the stars are clear enough. In the Levant the solar deity was a goddess, Shapsh, and it is probable that we should interpret Athirat (Asherah) as her *alter ego*.[35] El, in contrast, was originally a moon-god. Here it is possible that the bull's horns were seen in the artist's mind's eye as the crescent moon bearing the god's solar consort across the heavens. But the bull is also the heavens in their vastness, echoing the

Mesopotamian mythologem the bull of heaven,[36] carrying as well as his wife his myriad offspring, represented here, as in Job 38.7, as the stars. The bull then is an icon not merely of the bull-god, but in the form of the one animal of the whole pantheon, an eloquent expression of the incipient monotheism which can sometimes be detected even in the Canaanite evidence, contrary to the common view. Of course a discovery of this kind in Tyre tells us nothing directly about the calves of Jeroboam. The use of the term *ʿgl* ('calf') might be construed as pointing to the younger looking shorthorns referred to above, but these are no more corroborations of the view that the calves represented Baal than is the Tyrian example that they represented El. We have only the literary evidence to go on, and if the analysis offered above is cogent, this offers no support for the Baal theory, but does so for the El theory. (Of the other views mentioned, the only serious candidate is Yahweh himself, and this is also to be discounted, both for the reasons given above, and by the accumulation of arguments to come, to the effect that Jeroboam's policy was specifically to discontinue the cult of Yahweh in the north). El is then the bull-god of the northern cult.

Perhaps we should here consider what other evidence there is to support this theory. The first thing to note is the inseparability in the passages cited (1 Kings 12.28 and so on) between the identity of the god and the event. This is presumably why scholars have supposed that it must be Yahweh: he, after all, was the saviour god of the ancient kerygma.[37] But we are entitled to ask whether this had always been so. After all, even a conservative reading of the Priestly Work has to admit that it was only at a certain point in history that the divine name Yahweh was revealed. Since the accounts of this (Exodus 3 and 6) are replete with theological reflection on the event we may well wonder if they do not contain as much interpretation and indeed reinterpretation as reflection. Furthermore, the witness of the Pentateuch is scarcely consistent on the matter since the divine name is first used in primordial times (Genesis 4.1,[38] 4.26),[39] by Abra(ha)m (Genesis 12.7-8), or is revealed to Moses in Midian (Exodus 3.1ff.) or in Egypt (Exodus 6.2, 28). If on so fundamental an issue as the original revelation there was room for variation, and a concern to preserve such diverse traditions as existed, perhaps on the matter of the kerygma there was similar variety. I have argued elsewhere[40] that this is the case with Exodus 3. A summary of this argument is useful as a preliminary to a consideration of various other passages which provide evidence of the kind we are concerned with. My starting point was a previous discussion of the problem of the so-called 'god of the fathers', and the suggestion that contrary to the view proposed by A. Alt,[41] and subsequently widely endorsed, we have in the oldest singular form (*'lhy 'byk*) an echo of an older formula *'l 'byk*, which has been transformed for polemical reasons into an intermediate **'lhm 'byk*, which subsequently, on a different interpretation of cult-continuity, perhaps to be seen as influenced by the independent plural form *'lhy 'bwtk*,[42] gave way to the form *'lhy 'byk*.[43] The result of the application of this argument to Exodus 3 is to transform the narrative normally allocated to the pentateuchal source E into one in which El was the deity who addressed Moses on the mountain and subsequently brought the Israelites out of Egypt. The key to the interpretation of the narrative along these lines is v. 6, in which the deity announces himself to Moses as 'the god of your father'. On my argument, what he actually says is 'I am El your father...' This in turn leaves no room for vv. 13-15, since there is no question of Moses having to ask his name. This section belongs to the final redactional stage of the narrative, into which the story of the burning bush, of exilic origin,[44] has previously been grafted. All this may appear to be highly speculative to the reader, but it does find some corroboration in a number of other references to precisely such a tradition. Let us consider them.

In Numbers 23.22 and 24.8 we have a bicolon within the body of Balaam's oracle which reads as follows:

> *'l mwṣy'w*[45] *mmṣrym*
> *ktwᶜpt r'm lw*

The *'ēl* here is commonly construed simply as a poetic variant for *'ᵉlōhîm*.[46] This may well have been a sustainable argument back in the nineteenth century, but is no longer so. It is plainly the divine name El. Indeed this is a general principle: wherever *'ēl* appears in the Old Testament with a divine reference, the first line of interpretation should be to take it as the divine name. Just occasionally it has been altered into an appellative by the addition of an article, perhaps for polemical reasons.[47] The onus of proof lies on any alternative approach. The bicolon is therefore to be translated as follows:

> El brought him out of Egypt;
> he is like the horns of the wild bull to him.[48]

Balaam's oracle has been argued to refer in its ideological content to the monarchy of David,[49] and so may date from this period, and is at any rate to be construed as southern in origin, which is the important point for our concern, since its survival (where we might expect it to be changed to Yahweh on polemical grounds were it northern) depends on the typical southern equation of Yahweh and El. The bicolon nicely combines the two motifs, the bovine aspect of the god and his role in the exodus tradition.

Psalm 106.19-22 refers with disapproval to the golden calf tradition (specifically the Exodus version, on the basis of its molten nature, and is therefore a late – exilic? – psalm). Nevertheless it appears to accept the kerygmatic association with El:

> They made a calf at Horeb
> and bowed down before a molten image;
> and they exchanged their Glory[50]
> for the likeness of a grass-eating bull.
> They forgot El who had saved them,
> him who had done great things in Egypt,
> wondrous things in the land of Ham,
> fearful things at the Sea of Extinction.[51]

Here we have the conventional Yahwistic rejection of idolatry, but not in a Yahwistic framework. To be sure, the psalm as a whole incorporates this ancient version of the kerygma into its own purview, and the epithet **ᶜelyôn*[52] in v. 7 indicates that we have in fact the common psalmodic parallel: *yhwh* || *'ēl ᶜelyôn*. But if El Elyon is a southern form of El, the kerygma of the exodus is drawn on the contrary from the northern tradition, and thus incorporated here into the southern (now Jewish) amalgamation of northern and indigenous lore.

Hosea 7.16 may be seen to contain a further allusion to the El-tradition. To appreciate this, we must first however consider the following verses, 8.4-6, which belong with it;[53] a number of other allusions in the book may also be considered, for cumulatively they point to the likelihood that the entire book is a sustained attack on the cult of El. In 8.6 the opening phrase in MT, *kî miyyiśrā'ēl*, is quite without meaning in the context, and the versions are of no help in restoring a coherent text. H. Tur-Sinai proposed that the consonants be simply regrouped, to *kî mî šōr 'ēl*, with the minor alteration of the *sin* to *šin*,[54] which would be of no significance before the text was pointed. This gives the sense 'for who is Bull El?' which is unprecedented in the Old Testament, but echoes the common title of El (*ṯr il*) in the Ugaritic literature.[55] This fits very well into the broader context of vv. 4-6:

> They have made kings,
> but not by my authority;[56]
> they have established rulers,
> but I know nothing of it.
> With their silver and their gold they have made themselves
> idols...[57]

I reject your calf, Samaria,[58]
my rage is kindled against it.[59]
...[60]
For who is Bull El?
He is silent and is no god.[61]
Indeed, the calf of Samaria will become mere fragments.[62]

The acceptance of Tur-Sinai's emendation gives us a text which nicely plays off the formal title of El against the parody which is perhaps intended in the scornful use of *ʿēgel* ('calf').[63] This preserves the sexual potential, so to speak, while diminishing the actuality. To call the image a calf is to question the validity of the theological claims made on behalf of the god. This language belongs to the polemical tradition, to be sure, rather than to the cultic tradition which is under attack. Some of the discussion of Ugaritic El has attempted to present him as impotent and superannuated,[64] or even as castrated *à la* Ouranos,[65] but there is no warrant for such an assessment. El is rather the epitome of virility.[66] But Hosea and the Yahwist tradition thought otherwise. U. Cassuto proposed the following translation for Hosea 12.1b:

But Judah still roams with El,
and is faithful to the Holy Ones.[67]

On this construction the passage, far from contrasting Judah's fidelity with the apostasy of the north, attributes the same sin to both kingdoms. H.S. Nyberg argued that in a number of passages an abbreviated form of *ʿelyôn* appears in Hosea, as *ʿl(y)*, to be read in 10.5 (dubious), 7.16 and 11.7.[68] In such usage we would have an allusion to El by the epithet commonly found in southern tradition. It is 7.16 which concerns us here. The corrupt nature of the text is evident. I read it as follows:

They have returned to El Most High.[69]
they are a slackened bow.
Their princes shall fall by the sword,
their rulers by my indignation.[70]
For this has been their mockery
since they were in Egypt.[71]

The final bicolon may alternatively be read thus:

For this has been their calf
since they were in Egypt.

This would be to take MT *lʿgm* as a perversion, deliberate or otherwise, for *ʿglm*, 'their calf'. But the MT text may stand with the allusive nature of the 'mockery' evident to the reader and even the original listeners. On this interpretation the various calf-references in *Hosea*, which we have seen to refer to El (rather than Baal), are seen be connected with the kerygmatic motif of the exodus. Hosea was accusing the people of having turned away from recognizing their true saviour, Yahweh, not just now, nor at the time of the secession, nor even at the putative event described in Exodus 32,[72] but way back in Egypt, when they already worshipped El. But this is in accordance with our findings. Historically speaking, there was no new theological departure at the time of the exodus. The Israelites naturally attributed their 'rescue' (however it is to be assessed in historical or mythical terms) to their ancient deity.

To conclude this discussion of passages which offer some support to the proposal that El was the god originally connected with the exodus tradition, let us consider Exodus 18. This gives an account of how Moses and the Israelites encountered Jethro on their way to Sinai. The passage is the crux of the so-called Kenite hypothesis, which proposes that Yahweh was originally a Kenite god, whose cult Moses adopted upon marrying Jethro's daughter (Exodus 2.22).[73] There are in fact two quite distinct parts to this theory, which I shall call Kenite and Midianite respectively. I think there has been a tendency to confuse them.

Genesis 4 preserves an ancient tradition of the origins of the Kenites, tracing the birth of the eponym, Cain, as son of a divine couple, Yahweh and Eve, who bears all the hallmarks of a mother goddess.[74] In the present form of the narrative Cain is presented as the first murderer, in what is to become a tedious catalogue of human sin. The murder no doubt belongs to the oldest form of the story, in which we may suppose that the brothers were twins and that one was fated to kill the other (like Romulus and Remus, or Seth and Osiris). This is a typical myth of cultural origins. But in it we would expect the hero to be the first devotee of the tribal god. This is all the more probable in Cain's case since his mother had burst out at his birth with the deity's name (Genesis 4.1). But in incorporating the story into the Genesis narrative, the author has turned Cain into an anti-hero, and according to I. Lewy, the statement which would have followed 4.16, to the effect that Cain was the first to invoke Yahweh, has been taken from him and given to a third generation primal man, Enosh (4.26).[75] Even admitting that any alterations to or reconstructions of the text here are conjectural, this remains the most substantial part of the Kenite hypothesis. Of course, there is no reason to credit the story with any historical content. The important issue with regard to its relevance to questions of the history of Yahwism is that Cain, as eponym of the Kenites, would be the ultimate ancestor of the Rechabites of the Old Testament, who appear as a paradigm for devotion to Yahweh in 2 Kings 10.15-27 and Jeremiah 35.1-11. There is no evidence that in historical terms they were responsible for the origins of the cult of Yahweh in Palestine – that is, as the people who transmitted it directly to Israel and Judah. But the note in 1 Chronicles 2.55, which identifies the Rechabites as Kenites and also states that they came from Hamath (in Syria), may indicate that they had connections with the cult that is apparently present in the region in the early Iron Age, to judge from the name of King Iau-bidi.

So much for the Kenite hypothesis. The Midianite hypothesis is concerned with Moses' connections with the land of Midian and the priest of Midian, Jethro. There is in fact some dispute about the name, and three variants are found. He is called Jethro, priest of Midian, in Exodus 3.1, 4.18 and 18 *passim*. Exodus 3.1 implicitly identifies him with the anonymous priest of Midian who appears in 2.16, 21. But in 2.18 this figure is identified as Reuel, and in Numbers 10.29 Reuel the Midianite is father of Hobab. One of them, it is not clear which, is father-in-law of Moses. The latter is said to be so in Judges 1.16 and 4.11, where he is said to be a Kenite. Apart from the reference in 1 Chronicles mentioned above, the Kenites are always associated with the Negev, which separates them geographically from the Midianites, who would have occupied territory east of Aqaba. Thus apart from the passages in Judges, which mention the Kenites, the identity of the father-in-law is in doubt, there perhaps being at least three traditions, and there is no ground simply to lump them all together and equate Kenites and Midianites.[76]

The crux of the Midianite hypothesis lies in the exegesis of Exodus 18. Moses has led the Israelites out of Egypt, and is met by Jethro, who offers sacrifices. In vv. 10-11 he praises Yahweh:

> Blessed be Yahweh...who has rescued you from the hand of the Egyptians and from the hand of Pharaoh, who rescued the people from beneath the hand of the Egyptians.[77] Now I know that Yahweh is greater than all the gods...

J. Morgenstern argued that Jethro's praise of Yahweh was 'not the exclamation of a recent and enthusiastic convert, but the proud and gratified utterance of an old and loyal devotee...'[78] He took it that Jethro was a priest of Yahweh, which explains his sacrifice in the following verse. However, C.H.W. Brekelmans and R. de Vaux were led to the opposite conclusion by the same evidence.[79] The passage at large offers some help out of the quandary, because of its clearly composite state. Verses 1b, 8-11, which refer to Yahweh, are intrusive in an older text.[80] If these are removed, a coherent narrative emerges in which Moses and his family meet, and a sacrifice of thanksgiving is offered by Jethro, not to Yahweh, but to *'elōhîm*. We saw above that this term at times appears to have been amplified from an original *'ēl*, and it seems that at worst we may say that Jethro sacrificed to 'God' or even 'the gods', but at best he may have sacrificed to El, which is entirely consonant with the other allusions we have found linking El with the exodus tradition. What we may say with confidence is that he did *not* sacrifice to Yahweh. We may finally note that while the priestly source attributes the exodus to Yahweh in Exodus 6.2ff., it does so in a context in which he is explicitly identified with El Shaddai. A number of theological and literary motives may underlie the passage, but it evidently contains a further allusion to the El tradition.

In our discussion so far we have ranged fairly widely. We may summarize our argument as follows. As monarchy develops as a governmental system in Palestine, it is evident that two independent kingdoms, of Israel and Judah, are established. This is of paramount importance. Among other things, it means that the sense of identity of the peoples is diverse. The common practice in scholarship of using the umbrella term Israel to denote either of the two kingdoms is misleading from a historical perspective, however justified it may be felt to be on theological grounds. It glosses over differences not merely of prehistorical experience and ethnic diversity, but above all of religious practice. To assume that Yahweh always was and always remained the god of both nations is simply not supported by the evidence. The division of the kingdom, which was briefly united under David and Solomon, was merely a reversion to the norm. The religious policies of Jeroboam are to be explained not in terms of a dissident form of the cult of Yahweh or an act of disgraceful apostasy, but rather as the rehabilitation of a cult which had always been present, and which opinion of his day appears to have regarded as having been suppressed by the religious policies of David and Solomon.

Endnotes

1. Östborn 1955: 3.
2. Day 1985: 124-25, 152, 165-66, 174; Kloos 1986: 93 (cf. 94), 123-24, 213. Cf. M.S. Smith 1990: 12-15, 41-79.
3. Aberbach and Smolar 1967.
4. Cf. Syr., Vg. (BHS).
5. The first three terms are prefixed by the preposition *'l*, the final three by *ʿl*. Perhaps the first three represent an expansion of the text.
6. Cf also the offer of Merab, on which Saul subsequently reneges (1 Samuel 18.17-19). See also Nathan's words in 2 Samuel 12.8, and discussion in Wyatt 1985d: 51, nn. 23, 24.

7. The strictly historical status of all this information remains an open question, in view of the total lack of external corroboration, and the generally agreed novelistic quality of the narrative. But this need not reduce the value of the information given, however historically spurious, since it reflects the view of the narrator, and thus indirectly mirrors the conditions of the time.

8. Aberbach and Smolar 1967: 129-34.

9. See literature cited in Bailey 1971: 97, n. 2. See also Nicholson 1973; Ramsey 1982: 59; Vermeylen 1985.

10. Nicholson 1973.

11. Paton 1894: 80-81; Obbink 1929: 268; Albright 1940: 229; de Vaux 1943: 80-81; Bič 1949: 52; Dumermuth 1958: 83; Weippert 1961; Gray 1964: 290; Aberbach and Smolar 1967: 135; Jagersma 1982: 132; Jones 1984: 259; de Vries 1985: 162. Donner (1973) is among these scholars, but presents an interesting theory of 'poly-Yahwism' or 'dyo-Yahwism'. (See now Wyatt 1995b.)

12. Albright 1940: 229; Würthwein 1977: 165; Jones 1984: 259.

13. Östborn 1955, 15, 23, 26. So also Dus 1968: 111; Würthwein 1977: 165.

14. *ANEP* §500. Cf. §§534, 537.

15. See Yadin 1961: pll. cccxxiv, cccxxv; *idem* 1972: 95 and pl. xxa.

16. KTU 1.5 v 1-25.

17. Montgomery 1951: 255.

18. Graetz 1888: IV, 89; Pfeiffer 1926: 217-18; *idem* 1961: 75.

19. Oesterley 1942: 239; Danielus 1967-68.

20. As pointed out by Bailey 1971: 42, 102, n 30. His alternative explanation for Nebat, 110, is much better.

21. Sasson 1968; *idem* 1971: 151.

22. On Deuteronomy as northern see for instance McCurley 1974.

23. Cf. J. Lewy 1945-46; Key 1965; Bailey 1971.

24. Judges 5.5; Psalm 68.9 (EVV 8). On the form see Grimme 1896: 571, 573, n. 1; Albright 1936: 30; *idem* 1950-51: 20; Allegro 1955; Lipiński 1967: 198-99, nn. 1-3; Dahood 1965-70: II, 139. Cf. Ugaritic *d* in *dpid,* Epigraphic South Arabian *d* (f. *dt*) in Jamme 1947, *passim*, especially 64-65.

25. Cf. von Rad 1966b: 1-78.

26. Schaeffer 1966: 16. M.S. Smith 1990: 51, hinted at the possibilities of this, but did not enlarge.

27. GK: 463, §145i, though denied of Exodus 32.4. Cf. Bailey 1971: 99 and n. 16; Donner 1973: 46-47.

28. There is the possibility that Nehemiah 9.18 has actually picked up the archaic reference in Judges 5.5 and Psalm 68.9 (EVV 8) to Zê Sinay, but in view of the pejorative allusion this is unlikely.

29. BDB 41a cites Genesis 19.8, 25; 26.3, 4; Leviticus 18.27; Deuteronomy 4.42; 7.22; 19.11; 1 Chronicles 20.8.

30. Ugarit: Caquot and Sznycer 1980: pl. vi; Hazor: Yadin 1972: 94 and pl. xxb.

31. *ANEP* §500.

32. Schaeffer 1966: 15, fig. 10. While this is largely influenced by Egyptian models – see n. 33 – we may also compare the aurochs probably represented in the much earlier Alaça Hüyük sanctuary – *idem*: 10, fig. 6.

33. See Schaeffer 1966: 17, fig. 11.

34. The only other example of this pattern to my knowledge is on the bust of the so-called priest-king from Mohenjo-Daro in Pakistan. See Wheeler 1968: pl. xviii.

35. Cf. Wyatt 1983: 273.

36. *Gilgamesh* 6.117-162 (*ANET*[3]: 505, 85).

37. 'Indubitably, no one but Yahweh had led Israel out of Egypt': Donner 1973: 48.

38. See Wyatt 1986e.

39. See I. Lewy 1956.

40. See Chapter 2.

41. Alt 1929; 1966.

42. May 1941.

43. See Chapter 1.

44. See Chapter 3.

45. *-ô* in Numbers 24.8, *-ām* in 23.22. The former is preferable, as agreeing in number with the *lô* following.

46. E.g. Noth 1968: 187. M. Smith 1987: 162, n. 53, argues against the consensus. Cf. M.S. Smith 1990: 51.

47. E.g. Genesis 35.1, 3. Cf. Chapter 1.

48. Cf. RSV: 'he has as it were the horns of the wild ox'. Both terms in the second colon are obscure. The term *tʿph* (√*yʿp*: BDB 419) is generally taken to mean 'horns'. *r'm* (BDB 910a) is to be taken in accordance with the parallel in Psalm 29.6: *ʿgl* || *bn r'mym*, where indeed the *r'm* of the formula – to be construed as an archaic genitive singular? (cf. Wyatt 1990d: 210) – may denote El himself. The aurochs would have been replaced by some domestic breed of bull in proto-historical times, when it became extinct. On *šwr* see Peter 1975.

49. Eissfeldt 1965a: 200.

50. *Kābôd* here to be taken as a divine title. Cf. Dahood 1965-70: III, 357 – of Psalm 149.5. He does not recognize it of the present psalm (p. 72) where it would make much better sense than his 'adoration'. He also sees the divine title in Psalms 3.4 (EVV 3); 3.43 (EVV 2) and 29.9 (1965-70: I, 18, 23, 179-80), and 62.8 (EVV 7) (1965-70: II, 92).

51. On the cosmological significance of *yam sûp* see Montgomery 1938; Snaith 1965; Batto 1983; *idem* 1984; Wyatt, Chapter 5 above; *idem* 1990c.

52. MT *ʿl-ym*. Read *ʿlywn* with BHS app.

53. Perhaps Hosea 8.1-3 are intrusive in the context? Note the singular 'Israel, him' in v. 3, clashing with the plural 'they' (sc. the people of Israel) in v. 4.

54. H. Tur-Sinai 1964: I, cols 31-33, followed by NEB.

55. KTU 1.1 iii 26 etc.

56. It is possible that both the kings (*mlk*: here a verbal form is used) and the rulers (*šrym*) have a divine reference, in which case the first term might denote 'Molek' (cf. C.A. Kennedy, unpublished, as discussed in Heider 1985: 313; cf also Day 1989: 76-77); while the second (read not *śrym* but *šrym*; cf. Tur-Sinai 1964) could denote bull images of El.

57. Omitting *lmʿn ykrt* of MT, with BHS app.

58. Reading *znḥty* for MT *znḥ* with BHS app. (a view rejected by Wolff 1974b: 132). Samaria here perhaps denotes the whole northern kingdom rather that the city – see Motzki 1975: 471. It may be genitive rather than vocative: see Andersen and Freedman 1980: 494.

59. Reading singular, in view of the singular *ʿgl* in v. 6.

60. Omitting v. 5c as a gloss.

61. Omitting *ʿśhw* and reading *whw' ḥrš*. Alternatively we may omit *whw'* and read *ḥrš ʿśhw* ('a craftsman made it'). MT represents a hybrid.

62. The initial *ky* is emphatic. Cf. Dahood 1965-70: III, 402ff.

63. Though cf. J. Lewy 1945-46: 449.

64. E.g. Pope 1955: 37ff., a view reiterated in Pope 1987.

65. Oldenburg 1969: 112ff., 125; cf. the assessment of his argument by L'Heureux 1979: 24ff.

66. Gaster 1966: 429-30; Wyatt 1977: 380; L'Heureux 1979: 10ff. In KTU 1.23 El makes love to his wives (two of them) seven times on one occasion! (For a revised estimate of this episode, based on Tsumura 1978, see Wyatt 2002a: 332-33.)

67. Cassuto 1971: 57. Cf. NEB.

68. Nyberg 1935-36: 58ff., 90, 120; *idem* 1938. Cf. Lack 1962: 46, n. 24, 48; NEB. Also Dahood 1965-70: III, 185 etc.; Pope 1973; Andersen and Freedman 1980: 466.

69. MT reads *yšwbw l'ʿl*, which is to be read as *yšwbw l''l ʿly*: a *l* has dropped out.

70. On possible divine references here see n. 56. For MT *mzʿm lšwnm* I have read the *mzʿmy mšlm* of BHS app. *mšlm*, 'their rulers', could on a theological reference have replaced an earlier **mlkm*.

71. 'This' in the final colon (*zw*, archaic for *zh*) refers to the deity, and may have been an evocation of the formula discussed above (see references in n. 24). 'Since they were in Egypt' – lit. 'from the land of Egypt', taking *b* as 'from': Gordon 1965: 92, §10.1; Dahood 1965-70: III, 391-93, 397.

72. The narrative of Exodus 32(–34) certainly postdates Hosea, in which case he would not be familiar with it. He was rather relating the falsity of contemporary religion directly with an ancient tradition. The gist of his argument is that the ancient claim that El saved Israel from oppression in Egypt is false. Yahweh was the author of the event. Hosea's historical knowledge would of course be limited to the data as preserved in Yahwistic tradition, and in the El-tradition which appears to have been prevalent in Israel. In view of the element of sectarian finesse which really underlies the point he is trying to make, it is all a storm in a teacup. On the ritual and mythological allusion of Hosea 11.1 (which may be the source of all exodus language), see Chapter 5.

73. For discussion and references see Weippert 1971: 105-106, n. 14. The theory also has its opponents: Meek 1920-21; *idem* 1950: 97-98; Brekelmans 1954; de Vaux 1969; *idem* 1971: I, 313-21.

74. See Heller 1958; Gaster 1969: 21; Kikawada 1972; Wyatt 1986e: 91-92.

75. That is, as the first man. See I. Lewy 1956; Wyatt 1986e.

76. The Kenites were evidently tinkers (cf. Genesis 4.22 and the etymology of Cain: Wyatt 1986e: 89-90); the Midianites appear as caravan traders (see Genesis 37.28a: in 25.28b, Ishmaelites are involved, while in Judges 8.22-24 Ishmaelites and Midianites seem to be interchangeable terms) and camel-owners (Judges 7.12, 8.26 – cf. Genesis 37.25).

77. The text is overloaded. Either the 'you' clause or the 'people' clause should be omitted. 'Egyptians': MT reads 'Egypt' in both instances.

78. Morgenstern 1920–21: 249.

79. Brekelmans 1954; de Vaux 1969.

80. Cf. Noth 1962: 147.

Chapter 8

The Darkness of Genesis 1.2*

It is commonly observed that in cosmogonic accounts, darkness precedes light, and is in opposition to it: it represents the chaos which precedes the cosmos. There is a half-truth in this. It is certainly the way in which mythology may express a creation story in its choice of surface language. But to stop at this point, concluding that this is what the myth is about, is perhaps to miss the deeper levels of meaning that are available merely by asking simple questions of the precise vocabulary used, its affective ranges, the order in which words occur in a text (or oral narrative), and even the simple question, are we dealing with prose or poetry?

The account of creation in Genesis 1.1–2.4a begins with perhaps the most discussed verse in the entire Hebrew Bible. The only aspect of it which need detain us is the precise nuance of the term *'ereṣ*. Its Ugaritic counterpart, *arṣ*, is notoriously difficult to pin down, which is perhaps understandable, given the mythological nature of much of the literature. At times it simply means (1) the ground on which we stand. At others it refers (2) more specifically to what lies underneath the ground, that is, the realm of darkness and death, the abode of the dead. And sometimes it is (3) ambiguous, carrying the overtones of both senses. Context alone guides us in the right direction when trying to interpret it.

A good example of the second use in Ugaritic is the formula *yrd (b)arṣ*, occurring for instance in KTU 1.4 viii 7-9 and 1.5 v 15-16. The former passage reads:

wrd bt ḫpṯt arṣ	and go down into the 'house of the couch'[1] of the earth,
tspr byrdm arṣ	be numbered among those who go down into the earth.

The key phrase used here, *yrd arṣ*, corresponds to the Hebrew *yrd š'wlh* (Genesis 37.35) or *yrd bwr* (Psalm 88.5 [EVV. 4]). *'ereṣ* clearly has the same sense of 'underworld' in such passages as Isaiah 14.12, 1 Samuel 28.13, Psalms 71.20, 143.6,[2] Job 4.23 and 15.29 (Dahood 1965-70: III, 305). More relevant to our present context is the threefold division occurring in Psalm 89.12 (EVV. 11):

lk šmym	The heavens are yours,
'p-lk 'rṣ	and the underworld is yours,
tbl wml'h	the world and its fulness:
'th ysdtm	you established them.

The term *tēbēl* occurring in the third line of this tetracolon represents the habitable and culture-orientated world lying between the heavens above and the underworld below, and separating them. This is in effect a figure for the world-constructional role of culture, keeping apart as two separate parts those features of reality which, allowed to come together again (as for example in the flood story), would involve a reversion to chaos. The same threefold division may be discerned in 1 Samuel 2.8, where the opposition between the bicola in *a* (the dust || the ash-heap) and *b* (enthroning || a seat of honour) is that between the condition of the underworld and that of the land of the living, and anticipates the opposition within *c*:

ky lyhwlz mṣqy 'rṣ	For to Yahweh belong the pillars of the underworld,
wyšt ʿlyhm tbl	and he has set over them the habitable world.

Dahood suggested (1965-70: II, 232) that we have the same division in Psalm 77.19 (EVV. 18):

qwl rʿmk bglgl	The voice of your thunder is in the vault of heaven;
h'yrw brqym tbl	lightnings illumine the habitable world;
rgzh wtrʿš /h'rṣ	the underworld shudders and quakes.

This is part of a description of Yahweh's fight with the sea, and of relevance to our present discussion is the fact that the entire universe, on Dahood's approach, in all its three levels, responds to the divine manifestation of power. That is, even the underworld is subject to Yahweh's influence. It may be argued, however, that his interpretation of *glgl* as 'vault of heaven' is less than certain.

I think it likely that *'ereṣ* in Genesis 1.1 may be an example of the ambiguous use of the term, allowing for the *'ereṣ* as the environment of the creatures who later appear and belong to neither the sky nor the sea, while at the same time inviting the sense 'underworld' in the implicit opposition of the merismus *haššāmayim wᵉ...hā'āreṣ*. The obvious sense of the word in its use in v. 2, where it is qualified as *thw wbhw*, 'chaotic and empty', confirms the line I have taken. Indeed, whether or not we follow the interpretation of v. 1 as a subordinate clause, there is a sense in which the *'ereṣ* of v. 2 at least logically, if not temporally, precedes that of v. 1. For it is not yet defined by opposition to the *šāmayim*, but is instead characterized precisely by the quality of chaos. Like *'ereṣ* in v. 1, however, it remains ambiguous, and may therefore be translated as 'earth' (as distinct from '[habitable] world' – exclusively the upper dimension – or 'underworld' – exclusively the lower dimension). It may be considered to contain undifferentiated within it the later oppositional senses (1 and 2) of the word.

Apart from my discussion and the conclusions reached so far there is another important reason for understanding *'ereṣ* in v. 2 to be ambiguous. This is that the verse is poetry.[3] This can be seen by grouping the text according to its cola:

(w)h'rṣ hyth thw wbhw	(Now) the earth was chaotic and empty,
wḥšk ʿl-pny thwm	and darkness (was) over the face of the deep,
wrwḥ 'lhym mrḥpt	and the spirit of God was brooding
ʿl-pny hmym	over the surface of the waters.

At first glance it appears to be a tricolon, but the second and third cola are structurally distinct, and may alternatively be analysed for the sake of argument as a classic bicolon with synonymous parallelism, linked to a preceding monocolon by the *w* of *wḥšk*, which demands an antecedent. This also seems a satisfactory analysis of the prosody, though in fact the structure of the whole verse is more subtle than this suggests, as we shall see.

The structure of the bicolon (ll. 2-3), to follow this line of reasoning, is *ab, acb*, an unexpressed copula being implied in the first colon (or even the hiatus due to the lack of a verb anticipating a double-duty use of *mrḥpt* in the second). Recognition of the structure is important for purposes of interpretation, since it brings to the fore a hitherto unrecognized feature of the verse – the significance of *ḥšk* – as well as resolving a problem in the interpretation of a second item of vocabulary, *rwḥ 'lhym.* The two *b* items in the bicolon, *thwm* and *mym,* both refer to the primordial condition of the waters which after the cosmogony is complete will continue to exist above the firmament and below the netherworld, ready to irrupt and bring destruction to the cosmos in any breakdown of the system, but at the same time ready to be harnessed by proper cultic procedure for the nourishing of the world. At the same time they are evocative symbols of the underworld, as Tromp has shown (1969: 59-69). Death always contained in ancient Semitic religious thought a greater or lesser fear that it constituted total annihilation. Such a fear surely lies beneath the choice of vocabulary of a literary composition that reached its final form in the heart of the exilic experience.

But if the two *b* terms belong together, the same is true of the *a* pair. The darkness therefore must correspond in some way to the spirit of God. It is arguable that the two terms form a contrasting pair:

> and darkness (was) over the face of the deep,
> but the spirit of God was brooding over the surface of the waters.

But I suggest that, while this is generally assumed to be the case, it is a false assumption. It is, of course, possible to take the latter expression, *rwḥ 'lhym*, in the neutral sense proposed by some recent commentators and accepted in the NEB (contrast the REB) translation, that is, 'a mighty wind', but it seems unlikely that the writer of Genesis 1 would allow such a diminution of one of his key terms by its use as a mere superlative. We may perhaps take it as 'the wind of God', but the deity who is in total control of the cosmogonic process is surely present, even perhaps in the notionally neutral form of his 'wind', from the beginning.[4] Verse 2 is the beginning grammatically (I reject the view that v. 1 is a main clause) and therefore logically, and its heavy stress on *hā'āreṣ* by its initial position, preceding its verb, draws attention to its pregnant, ambiguous nature. Now, if *rwḥ 'lhym* denotes some divine quality, it follows that *ḥšk*, unless contrastive, as commonly assumed, must also denote a similar quality.[5] We have been misled by our habit of reading Genesis 1.2 as prose into supposing that darkness is no more than the primordial entity later split into two constituent parts, darkness and light (v. 4). It is indeed that, but does not simply have negative connotations, having rather a richness of content of which commentators have apparently been unaware.

An assertion based on no more than the discussion above may be felt to be unconvincing. But an excellent corroboration is to be found in Psalm 18.12 (EVV. 11), appearing also with some variation in 2 Samuel 22.12. The Psalm verse reads as follows:

> *yšt ḥšk strw sbybwtyw*
> *sktw ḥškt-mym ʿby štqym*

I suspect that there are glosses to both cola here (though the matter is not vital to our discussion), so that an original form, underlying both the Psalm version and that of 2 Samuel, would have read:

> *yšt ḥšk strw* — He made darkness his hiding place,
> *sktw ḥškt-mym* — his shelter the darkness of the waters.

This passage paradoxically makes darkness the locus of the invisibility, and therefore perhaps of the spiritual essence, of the deity. Furthermore, it links darkness explicitly with the waters, and, I suspect, with the primordial waters in mind, as the extraterrestrial location of God. Indeed, the chiastic structure of the bicolon cleverly envelops the dwelling (*str, skh*) in the darkness and the darkness of the waters, a graphic verbal presentation of the secrecy of the divine abode. In a context of primordiality, we may see here a thought-process similar to that of the ancient Hermopolitan cosmogony of Egypt, in which Kuk and Kauket feature as a male and female pair of primordial deities, representing darkness, and Amun and Amaunet appear as the deities of invisibility.[6]

Another biblical usage occurs in two passages describing darkness as an important element in a theophany. These are Deuteronomy 4.11 and 5.23. The first reads awkwardly, since the final three words hang rather limply in apposition as attributes of heaven:

> *whhr bcr b'š ʿd-lb hšmym ḥšk ʿnn wʿrpl*
>
> and the mountain was burning with fire to the midst of heaven,
> (amid? with?) darkness, cloud and deep gloom.

The second passage is more graphic:

> *wyhy kšmʿtm 't-qwl mtwk hḥšk*
>
> And when you heard the voice from the midst of the darkness...

In this context, darkness seems precisely the appropriate medium for the divine voice. It is a figure for invisibility. And it is out of the primordial darkness that the voice of God is uttered in Genesis 1, initiating the creative process, the manifestation of his glory. It is out of the darkness of v. 2 that God's voice comes, uttering the first word in v. 3: 'Let there be light!', whose climactic nature is due precisely to its surprising implication that the light proceeds from the darkness.

Deuteronomy 4.11 has combined the darkness idiom of 5.23, which belongs to the same formulaic context as Genesis 1.2, with the alternative idiom of the storm-cloud as the veil for the divine glory. This is not inappropriate, if we recall, following Day's analysis, that Genesis 1 is an extensively reworked version of the fight with the sea.[7]

I have suggested that the putative bicolon we have discussed in Genesis 1.2 follows a monocolon, the two units forming the present body of the verse. The first colon, omitting the initial *w* which was perhaps added to link the verse to the preceding one, would have read:

> *h'rṣ hyth thw wbhw* The earth was chaotic and empty

Let us note the structure. I characterized the following bicolon in prosodic terms as *ab, acb* (above). But while the preceding monocolon may be construed as an independent unit, having a different structure, with copula[8] but no prepositional phrase, it nevertheless has a peculiarly intimate relationship with the first stich of the bicolon. These two lines can also be isolated and taken together:

> The earth was chaotic and empty
> and darkness was over the face of the deep.

The absence of the copula in the second line now makes sense on the ground that *hyth* in the first performs double duty, and the obvious analysis of the lines is as *abc, ac*: *h'rṣ* || *ḥšk*, and *thw wbhw* || *thwm*.[9] In view of the impossibility of separating the second and third lines of the verse, we may conclude that it is after all a tricolon. Prosodically, we have *abc, ac, adc* through the three lines of the verse. In the first stich, the effective equating of *a* and *c* binds not only these two terms together, but also the *a* and *c* terms of the following stichs. There is thus an overall chiastic structure with further reinforcements throughout (such as the assonance of the gutturals; there are no less than seven *h*s and three *k*s), which serves to emphasize the central theme, of the darkness over the face of the deep. The omission of the copula in the second stich also enhances the chiasmus, and the possibility noted above that the hiatus in the central stich also anticipates the *mrḥpt* of the third gives it a peculiar prominence, as though the 'grammatical void' were itself a religious symbol.

It may be argued that, while all that has been discussed so far is reasonable, it is absurd to imply that the formula *thw wbhw* can seriously be taken as tantamount to a designation of the deity, or of the aura of his presence. But this seems to be an implication of what I have said. Within the context of the verse, I may make two points. Firstly, we have to proceed on any exegetical path with regard to what the text says, and not what subsequent generations have made of it; and certainly we cannot allow a later theology to determine what an exilic or earlier writer may or may not have said or meant. Secondly, the logical structure of the verse indicates that a process is being identified within the verse. This process involves the initial stages in the self-manifestation of the deity. It is, in somewhat unusual form, an account of a theophany. It describes three stages in it: first, there is the seemingly improbable condition of primordial chaos in which it is to occur. Secondly, there is the inchoate medium of revelation: the darkness. And thirdly, there is the spirit of God intuited rather than seen traversing waters as yet unordered.

The term *thw* occurs some twenty times in the Hebrew Bible, on three occasions in conjunction with *bhw*. These three passages are instructive, and perhaps significantly, they probably all belong to the same general historical period, that of the exile. They are the following: Genesis 1.2, Jeremiah 4.23, and Isaiah 34.11. Job 26.7 is also of interest, and these further three passages may be cited in turn:

Jeremiah 4.23[10]

r'yty 't-h'rṣ	I looked at the underworld
whnh thw wbhw	and lo, chaos and emptiness!
w'l hšmym	And to the heavens,
w'yn 'wrm	and they had no light.

Isaiah 34.11

wnṭh ʿlyh qw-thw	And over it he stretches the measuring-line of chaos
w'bny-bhw	and the plumbline of emptiness.

Job 26.7

nṭh ṣpwn ʿl thw	He stretches Saphon over chaos
tlh 'rṣ ʿl-blymh	and hangs the netherworld over nothingness.

The Jeremiah and Isaiah passages both occur in contexts of judgment oracles, and might therefore be argued to have no useful connection with our present discussion. But the point of each of them is that the prophet has a vision of destruction in which there is a reversion to the primordial situation. It is particularly interesting to note that Jeremiah uses the notions of chaos and darkness ('no light') in parallel. But the Isaianic passage is even more interesting, and shares a significant feature with the bicolon in Job. This is the use of the verb *nṭh,* the precise meaning of which is to stretch out the fabric of a tent, or to pitch it. This, as N.C. Habel has eloquently shown,[11] is a figure for cosmogony, in which the archaic image of a tent-shrine is used to describe the canopy of heaven. The whole earth (that is, the universe) is the divine shrine. And while in context the plumb-line image of the passage may evoke Amos, it is of course a constructional, architectural metaphor, appropriate as much to a cosmogonic as to a forensic context. The bicolon from Job is the most interesting to us, since as well as being strictly cosmogonic, it incorporates the ancient Canaanite figure of the cosmic mountain, abode of the whole pantheon (and not just to be associated with the storm-god: see the designation of KTU 1.47 *il ṣpn*: 'the gods of Saphon'). The point in the bicolon is that the deity dwells everywhere: he is as much at home in the underworld, which he controls as cosmic overlord, as on Mount Saphon. At the same time,

Saphon and the underworld are significantly located in relation to *thw wbhw*, even though for *bhw Job* employs the synonymous expression *blymh*. A further point to this passage, which requires more detailed analysis, is that M.C. Astour's suggestion that *ṣpn* and Greek Τυφων are related[12] suggests that at least in mythological contexts the former was personified and implicitly identified as Yam, since the Greek myth of Zeus and Typhon (Hesiod, *Theogony* 820-68, and others) is a variant of the Baal-Yam conflict.[13] Astour's suggestion has interesting implications for Psalm 89.13 (EVV. 12), where MT reads *ṣāpôn w^{e}yāmîn*, but LXX reads και θαλασσας or και την θαλασσαν, suggesting that the second word be corrected to *yām(m)îm* (see BHS app.), and explained as an appositional equivalent to *ṣāpôn* ('Typhon' || Yam) rather than the MT's contrasting complement (north || south). It also has a bearing on Job 26.7, which may be construed as indicating that Yahweh uses (the corpses of) Yam (=*ṣāpôn*) and Mot (= *'ereṣ*) as the raw materials of his cosmogonic activity.

We have encountered a wide range of associated motifs – *thw wbhw, blymh, thwm, mym, 'rṣ* and *ḥšk* – which are figures for the same thing, the invisibility of God with particular reference to the primordial context of cosmogony. If we return briefly to the bicolon in Psalm 18.12, there is a further term which may have considerable importance in our overall understanding of this language. This refers to Yahweh's hiding place and his shelter (*str* || *skh*). Now while the former of these terms is relatively neutral, merely referring to the hiddenness of the deity, the latter is replete with cultic overtones. It is possible that it should be viewed neutrally, in conjunction with *str*; but given the cultic *Sitz im Leben* of the psalm, in which a cry for help results in a theophany, so that the choice of vocabulary is determined by the cultic milieu, it seems more credible to see in *skh* the technical term for a booth used in the seasonal festival, the chief function of which was the sexual rituals of cosmic fertility. While this must remain conjectural, I propose that we lift this entire cultic ambiance, and recognize its presence, implied rather than explicit, to be sure, in the cosmogonic language of the darkness from which the divine voice calls in Genesis 1.2. That is to say, whatever theological nuances are to the fore in the creative language of Genesis 1, with its systematic use of such verbs as *br', bdl* (hiphil), *qr', 'mr, qr'* and *nṭh*, there lies behind the altogether less cerebral discourse of v. 2 the older mythological overtones of the primordial *hieros gamos*, which initiated all things. That this is by no means alien to the thought of the biblical writers is clear from the content of Psalm 19, which in vv. 2-7 (EVV. 1-6) narrates the sacred marriage of El and the sun. While there is a constant pressure among scholars to see such allusions in the biblical text, and in particular when their pre-biblical origin is (sometimes reluctantly) acknowledged, as thoroughly demythologized in their present context, this is surely to diminish, not to enhance, the material in question. It is in the pervasive nature of myth that its literary use is one further twist in the mythological plot.[14]

There remains one final issue: the matter of the origin of the snatch of poetry I have detected in Genesis 1.2. Its poetic nature is hardly in dispute, since its whole structure is entirely in accordance with the rules of Hebrew poetry. Nor is the isolated presence in Genesis of a short poetic passage cause for surprise.[15] For instance, the JB and the REB print Genesis 1.27 as poetry within a prose context, and treat 2.23, 3.14-15 (disagreeing about where the poetry begins), 16, 17b-19 in similar fashion. The REB in addition reads 4.6-7 as poetry, and is joined by the JB in its similar treatment of 4.23-24. The same sporadic incidence of poetry, often unrecognized by older editors, is found widely in modern versions. The same belated recognition may be seen with reference to the layout of the text in BH^3 and BHS, which acknowledge most of the above. Examples of such poetic passages will no doubt continue to be discovered. Genesis 1.10a is a further case, for instance, having the structure *abcd, cad*. The question is whether the present instance is a quotation from a larger composition, such as a poem about creation, or is the result of a poeticizing tendency by the writer of Genesis 1.

It is impossible to determine this. Genesis 1 certainly exhibits a distinctive prose style, with its constant, refrain-like repetition of many phrases, as though it served a liturgical purpose. Its use of alternative verbs for creation (*br'*, *ʿśh, hbdyl*) could be argued to be evidence of multiple authorship – not a view I would espouse – in which parts of a poem had as legitimate a place as the prose elements. Even if its unitary nature be accepted, an author might spontaneously cite excerpts of a poem (vv. 2, 10a, 27 are obvious, and a case might be made for others)[16] to which his prose account was parallel. Alternatively, his 'poetic prose' may be seen to have tipped over from time to time into the classic structure of verse.

Endnotes

* First published in *VT* 43 (1993): 543-54.

1. Wyatt 1996b: 106 and n. 170; *idem* 2002a: 113 and n. 176, 124. For this interpretation of *bt ḫpṯt* (= Hebrew *bêt ḥopšît*) see Tromp 1969: 157-59. He makes a good case for *ḥopšî* in Psalm 88.6 (EVV. 5) meaning 'my couch'. Cf. Dahood 1965-70: II, 301, 303-304.

2. On the last passage, see Dahood 1965-70: III, 324.

3. See Kselman 1978: 163. As will be seen, I disagree with his association of parallel terms (*'rṣ* || *thwm* || *mym*).

4. On the expression see P.J. Smith 1980.

5. The formal association of the two terms is argued by Blythin 1962.

6. See Sethe 1929, *passim*, for Kuk, Kauket: 65, 76; Bonnet 1952: 5; Brandon 1963: 54-55, and 148 (cross-reference to Genesis 1.2). See also Kilian 1966.

7. Day 1985: 49-53. I disagree with Day's assessment that Genesis 1 has demythologized the event, reducing it, in his words, to 'simply a job of work'. See my comments in Wyatt 1985b: 376, and Chapter 11 below. His whole approach is questioned by Tsumura 1989: 62-65.

8. For the nuance of the verb *hyth* see Lane 1963: 70-71.

9. The two terms *thw* and *thwm* are unrelated etymologically (see Tsumura 1989: 17-18, 51-52), though their assonance is of course of value here in interlocking their complementary resonances.

10. See Fishbane 1971.

11. Habel 1972. See also Wyatt 2001a: 173-76.

12. Astour 1967: 216-17. The older form of Typhon, Τυφωευς, may be tentatively explained as from **ṣāpūy*, 'stretched out' (cf. Hebrew *ṣāpâ*) on C.H. Gordon's argument (Gordon 1969: 288), that Greek names in *-eus* are derived from pre-Greek Near Eastern names. Astour 1967: 175, argues that the ending is related to West Semitic passive participles. Cf. Chapter 9.

13. Fontenrose 1980: 129-38.

14. Cf. Lévi-Strauss 1977: he insists on taking into account all versions of a myth as the basis for analysis. This would ultimately take into account, for instance, J. Anouilh's treatment of the Oedipus myth in *Antigone*.

15. See Westermann 1984: 90-91: 'Gen I contains a fusion of poetry and prose that is unique in the Old Testament'; Wenham 1987: 10: 'It is indeed a great hymn...elevated prose, not pure poetry...' See also Kselman 1978.

16. Thus Kselman argues, in addition to 1.10, 27, for 1.5, 16 and 20, as well as for verses in later chapters, 1978: 164-65; and Porten and Rappoport 1971: 368-69, make the case for 1.22. (Cf. my layout of the text of Genesis 1.1-9 in Wyatt 2001a: 72, §2[15].)

Chapter 9

The Significance of *Ṣpn* in West Semitic Thought: A Contribution to the History of a Mythological Motif*

A paper on the theme of the History of Religions and Ugaritic myth could lead in a number of directions. Those that are entirely theoretical, in the sense that they would deal with problems in the theoretical approach to the discipline, are to my mind not terribly helpful, since grand theory always has to give way to awkward fact. The problem I shall treat is no less theoretical, of course, but at least it is testable, and seeks to answer a specific, and ultimately historical problem, rather than simply indulging in airy speculation, or more dangerously, in the promotion of an ideological stance. The 'History of Religions' indeed raises a problem of reference: the English expression is fairly neutral, simply denoting the study of religions within a historical framework, considering historical developments and so forth, while as I understand it the German term *Religionsgeschichte* can have a more restricted sense, denoting this approach applied to Israelite and Judahite religion in historical context, so that it merges with Comparative Religion and the History of Tradition (*Überlieferungsgeschichte*). It can then take on a significant polemical role, which I do not see it as my brief to defend.[1]

The 'History of Religions' is better pursued in the former sense, but at the same time it is preferable to approach it *ad textum* or *ad contextum* rather than in the abstract, and the problems associated with *ṣpn* seem to me an excellent field for enquiry in this context. Inevitably, since this topic also impinges on biblical matters, it becomes a study bridging the divide noted above.

There has been considerable discussion concerning the etymology and meaning of the Ugaritic term *ṣpn*, appearing in Hebrew as *ṣāpôn* ('Saphon'). The vocalization problem, which has taken up an inordinate amount of discussion, may be summed up as follows:

i. the unvocalized Ugaritic form is *ṣpn*.
ii. in Akkadian it is normally transcribed as *ṣapunu* (nominative) as in

ṣa-pù-núm^{KI} (TM.75.G.1642),[2] or *ṣapuna* (oblique), as in the form *gir ṣa-pu-na,*[3] *šadû ba-'-li-ṣa-pu-na,*[4] also *ba-'-il-ṣa-pu-na,*[5] or even as *ṣapuni* (oblique), as in ^{URU}*ṣa-pù-u*$_{4}$*-ni*^{KI} (TM.75.G.2231 rev ii 9).[6] This presupposes a second vowel *u*.

iii. in the Akkadian of Ugarit it appears also to be written *ṣa-pa-n*u,* if we accept Albright's restoration of RS 17.11 6.3,[7] followed by E. Lipiński.[8] But this depends on a restoration, and therefore hardly outweighs the evidence noted above. E. Lipiński proposed a sense 'floating', deriving the form from *ṣup,* 'to float',[9] and understands this etymon at Job 26.7, and considers the original meaning of *bʿl ṣpn* to be 'lord of floating', the sense of '[the storm-god of] Mount Sapan (*sic*)' being a later nuance. 'The rituals have preserved in the meantime', he averred, 'the souvenir of a distinctive deity *Ṣpn,* identified with the mountain itself.'[10] It seems to me that we should appeal to Ockham's razor here. If we concede E. Lipiński's alternative etymology, we would have to think of a distinct south Palestinian and Egyptian god, quite independent of the Ugaritic Baal. The Mami stela, thoroughly Egyptian in style and language, yet coming from Ras Shamra, and presupposing the common equation of Seth and Baal, would seem to frustrate such an approach. In any case, reverting to the problem of vocalization, the text in *PRU IV* is anomalous if restored as proposed, in that we should expect ^{d}IM ^{HURSAG} *Ḫa-zi.*

iv. in Egyptian it is transcribed as *Djapuna*: *ḏ3-pw-n3* appearing twice on the Mami stela from Ugarit, ('Seth of Sapuna'), the *u* sound confirmed by the separate signs used in the two occurrences (Gardiner G43, Z7). It occurs also in this form in P. Sallier from Egypt,[11] and perhaps on the 'Job-stone', though this seems illegible to me, on which W.F. Albright read, tentatively, the form *i3tn-ḏ3-p3n3* ('Lord of Sapan').[12] Albright noted the anomaly of *p3*, and indeed questioned the whole reading. The latter monument is best left out of account, in which case the *u* is the most secure Egyptian form.

v. in Hebrew it is vocalized *ṣāpôn* (e.g. Psalm 48.3 etc.) or *ṣ*^{e}*pôn* (e.g. Exodus 14.1 etc.). This could be explained both as NWS *ā* > *ô*, a regular shift, as for instance in Ugaritic *Dāgān* = Hebrew *Dāgôn,* and as a reflection of an older *u*. The fact that there is a choice precludes an automatic appeal to the first possibility. The Akkadian and Egyptian evidence cited weighs in favour of the second explanation.

vi. An appeal to EA Akkadian *ṣapanu* (147.10, *ṣa-pa-ni-šu*) is probably irrelevant; this word is generally agreed to be the Akkadian infinitive, meaning 'to hide', taken as a WS loanword by *CAD* xvi 96. The valiant attempt by C. Grave[13] to prove that the EA lexeme is the same as the Ugaritic one under consideration begs the question, to my mind, though taken up by W.L. Moran in his new edition of the letters.[14] There is no internal evidence from Ugarit that *ṣpn* means 'north', as later in Hebrew, much less 'north wind'.

The outcome of this seems to me to be that the *u* value of the second vowel is well attested, while the *a* sound claimed or assumed by many scholars leaves many unanswered questions, is scarcely beyond dispute, and indeed is not likely. It may owe its popularity to the dubious influence of Albright, who in the very midst of citing all the evidence to the contrary, could write that 'the vocalization of the word in Ugaritic is uncertain, but may well have been *Ṣapanu*'.[15]

The vocalization **ṣapunu* will have an important bearing on etymology, as will become apparent below.

The Hebrew form has commonly been translated as 'north' in most of its occurrences in the Bible.[16] This common geographical sense seems entirely appropriate in most instances. But there are a few occurrences in which a more pregnant sense is required. What are we to make, for instance, of the following bicolon in Job 26.7:

nōtê ṣāpôn ʿal-tōhû	He stretches Saphon over chaos
tōlê 'ereṣ ʿal-bᵉli-mâ	and hangs the underworld over nothingness.

There is a double problem here. Firstly, are we to understand 'north' – an abstraction – to be 'stretched' as though having substance?[17] Secondly, what kind of relationship are we to understand to exist between 'north' and 'the underworld'? It may seem that an appeal to external, in this case the Ugaritic, material, provides the most likely solution; but we should appeal first to any help available within the biblical tradition.

There is fortunately a passage in Psalm 48 that seems to have something to offer. Consider the following lines:

har-qodšô yᵉpê nôp	His holy mountain is as beautiful as Memphis,
mᵉśôs kol-hā'āreṣ	the exaltation of the whole earth,
har-ṣiyyôn	Mount Zion,
yarkᵉtê ṣāpôn	the recesses of Saphon,
qiryat melek rāb	the city of the Great King.
	(vv. 2d, 3 MT)[18]

While elements in this chiastic pentacolon are open to alternative explanations, the gist of the structure is clear enough. Mount Zion is being compared, even identified with, the great symbols of cosmological plenitude of the Egyptian and Canaanite worlds. Memphis to the south, the

Great Seat of Ptah, and Mount Saphon to the north, dwelling of the gods of the West Semitic pantheon. The poetic resonances and subtleties of the passage are considerable.

But has an appeal to this passage really solved our problem? Are we to think of a *mountain* 'stretched out' in the Joban verse? And how does this relate to the underworld? After a fashion, of course, this bold metaphorical language makes good sense. The mountain may represent the superstructure of the world, while the underworld, *'ereṣ*, is its substructure. The two aspects complement each other perfectly. In addition, the metaphor of 'stretching', that is, pitching a tent, using the different verb *nāṭāh* (*nāṭâ*), has been shown by N. Habel to be one of the dominant figures for cosmogony in the Hebrew Bible.[19] The image is drawn from the construction of tent-shrines to house divine images, no doubt a cultic practice of great antiquity, surviving in the structural details of shrines in Egypt,[20] in the form of the priestly Tabernacle in Exodus, and no doubt in a tent shrine before the building of the Jerusalem temple (see 1 Samuel 7.6-12: v. 13 reconciles this with the Solomonic construction), and in Ugaritic allusions to the gods such as KTU 1.15 iii 18-19:

tity ilm lahlhm	The gods went away to their tents,
dr il lmšknthm	the family of El to their dwellings.[21]

One further biblical passage is relevant to our enquiry. This is Isaiah's great taunt against a Babylonian or Assyrian king in Isaiah 14.7-21. Verse 13 reads as follows:

haššāmayim 'e^{ce}lê	I shall scale the heavens:
mimmaʿal l^{e}kôk^{e}bê-'ēl 'ārim kis'î	above the Stars of El I shall raise my throne,
w^{e}'ēšēb b^{e}har môʿēd	and I shall sit in the Mount of Assembly
b^{e}yark^{e}tê ṣāpôn	in the recesses of Saphon.

Again, the text is based on an allusion to the Canaanite substratum of tradition. Before we turn to the Ugaritic treatments of the motif, let us note that in these translations I have, provisionally, accepted the common rendition of *yark^{e}tê* as 'recesses'. This is a *pis aller*, and we shall perhaps be able to justify an improved translation when we have examined other matters.

We have preferred to recognize in Hebrew *ṣāpôn* in these passages the name of the cosmic mountain rather than a simple references to the north, in accordance with the broad consensus among scholars. But we have hinted, especially with reference to Job 26.7, that there may be more to this mountain than meets the eye. Is there, perhaps, a more overtly mythological rather than simply cultic or cosmological allusion here? Let us leave this for the present as a rhetorical question, because the answer I shall propose will take us far afield in both space and time.

I have published a number of papers in recent years[22] in which I have examined the possibility of links between not simply the Canaanite and biblical worlds – this is almost parochial on the scale I envisage – but between the broader Semitic world and the whole of Eurasia to the north, and closer to home, the Aegean to the west. The results of investigations by a number of scholars, notably J.A. Fontenrose, are that a wide range of *Chaoskampf* myths are in all probability cognate, with an Indo-European prototype being brought to the Near East by the 'Proto-Indo-Aryans' in the middle of the second millennium.[23] A clear historical record of these people is found in Ugaritic and Egyptian documentation, referring to the *mariannu* class of chariot-owning warriors.

The term by which they are designated is derived from the early Sanskrit *marya,* meaning 'youth', 'hero' or 'warrior'. The archaeological record, most useful in terms of the texts it has revealed for examination, speaks for itself. The historical interpretation of the raw data is perhaps more open to constant reassessment, and this must apply all the more to larger interpretations about world-views, mythology, and metaphysics.

The *Chaoskampf* mythological tradition in the Indian material has spawned a vast number of versions. In earlier work I have suggested that the purāṇic version of Viṣṇu and Hiraṇyakṣa bears a close relationship to the Baal-Yam conflict, particularly when the Greek derivative of the Canaanite myth, Perseus and Andromeda, is taken into account.[24]

Here I want to draw attention to features of the earlier Indian version, as found in the *Ṛgveda*. In this older tradition the Vedic war-god, the first of the Devas, later also a weather-god, fights with Vṛtra, an Asura. Already the myth is extremely complex, with numerous obscure ideological overtones, and more to the purpose, a wide variety of descriptive metaphors for the various phases of the combat. Some verses from *Ṛgveda* 1.32, our most important single source for the myth of Indra's combat with Vṛtra, will illustrate the point:

1 He killed the dragon and pierced an opening for the waters:
he split open the bellies of mountains.
2 He killed the dragon who lay upon the mountain…
like lowing cows, the flowing waters rushed down to the sea.
…
5 Like the trunk of a tree whose branches have been lopped off by an
axe, the Dragon lies flat upon the ground.[25]

This passage allows us to reconstruct a composite portrait of Vṛtra. His name is generally explained as 'Obstruction', but it is worth noting that a wordplay in *Śatapatha Brāhmaṇa* 1.6.3.9 explains it by the radical *vṛt*, meaning 'rolling onwards', which is conceptually similar to the epithet *ʿqltn, ʿaqallatôn* occurring of Litan in KTU 1.5 i 2 and of Leviathan in Isaiah 27.1. Vṛtra is at once a dragon, with watery associations, a mountain, and can both 'lie upon the mountain' and 'lie flat upon the ground'.

It is not going too far to suggest that his cadaver, spread out upon the ground, is mountainous in form. The frequent Vedic image of his death being associated with the releasing of pent-up waters, which then flow down from his flanks, suggests the identification of local landmarks with Indra's victim. There is also a cosmogonic dimension to this myth, though it is allusive rather than explicit. It is bound up with a complex of symbolic allusions to war, sacrifice, the creation of 'space' or 'territory' (*loka*), in which the Vedic war-god is championing Aryan claims to India. But even if we concede that the Baal-Yam conflict is related to the Vedic account, and that Vṛtra appears to be mountainous in form, we have not solved the problem of the term *ṣapunu*.

Let us return to the Syrian theatre. U. Oldenburg drew attention to a curious remark of Strabo, concerning the River Orontes. 'Though formerly called Typhon, its name was changed to that of Orontes, the man who built a bridge across it.'[26] If there is any truth in this tradition, 'Typhon' must be a Semitic name. Astour confidently identified the name with *ṣāpôn*.[27] It is, of course, the name of the Titan, the monstrous serpentine offspring of Hera, who wanted to avenge herself on Zeus out of jealousy for his ability to generate Athena without her assistance.[28] Oldenburg suggested that it is the Orontes which gives rise to Yam's sobriquet *Naharu*, 'River'.

Let us explore the Typhonian tradition a little further. Typhon is said by Homer to be among the 'Arimoi',[29] whom Fontenrose reasonably supposed to be the Arameans.[30] His sexual dalliance with Echidna is also said to have taken place in Syria (*Theogony* 304). Furthermore, during the struggle with Zeus, the wounded Typhon is said to have fled to Mount Kasion, that is, of course, Mount Ṣapunu of the Ugaritic tradition. At a further crisis in the battle, Typhon fled to Nysa, according to Apollodorus (1.6.3), which is surely to be identified with Beth Shean[31] and therefore represents another Syrian stage of the battle before it shifted to Thrace and on to Etna. The reference to Etna, opening up the world of the western Mediterranean, is clearly no more than a Greek embellishment.

If the Greek tradition is derived most directly, as some opine, not from the West Semitic, but from the Hittite world, it is of significance that Mount

Kasion is also the location, as Mount Ḫazzi, of the battle in the Hurro-Hittite version.[32] This version is, of course, directly dependent on the Ugaritic tradition.

Mount Typhaonion in Thebes, Boeotia, a locale saturated with Semitic tradition, as hinted at by the Kadmos traditions,[33] claimed to have Typhon's body below it,[34] and indeed the mountain is doubly duplicated, as Typhon and Typhaonion, the former with twin peaks Basileos and Tyrannike.[35] There may be something in the tradition which called for an identification of a twin-peaked mountain with the conflict.[36]

Thus far our discussion may appear to have been avoiding altogether the Ugaritic traditions concerning *ṣpn*, while exploring every other possible theme. But in treating the problem of how, or even whether, the diverse fragments of myth and legend we have so far encountered are to be related, it is to these that we must turn for an answer. And the answer which I believe is waiting to be unravelled from the texts provides a most interesting example of the interlocking of diverse cultures in what was later to become one of the dominant myths of western culture.[37]

The Baal cycle itself, KTU 1.1-6, makes no explicit connection between Yam and Ṣapunu. The setting of the conflict may, however, be tentatively reconstructed from the following fragments, and such a connection established.

El appears from KTU 1.1 iii 12 to be resident on Mount 'Kas' (*ks*: 'Kasu', 'Kisu'?), and this location is usually restored in gaps in the text in ll. 16 and 22.

Thereafter some 60 lines at a minimal estimate are missing, followed by the account of the coronation of Yam by El (KTU 1.1 iv 12-32: the ceremony concludes with sacrifices). The narrative is severely disrupted from now on, and we cannot say with any certainty how much text is missing.

When it next becomes coherent, in KTU 1.2 iv, Baal is cowering, presumably a prisoner, beneath Yam's throne (*tḥt ksi zbl ym*, l. 7), and it is from here that Kothar summons him to the battle.

Now let us conjecture for a moment. If the battle takes place in the vicinity of Yam's throne, and we may not unreasonably suppose this throne to be the same place where Yam had been crowned king, then we may suggest that Yam's throne is on Mount 'Kas'. We have no reason to suppose that El has left his mountain for the ceremony. Now where is this place, and how does it fit into the discussions concerning the matters discussed above? I think that the answer has been staring us in the face, but we have failed to recognize it. Consider for example the remark of A. Caquot *et al.* on Mount 'Kas':[38] 'This must be another name for the mountain of El. It cannot be identified with Khazzi, the Hurrian name of Sapon which is Baal's residence.' This view has been universally accepted. It involves two questionable propositions: firstly that El's dwelling is not on Mount Ṣapunu, and is at a great distance from there; secondly, that the equation *kasion* = *ṣapunu* = *ḫazzi* means that the word *kasion* is derived from *hazzi*. This was justified by M.C. Astour in his discussion of *ṣpn*[39] on the ground that equations can be made between Greek *k* and near eastern *ḫ*, in the transcription of toponyms. He cited *Ḫilakku* – *Kilikia* and *Ḫubišna* = *Kybistra*. Everything that is taken for granted in this discussion seems to go back to the view A. Goetze proposed in 1941,[40] taken up by W.F. Albright,[41] championed by Clifford,[42] and recently reasserted by W. Fauth.[43] A. Goetze stated baldly that, 'it seems that the name *Casius* derives from our *Ḫa*(*-az*)*-zi*', but offered no further arguments.[44] R.J. Clifford wrote of the phonetic equivalence of *Kasios* (read *Kasion*) and *Ḫazzi*, but a strict phonetic equivalence is precisely what there is not.

Kasion, then, is generally taken to be the Greek form of *Ḫazzi.* It seems to me however that a much better equation would be the following, accepting for the moment the received text: *Kasion* = *ks,* perhaps vocalized '*Kas*', *kasu*, or *kisu*. The latter I would provisionally explain by reference to West Semitic *ks'*, Ugaritic *ksu,* Hebrew *kissē'*.

Let us pause for a moment on the matter of the reading. I think that the reading **ksi,* or *ks,* and the equivalence I have proposed, could be defended on the ground that an ancient name might preserve an archaic biliteral root from which the triliteral *ks'* subsequently developed. But before we consider this matter, let us consider the actual epigraphy of the tablet.

There is clearly a difficulty with the reading on the tablet at KTU 1.1 iii 12. The *ǵ, r,* read clearly enough, followed by a bold word-divider. But there then follows after *ks* a very timid, indeed diminutive, word-divider, much smaller than the others appearing on the tablet. This in turn is followed by what is usually taken to be a *d,* written with the same apparent hesitation. But this is a curious *d,* and I am not convinced beyond doubt that the three superimposed horizontal strokes of a *d* are present.

Let me offer the following proposal. The scribe intended to write *ǵr ksi dm*, that is, 'the mountain of my throne, for...' (**ksi* might stand for **ksiy*).[45] But he confused his *alephs:* instead of the *i aleph* appropriate to the genitive or the possessive, or even the voiceless *aleph,* his mind wandered ahead to the predicted *dalet,* and he produced a hybrid. The sign, written , is evidently a mixture of  (*i*) and  (*u*), which has been read by modern scholars as a  (*d*). He either failed to notice his mistake, or gave up trying to correct it, because he had to press on. The tentative markings suggest a hesitation which we can only imagine. A photograph of line 12 shows details.

KTU 1.1 iii 12

The transcription of the text in this line 12, on this argument, should thus be:

*ǵr.ks<i>.*dm.rg*[*m*...]

or better:

*ǵr.ks*i. <d>m.rg*[*m*...]

The other two occurrences of *ks* cited are of course restorations, and so add nothing to our discussion. Thus, if this argument be accepted as cogent, the name of the mountain is *ksu*, (vocalized perhaps *kasi'u*?) that is 'Mount Throne', all along, and is simply transcribed into Greek. Alternatively it is to be read *ǵr ksi*, as above, being in the genitive following the construct: 'the Mountain of the Throne', as provisionally proposed for KTU 1.1 iii 12.

I agree that the above is only hypothetical. But it does get us off the hook of a *ks* for which no scholar has provided a plausible explanation, and it provides a more convincing etymon for *Kasion* than *Ḫazzi*. Of course, this leaves us with the Hurro-Hittite name of the mountain unexplained. But this might in turn, tentatively, be explained as a transcription of the proposed **ksu*: that is, the equivalence of Greek *k* with an Oriental *ḫ* would simply be shifted further eastward. I am not myself convinced that this is very likely, but the difficulties involved here do not, on my argument, have any bearing on the equation *ksu* = *Kasion*. I shall propose an alternative explanation for *ḫazzi* below.

In fact the whole discussion above is really concerned to explain the *i* in *Kasion* as derived from an *aleph*. If there were not the need to explain this, we could equally appeal to Hebrew *kēs*, appearing in Exodus 17.16 and in modern Hebrew,[46] for 'throne', and read the putative <*i*> of my restored text as the possessive indicator, which could in any case be presupposed on the biliteral Reading *ks*.

The equation of West Semitic *k* with Greek *k* is at least as well attested as the one noted above.[47] And this proposal finds support from an unexpected quarter, the name 'Mount Thronos' which is one of the names of

Anti-Casius, the Mount Nanu of the *Keret* story.[48] This is a lower, south-western outcrop of the massif of Jebel el Aqra, lying west of Kassab (ancient *Ḫlb ḫuršan Ḫazzi*). Thus *Kasion*, I suggest, is a Greek transcription of the West Semitic term for the 'throne' of a god, subsequently translated into the Greek toponym *Thronos*. The form *Kasios* is initially the epithetal form accompanying the DN *Zeus*, but may have become masculinized by recognition of its equivalence with *Thronos*.

Mount Nanu appears in parallel with *ṣpn* in the *Keret* text (KTU 1.16 i 6-9, ii 44-47), as recently recognized by P. Bordreuil:[49]

tbkyk ab	They weep for you, father,
ǵr bʿl ṣpn	the mountain of Baal, Sapunu,
ḥlm qdš nny	the holy stronghold of Nanu,
ḥlm adr	the mighty stronghold,
ḥl rḥb mnkpt	the citadel of vast expanse.

Now while *we* differentiate between Nanu and Ṣapunu, and indeed differentiate the two from Inbubu and Aruru, and it is clear that for administrative purposes the Ugaritians did so as well, it is evident from this pentacolon that the names of the different parts of the massif could be used as poetic equivalents, just as Siryon and Lebanon can be used in parallel in Psalm 29.

This proposal falls short of proof, but as much can be said of all the alternatives. Yam was once enthroned, then, I am suggesting, on a mountain which we can identify as part of the Ṣapunu massif. I think that this is also where El dwelt, and that attempts to put the god away in the underworld or on Mount Hermon or elsewhere, from an Ugaritic perspective, are misplaced.[50]

Though Ṣapunu is not involved by name in the Baal-Yam myth of KTU 1.1-2, it does occur in KTU 1.10 iii 29-31:

w tʿl bkm barr	Then she climbed up on Aruru,
bm arr w b ṣpn	up on Aruru and Ṣapunu,
b nʿm b ǵr tliyt	up on the sweet place, the mountain of victory.

The victory alluded to here is undoubtedly that of Baal's mythological triumph over Yam, referred to as the 'hill of victory' *(gbʿ tliyt)* at KTU 1.3 iii 31, in parallel to *ǵry il ṣpn, bqdš b ǵr nḥlty*, 'my divine mountain Ṣapunu, in the sanctuary on the mountain of my inheritance'. The equivalence of Aruru and Ṣapunu is to be noted. KTU 1.10 iii 11-14 has previously alluded to Baal taking his place upon his throne:

yʿl bʿl b [ǵr]	Baal went up onto the moun[tain of Aruru],[51]
w bn dgn b š[ ]	yea, the Rainy One up onto [ ];
bʿl yṯb lks[i mlkh]	Baal sat down on the thron[e of his kingship],
bn dgn l kḥ[ṯ drkth]	the Rainy One on the sea[t of his dominion].

By the same token that the victory indicates the location of the throne, we may say that Baal in fact takes possession of the throne previously belonging to Yam. He has taken his place. This physical act seals the victory.

The same implications may be recognized in the opening lines of KTU 1.101, (ll. 1-3), which however take us considerably further in our enquiry, since they bring us back to the allusive Vedic hymn discussed above:

bʿl yṯb kṯbt ǵr	Baal is enthroned as a mountain is enthroned,
hd r[bṣ] kmdb	Hadd li[es down] like the ocean,
btk ǵr h il ṣpn	on his divine mountain, Sapunu,
b[tk] ǵr tliyt	on the mountain of victory.

D. Pardee has drawn attention to two remarkable passages in Genesis 49.25 and Deuteronomy 33.13, which allude to the cosmic ocean (Hebrew *tᵉhôm*) in connection with the verb *rbṣ*, proposed as a restoration in l. 2 by J.C. de Moor:[52]

mēʾēl ʾābîkā wᵉyaʿzᵉrekā	By El your father[53] – may he help you,
wᵉʾēt šadday wîbarkekā	and by Shaddai, may he bless you,
birkōt šāmayim mēʿal	(with) blessings of heaven above,
birkōt tᵉhôm rōbeṣet taḥat	blessings of the ocean lying down beneath,
birkōt šadayim wārāḥam	blessings of breasts and womb.
mᵉbōreket yhwh ʾarṣô	Blessing of Yahweh (be upon) his earth,
mimmeged šāmayim miṭṭal	from the gifts of heaven, from the dew,
ûmitᵉhôm rōbeṣet tāḥat	from the deep lying down beneath![54]

The term *rbṣ* seems here to describe a distinctive quality of the ocean, the cosmic sea which surrounds the habitable world. This was of course identified mythologically with Yam in Ugaritic tradition. Yam's characteristic posture is now copied in KTU 1.101.1, if we accept this restoration, by his conqueror.

The first bicolon of KTU 1.101 suggests more than an echo of Yam's posture by Baal, but more formally the equation *ǵr* = *mdb*. There is in fact a clever *double-entendre* here: not only does Baal lie down 'like...', but more to the point, the bicolon invites us to imagine, he lies down 'upon'. He takes up his position on the shattered body of his foe, who was the sea, but is now a crumpled corpse, and forms the mountain of his throne. The *yarkᵉtê* of the Hebrew version may even be tentatively regarded not simply as a geographical metaphor, but more specifically as the '*flanks*' of the sea-god's cadaver. This in turn raises the intriguing question of the precise sense of *ṣrrt* in the phrase *ṣrrt ṣpn*. Is it simply the highest parts of the mountain,[55] or does it perhaps play on the term *ṣrrt* with the sense of 'inward parts'?[56] Perhaps Bordreuil's proposal that *ṣrrt* means 'folds' may be construed as a geographical formation recalling the coiled intestines of the dead Yam. Does Baal sit enthroned in triumph on the shattered body of his foe? Such a wordplay is not inconsistent with alternative etymologies *sensu strictu.*

We are now, perhaps, in a position to reopen the etymological question of *ṣpn,* because we have new evidence at our disposal. We have seen that Yam was previously enthroned on Mount Kasion, as it later came to be called. We have every reason to regard the Greek and Ugaritic myths of the *Chaoskampf* as cognate, so that an equivalence between Typhoeus and Typhon on the one hand, and Yam on the other, is beyond reasonable doubt. And we have seen that the Greek tradition itself appeals to this locality for episodes in the tradition. The body of Yam has come to be equated with the mountain, so that as the throne changes hands (or seats) Yam himself forms Baal's throne. This conclusion may be argued to be supported by a further biblical allusion. In Psalm 89.13 (EVV 12) we read:

ṣāpôn wᵉyāmîn 'attâ bᵉrā'tām North and south, you created them.

Such is the apparent meaning of the MT, with Tabor and Hermon following on, as though the geographical limits of the world are balanced by the sacred mountains of Palestine. R. de Langhe wonders whether *yāmîn* signifies Amanus, the mountain range, thus giving a quartet of mountains.[57] But LXX has θαλασσαν for *yāmîn,* which presupposes a reading *yāmîm.* If we accept this reading as older, we have:

Saphon and Sea (or: Yam), you created (or: divided)[58] them.

This sense can be construed as equating the two things created, *ṣāpôn* being not just a reference to, but more strictly a title or name of, the sea-god. On such an understanding, we should conclude that the present reading of MT has taken *ṣāpôn* as a *nomen montis,* triggering off the addition of two further mountains in the following colon.

This allows us to suggest a plausible etymology for *ṣpn.* I take it to be a noun-formation with post-positional *n* from the verbal radical *ṣpy.* This is to be explained by reference to Hebrew *ṣāpâ* (*ṣāpāh*) II,[59] which in the Qal appears to have the sense of 'spread out', as in Isaiah 21.5, where it is used of rugs. This would correspond to the G stem in Ugaritic, which as an internal passive participle would be vocalized something like *ṣapuy,* becoming when substantivized *ṣapunu,* exactly the form in which it is transcribed into Akkadian, or written out phonetically in Egyptian (Mami stela).

This explanation also explains rather well the double form of the Greek opponent of Zeus. The form *Typhoeus* is to be explained on the participial form, while *Typhaon, Typhôn,* is to be explained on the nominal form.[60]

This etymology is also to be linked with the motif of Yahweh 'stretching out the heavens', which has developed the mythological allusion into a more specific cultic metaphor, the cadaver of the vanquished enemy of the *Chaoskampf* becoming the raw material of which the cosmos is made. This is precisely what we find in both the Vedic and Mesopotamian versions. The two figures, of tent-pitching and theomachy, are combined in two biblical passages – Job 9.8:

nōṭê šāmayim l^{e}*baddô*	(Yahweh) stretching out (the) heavens by himself
wedōrēk ʿal-bām^{o}*tê yām*	and striding on the back of Yam.

and Psalm 104.2-3:

nōṭê šāmayim kay^{e}*rîʿâ*	(Yahweh) stretching out (the) heavens[61] like a tent-curtain,
ham^{e}*qārê bammayim ʿaliyyôtāyw*	fixing on the waters the beams of your store-chambers.[62]

In the former passage we can imagine Yahweh striding back and forth triumphantly on Yam's back and pulling his skin into shape, while in the latter the architectural metaphor of world-construction is developed in the second colon, a permanent building balancing the more temporary tent-construction of the first. The tent of the sanctuary is a microcosm. We see this specifically cosmogonic treatment of the motif also spelt out at length in the *Enuma Elish* (4.104-106, 128-46 and catch-line).

It seems that Astour's claim that Greek *Typhôn* is 'certainly from W-S Saphon'[63] may not be so wide of the mark after all.

But we know how elusive are etymologies of ancient toponyms, and indeed of virtually any proper noun from an ancient tradition. We look for a scientific etymology, which we can accept, monogamously, to the exclusion of all others. In fact, of course, etymology is not an exact science, and least of all when mythological considerations have to be taken into account. We may therefore be sure that the people who encountered Jebel el Aqra in antiquity would give it a variety of explanations, depending on the context in which they were working. The above explanation, I submit, makes excellent sense in the context of the Baal-Yam conflict, and as we have seen, most aptly explains derivative forms such as *Typhoeus* and *Typhôn*.

But the mountain had an altogether more practical significance. It was the landmark for seafarers along many miles of coastline to north and south. And the gods of Ugarit, not least Yam and Baal, who may almost be said to represent the unruly sea and its divine tamer,[64] would have been periodically invoked for protection against storm and shoal as ships mercantile and naval butted through the coastal surge. Recent work at Ras Shamra, where considerable numbers of votive anchors have been discovered in the Baal temple, has led M. Yon and colleagues to conclude that the two main temples at Ugarit, those of Baal and – tentatively – Dagan, were built in a specific relationship to each other, providing an important landmark for craft entering the harbour at Minat el Beida.[65] We may even surmise that beacons would be lit on their towers at dusk, acting as primitive lighthouses.

In his discussion of the formation of the term *ṣpn*, O. Eissfeldt looked to the root *ṣāpâ*, 'to look out', and noted the similar structure of *ḥāzâ* and *ḥāzôn*.[66] R.J. Clifford explained the etymology of the verb similarly.[67] But neither made anything of the possibility that Ugaritic *ḥdy* (Hebrew *ḥāzâ*) may be the explanation of the Akkadian and Hurro-Hittite form *Ḫazzi*. M.C. Astour however did make this connection, citing *ḫaz*(*i*)*anu*, 'mayor, literally inspector' as an example of the etymon in Akkadian.[68] I think that this etymon is exactly the source of this form. Thus the mountain, replete with cosmological significance, was also a useful *point-de-répère* for seafarers, which as the sacred mountain of the gods, served as *their* lookout, from which they were imagined to be gazing down on coastal craft, guiding them in due course safely into the haven.

It is also possible that by further *jeux-de-mots* the sense of *ṣāpan* I, 'hide', perhaps with the sense of 'protect', was also perceived of the mountain, with the sense that Baal looked down protectively upon his people.

We may summarize the etymological discussion by saying that the idea of 'spread out' or 'stretched out' has given rise to the Greek forms, while that of 'look out' has given rise to the Hurro-Hittite and Akkadian form. It is, however the former which is primary in terms of the strict etymology of *ṣpn*, because the Greek and Egyptian forms, with the *-oeu* or *-u* in the second syllable, can be derived only from a passive form, and hence from **ṣāpuy*, which can hardly be secondary to an Ur-form *ṣpn*.

This may be conveniently set out in the form of a chart.

GREEK	UGARITIC-HEBREW	HURRIAN-HITTITE-AKKADIAN
	A **'(Mount) Spread Out'**	
	√*ṣpy*/*ṣph* I 'spread out'	
Τυφοευς	< *ṣapuy* (*qatul* pp. passive)	
	ṣapuy > *ṣapunu*, *ṣāpôn*	
Τυφαων	< *ṣapunu*	
Τυφων		
	B **'(Mount) Look Out'**	
	√*ṣpy*/*ṣph* 'look out'	
	ḥdy/*ḥzh* 'look out'	
	ḥadiy (act pt *qatil*) >	*Ḫazzi*

	C '(Mount) Throne' *ksu, ks* (Ugaritic *kasi'u, kasu* Hebrew *kissē', kēs*)
Κασιον (adj. Κασιος), LATIN *Cas(s)ius*	< (TRANSCRIPTION)
Θρονος	< (TRANSLATION)

It is a commonplace that the most important aspect of the history of religions is philology. Until we have solved problems of this kind, any further enquiry is premature.

We have argued that the same throne is intended at all stages of the Baal and Yam myths. Baal is also buried on *Sapunu* – KTU 1.6 i 14-31 – and Baal and Mot fight at *Ṣapunu* – KTU 1.6 vi 12-33, and Baal is enthroned anew at the same place in ll. 33-35. It thus transpires that the entire action of the Baal cycle takes place in the one location. All the language of journeys of enormous length is merely a theatrical fiction for changes of scene.

The same throne is used for the coronation of Athtar, though he descends from it to reign in the *arṣ* below (KTU 1.6 i 56-59, 63-64):

apnk	Then
ʿṯtr ʿrz yʿl bṣrrt ṣpn	Athtar the Brilliant went up into the recesses of Sapunu,
yṯb lkḥṯ aliyn bʿl	he sat down on the throne of Valiant Baal...
yrd ʿṯtr ʿrz	Athtar the Brilliant came down,
yrd lkḥṯ aliyn bʿl	he came down from the throne of Valiant Baal...

I have argued previously[69] that the royal rituals implicit in this episode are to be discerned in the myths of Ezekiel 28 and Isaiah 14. There they are parodied. In other biblical passages they are not. Thus the ascent of Moses on Mount Sinai is shaped according to a ritual form. There are two remarkable episodes on this theme which have perhaps not been adequately evaluated. 1 Chronicles 29.23 is particularly striking:

> *wayyēšeb šlōmô ʿal-kissēʾ yhwh lammelek taḥat-dawid*
> Then Solomon sat upon Yahweh's throne to reign (read *limlōk*) instead of David.

A similar, but periphrastic, phrase is used in 1 Chronicles 28.5, when David refers to Yahweh 'choosing my Solomon my son....

> *lāšebet ʿal-kissēʾ malkût yhwh*
> to sit on the throne of Yahweh's kingship.

In either case, the throne belongs primarily to the deity.[70] The king ascends to it during his enthronement and coronation rites. This is undoubtedly the allusion intended in Psalm 110. 1:

n^{e}*'um yhwh*	Oracle of Yahweh
la'dōnî šēb lîmînî	'O my lord: sit at my right hand,
ʿad-'āšît 'oy^{e}*bêkā*	until I set your enemies as a footstool
h^{a}*dōm l*^{e}*raglêkā*	for your feet.'

There is perhaps a direct link between the royal cultus of Judah and the common mythological tradition preserved in the Song of the Sea in Exodus 15.17. This reads as follows:

t^{e}*bī'ēmô w*^{e}*tiṭṭāʿēmô b*^{e}*har naḥ*^{a}*lāt*^{e}*kā*
mākôn lešibt^{e}*kā pāʿaltā yhwh*
miqdāš '^{a}*dōnāy kôn*^{e}*nû yādêkā*

You brought them and planted them on the mountain of your inheritance,
the foundation (which) you made into your place of enthronement,[71] Yahweh,
the sanctuary, My Lord, (which) your hands established.

Given the debt of the biblical royal rituals to the *Chaoskampf* and of the latter to the Ugaritic tradition, it is hard to escape the allusion in *lešibt*^{e}*kā* to the place where the triumph of the cosmos-deity over the chaos-deity is sealed in coronation rites. Exodus 15.17 is surely to be construed in the same conceptual world as the 'mountain of victory' met with in the Ugaritic tradition. We cited KTU 1.10 iii 11-14, 29-31 and 1.101.1-3 above. The following Ugaritic passage has an even closer connection:

KTU 1.3 iii 29-31 (= iv 19-20):

btk ǵry il ṣpn	in the midst of my divine mountain Sapunu,
bqdš bǵr nḥlty	in the sanctuary, in the rock of my inheritance,
bnʿm bgbʿ tliyt	in the delightful place, the hill of victory.

The expressions *ǵr nḥlt* and *har naḥ*^{a}*lâ* are clearly equivalent.[72]

I have endeavoured in this discussion to do more than solve a related group of Ugaritic problems. Our topic is of considerable concern to several related cultures, and thus plays a pivotal role in the kind of intercultural discussion which is necessary in the field of the history of religions. It is very easy to draw loose parallels between similar traditions; it is quite another to establish formal links between them. And while thematic links can be very intriguing, it is only in the establishment of real historical (and indeed, philological) connections that we can trace mutual influences and processes of development. This does not ease the difficulty of adequate assessment in each area in which a motif or ideological form is used. But it does provide firmer ground on which to stand as we undertake such enquiries.

While the present generation is well aware of the dangers of historicism, to which past biblical scholarship in particular has been prone,[73] we must also remain alert to its mirror image, the anti-historical prejudice which often masquerades as a concern for common currents, common themes, or universal principles. It is a fact of life that everything, scholarship, no less than all the evidence which we treat, is conditioned by its history. The only legitimate use of the comparative approach, which can open up new levels of understanding, is in the full recognition of its historical context.

The present exercise has been of use, I submit, in both senses in which the 'History of Religions' is applied: in terms of the general cultural history of the ancient Mediterranean region it emphasizes the considerable importance of Ugarit and its traditions as a source for many surrounding mythological and cosmological traditions. The one site of Ugarit has yielded more information about the whole of the history of religious developments in the Levant throughout the last two millennia BCE (even though it was destroyed in the first of these) than all other excavated sites and literary discoveries together, outside the Hebrew Bible. On this score alone the importance of the mythological texts is paramount to the development of our knowledge in the field. In selecting one single word from one of the mythological traditions from the city for analysis in this paper, I have been able to make connections with cultures that are habitually dealt with by unrelated branches of scholarship. Ugarit more than any site in the near east, perhaps, exemplifies a fact of ancient history which is all too easily overlooked in an era of increasing specialization. This is that trade, war and diplomacy carried ideas over vast distances, and the most powerful of these, couched typically in the language of poetry and myth in the ancient world, could not only pervade the region, but through the further ramifications of empire and ideology remain with us today.

In the narrower sense in which 'History of Religions' applies to biblical studies, I hope that this discussion has put one further nail in the coffin of academic exclusivism. If ideology is an ever-present danger to scholarship, then its greatest enemy is the openness and perhaps even the relativism which Ugaritic scholarship must by its international nature promote. The study of Ugarit and its literary and religious traditions should be on the agenda in every theological faculty. This offers no threat to serious theological discourse, which must surely be open to all the implications of historical research, but sets it in a wider symbolic context.

There is one final aspect of our topic which requires periodic airing among Ugaritic scholars. This is the question of the adequacy of our assessment of Ugaritic religion. In a general treatment of this problem,[74] P.D. Miller has rightly queried K. Kenyon's description of Canaanite religion as 'basically a fertility religion'. This has always been a rather vacuous cliché, since all religions are concerned with fertility as much as with other aspects of life, and as much with other aspects as with fertility. But it has been a particularly dangerous cliché given the agenda of the institutions where Ugaritic is commonly taught. If it becomes merely shorthand for the superficial nonsense of the religious beliefs and practices of 'Israel's' predecessors, which the prophets so rightly denounce, and which serious students of theology can find so repulsive in imagination that they find themselves defending and rationalizing the genocidal demands of Deuteronomy 7, then we are on dangerous ground.

Here we have a people, in a sophisticated, polyglot society, who contributed to the invention of the alphabet, communicated far and wide, and had a demonstrably profound influence on the traditional heroes of European intellectualism, the Greeks, as well as on biblical thought, the roots of our spiritual tradition. Their myths remain vital today in their derivative forms, which are found in the three western monotheisms, and in the whole European literary tradition. It is satisfying to be able to honour the debt.

Endnotes

* First published in M. Dietrich and O. Loretz (eds.), *Ugarit: ein ostmediterranes Kulturzentrum im Alten Orient* (ALASP, 7; Münster: Ugarit-Verlag, 1995): 213-37

1. For a useful treatment of the problem, including problems of translation, see Hahn 1956: 83-118.

2. Cited by Grave 1982: 161, n. 2, with sources. Also in the Esarhaddon treaty with Baal of Tyre (*ANET* 533-34): Eissfeldt 1932: 6; Aimé-Giron 1941: 455; de Savignac 1984: 273, read the DN as Baʿal Ṣapunu (from Scheil, *Le prisme d'Assaraddon* 37).

3. Cited by Clifford 1972: 62.

4. Eissfeldt 1932: 8; Albright 1950: 2; Lipiński 1971: 63, n. 252; Astour in Fisher 1972–81: II, 319, §viii 89e.

5. Albright 1950: 2; Lipiński 1971: 63, n. 252; Astour in Fisher 1972–81: II, 319.

6. Grave 1982: 161, n. 2, with sources.

7. Nougayrol 1956: I, 132; II, pl. xii. 3; Grave 1982: 16,1 n. 2 referred erroneously to Albright 1957: 35, for the restoration. The correct reference is to Albright 1968: 109, n. 38. The text was read by Nougayrol thus: [*ša* ^{al}(??) ?-]? *-ba-ni* ^{il}*bi-it-ra-i*, and he pointedly declined to attempt a restoration (n. 1).

8. Lipiński 1971: 61 and n. 243. Cf. discussion in Grave 1982: 161, n. 2. She evidently accepted the vocalization *ṣapanu* as primary, as is clear from her two discussions, here and in 1980: 221-29.

9. Lipiński 1971: 61-62.
10. Lipiński 1971: 64.
11. See Aimé-Giron 1941: 453.
12. Albright 1924–25: 4-6, n. 104. Cf. *idem*, 1950: 8, n. 4; R. Stadelmann 1967: 44-47; de Moor 1990, 125-26 and nn. 117, 118 for bibliography. On the Mami stela the name is written thus:  and ; on the Job-stone it is read thus: . There seems to be a tension here; in the former cases it is certainly to be read *-pu-* (so W. Helck orally at Münster, 11 February 1993) as this is the convention in monumental writing. De Moor also accepted that a reading *pu* is possible, 1990: 126, n. 118. In the second case, the biliteral  is conventionally read as *p3*, though it is wrong to conclude automatically that an *a* vowel is presupposed. On the contrary, the aleph is at best neutral. In so far as it is biliteral, that is, indicating two successive consonants rather than a singular nexus, it is still open to a reading **pu-3a*.
13. Grave: 1982: 161-82.
14. Moran 1987: 378.
15. Albright 1950: 2, n. 2. Taken up for instance by Clifford 1972: 57; H.P. Mullen 1980: 85; Grave 1982: 161, del Olmo 1981: 615; de Moor 1987: 1; M.S. Smith 2002: 79-80.
16. See BDB 869b.
17. The problem was recognized by Roberts 1975, and he usefully drew attention to K. Budde's observation, *Das Buch Hiob*, 145, that there is a progression through from the underworld to the heavens over the passage (vv. 5-11). However, I think he failed to recognize the particular nuance of *ṣāpôn*. The point was entirely missed by Day 1985: 38, n. 106, where on the strength of the 'stretching' image he considered *ṣāpôn* 'to allude to the firmament of heaven...'.
18. *yepê nôp*, lit. 'the beauty of Memphis'. None of the commentaries recognizes this sense of the present passage. So Delitzsch read 'rising beautifully' (1888: II, 118); C.A. Briggs and E.G. Briggs, 'beautiful in elevation' (1907: I, 400); ditto Weiser 1962: 379; Dahood, 'the most beautiful peak' (1965: 188-89). Dahood did note the possible connection with KTU 1.3 vi 9, but did not expand. Gibson 1978: 54, n. 9, following the view of J. Sanmartín, *UF* 10 (1978): 352, n. 26, acknowledged the possible reference there to Memphis, as did del Olmo 1981: 591. 'Noph' clearly refers to Memphis in the following biblical passages: in Hosea 9.6; Isaiah 19.13, with Zoan (Tanis); Jeremiah 2.16, with Tahpanhes (*t3 ḥwt p3 nḥsi*, Daphnai), 44.1 with Migdol and Tahpanhes (see also 43.7-9) and 46.19; Ezekiel 30.14-19, with Pathros, Zoan, No (*niwt*, Thebes), Sin (Pelusium or Sais: W. Eichrodt 1970: 414), Syene (Aswan), On (*iwnw*, Heliopolis) and Tahpanhes. The Hebrew form appears to be a contraction of the Egyptian form *mn-nfr*.

These several references indicate that the biblical writers were thoroughly conversant with Egyptian place-names, and it is entirely possible, in my view highly probable, that the psalmist intended such a reference here, thus assimilating Zion, by way of enhancing its prestige, with two of the great cosmological 'centres' of the known world. The fact that one lies to the south, and the other to the north, may even be understood to be a subliminal allusion to Zion's greater claim to be the true Omphalos. Their traditions are, so to speak, fulfilled here. Cf. Ezekiel 38.12, which alludes to the *ṭabbûr hā'āreṣ*, and Ezekiel 28.2, 12, 14, where the paradise language, at the pen of the same prophetic tradition, is undoubtedly based in Judahite cosmology. BDB's '*mop*' is erroneous.

While it is peripheral to our discussion, it is worth noting that Baal Saphon was known in Memphis, as well as at the well-known sanctuary of Baal-Saphon on the Egypto-Levantine frontier (for which see Exodus 14.2, 9, Numbers 33.7). See Albright 1950: 9. Aimé-Giron 1941 has also shown that the same deity was worshipped at Tahpanhes. It is conceivable this tradition of Egyptian Baal-Saphon (Baal was systematically identified with Seth following the Hyksos invasion) is in the poet's mind, the 'double Saphon' thus forming an *inclusio* round Zion.

The wording of this verse may be compared with Lamentations 2.15, though the reference to Memphis is not present there. Cf. the remark of Robinson 1974: 123.

19. Habel 1972. The motif occurs at Isaiah 40.22, 42.5, 44.24, 45.12, 51.13, Jeremiah 10.12, 51.15, Zechariah 12.1, and in Psalm 104.2-3 and Job 9.8. The last two passages are relevant to our present discussion.

20. See Kemp 1989: 69-71, 92-100.

21. Cf. KTU 1. 17 vv. 31-33:

tbᶜ kṯr lahlh	Kothar departed to his tent,
hyn tbᶜ lmšknth	Hayin departed to his dwelling.

22. Wyatt 1988a, 1989, 1990a.

23. On the general movement of peoples See Mayrhofer 1966, with extensive bibliography. See also Wyatt 1989. For the mythological aspects see Fontenrose 1980, Forsyth 1987, Wyatt 1988a.

24. Wyatt 1988a.

25. O'Flaherty 1981: 149-50.

26. Strabo, *Geography* 16.2, 7, cited Oldenburg 1969: 32-33. Astour 1967: 214, referred to various traditions which had the Orontes arise from the remains of the dying Typhon, who crawled into its source. He identified Typhon with Yam here.

27. Astour 1967: 216.

28. *Homeric Hymn to Apollo*, 305-57.

29. *Iliad* 2.781-83. See also Strabo 13.4.6 and 16.2.7.

30. Fontenrose 1980: 70-71. Hesiod, *Theogony* 304 has Echidna dwell ἐν 'Αριμοισιν. She mates with Typhaon (306-307), who must be a doublet of the Typhoeus borne by Ge (820–22). In the *Homeric Hymn to Apollo* (n. 30 above), it is Hera who bears Typhaon.

31. See Astour 1967: 313, n. 1.

32. Tablet 2 of the Ulikummi myth. See Hoffner 1990: 55. See also Oldenburg 1969: 78.

33. See Walcot 1966: 104-30, Astour 1967, *passim*, and Chapter 12 below.

34. Fontenrose 1980: 78-79 and n. 6, citing *The Shield* 32, Dion Chrysostom 1.67, Hesychius T1698, etc.

35. Dion Chrysostom 1.67, discussed by Fontenrose 1980: 79.

36. There is no time in the present discussion to pursue this point. See Dijkstra 1991 for the most recent discussion.

37. This much is evident from the huge number of versions dealt with by Forsyth and Fontenrose. In addition we may note the 40 odd examples in the Hebrew Bible — mostly found in Day 1985, the Khadir (also Khidr) traditions of Islam (on which see de Moor 1971: 200, n. 8; 219, n. 12; 238, n. 13, with references), and Campbell 1911.

38. Caquot *et al.* 1974: 304, n. g.
39. See Fisher 1972–81: II, 318-24 (§89).
40. Goetze 1941: 32-34.
41. Albright 1950.
42. Clifford 1972.
43. Fauth 1990: 107-108.
44. Goetze 1941: 33.
45. An example of a possessive not indicated by a suffixed *y*, such as this argument presupposes, is found in KTU 1.17 vi 36-37:

spsg ysk [l] riš	a libation-cup will be poured on my head,
ḥrṣ lẓr qdqdy	oil on top of my skull.

This is to be explained in terms of a simple vowel suffix, *-i*, in the first colon, followed by the longer form *-iya* in the second. (This bicolon is interpreted slightly differently in Wyatt 2002a: 274 and n. 115.)

46. See BDB 490b, *sub kēs*, with cross-reference to *kisse'*. BHS apparatus predictably proposes an emendation to *kissē'*, following the difficulties of some of the versions. The whole of Exodus 17.15-16 would repay re-examination. Has *nissî* in v. 15, for example, been 'corrected' or misread from an earlier *kissî* (*kēs* + i suffix)? It seems to me that the passage makes excellent sense along the following conjectural lines:

> *wayyiben mōšê mizbeaḥ wayyiqrā' šᵉmô yhwh-*kissî wayyō'mer kî-yād ʿal-kēs yâ milḥāmâ layhwh baʿᵃmālēk middōr dōr*
>
> Then Moses built an altar to Yahweh and named it 'Yahweh is my throne', and he said: 'As (my) hand is on the throne of Yah, there will be war by Yahweh against Amalek for ever!'

'Throne' seems a more appropriate name for a solid object like an altar than 'banner', 'standard' or the like, and is consonant with the words of the ensuing vow, however precisely understood. I take it that Moses rests his hand on the altar or holds it above the altar, while uttering the vow. *ʿal* may carry both nuances.

47. See for instance *kôs* ('owl') > Kos, the island, *kṯr*, the DN > *Kousôr*, *kinnôr* > *Kinyras*, examples proposed by Astour. The very names of the letters *kaph* and *kappa* state the phonetic equivalence in the first case. Greek *k* also transcribes *q*, in *Qadmu* > *Kadmos*.

48. See Bordreuil 1989b, 275-79. He proposed this reading for *KTU*'s reading *any* at KTU 1.16 i 8, ii 46 (corrected).

49. Bordreuil 1989b: 275-79.

50. So Pope 1955, and Lipiński 1971. El is shown to be at the very heart of the universe by the formulae at KTU 1.1 iii 23-24 and ||s, and 1.3 vv. 10-12 and ||s. (On the identity of El's, Yam's, Baal's and Athtar's throne, all located on Mt Saphon, see Wyatt 1996b: 34-48; *idem*, 1996c.)

51. So de Moor 1987: 115.

52. Pardee 1988: 132; de Moor 1969b, 180-81.

53. For this understanding of *'ēl 'ābîkā*, see Chapter 1. This can be taken with *šadday* of the following colon as an example of the poetic division of a binominal, or alternatively the *'et* of the following colon may be taken to be an altered *'el*. The former is to be preferred, as involving no unnecessary textual emendation.

54. This blessing is to be contrasted with the curse occurring in 2 Samuel 1.21, restored on the basis of the similar form in KTU 1.19 i 44-45. See Ginsberg 1938: 209-13. The same three sources of life-giving water are involved. The 'gifts of heaven' can only be rain. See also Wyatt 2001a:291-92 (§11 [28, 29]).

55. See de Moor 1971: 76-77, van Zijl 1972: 334-36, Astour in Fisher 1972–81: II, 322, Dietrich and Loretz 1990.

56. Cf. Driver 1956: 150, n. 18.

57. De Langhe 1945: II, 235-36.

58. While *bārā'* is the Bible's specific word for 'create' in the cosmogonic sense, its basic meaning appears to be 'to divide', so that it may here have the more fundamental sense of Yahweh actually carving up Yam in his differentiating procedure. See Danthine 1961: 441-51. De Langhe takes the text underlying LXX, viz, *yam* (*sic*) to mean 'west': 1945: II, 236.

59. See BDB 860a.

60. The only morphological problem here is the *y* of the first syllable (Greek *upsilon*). This is perhaps to be explained as a *šᵉwa*, such as appears in the Aramaic form *ṣᵉpôn*, in the toponym Baal Zephon, which has subsequently been attracted into *upsilon*, which has the approximate phonetic value of the short [*i*].

61. MT reads *šāmayim*: should we envisage an original *māyim* to parallel *yām*? If this were the case, we would have a specific allusion to the stretching of the sea-god: the *nāṭâ* of the Hebrew would be equivalent of the conceptually similar **spy*. The amendment is not, however, necessary: in the ancient conception of the cosmos, the heavens were covered in waters (cf. following note), and thus were themselves of an aqueous nature. I know of no deliberate wordplay, but the fertile Semitic mind was hardly unaware that the heavens were 'of the waters' – *še* + *mayim*. (Cf. Chapter 12.)

62. The *ᶜᵃliyôt* is or are structure(s) containing the rain, as part of the firmament: see v. 13. The *šāmayim* are, of course, a container of waters ('the waters above the firmament'), and the wordplay *šāmayim* : *māyim* emphasizes the link.

63. See Astour 1967: 216.

64. I do not intend this in any way to be taken as a naturalistic, and therefore reductionist, assessment of either god. The gods do not simply personify natural realities.

65. See Yon 1990: 326-27; 1992: 116; Frost 1991: 356.

66. Eissfeldt 1932: 16-18.

67. Clifford 1972: 57.

68. Astour in Fisher 1972–81: II, 319-22. Grave rejects his arguments, 1980: 224-26.

69. Wyatt 1986a.

70. Cf. the following lines from Ezekiel the Tragedian: 'On Sinai's peak I saw what seemed a throne so great in size it touched the clouds of heaven. Upon it sat a man of noble mien, becrowned, and with a sceptre in one hand while with the other he did beckon me. I made approach and stood before the throne. He handed o'er the sceptre and he bade me mount the throne, and gave to me the crown; then he himself withdrew from off the throne...' (*Exagoge* 68-76; ET R.G. Robertson in Charlesworth 1985: II, 811-12).

71. This interesting expression recurs at 1 Kings 8.13, 39, 43, 49 = 2 Chronicles 6.2, 30, 33, 39. The first reference in each book is a poetic fragment. In the other cases the divine dwelling is located in heaven. This is Solomon's dedication prayer, which clearly

establishes the cultic principle 'as above, so below'. The loftiness of the dwelling is clear from Psalm 33.13-14: it is again in heaven, and Yahweh surveys the world from it.

72. While Exodus 15 mentions no 'hill of victory', cf. the *ṣur yᵉšuᶜātô* of Deuteronomy 32.15, Psalm 89.27 (EV 26) etc.

The expression *ǵr ll* (*hapax* at KTU 1.2 i 20-21, restored by some at l. 14) has raised problems. It is in parallel with *pḫr mᶜd*, which suggests that Ṣapunu is meant. It is read *ǵr il* by Clifford 1972: 42, del Olmo 1981: 169. The place where the gods meet in council is scarcely to be separated cosmologically from Ṣapunu. The biblical tradition certainly equates the two at Isaiah 14.13. Cf. the *har ᵉlōhîm* of Ezekiel 28.16. The proposal of W. van Soldt (orally, Münster 11 February 1992) that *ll* is an allusion to the Hittite sacred mountain, Lalu, is interesting. I prefer to correct the text (to *ǵr il*), but we may conjecture that a scribal error arose because of an association with the Hittite tradition.

73. The most hard-hitting analysis of the problem remains Thompson 1974.

74. Miller 1981.

Chapter 10

THE VOCABULARY AND NEUROLOGY OF ORIENTATION: THE UGARITIC AND HEBREW EVIDENCE*

I

So engrossed do we become in arcane and highly metaphysical questions in our analysis of ancient traditions that we may easily remain blind to the obvious, and fail to see features which may be of some significance, are staring us in the face, and yet remain unseen by their very familiarity. The present discussion may appear to treat matters of no importance at all, and yet they not only determine all that we may say in consequence, but also root the culture we are examining into its very foundations in the structure of the human mind and body.

I shall discuss here four Ugaritic words and their semantic fields: between them they encompass the entire experience of time and space as evidenced in the surviving texts in the Ugaritic language, and thus serve to locate all cultural experience and activity within an orderly framework, such as we understand in speaking of a culture's 'cosmology'. Their cognates also occur in Hebrew, at the same time allowing a window into interesting aspects of Hebrew cosmology and religious psychology, and providing a useful control upon our understanding of the Ugaritic evidence.

The broad principles of our concern have been examined by E. Lyle (1990), who suggested a useful term to identify our topic: 'canonical orientation'. The term is the more useful in recognizing that different orientations may obtain for different practical purposes; we are dealing here, if you will, with what may also be called 'ritual orientation', as observed in cultic contexts, which are concerned with the location of the worshipper (priestly officiant) with reference to cardinal points, celestial loci, the home of the gods, and so forth. Other terminologies will also be noted below. Apart from general studies (e.g. C.H. Brown 1983) there has been some brief discussion of some aspects of these matters in the biblical context (see Boman 1960, Stadelmann 1970, Malamat 1989, O'Connor 1991, Rosén 1991, Drinkard 1992), while J. Chelhod (1964) has explored some of the Arabic dimensions of the issue; but I am unaware of its extension into the field of Ugaritic studies, nor do I think that everything useful on the subject has been said in these other areas.

II

i. *Behind* (aẖr)

Ugaritic *aẖr* and its derivative forms (*uẖry, uẖryt*) probably have a basically spatial sense, 'behind', which is used metaphorically in a temporal sense, with reference to the future. We can see this most graphically by reference to its Greek cognate. It was shown long ago by H. Lewy (1895: 229, noted by Astour 1967: 314-15) that the Greek name Acheron ('Αχερων), given to the river of the underworld, has a West Semitic etymology. The fact of the choice of direction, referring to what lies *behind* (that is, in spatial terms) the person experiencing a *temporal* process, tells us important things about the sense of position in space and time of the culture concerned, a point on which I shall remark further below. This is also the sense of *'aḥar* in Hebrew. Usage in Ugaritic is as follows:

aẖr	Then
tmǵyn.mlak.ym	the messengers of Yam arrived,
tˁdt.tpṭ.nhr	the embassy of Lord River.

KTU 1.2 i 30

The force here is adverbial, relating the present action to that immediately preceding. It could also be translated 'when', or 'afterwards'. I have treated it here as an anacrusis. The same usage occurs in KTU 1.4 iii 23-24:

aẖr	Then
mǵy.aliyn.bˁl	Valiant Baal arrived,
mǵyt.btlt.ˁnt	Virgin Anat arrived.

The same grammatical, though not necessarily prosodic, purpose is served in the monocolon of KTU 1.4 v 44:

aẖr.mǵy.kṯr.wẖss	Then Kothar-and-Hasis arrived.

A more specific temporal allusion may be intended in the expression *aẖr.špšm*, occurring in KTU 1.14 iv 32-33, and 46. This is variously understood. Gibson (1978: 87-88) translates it by 'afterwards with the sun (on the third/fifth day)' (correcting *brbˁ* to *bẖmš* in l. 46); del Olmo (1981: 298-99) has 'with the coming out of the sun (on the third/fourth day)', while de Moor (1987: 199-200) has 'after sunset (on the third/fourth)'. The precise sense is obscure, and this is reflected in the disparity of these approaches. But it seems to be prepositional, though the *m* at the end of *špšm* turns the whole phrase into an adverbial one.

The form *uḫry* occurs in a formulaic phrase in the account of Danel's cursing of the land, in KTU 1.19 iii 49, 56, iv 7:

ʿdb.uḫry.mṭ.ydh

As with the previous instance, the meaning is not entirely clear. Gibson (1978: 119-120) has 'let every last one make ready a staff for his hand', as part of Danel's curse. Del Olmo (1981: 396-97) takes it to mean 'whose staff should be set down finally', also as part of the curse. De Moor (1987: 259-60) has 'he put down the tip of his walking-stick' (cf. Dijkstra and de Moor 1975: 209), taking it to be a symbolic gesture reinforcing the curse, and citing the use of *'aḥᵃrê* in 2 Samuel 2.23. Margalit (1989: 163-64, cf. 433) took it to mean 'stooping, he picked up his walking-stick'. Aitken (1990: 73-75) read 'finally he picked up his walking stick', following Ullendorf (1962: 343-44) who took it to mean 'thereupon'. The word is thus variously translated by these scholars as adjective, adverb, noun, conjunction and verb (participial)!

uḫryt appears once, in KTU 1.17 vi 35:

mm uḫryt mh.yqḥ

The initial *mm* is corrected by *CTA*, KTU to *mt*. Gibson (1978: 109) has 'As (his) ultimate fate what does a man get?', citing Numbers 23.10 and Qohelet 6.12 in support. Del Olmo (1981: 378) is similar: 'what can a man obtain as ultimate destiny?' De Moor (1987: 239) understood it to mean 'Death in the future, what can take (it) away?' Margalit[1] (1989: 151, 433) took an entirely different approach, understanding the word to mean 'posterior'. This is unconvincing in the context, and seems a forced interpretation. The other views cited, however, already show the intractability of the text. Whichever approach we accept, however – my preference being for that of Gibson and del Olmo – it appears that *uḫryt* is a substantive form from *aḫr*. Its meaning is fixed by the parallel term *aṯryt*, based on the preposition *aṯr*, 'after'. This too can evidently have both spatial (primary) and temporal (secondary) aspects.

ii. *Before* (qdm)

The radical *qdm* may be defined as the spatial and temporal antonym of *aḫr*. In the former aspect, it may have a strictly prepositional force:

št.alp.qdmh	He set an ox *before* her,
mria.wtk.pnh	a fat ram as well in front of her.
	KTU 1.3 iv 41-42

The same formula occurs at KTU 1.4 v 45-46.

The verb *qdm*, meaning 'to approach', comes in the *Keret* story:

bt.krt.tbun	To the house of Keret they came,
lm.mṯb.atw	to the dwelling they walked,
wlḫm{m}r.rqdm	to the winevat *they drew near.*

(KTU 1.15 iv 21-23 restored; the tricolon may be restored at 1.15 vv. 5-7.)

In KTU 1.100.62 we have the following sentence:

ykr.ʿr.dqdm.

Pardee (1988: 203) understood this to mean 'he goes to the *eastern* city', de Moor (1987: 153): 'he left the city *of the east*'. This is the sense commonly read in the Hebrew term *qedem* occurring in the story of the Garden of Eden in Genesis 2.8. In this passage however it means rather '*in the beginning*' (Wyatt 1981: 13: cf. also Landy 1983: 330, n. 8), having something of the primaeval nuance of the following passage. In KTU 1.12.8 there is insufficient context to permit translation of the word. In KTU 1.4 vii 31-34, also fragmentary, but recognizably a tetracolon, I propose the following tentative reading:

qlh.q[dš.]trr.arṣ	At his h[oly] voice the earth qu[ake]d,
bgʿrth[2] *ǵrm.tḫšn*	[at his roar] the mountains shook,
rtq [ǵrm[3]*] qdmym*[4]	the ancient mountains were afraid,
bmt.ar[ṣ.] tṭṭn	the hills of the earth tottered.

The text at KTU 1.4 vii 40 is to be read rather as **qrdm*, I have suggested (Wyatt 1990e), and therefore has no bearing on the present discussion. In a private communication, Wilfred Watson has suggested to me that the reading *qdm* may be retained (citing Durand 1984: 279; Mayer 1989: 268, *qa-du-mi* 'axe'), but still having the sense 'axe' I have proposed. It thus remains irrelevant here.

The passages cited illustrate much the same range as the Hebrew equivalent. The basic sense appears to mean 'before the face', which then leads on to the idea of approaching something (which a subject is facing). This can give the sense of 'eastwards' when a person is facing east.

The metaphorical and temporal sense, 'before', that is 'past', and often with a sense of ancientness, of primordiality, as in the case of Genesis 2.8 noted above, presupposes an eastward orientation, with the west behind. When the temporal senses of the terms *qdm* and *aḫr* are used, it is with a nuance of facing back – or more accurately facing *forwards* – into the past, and of having the future behind the back. This is perhaps most powerfully illustrated in a relief on the wall of the Seti I temple at Abydos in Egypt

(Kemp 1989: 22 and fig. 4). Seti stands with his son (the future Rameses II) contemplating rows of cartouches of the kings of previous dynasties. The past is *before* them. No better illustration could be cited to rebut the common assertion that the ancients (apart, of course, from 'biblical man'!) had no sense of history.[5]

We may cite two examples from the Ugaritic texts which illustrate the same principle, lacking only the overtly directional element: these are the list of divinized dead kings in KTU 1.113, and the invocation of dead kings in KTU 1.161. Only a type of memory which is essentially 'historical' – that is, as capable as ourselves of appreciating 'history', though they may have lacked our conceptualizing, 'logico-scientific', tendencies – could address these figures of the past to the present mind in a linguistic form. The same may be said of all the other king-lists, invocatory rituals, and annalistic writings from the ancient world.[6]

The significance of orientation has some interesting implications in other areas of cognition. Firstly, it raises serious questions about views of time. The experience of time expressed by means of an orientation into the past, towards memory and tradition as in the range of vision, and as vital for the present well-being of society, illustrates both a growing awareness of temporality, and also of its ancient roots in seeing (perhaps in dreams and visions). The idea that you can contemplate your past either in real vision, or in your mind's eye, and determine your position in the world primarily with reference to such a concern, can readily be seen to have enormous intellectual and social implications. Tradition, conservatism, well-tried procedures, established patterns, all show how a society feels its way into the future by way of its security in the past. Religion, with not only its rituals and specifically sacred traditions, but also its critical role in the management of the economy of ancient societies, since it effectively determined agricultural practices through its cultic demands, and temples served as the banks of the ancient world, is simply the epitome of such processes, all the more important in pre-secular antiquity precisely because it sanctioned and legitimized social procedures, affirming their worth.[7] Secondly, there are further spatial implications which are worth noting. We shall examine these as separate categories.

iii. *Right* (ymn)

The term *ymn*, with the primary sense of '*right* (hand)', and the extended meaning of 'south', presupposes the orientation to the east we have mentioned. This must be the way in which the word developed, from the physical experience of the right hand to the geographical and conceptual application. Let us consider some examples of the usage of the word, for it is particularly *nuancé,* and carries some overtones which are of considerable significance for religious thought.

Perhaps the most conventional use in poetry is in the seemingly neutral word-pair *yd* || *ymn,* meaning '(left) hand, right hand'. On the sense 'left hand' for *yd,* see Dahood (in Fisher 1972-81: Introduction 7d; II, 218d). (While I have considered that the verbal root *ydd,* variant *dwd,* may lie behind the term *yd* meaning 'penis' [1994a: 416], we may wonder whether an alternative etymology does not in fact lie in the term presently under discussion, with the emphasis on its sinistral quality. It would thus be the 'toilet-hand' associations which determine the secondary anatomical designation. This would still be a better explanation than the usual one of euphemism.) At times the usage we have isolated, the word-pair *yd* || *ymn,* appears to be merely conventional, though it may involve a sense of progression. Typical examples are such as the following:

aḫdt.plkh.[bydh]	She (i.e. Athirat) took her distaff [in her hand],
plk.tʿlt.bymnh	the whorl[8] in her right hand.
	KTU 1.4 ii 3-4

There seems to be no particular progression here. Cf. also KTU 1.15 ii 16-18.

A development *does* appear to take place, however, in KTU 1.4 vii 40-41:

ʿn.bʿl	Baal spoke (or: looked):
q<r>dm[9] *ysh.ktǵd̲*	the axe his (left) hand indeed brandished,
arz.bymnh	the cedar(-spear) in his right hand.

In this case there appears to be a differentiation of two weapons. Cf. also KTU 1.14 ii 13-15, where the final *kl[atn]m,* 'both of them', embraces the two hands mentioned.

The following passage deals with a single weapon, a bow and its arrows, but with the parts distributed between the cola:

qšrh.aḫd.bydh	He took his bow in his (left) hand,
Wqṣ ʿth.bm.ymnh	and his arrows within his right hand.
	KTU 1.10 ii 6-7

Whether or not *yd* is here the left hand is moot. In Assyrian iconography of the first millennium (Wilkinson 1991: 86 pl. 2) kings commonly hold bows and arrows in the same hand. It is however conventionally the left hand, as it is for a bow held by itself, suggesting that the specific mention of the right hand in the present passage is intended for purposes of differentiation. That is, *yd* is very probably to be understood as the *left* hand. This seems to be the convention on the ivory panel from Ugarit, showing the king holding a bow in his left hand, and a harpé in his right (Caquot and Sznycer 1980, the situation here is complicated by the presence of a second figure).

KTU 1.2 i 39-40 contains an interesting chiasmus:

[yuḫd].byd.mšḥt	In his (left) hand he seized a knife,
bm.ymn.mḫṣ	within his right hand a weapon,
ǵlmm.yš[ ]	the divine assistants of Yam [to slay?].
[ymnh ʿ]nt.tuḫd	His right hand Anat seized;
šmalh.tuḫd. ʿṯtrt	his left hand Athtart seized.

In the first bicolon, we are not certain of the number of weapons involved (cf. the two double-bladed axes later used by Baal, in KTU 1.2 iv 11-26, and the pair of weapons in 4 vii 40-41 above), and cannot be sure that *yd* really has the force of 'left hand'; if this sense is potential rather than realized, we may then discern an unfolding of the implication in the final bicolon, where the point becomes explicit in *šmal*. At any rate, the passage moves forwards to the full force of a right hand wielding a weapon, and after identifying the intended victims in the central monocolon, resolves the diplomatic crisis by having the weapon-hand seized first, thus neutralizing Baal's threat. All these examples are fairly neutral in terms of the symbolism that concerns us here, though there may often be a dead metaphor element, with the meaning somewhat eroded by conventional usage.

An altogether more pregnant sense is surely to be discerned, however, in KTU 1.4 v 46-48, describing the arrival of Kothar):

tʿdb.ksu	A chair was prepared
wyṯ ṯb lymn aliyn.bʿl	and he sat at the right hand of Valiant Baal,
ʿd.lḥm.št[y ilm]	while the gods ate and drank.[10]

This passage illustrates graphically the social significance attached to the right hand. To sit at someone's right hand is to take the place of honour, in this case to be the special guest, in whose honour the feast is given. In so far as cultic practice may be echoed in mythological language, we may discern a hierarchical concern in the arrangement of divine images in a shrine, perhaps in descending order of precedence from right to left, from the perspective of the images facing the worshippers. The passage cited may be compared with the biblical expression, found with the fullest theological significance in Psalm 110.1:

n^{e}'um yhwh	Oracle of Yahweh:
la'^{a}dōnî šēb lîmînî'	O my lord:[11] sit at my right hand,
ʿad-'āšît 'oy^{e}bêkā	until I make your enemies
ḥ^{a}dōm l^{e}raglêkā	a footstool for your feet.'

iv. *Left*

The Ugaritic term is *šmal*, the equivalent of Hebrew *s*ᵉ*mō'l* (var. *s*ᵉ*mô'l*). We have met it above in KTU 1.2 i 40. Its only other literary occurrence in Ugaritic is in KTU 1.23.63-64:

ndd.gzr.l<g>zr	And wandering abroad, piece by piece
yʿdb.uymn.ušmal.bphm	they put (things) from both right and left into their mouths
wl.tšbʿn	and are not satisfied.

This passage is interesting, in that in view of the context, which describes the general depredations of the two gods Shahar and Shalem, as all-devouring, the two words *ymn* and *šmal* may here denote not just the space around them, to right and left, but more specifically the cardinal points, respectively south and north. (Cf. the Aramaean kingdom of Sama'l, and the Arabic *šamāl* meaning 'north wind'. See also Chelhod 1973.) If this is the case, it would be the only instance of this usage so far occurring in Ugaritic. In any case, the terms serve as a merismus, meaning 'all around them'.

In KTU 1.109.26-27, a ritual text listing sacrifices on the fourteenth day of the month, the following passage occurs:

lgṯrm.ǵṣb.šmal d.alpm.walp.w.š
For the *gṯrm*, the left protuberance of two bulls, and a bull and a sheep...

This translation reflects the analysis of P. Xella (1981: 51). The text remains thoroughly obscure, but appears to involve some part of the animal which is duplicated (horns? shoulders? some part of a leg? testicles?), where the left one is offered. This cannot be without a serious symbolic purpose, as we should expect, where a differentiation is made, that the right hand one would be favourable, and the left hand one unfavourable. I take it that a kind of homoeopathic symbolism operates here, where a dangerous contingency is avoided by meeting it with a symbol of equivalent danger.

Another difficult passage comes in KTU 1.92.8-9:

ṯṯb.ʿṯtrt.bǵl [ ]	Athtart sat in[12] the marsh(?) [ ]
qrẓ.tšt.lšmal [ ]	she placed the *qrẓ* on the left of[13] [ ]...

It is impossible to reconstruct with any confidence a context for this passage. Whatever she is about, it seems that the point of Athtart's placing something unidentified on the left hand side of or to the north of something or someone is of significance. It may be provisionally inferred that something of the kind noted above is to be understood.

Gordon (1965: §19.1107) associated the Semitic *ymn*, 'right hand', with the Egyptian *imn*, having the same sense, and giving the derivative *imnt*(*t*), 'west', which he explained by an eastward orientation for Semitic peoples, but an upstream orientation for the Egyptians. Actually the question of Egyptian orientation appears to be extremely complex, with the respective positions of Horus and Seth to north and south suggesting a westward orientation for some purposes, while the dead were buried facing, or head to, the east. The Egyptian forms cited above may equally well be derived from *imn*, 'unseen'. Oden's analysis[14] of the spatial movement in *The Contendings of Horus and Seth*, from the east to the west bank of the Nile by way of an island in the midst, reflects the temporal progression of the story, with the east implicitly in the past. In this case, the positions of Horus and Seth are the reverse of what we might expect, that is, Horus' natural position on the right ought to be to the south. Perhaps the deliberate reversal implicit here is itself symbolic of the reversal of fortunes which the myth explores, and is comparable to the inversion of the cardinal points in the game of Mah-Jong. As noted, there appears to be only one Ugaritic example of *ymn*, meaning 'south' (tentatively, KTU 1.23.64), but even if this interpretation be rejected in this instance, that is not to say that Ugaritic cultural thought was unfamiliar with the common Semitic sense of orientation as outlined.

III

Given the particularly close cultural and linguistic links between Ugaritic and early biblical literature (the latter amply attested by the evidence presented in Fisher 1972–81) we may turn briefly to Hebrew usage by way of a control on the Ugaritic material. If we find that the same broad principles obtain, then it will be clear that we are dealing not with a peculiarity of one language, which might, for the sake of argument, be dismissed as based on too restricted a textual repertoire, but rather with a wider issue. One biblical passage, cited by Malamat (1989: 67) lists all our key terms, and will therefore serve as a useful point of entry: namely Job 23.8-9:

hēn qedem 'eh^{e}*lōk we'ênennû*	Look, I go forward, but he is not there;
w^{e}*'āḥôr w*^{e}*lō'-'ābîn lô*	and backward, but I do not discern him.
s^{e}*mō'l ba*^{ca}*sōtô w*^{e}*lō'-'āḥaz*	to the left I go but I do not grasp (him);
yaʿṭōp yāmîn w^{e}*lō' 'er'ê*	I turn to the right but I do not see.[15]

This passage really contains the whole nub of our discussion in a single tetracolon. It entirely confirms our findings from the Ugaritic evidence. We could give further examples, but they would only be a repetition of data.

One interesting feature of Hebrew is its varied terminology for directions. This has been treated by M. O'Connor (1991), and some broader issues have been covered by Rosén (also 1991). O'Connor listed a number of passages in which an entirely different vocabulary occurs. It transpires upon examination that there are not one or two, but three (or possibly even more) different systems employed, depending on the perspective from which the writer is operating. O'Connor (1991: 1145) distinguished the different perspectives as 'homuncular', 'cosmological' and 'topographic'. For the same categories, Rosén (1991: 1339) used the terms 'religious', 'solar' and 'topographical'. We can usefully draw up a table of the terms in use, and in doing so I have added the Ugaritic vocabulary. The first category in each case corresponds to the 'canonical' or 'ritual' labels applied above.

TABLE OF VOCABULARY[15a]

	Homuncular/Religious	*Cosmological/Solar*	*Topographic*
		I HEBREW	
East	*qedem*	*mizraḥ*	—
	qadmōnî	*mōṣā'*	
West	*'aḥar*	*ma*^{ca}*rāb*	*yām*
	'aḥ^{a}*rôn*	*mābō'*	
North	*s*^{e}*m'ôl*[16]	—	*ṣāpôn*
South	*yāmîn*	—	*negeb*
	tēmān		*dārôm*[17]
		II UGARITIC[18]	
East	*qdm*	*ṣat*[19]	—
West	*aḫr*[20]	*ʿrb*[21]	—
		(*ṣba*[22])	
North	*šmal*	—	(cf. *ṣpn*)
South	*ymn*	—	—

The Hebrew *ṣāpôn* frequently means simply 'north', with no apparent consciousness of a mythological dimension, though the term is derived from *ṣapunu*, which *does* have such a nuance. We should, of course, be cautious about reading into the Hebrew usage a principle of systematic demythologization. This may be simply an instance of a dying metaphor, and indeed I have examined some biblical passages in which the mythological dimension is emphatically present, reflecting the etymology of the term, which is itself rooted in mythology. No such strict sense, as 'north', appears to occur so far in Ugaritic, yet of course, the sacred mountain *did* lie to the north, and therefore from an orientational perspective on the left. There is no evidence that the Ugaritic *ṣpn* is used in the purely geographical sense. It is possible that some instances are to be interpreted in this manner, and that we have simply over-interpreted it on the basis of the mythological usage, but the onus of proof lies on whoever would insist on a more neutral sense. While we simply do not have the evidence from Ugarit, then, which allows us to sense all the subtleties of the term *ṣpn*, the pregnancy of the Hebrew usage in Jeremiah 1.13-15, 4.6, 6.1, and so on is evident. The whole point of the usage here is its reliance on a tradition in which *ṣāpôn* carries powerful overtones of the sinister, which is exactly *le mot juste* for the resonance that concerns us here. An enemy from the north is specifically a divine visitation.

It is this element, also evident in other biblical poetic passages, of the unspoken aura of danger associated with divine transcendence and the numinous abode of the gods, which must surely have been felt in the Ugaritic word, particularly when religious or mythological themes were to the fore. But of course the skeleton of the word (see Chapter 9) preserves little of the emotional flesh. As for the general use of the term in Hebrew, for 'north', we can see from the other terms in the 'topographical' category that it is chosen from a specific geographical feature, a mountain, rather than from abstract notion of the north, thus confirming the etymological pathway the Hebrew word has traced.

The comparison of the tables is instructive. Since only the 'religious' set of terms is complete in Ugaritic, and common to both languages, it is arguable that it is an older vocabulary, more personal and affective by nature, which has given way to the more neutral, objective vocabulary of the other sets. While there is insufficient space to pursue the matter here, we may predict that a study of the wider Semitic vocabulary would probably bear this out. The oldest category, then, is in relation to aspects of the body; the second category extends this with regard to the movements of the sun and other celestial bodies (which is certainly still as much a religious as a secular category in the ancient world), while the third belongs to an enlarging horizon of geographical features at some remove from one another (as clearly with a northern mountain and a southern desert zone). The incomplete nature of the second and third lists, though no firm conclusions can be drawn in view of their possible incompleteness due simply to the small pool of evidence, nevertheless suggests that they have developed far more restricted purposes (such as the east–west axis of the movement of celestial bodies in the case of the second category) to complement an older and more basic system of classification. The fundamental importance of that older system, based above all on self-awareness, for purposes of understanding the psychological roots of orientation will become clear in our further discussion.

IV

Since we have more or less exhausted the Ugaritic source-material on the subject, which is also evidently the source for Hebrew usage, it is clear that we cannot go much further on surviving evidence in analysing the religious and social attitudes involved in the matter of orientation. But here we should perhaps dwell briefly on the significance of left and right, since there are universal elements at work here which are true irrespective of the absence of local evidence. It is precisely the universality of experience which emerges from even the simplest further analysis which indicates that we are dealing with a pre-linguistic, and thus extremely archaic, factor.

One of the reasons why left and right have the emotional and moral nuances they bear in all cultures derives from the facts of human anatomy and neurology. It might be expected that we should begin a discussion on the matter with neurological issues, but it is possibly another anatomical fact, the location of the primate and human heart in the left side of the thorax, that is the primary determinant in the issues that follow. It has been observed that primate suckling mothers, while of course breast-feeding from both sides, conventionally hold their infants to the left breast for purposes of comforting, where the mother's heartbeat can be most readily sensed by the offspring, and a sense of security obtained. This is also the case with human mothers and their children, with 'an average of about 80 per cent left-side cradling established from large samples of human populations' (Manning and Chamberlain 1990: 1226, citing a number of authorities: cf. also Hopkins *et al.* 1993 for more recent work). Its conventional treatment in art merely reinforces and reflects the social fact. This was explained by Manning and Chamberlain on the ground that the sensory data received by the mother are processed in the right hemisphere of her brain, where emotional experience tends to be located. But it may be selective pressures making the holding of infant offspring to the heart (that is, on the left-hand side) a beneficial strategy which has contributed to the lateral-specific developments of neurology. While for the mother the emotional bond of the child represented in physical terms is experienced on the left, from the infant perspective security is located primarily on the right side (the right being against the mother), which may give rise to the later intellectual experience of the right side as representing control and stability, the counter to the maternal experience. These positions are periodically reversed during suckling, but perhaps the very change from a norm serves to reinforce the norm. Basic lateral locations of emotions seem therefore to be expected in the development of human psychology.

The degree to which elements in this area have a structural influence on neurological patterns is perhaps uncertain, although there do seem to be at least superficial correspondences between the two. In view of the 'standard' position, we should expect the more deeply rooted emotions to reflect the physical fact. Thus for the infant, security is experienced on the right side, while the left side, potentially open to danger from without, is furthest from the mother, though protected by her embracing arm. While the infant experiences emotional concerns on both sides, the left side is associated more directly with the possibilities of instability and trauma. The mother, alert to the surrounding world, is nevertheless involved very specifically on her left side with the infant she suckles.

The brain and its functions have long been recognized as being bilateral. The left hemisphere of the brain relates most closely to the right side of the body, and the right hemisphere to the left. The former is the location of language (more specifically, speech), and in particular its rationalizing and ordering capacity, the latter of rhythmic experience, music and affective sentiment (Lex 1979: 125). This is a simplified view, however, since in cases of left-handedness or ambidextralism, as well as in cases of lesions and atrophy of one hemisphere, the other is capable of compensating for its loss by undertaking the missing function, particularly when damage occurs in early life. The division of labour is also apparently developed after birth (Gardner 1975: 386).

In spite of this qualification, there would be enormous pressure, at first biological selectivity, and later cultural conformity, for behavioral conventions of the kind which would reinforce laterality, and more importantly, would reinforce the symbolic potential associated with each dimension, as in the use of hands for toilet and eating functions, in ritual contexts and in general social interaction. All this hardly needs spelling out, and is the substance of several recent discussions of consciousness, its neurological base and its cultural implications (Jaynes 1976; Changeux 1985; Ornstein 1986; Donald 1991). It is important to remember that culture is not itself, in its strictly human sense, the foundation of the neural structures. These developed with the concomitant evolution of the primate line, so that lateralization was essentially a survival and adaptation strategy of the particular branch that developed into *Homo Sapiens Sapiens,* arising out of the progressive specialization of certain regions of the cerebral cortex, with differentiation between the left and right hemispheres (see Dimond and Beaumont 1974; Pugh 1978: 126-49). The famous Penfield and Rasmussen cartoons of the homunculus and his cortical links (1950: 24, 44, 57, figs. 9, 17 and 22) demonstrate graphically the enormous importance of cortical evolution in the development of specialist areas, with a marked dedication of areas in both hemispheres of the human brain to manual dexterity and facial mobility, and in the left hemisphere to speech functions. Donald (1991: 264) pointed out that phonology – the foundation of speech – is lateralized on the left in spite of its dependency on the facial-muscle control required from both hemispheres. Thus, in this instance, a bilateral specialization has subsequently become concentrated in one hemisphere.

Dextrousness in the more restricted sense, that of right-hand dominance in terms of the use of the hands, also has ancient roots. Schick and Toth (1993: 140-43) have studied early hominid toolmaking at Olduwan sites in East Africa, and by their own experimentation have shown that right-handed use of hammer stones was the norm at least one and a half million years ago. Denison (1995) reported examples of chimpanzees showing the same trait, while Westergaard (1995) has seen the trait among New World capuchin monkeys, which suggests either convergent evolution among primates in this respect, or that its roots go back the forty million years that the separate development of New World primates suggests. This development must have interacted with the general structuring of the cortex, with its other neurological and psychological implications.

R. Hertz (1973: 4) criticized the view of a purely anatomical account for right-hand dominance (I take it that this is what he meant by 'the organic cause'). To Broca's famous dictum that 'we are right-handed because we are left-brained' he countered with 'we are left-brained because we are right-handed' (Hertz 1973: 4). This neatly epigrammatic treatment of our theme must, however, be judged superficial, in the strictest sense of the term, because it belongs to more superficial levels in the deposition of structuring processes in the phylogenetic development of the brain. It can hardly be the case that the cultural dominance of the right hand precedes or in any way causes the lateral asymmetry of the brain, with the (supposedly) richer neuralization of the left hemisphere. Indeed Hertz finally retreated to an anatomical explanation of things (Hertz 1973: 21) though he was hardly very specific as to what was responsible. He wrote rather vaguely that 'an almost insignificant bodily asymmetry is enough to turn in one direction and the other contrary representations which are already completely formed'. Chelhod's judgment (Chelhod 1973: 245) that Hertz had betrayed his own instincts in this retreat, followed by his own reiteration of an older explanation based on the rise and pathway of the sun, illustrated from Arab culture (Chelhod 1973: 249-253), must similarly be judged not just superficial, but trivial. He has, to change metaphor midstream, placed the cart before the horse. I would be the first to concede that while the sinistral location of the heart is to be seen as the starting point of all that follows, once any cause-and-effect processual development was under way, it must have advanced in a dialectical, that is two-way, manner. There is no teleology to be discerned here: it is simply that one implication for B of such and such a development in A would in turn redound upon A, and so on in reciprocal fashion. The advent of human culture would complicate such a process tenfold.

The point I have tried to make in the previous paragraph cannot be over-emphasized. It is all too fashionable in the cultural (and above all cultic) disciplines to wield a philosophical big stick, declaring that any account of a human cultural fact in terms of its biological foundations is reductionism. This term has become a short-hand cipher for an abdication from serious analysis. All causal explanation, which regresses through the causal chain to a primary datum or axiom, whether scientific, philosophical or theological, is of course reductive, in that it reduces a complex effect to its usually less complex cause, since complexification, by adaptation, random mutation or sheer serendipity, tends to be inherent in development. Those who are unhappy with such procedures commonly denigrate them as 'reductionist'.

The fact remains, in our present context, that the foundation of our lateral symbolism can lie nowhere else but in the biological facts of our physical structure. The only element of asymmetry which could have been *known* in antiquity, before the rise of neuro-anatomy, was the location of the heart, which could provide just the kind of symbolic impetus to further neurological, psychological and cultural developments of the kind I have outlined. If we regress to a pre-conscious time (for symbolism does not arise out of conscious reflection), seeking the only element of asymmetry which satisfactorily explains all the other features we have isolated, which cannot have been prior to or independent of a hard anatomical fact such as this, we are again forced to see the heart as the only serious candidate. While in a dextrous use of the hands, such as the making or using of tools by primitive hominids, or their use by earlier primates, a dominance of one side might well develop within a community, it is above all the *cultural*, not the anatomical aspects, which create the human dominance of the right. Therefore it can hardly be a first cause, when an anatomical feature is already present which fulfils this purpose.

These observations have an evident bearing on the question of the left–right symbolism we have noted. But one may reasonably ask, what have they to do with the other axis, of before–behind, east–west? Here again neurological studies have a serious contribution to make. It was once regarded as a commonplace that the human brain, like many other structures in nature, recapitulates in its development the whole evolution of the central nervous system. While this has been discredited, one aspect of it, that the brain has a threefold structure, the upper two parts being superimposed upon a more archaic core, is still accepted. Thus the brainstem is sometimes called "the reptilian brain" (Maclean 1982) in so far as it preserves the structure and some of the ancient functions which developed long before mammalian, let alone primatial and hominid, development occurred. Before the development of the laterally divided brain, according to Dennett's interpretation of Kinsbourne 1978,[23] (see summary in Dennett 1993: 181) the two specialized areas of the primitive brain were dorsal and ventral. The dorsal brain dealt with external stimuli and reaction to them, while the ventral brain had the leisure for more detailed analysis of the immediate locality and its own concerns. This arrangement was subsequently reorganized into the left–right differentiation, the dorsal brain corresponding to the right hemisphere, working in intuitive relation with the world of the senses, the ventral to the left hemisphere, with its powers of analysis and introspection. If this sounds incredible, consider the case of the flat fish! On the basis of the principle of recapitulation (though this is now questioned), we might therefore expect the importance of the before–behind axis to be even greater, and certainly, in terms of its importance, incomparably older, than that of the left–right axis. In purely physical terms, we would expect the relationship of the two axes to conform to this, the question of whether something is visible (in front of the subject) or invisible (behind the subject), being a more pressing issue in the first instance that whether it is to the left or the right. We have reason to suppose that the whole tenor of all human culture is conditioned by these factors, and that this was *a fortiori* undoubtedly the case in Ugarit (as it was for all the neighbouring cultures, so far as we know).

One elegant observation of J. Jaynes neatly encapsulates the point I wish to make here with specific reference to lateralization. He observed (Jaynes 1976: 73) that 'the gods were organizations of the central nervous system', hallucinated voices from the right hemisphere communicating in encoded form with the left hemisphere as a cerebral tool in responding to external stimuli and environmental and other problems (cf. d'Aquili and Laughlin 1979: 170). Now the voices of the right hemisphere would be spatially located by the experiencing person as being on the left, 'sinister' side. And the left hand, for a person with an Ugaritic orientation, would be on the north side. Hence the location of the gods on Mount Saphon.

We see then that it is more than an accident of geography which locates the Ugaritic pantheon on Mount Saphon (*Jebel el Aqra*). It is a combination of that – and of the atmospheric qualities of a mountain, periodically swathed in cloud, often snow-capped, and associated with the supernatural clap of thunder – with the facts of human neurology. It is of interest to see that the deities appear to have been associated collectively with this location (see Wyatt 1996b and 1996c, on the location of all stages of the surviving *Baal* cycle).[24] This suggests two things. First, it belies the view that ancient deities were simply personifications of natural forces. In this case they would be located in various places, not set together. This unification of their location may of course be part of a theological rationalization from more primitive experiences of a more generalized nature, but that process itself is worthy of note as a neurological organization rather than a conscious reflective process. Second, their common location indicates a processing of the various items of religious responsiveness which goes to make up the complex of a polytheistic culture, and a concern to express these in a unitary manner. How far this may be attributed to conscious decisions by a community or their religious specialists, we cannot determine. In Jaynes' terms, it is much older than consciousness. The site of Ugarit was settled from as early as the end of the eighth millennium BCE (de Contenson 1992: 12), and thus undoubtedly preserved as hallowed lore traditions far more archaic than those of the extant literary traditions of the Late Bronze Age, though these themselves might undoubtedly also represent late adaptations of older tradition.[25] In view of Kinsbourne's hypothesis, we may also state that the fact of the sun's rising in the east was just a curiosity of the natural world which acted as a stimulus to primary orientation, which was the root of the significance of a northern mountain (that is, experienced on the left). With another orientation, another landmark would have taken on the symbolic role of Jebel el Aqra.

In view of Chelhod's discussion, of the evident importance of the Ka'ba and of biblical imagery concerning left and right, which indicates that the sacred mountain ('Saphon' in Psalm 48.3) in the north is at the same time the omphalos, and therefore at the centre, and so is not on the left-hand side at all, we should dwell briefly on the likelihood, not as yet receiving any explicit textual support in the Ugaritic texts, that a kind of mystical identification of Mount Saphon some 20 miles north of the city with the city-acropolis and its temples in Ugarit was intuited in Ugaritic theology. The key to *our* understanding of this issue, and of *their* experience of it, must lie precisely in the principle of orientation. Thus when the conventional stance was assumed, facing the east, the gods in the temples at Ugarit – those of Baal and Dagan on the acropolis both having their cella to the north, on a north–south axial orientation – would be heard to speak from the left. Thus even when temple architecture, the probable omphalic nature of the site and the essentially human experience of a central location were operative, the element of laterality was by no means absent. As I suggested in an earlier discussion (Chapter 5) the purpose of cult was in part the unification in experience of centre and boundary (or limen), the liminal dwelling of the gods on Mount Saphon becoming assimilated in the cultic experience to the central locus of the *naos*. The insistent leftness of theological language from Ugarit, contrasting interestingly with the biblical imagery which makes much both of this background and of an alternative tradition which has Yahweh proceeding from Teman (that is, the south) in Habakkuk 3.3 (cf. Deuteronomy 33.2, Judges 5.3), bids us question the universality of Hertz's view (Hertz 1973), that the gods are always associated with the right, and demons with the left. The West Semitic gods evidently come habitually from the north, which is the left, according to the Ugaritic tradition. Yahweh is apparently different in the Sinaitic traditions, yet himself conforms to the common pattern in the language of Psalm 48.3. In our present context, Hertz can be judged to be correct only in a neurological sense (the gods speak from the right hemisphere of the brain), not in a geographical sense.[26]

There is an interesting peculiarity about ritual orientation as evidenced in the Bible. Taylor (1993: 143-58) has drawn attention to the following passages, in 1 Kings and Ezekiel.

First, 1 Kings 8.11b-14: taking into account the LXX displacement of vv. 12-13 to v. 53, and restoring a fuller text than MT, may be translated as follows:

> For the glory of Yahweh filled Yahweh's temple. Then Solomon said:
> 'Sun he set in the heavens,[27]
> but Yahweh has chosen to dwell in thick cloud,
> I have surely built a princely temple for you,
> a place for your eternal dwelling.'
>
> Then the king turned round, and blessed the entire assembly of Israel, while the entire assembly of Israel stood.

Secondly, 1 Kings 8.30 reads thus:

> 'And listen to the entreaty of your servant and of your people Israel, which they address towards this place (*'el-hammāqôm hazzeh*).'

Thirdly, Ezekiel 8.16-18 reads as follows:

> He took me into the inner court of Yahweh's temple, and at the entrance to Yahweh's sanctuary, between the threshold and the altar, there were about twenty-five men. Their backs were to Yahweh's sanctuary, and their faces towards the east, and they were prostrating themselves towards [the east, facing] the sun.[28]

In the final passage the prophet goes on to indicate that this orientation was an abomination. But presumably the men worshipping did not consider themselves to be acting except piously and in good faith. Taylor (1993: 150) explained the situation in the following manner. His study is concerned with the possible relationship of Yahweh with the sun, and the broad drift of his argument, despite all his caution in many contexts, is that Yahweh is to be identified with the sun – a position which I find untenable – but in a subtle fashion. He saw hints of an ancient Gibeonite solar cult which Solomon has brought to Jerusalem, and which the Jerusalem cult then 'purifies' by purging it of an iconic element, symbolized in the *volte-face* performed by Solomon, and evidently approved of by Ezekiel. Taylor argued thus (Taylor 1993: 150):

> The Deuteronomistic concern with orientation away from the sun reflected in both 1 Kings 8 and Ezekiel 8.16... is not a concern over syncretism or even solar elements in Yahwism *per se*, but with iconism. In other words, DH and Ezekiel 8.16-17 are probably not so much opposed to the worship of *Yahweh* as the sun, but with the worship of the *sun* (that is, a physical object) as Yahweh...

If the orientation of the Jerusalem temple was east–west (that is, with the cella at the enclosed western end, so that entrance was effected at the east, as is generally accepted), then we can see why there was a practical need for physical reorientation as the cult became established. But this might be perfectly compatible with an eastward orientation at appropriate junctures within the cult. Indeed, we need not suppose that the abomination performed by Ezekiel's contemporaries, of facing *east*, represented anything out of the ordinary until the circumstances of Ezekiel's time, that is the exile, enforced attention to a more important concern. For the whole point of a western orientation in terms of the insistence behind Ezekiel's attitude and the passages from 1 Kings cited, equally belonging to the period of exilic Judaism, surely has less to do with an intra-Jerusalem cultus than with the matter of *qibla*, the facing towards Jerusalem of exiles in Babylon. That is surely what Solomon's prayer is all about.

If my interpretation is right, then it was precisely an older eastward orientation which was normative in earlier times, which thus corresponds to what we saw to be the case in Ugarit. There too, the priests would of course face north at certain junctures in the cult, though it is perhaps highly significant that in the case of both the acropolis temples, conventionally attributed to Baal and Dagan, the niche for the cult image in the cella is in its *east* wall.

The view of Fronzaroli (1965: 257) according to which the eastward-facing Hebrew terminology may be compared to a southward-facing Mesopotamian one on the basis of their respective west–east and north–south axial alignment of temples, was discussed by Rosén (1991: 1341). Unfortunately, such a neat scheme as Fronzaroli proposed, dealing with cultural units on the grand scale, without reference to local variations, and taking no account of the problem raised by 1 Kings and Ezekiel, cannot be maintained, as in any given West Semitic site, for instance, a variety of temple alignments will be found, often within one cultural context. This is evident at Ebla, Lachish, Beth Shean, Hazor, Shechem, Megiddo and at Ugarit itself. In the last case, the 'temple aux rhytons' is aligned west–east, though the entrance is on the north side, while the Baal and Dagan temples are both aligned north–south. Indeed in the latter cases, at Ugarit, Mount Saphon (Jebel el Aqra) dominates the northern horizon beyond, formally the seat of Baal (though also of the other gods), while if El is the deity of the former, as the statue found in the neighbouring oil-press courtyard suggests, the eastward alignment may reflect his possible lunar traits. This factor, rather than a solar one, may also determine the orientation of Yahwistic temples.[29]

One final point brings us back to an overall perspective on the matters discussed. Stadelmann (1970: 132-36) offered some interesting observations on Hebrew cosmology, that is, the present issues with reference to usage in the Hebrew language, but said nothing at all about any relationship between the four cardinal points he isolates. Can we add anything useful? We began by noting the primarily spatial use of the terms, before noting that they can also be used metaphorically. It has often been observed that our species is to be distinguished not so much on physical grounds, as on what we have learned to do with our brains. Thus we are above all the symbolizing species, the speaking species,[30] the primates who with the development of language have been able to construct elaborate metaphysical structures over and beyond the merely physical environment in which we live (Teilhard de Chardin's 'noosphere'). The present instance not only provides a clear example of this process at work, but perhaps isolates one of the earliest developments – so that to discuss it in an Ugaritic context is merely to illustrate the principle from one relatively late example – without which many other abstractions would have been impossible.

Let us consider our four cardinal points as representing two axes: an east–west one, and a north–south one. These intersect at the location of a speaking subject. That is, as we have seen, the north is on *my* left, the south on *my* right, the east in front of *me*, and the west behind *me*, always with regard to *my* subjectivity. In a spatial use of this concept, then, for as soon as it is articulated in language it becomes a concept, I am at (or 'at the centre of') a spatial intersection of axes. But we saw that there are other meanings to each axis. Thus the east–west one is a metaphor for time, leading from the past in front of me to the future behind me. We may, to adapt current jargon, speak of it as diachronic. Its power, and the subject's central role along the axis, is well summarized by Winston Smith in his recitation of the party slogan in *Nineteen Eighty-Four*: 'Who controls the past controls the future: who controls the present controls the past' (1949; 1977 Penguin edition: 199).[31] The north–south axis is a metaphor for all the other values of culture which are non-temporal. We may think of these as synchronic. Thus the north is the affective side, the south the articulate side, the north the source of danger, of lack of control and dependence on external pressures, represented as the abode of supernatural powers; the south is the symbol of control over life, of well-being, of everything ordered. North symbolizes chaos, south cosmos. Since in orientation the subject faces east, the north, the left, is *sinister, nefas*, the toilet side, private and inscrutable, dangerous and unpredictable. The south, the right, is *dexter, fas*, the public and predictable side. The propensity of language to think in merismic terms ('good and evil' and so on), which is by no means peculiar to the Semitic languages, is undoubtedly a linguistic harnessing of these realities. The binary foundations of Lévi-Strauss' perception of myth can be explained in terms of a 'neurological dialectic' which is the interaction of the two hemispheres of the brain, of which the axes we have isolated are simply the most basic.

A host of symbolic constructions rests on these relationships, and the left–right axis and its influences upon the subject is merely compounded when the east–west axis is also taken into account. Thus, from spatial awareness of his or her place in the world, the subject becomes both temporally and morally aware. It is significant that the subject is located precisely at the intersection of the two axes: spatially, *I* am at the centre of the universe as I experience it; temporally, *I* am in the 'now', neither past nor future. We can readily see the efficacy of cult in actualizing and reifying these two potentials, realizing the true centre of all reality *in the subject*, and its experience of the 'eternal present' (Eliade's '*illud tempus*'). A behavioral pattern that can achieve this for entire communities is a powerful instrument indeed.

Two final observations will, I hope, draw these strands into a whole. We have spoken of spatiality. Humans, and probably only humans, experience what Jaynes (1976) and others have called 'mind space'. Jaynes wrote that

'Conscious mind is a spatial analog of the world and mental acts are analogs of bodily acts' (Jaynes 1976: 66; cf. Hall 1966). We have seen in our discussion the physical bases upon which this mind space is built. Its essentially symbolic nature in its final form is a necessity brought about by the half-way house inhabited by humanity. Berger remarked of our species that 'biologically deprived of a man-world, he constructs a human world. This world, of course, is culture' (Berger 1973: 16). This reinforces the observation of Marais that man lacks the sense of locality to be seen in other animals (Marais 1973: 124-27). It is culture that has provided symbolic substitutes, and it is the roots of these that I have been attempting to identify and characterize. There is nothing in this peculiar to Ugaritic or even broader West Semitic culture. These have merely been the medium through which we can articulate a universal principle.

Our discussion has also provided the basis for a revision of the whole problem of the relationship between myth and history. I shall deal with this in brief, at risk of simplification. Biblical scholars long argued that while the ancients at large were constrained by their essentially cyclical, non-historical world views, the thought of the Old Testament represented 'the emancipation of thought from myth' (the title of the final chapter in H. and H.A. Frankfort 1946). Freed from the meaninglessness of a world going nowhere, the Hebrew mind, it was asserted, was able to introduce the principle of teleology, and to see divine purpose and meaning in the linear flow of history. Perhaps the culmination of this line of thought, and certainly the most egregious expression of it, was G.E. Wright's study *God Who Acts* of 1952. The responses by B. Albrektson (1967), and T.L. Thompson (1974) were quite devastating, and J. van Seters has produced a series of studies (e.g. van Seters 1975; 1983; 1992) following up the same drift. The growth of historical consciousness in the ancient world was a long, cumulative process, and ancient writers were never really able to distinguish the mythical and legendary from the historical in our understanding of these terms.

The matter of vocabulary must have some bearing on the intellectual process involved in generating a historical sense. We have already invoked the Abydos relief of Seti I as an illustration of the idea of a historical sense orientated towards the past. But such a view of history, which sees the present as the culmination of all that is past, and perhaps, theologically speaking, as the outcome of past divine intentions, is not the same thing as a serious sense of teleology, which is essentially futuristic in orientation, and *looks forwards to a future* shaped out of past paradigms. Such an orientation implies a physical *volte-face*, in terms of our discussion. The

Ugaritic material already betrays a more neutral, less subjective usage, which is endorsed by the Hebrew evidence. Whether we should read a reorientation into this new vocabulary, so that the future comes into the view of a person looking forward, is a matter on which the evidence before us does not allow us to determine. But quite apart from whether this is the case, it would be broadly true to say that a religious orientation would continue, on grounds of conservatism, even when a new arrangement entered into social usage for other purposes, such as economic or administrative, just as old cultic calendars often continue in use even when new ones have been devised for practical purposes. And historiography might well be motivated as much by practical considerations of that sort as by religious or philosophical motives.

It is in another area of religious experience that we can see the beginnings of the new orientation. Religion served important predictive functions in the ancient world. Ritual techniques were developed on many fronts to see an indication of future events in every action from disembowelling sacrificial animals to pouring oil on water. Natural occurrences such as the flight of birds, the appearance of hailstorms and the dreams of wise men were all seen as media by which the gods revealed the future.[32] Above all, in the prophetic experiences first attested beyond doubt at Mari, progressing through the evidently ancient (though perhaps unquantifiable) tradition underlying the Numbers and Deir Alla texts concerning Balaam, and reaching their climax in the classical biblical material (see Malamat 1989), we see the gropings for meaning in the future which finally emerge into serious teleology. The fruition of this tendency lies in the apocalyptic tradition, which, however, characteristically uses the past as paradigm for the future. This is not far removed from the tendency in mythology for primordial events, occurring *in illo tempore*, to determine all events. Thus even a future-facing world-view remains conditioned by its past.

Endnotes

* First published in N. Wyatt, W.G.E. Watson and J.B. Lloyd (eds), *Ugarit, Religion and Culture: Proceedings of the International Colloquium on Ugarit, Religion and Culture, Edinburgh, July 1994. Essays Presented in Honour of Professor John C.L. Gibson* (UBL, 12; Münster: Ugarit-Verlag, 1996): 351-80.

1. In discussion of the term *aḫr* in the broad context of the paper (Edinburgh Ugaritic conference, 1994), B. Margalit suggested that it had the sense of 'following' a person as he walked towards the future. But this orientation cannot be squared with the implications of the use of *qedem*, or of the overall orientation of the vocabulary under discussion.

2. Proposal of Cross (1973: 149). KTU2: ṣat.[špt]h] (*sic*: two parentheses and text in Roman).

3. If *ǵr*(*m*) is restored here, it gives the (a : b : : b : a) chiasmus *arṣ*, *ǵrm*, *ǵrm*, *bmt arṣ* (f., m., m., f.). The elegance of the structure reinforces the argument for the restoration.

4. I have taken the word-divider to be an error, giving the epithetal *qdmy*(*m*) occurring at Judges 5.21.

5. This relief is a primary work of historiography in every sense of the word. In addition to the basic psychological principles outlined here, we have a very interesting example of history really being at the mercy of the historian, since Seti, not himself of royal birth, claims legitimacy (and by the very act turns a lie into a fact!) by descent from the royal ancestors: their number is selective, certain predecessors now being 'written out' of the record. A Soviet historian of the 30s would have been proud of this achievement!

6. Collingwood (1946) made the point, with his different kinds of historiography. 'Theocratic history', however unscientific, is no less history than modern scientific history. On the rejection of the supposedly non-historical experience of people outside the biblical world, see Albrektson 1967, and for the mythical dimension in history, and the cultural forces determining even modern views, see Gibbs and Stevenson (eds.) 1975.

7. J.C. de Moor raised in discussion the matter of the themes of space and time as dealt with by T. Boman (1960: 123-183) and the reaction of J. Barr (1961: 72-85). In no way do I wish to be seen as endorsing Boman's more improbable views. As Barr noted (Barr 1961: 77) there is no contrast between Semitic and Greek thought in the present area, for 'not only does the Hebrew language contradict "the Indo-European idea of time", but the Indo-European languages do so too'. I am concerned not with isolating a peculiarity of Semitic thought, but with recognizing a common feature of ancient thought, which would probably be widely paralleled. It is likely, of course, that there would be local variations on the theme under discussion. Other cultures, using other vocabularies, might well interpret space and time in a different manner. The underlying anatomical and neurophysiological structures would, however, require them to be analogous.

8. Lit. 'distaff of whirling'.

9. For this reading and sense see Wyatt 1990e. Alternatively read *qdm* with the same sense.

10. Or: 'until the gods had eaten and drunk', that is, during the feast, which is of course a sacrifice.

11. Taking the *l* to be a vocative indicator, not a dative.

12. Or: 'replied from...'?

13. Or: 'to the north of...' For a slightly different analysis see Wyatt 2002a: 371.

14. Oden 1979: 366 and n. 72.

15. As Dhorme noted (1926: 315; see also Malamat 1989: 67, and Pope 1973: 172) the terms used may refer to immediate direction (before, behind, left, right) or equally well in the broader geographical sense (east, west, north, south). It is even possible that the temporal and moral connotations we shall explore below are to be discerned in the two axes, E–W and N–S respectively. The Hebrew of v. 9 is particularly difficult. Cf. comments in Dhorme, *loc. cit.*, Pope, *loc. cit.* 3rd sg. forms are read above as 1st. sg. for consistency.

15a. Cf. the much extended table, with the vocabulary of nine languages and discussion, in Wyatt 2001a: 33-52. There is a misplacement of the Ugaritic vocabulary on p. 42, to be corrected according to the present arrangement. The Hebrew *l^e^pānîm* meaning 'formerly' should also be added to the table on p. 43, in the box containing qedem and its meaning.

16. As in Genesis 14.15, noted by Rosén 1991: 1340.

17. On the problems of *dārôm* see O'Connor 1991: 1146 and n. 22.

18. See O'Connor 1991: 1141, n. 7; 1145, n. 21 for some remarks on Canaanite (Ugaritic) and Aramaic usage. He does not discuss our data *in extenso*.

19. *ṣat.špš*: KTU 1.3 ii 8.

20. The expression *aḫr.špšm* occurring in KTU 1.14 iv 32-33 etc., discussed above, is uncertain. Is it the directional use of *aḫr*, or simply its prepositional (temporal) sense, followed by an adverbial sense for *špšm* (noun with adverbial suffix *m*) or adverbial use, with *špšm*, as elsewhere in the *Keret* story, itself having the temporal meaning? Cf. Caquot *et al.* 1974: 531 n. y. The latter has been interpreted as 'sunrise' (del Olmo 1981: 298; Caquot *et al.* 1974: 528) and as 'sunset' (Clear 1976 : 63). Some scholars (Ginsberg, Driver, Gibson) appear to want to avoid committing themselves.

21. *ʿrb špš*: KTU 1.15 v. 18 etc. Rosén was incorrect in stating (1991: 1338) that this etymon occurs only in Akkadian.

22. *ṣbia.špš* || *ʿrb.špš*: KTU 1.15 v. 18-99. For justification of this interpretation see del Olmo 1975 : 95-96, *idem*, 1981: 613. (See also Wyatt 2001b: 701-702, *contra* Pardee 2000: 199-202.)

23. Kinsbourne did not, on my reading of his two papers in 1978 (a and b), make as explicit a statement of these matters as Dennett attributed to him (he spoke in b of a 180° turn, not a 90° one). The form of the argument outlined here is apparently therefore primarily Dennett's.

24. I think that my argument can be sustained even in the light of the two alternative locations for El's abode put forward at the Edinburgh conference: he dwelt on Mount Hermon (i.e. Anti-Lebanon) according to B. Margalit (cf. Lipiński 1971), but on Mount Lebanon according to A. Naccache (both 1996, in Wyatt, Watson and Lloyd 1996). There is no contradiction either between them, or between them and myself, in so far as a social group situated in any location would tend to identify a local landmark as their Omphalos (as Shechem – Mt Gerizim, Mt Tabor – the name, *tābôr*, can only seriously be explained from *ṭabbûr*, 'navel' – and Jerusalem were so identified). A migrating population would take their tradition with them and relocate it in their new environment. Traditions too can migrate independently, by way of trade, war or other influence. It may be noted that various peaks in Boeotia were named after the Semitic foundation of the myth of Typhon (Chapter 9). The 'relocation' of Mt Sinai by Christian monks in the modern Sinai peninsula is also a case in point. The unity of location in the Ugaritic material in the Baal cycle, evidently a deliberate literary ploy, is the more striking in view of the cogent arguments of S. Meier (1986) for the non-unity of texts KTU 1.1-6. On the two issues, see also M.S. Smith 1994b: 225-34 and 12-14.

25. I am not making any judgment here on the ethnic composition of earlier settlements. The fact remains that even the earliest inhabitants of the site would have shared the same neurocultural presuppositions for which I am arguing, and would also surely have also regarded Jebel el Aqra as a sacred mountain.

26. Jaynes (1976: 89-90), in discussing the localization of the voices of schizophrenics, notes that in some patients there is a tendency to associate the good consoling voices with the upper right, while bad voices come from below and to the left.

27. LXX (v. 53): ‘Ηλιον ἐγνερισεν ἐν οὐρανου (κυριος) (= Hebrew *šemeš hēkîn baššāmayim*).

28. The sentence ends *q^e^dēmâ laššemeš*. There is evidently a redundancy here: both words are not required. Perhaps the point of their proskynesis, that it is towards the sun, has at some point in transmission of the text been misunderstood as a merely directional term, whose eastwards orientation is then glossed.

29. Cf. Appendices A-I in Taylor 1993: 266-81.

30. ‘The Praying Animal’: Jenson 1983.

31. My thanks to Simon Wyatt for drawing this splendid slogan to my attention.

32. See for instance Loewe and Blacker (1975) *passim*.

Chapter 11*

The Mythic Mind[1]

The Problem

The term 'myth' has endured a confused perception in recent years. On the one hand, there has been a long tradition of hostile intent towards it, typical for the most part, curiously, among biblical scholars and systematic theologians. Many have been at pains to distance themselves and the biblical literature from any association with it. I. Strenski, writing in a different context, even felt compelled to remark sardonically on its altogether false status:

> ...instead of there being a real thing, myth, there is a thriving *industry*, manufacturing and marketing what is *called* 'myth'. 'Myth' is an 'illusion' – an appearance conjured or 'construct' created by artists and intellectuals toiling in the workshops of the myth industry...[2]

He was here playing on the sheer elusive nature of the concept to deny it any real ontological or even conceptual validity. On the other hand, an increasing number of studies[3] has brought about a process of rehabilitation, bringing a prodigal son back into the fold, and enriching the discipline with the insights he had gained while out in the cold, among alien peoples such as anthropologists and psychologists. While there is undoubtedly a positive reception in many quarters, even among some biblical scholars, of such a revisionist view of a category long held in deep hostility within this discipline, some elements of that hostility remain, and are still vocal.

It still remains true to say that there is a powerful current of thought among biblical scholars that the Hebrew Bible is emancipated from myth.[4] Some would perhaps go even further, and claim that the religion of ancient Israel was also emancipated from myth.[5] One reason for this may be the explanation offered by H. Eilberg-Schwartz for the discontinuity often asserted between the subject matter of anthropology, that is 'primitive peoples' and 'primitive religion', and Judaism. He averred that

> Since the Enlightenment, Judaism has typically been regarded as superior to other religions, with the single exception of Christianity. Although inferior to Christianity, 'the absolute religion', Judaism was not considered sufficiently primitive to be classified with the religion of savages. This judgment gave rise to the conviction that interpreters of Judaism had little if anything to learn from either the discipline of anthropology or comparative enquiry.[6]

A similar point was made by M.M. Epstein, who observed that, '...the idea of *myth* did not fit their [Jewish scholars'] conception of what Judaism should be',[7] and went on to deplore the dogmatic avoidance of a useful literary category in the interpretation of the Hebrew Bible, from which scholars had deemed myth to be absent. In both instances, while it is explicitly Judaism which is represented as contrasted with 'primitive' religions, it is fair to say that the same judgment applies *a fortiori* to the Hebrew Bible, and explicitly so for Epstein.[8]

A slightly different account was given by H.-J. Kraus, who noted the excessively speculative nature of both S. Mowinckel's work concerning the enthronement and New Year festivals,[9] and what he evidently regarded as the pernicious influence of the British 'myth-and-ritual' school associated with S.H. Hooke.[10] He was unhappy with a broad application of phenomenological principles to Israelite religion. In a barbed passage, he criticized Mowinckel (along with Pedersen),[11] but was particularly scathing towards Hooke:

> Although the question must be raised whether this phenomenology of primitive religion offers the right presuppositions for a correct explanation of Old Testament worship, there is no doubt whatever that the essential background of Israel's cult is clearly brought out. The objection could be made that in Mowinckel as well as Pedersen the principles of interpretation of the ancient cults and rites are too uniform, and that they see the manifold reality too much as a uniform phenomenon of primitive life. But the danger of distortion in these two scholars is slight compared with the trends to which we must now turn.[12]

We may note here the use of the term 'primitive' which at least admits, if it is not deliberately intended to convey, something of the prejudice noted above. Kraus went on to criticize G. Widengren[13] and I. Engnell,[14] who characterized 'the still more extreme approach of the Uppsala school'. All these scholars were guilty of a 'tendency to lose sight of the distinctions in worship at different times and places behind a unifying and all-embracing phenomenology'.[15] A phenomenological, rather like a comparative approach to religion, was evidently in bad odour because it threatened to break down the sharp barriers that could be maintained between Israelite religion and other 'pagan' traditions, so long as the absolute distinction could be made. Kraus did not have much to say about myth in general, but complained (1966: 18) that the approach of the scholars cited tended to push history out of the arena in favour of myth, and finally (p. 207), in alluding once more to 'the dogma of the "pattern" school of thought', complained that, 'there is no evidence within the Old Testament of this idea of a "mythicizing" of Yahweh, the Lord of history'. At last his own particular cat was out of the bag! Kraus stated another common view of the issue, of the kind associated with the 'biblical theology movement' to which we shall refer below.

It is easy to sympathize with Kraus. But even though the views of the scholars he cited be viewed as excessive, it does not follow that every category with which they dealt (and here we are concerned with myth) is therefore to be banished. Kraus, like those he attacked, appears to have regarded myth and ritual as a largely indissoluble pair of categories, quite apart from his evident concern to grant to Israelite religion a privileged status.

Anti-mythic views of this kind have at times been taken as axiomatic, as though the problem is over and done with, so that we can now get down to the serious business of an adequate, non-mythological study of the text and the religious beliefs to which it bears witness. Unfortunately, however, myth remains obstinate. Even apparently outvoted, it will not go away, and returns again and again to haunt us.

One of the problems which besets the whole issue is that no adequate definition of myth has ever been agreed,[16] and this is perhaps especially true among among biblical scholars, with the result that inadequate definitions have been paraded briefly, adopted uncritically, applied indiscriminately, and used dismissively.

The brothers J. and W. Grimm once defined myths as 'stories about the gods',[17] a definition taken up by H. Gunkel[18] and O. Eissfeldt,[19] thus conveniently excluding from the genre stories about God (singular) or stories about people (not gods). This somewhat restrictive view was attractive to generations of biblical scholars who felt constrained to contrast the allegedly mythical and primitive world-view of the surrounding cultures, to their disparagement, with the allegedly non-mythical and mature world view of ancient Israel. It spilled over into all the agonized debates as to the precise genre into which individual compositions were to be fitted, and was paralleled in New Testament Studies with the 'demythologization' programme of R. Bultmann and his allies, even washing up on the shores of systematic theology.[20]

H. Frankfort (1946) had already anticipated Kraus' objection, contrasting the personal, mythological world-view of the ancients with the non-personal, historical world-view of ancient Israel. This simple, not to say simplistic and convenient contrast played into the hands of the 'biblical theology movement' associated with such names as G.E. Wright.[21] This was to obtain the desired cultural contrast from another measure of rationality. The cyclical and ultimately purposeless experience of time allegedly to be found in all the other cultures of the near east contrasted, *mirabile dictu*, with the historical and linear view of Hebrew thought. This was self-evidently right, for it coincided with modern western perceptions of time! Thus from another perspective the convenient opposition between primitive and advanced thought could be maintained.[22]

The most important exponent of the widespread paradigm of *Heilsgeschichte* which grew round this approach was G. von Rad. Acknowledging the earlier foundations of the cultic structures of Israelite religion, he wrote of

> the historici[z]ing of what were previously purely agrarian festivals, that is, the rooting of them in the saving history, the legitim[iz]ation, indeed, of every ritual event on the basis of historical implantations on Jahweh's part. Here a rigorous demythologi[z]ing process, by means of which Jahwism appropriated cultic ideas and usages which derived from completely different cultic spheres, had been effected in utter secrecy.[23]

This passage takes it as axiomatic that myth and history are incompatible, and that the redirection of ancient rites to new circumstances involves an intrinsic programme of demythologization.

In my view neither of these suppositions bears examination. Firstly, the old opposition of myth and history, while at times a useful category distinction, suggests mental dispositions of an entirely different kind. It may work if the kind of history (more usefully historical thinking) is of the modern, quasi-scientific kind, with rules of evidence and objectivity as its main aspiration. But given the 'theocratic history' (R.G. Collingwood's expression)[24] of the ancient world, with its uncritical amalgamation of historical, legendary and mythological features, it is simply unconvincing to claim a complete mental transformation on behalf of Israelite writers. Both are types of narrative thinking, as well as narrative composition, of the type to be discussed below. Besides this, the historical status of the events lying behind Israel's festivals is scarcely secure; they constitute legends rather than any kind of sober history, and the narratives, for example that of the Passover, *function* as myth in their relation to the festivals. G. von Rad's assertion regarding the 'rigorous demythologi[z]ing process' of the biblical writers is merely a rhetorical flourish. No evidence is adduced of what constitutes the process, let alone its 'rigorous' nature. The process of which von Rad writes, it seems to me, was going on in his own head, not those of the narrators.

The influence of such expositions as I have outlined above lies partly in their capacity to express a half-truth. Myths may indeed be 'stories about the gods', for instance. They may even, as Eissfeldt asserted, involve a conflict between two gods. It is the implicit exclusion of all other possible story-lines from such a definition, to say nothing of matters of personnel and characterization, or even perhaps the formal insistence on a storyline in the first place, in view of other possible approaches, which makes it at best unhelpful in examining more fundamental features of the type.[25] Myths are certainly to be distinguished from sober history[26] as well, though that is not to say that we can make the simple opposition, myth *versus* history, into an inflexible principle. Myths may well contain elements of history,[27] just as history may contain elements of myth.

The half-truth contained in these and other inadequate definitions lies partly in the fact that human minds are perfectly able to inhabit two or more conceptual worlds, and frequently at the same time. Thus H. Frankfort was quite right to draw attention to the 'personalized' world of the experience of ancient people. But he omitted to say that the very same minds constructed engineering wonders, invented and developed mathematics and astronomy, managed complex societies, and were clearly as much at home in the real world of hard facts and pragmatic decisions as the rest of us. He also implicitly, and later explicitly, excluded 'Israel' from such an experience, by the blanket-application to all Hebrew literature of features of only one of its genres, historiography.

A view expressed by a number of these writers is that Israel did not invent any myths, but only (where this is reluctantly conceded), adopted and adapted the myths of others. Certainly so far as the main mythic themes of the Bible are concerned, they are not generally late inventions, but are the perpetuation of ancient forms, of which the antecedents may indeed be traced, particularly in the Ugaritian and Mesopotamian traditions. But why should this somehow be construed as exonerating Israel from the implied moral opprobrium of using them? It is almost as though they had been discovered fencing the goods! The view is expressed half apologetically, as though the biblical writers ought really to have known better. But how else could they express their tradition except in traditional form? It is no more than saying that for various Greek myths we can find an Ugaritian, Mesopotamian or Egyptian *Vorlage*. This does not oblige us to make similar pleas on behalf of Greek writers. Why should biblical writers be subject to such opprobrium, unless it is felt that they have betrayed a unique situation? That may be a perfectly valid theological standpoint,[28] though it strikes me as rather naïve, but it will not do for the historian of religions. Having established literary debts, in any context, we can then go on to see how a distinctive use is made of the same theme in its different historical manifestations. It is here that the peculiar qualities of the host community may be discerned.[29]

Perhaps in using other people's myths (if that is the way it was) the people of ancient Israel felt that these were meaningful and powerful forms; perhaps in adapting them they were using them in the time-honoured way, by actually shaping and articulating their own experience by means of mythic expression, for this is an important quality of myth; and perhaps they did not feel, as do many of their modern interpreters, a compulsion to deny the long-standing intellectual perception of this traditional past in favour of post-Enlightenment categories.

In broaching the subject again, I am reminded of the apocryphal story of the man who stopped a passer-by in O'Connell Street in Dublin and asked him the way to Limerick. 'If I were you, I wouldn't be starting from here', was the reply. To start from here would merely bog our discussion down in controversy which tends to be inconclusive, since all the evidence shows that scholars of opposed convictions are merely talking past one another. So let us begin from somewhere altogether different.

A New Starting Point

Another discipline which has suffered quite as many upheavals in recent years as Biblical Studies, and has seen quite as many wars of words, is Palaeoanthropology. The study of our past fascinates us like no other subject, except perhaps sex, and discoveries emerging from the fossil record or the laboratories of our universities require paradigm shifts almost as frequent as a change of socks. Lest any reader be tempted to put this article aside on the ground that I may not legitimately mix disciplines, I reply that the boundaries of our present academic disciplines are administrative conveniences, established or at least maintained by university administrators, not scholars. In legitimate scholarly enquiry, there are no boundaries, for each discipline shades off into associated disciplines, and biochemists, neurologists and psychologists, to say nothing of anthropologists and linguists ('linguisticists'!) have as much to contribute to our discipline as archaeologists, economists, historians, iconologists, philologists and the various kinds of scholar of religion. Our study is Man, *homo sapiens,* and any contribution to our understanding of this extraordinary creature, from whatever source, should be thankfully received. Even the study of God can be approached only by means of Man, since it is through human experience, human rituals, human language and literary forms, in short the activities of the human mind, that he, she or it may be perceived or conceptualized.

We are now used, in Biblical Studies, to a world in which there are no longer any fixed points. We drift in a sea of uncertainties, unsure whether the lights we see in the distance are from lighthouses on *terra firma,* or from other ships drifting as blindly as ours. Let no scholar of certain mind assure us on theological grounds that the lights are indeed fixed points, for our academic discipline finally steps outside its legitimate boundaries when it invokes theological axioms to anchor its paradigms. In an intellectual, human pursuit, we are obliged to obey the rules of the game, which are the implementation of logical procedures, and the assessment of evidence before us, and not the conjuring up of a *deus ex machina* to solve our problems. Nevertheless, the search for the fixed point, the assured datum, does provide sufficient motivation to pursue our enquiries wherever they lead. It is a heuristic tool in the process of our quest, if a dubious goal in the progress. Even if it be conceded that it is unobtainable, we can imagine it, though qualifying it *sotto voce* as 'relatively fixed'. It has catalytic value.

Perhaps in expressing the problem in the somewhat oppositional terms I have used above we have identified the real fly in the ointment. We are dealing with not one discipline, but two. Theology may quite rightly accept a number of exegetical principles in accordance with a broad confessional framework, and one of these is certainly to reassess past tradition in terms of present perceptions. The History of Religions, the discipline in which I see myself working, and which overlaps to some extent with Biblical Studies,[30] should however be very cautious in dealing with such an approach. It should strive always for a kind of objectivity which is inevitably secular, humanistic, and as far as possible value-free. By this I do not of course mean that it merely accepts the obscene and the perverse without judgment; but, on the other hand, it will be a lot more tolerant of the bizarre and the exotic, and will recognize a certain moral relativity. It seems to me that some of the former group of scholars in particular have at times confused the two disciplines, to the point of introducing theological judgments (on say, myth, or the 'morality' of Canaanite religion)[31] into the History of Religions, thus presenting as sober historical judgments, prejudices that are nothing of the sort. Its caution will be in direct proportion to its recognition that we never have the full picture, and that every judgment remains provisional.[32] The problem raised by the term 'myth' is a product of this duality of discipline and duality of purpose. To use the term in the context of theology is evidently considered by some of its practitioners as a slight on the truth-value of the subject matter, because myths are commonly considered to be false stories.[33] Within the field of the History of Religions, however, the term is entirely naturally used to denote a widely attested type of literature which communicates religious values, doctrines, convictions and paradigms.

Palaeontology is as full of uncertainties, and we are, while striving for those elusive hard facts, beset with competing theories on every point of detail.[34] But it can at least be said here that knowledge is a little more objectively based, if only because scientific procedures such as the use of carbon dating or thermo-luminescence techniques are objective, however imperfectly applied or interpreted. Furthermore, while strong opinions are to be found, and the usual claims of ideological bias are hurled from time to time at the opposition, palaeontology does at least work in theory on the principle of falsifiability.[35] In our disciplines, where commitment may be part of the equation, that is at times impossible to concede. Belief in the truth of the material you study has its drawbacks, and the last thing Theology seeks is falsifiability!

Let us begin, then, at the beginning, or at least in remote prehistory. The later hominids have evolved, *homo habilis* and *homo erectus*, the latter colonizing the world beyond Africa, and Neanderthals (*homo neanderthalensis*) and Cro-Magnon (*homo sapiens*) have lived in close proximity for perhaps 30,000 years in the Near East and Europe. Symbolizing skills have slowly evolved,[36] and finally speech is developed. The advent of speech unleashes hitherto impossible dimensions of experience. Whether it be interpreted as 'distance grooming' (Dunbar 1993) or as a phonetic extension of non-linguistic communication, a sort of verbalized pheromone, the development of speech interacted with the new symbolizing capacity of the early human brain,[37] each reinforcing the other on a feed-back loop principle,[38] and combining with other distinctive hominid developments such as bipedalism, opposed thumbs and increasing manual dexterity, the enormous growth in brain-size and above all of the cerebral cortex, to produce an ever-more complex world of symbolic capacity and achievement, which over immeasurable centuries transformed our ancestors from biological into cultural organisms.

M. Donald (1991) examined this development, and proposed a number of discrete stages in the development of one crucial feature in this nexus of processes, that of human memory. He postulated the following kinds of memory (he also used the following terms in conjunction with 'thought' and 'culture'), developing in this sequence:

1. 'procedural memory'. This is shared by large numbers of organisms. It is fair to say that evidence of primitive 'consciousness' is being constantly pushed back down the phylogenetic line.

2. 'episodic memory'. This is restricted to birds and mammals, that is, relatively late life-forms in evolutionary terms. It is greatly enhanced in the great apes.[39] To contrast this with the following type, we may cite Donald's comment that

> from a human standpoint, the limitations of episodic culture are in the realm of representation. Animals excel at situational analysis and recall but cannot re-present a situation to reflect on it, either individually or collectively. This is a serious memory limitation; there is no equivalent of semantic structure in animal memory...

3. 'semantic memory'. This final form is found only in man, although conceivably elementary forms also appeared among the earlier hominids, depending on how far back the genesis of language is pushed. But it distinguishes the hominid from the simian and pongid lines: 'Semantic memory depends on the existence of abstract, distinctively human representational systems. The cognitive element in human culture is, on one level, largely the development of various semantic representational systems.'[40]

None of these stages replaces or displaces the earlier stages,[41] but is superimposed on them. What Donald was here describing is the development of a means of storing and retrieving information. While it is 'abstract', in the strictest sense that language is itself an abstraction, a phonetic code for communicating complex ideas, and giving ideational form to feelings, sensations, and memories, it is of course not so in the more general sense of abstractions and conceptions of the kind represented in mathematics or philosophy. In this regard it is entirely concrete, for the materials encoded in early systems of thought and communication would be concerned above all with biological survival, and its many by-forms such as territorial control, social hierarchy and group-dynamics. The central key to such systematization of experience was the symbol. Language allowed for the first time a real semantic process, in so far as it allowed ideas to be related in the mind.[42]

In his consequent analysis, Donald dealt with two further matters of relevance to our present discussion. The first is an observation on the distinction between mimicry, imitation and mimesis:

> Mimicry is literal, an attempt to render as exact a duplicate as possible... Imitation is not so literal as mimicry; the offspring copying its parent's behaviour imitates, but does not mimic, the parent's way of doing things. Mimesis adds a representational dimension to imitation. It usually incorporates both mimicry and imitation to a higher end, that of re-enacting and re-presenting an event or relationship.[43]

Mimesis, he went on to argue, is essentially a public interpretation and expression of communicable information (we might add, stored in semantic memory), still in evidence in the arts. 'The "mimetic" customs of a group', he suggested, 'would serve as the collective definition of a society'.[44] While the emphasis in the arts today may be individual self-expression and virtuosity, they have historically been concerned above all with the reinforcement of social mores. Human rituals are those mimetic events which are taken with the utmost seriousness, and tend to have not only social but above all sacred value. M. Eliade's insistence on the link between sacredness and ontology, that the 'sacred' is the 'real',[45] has a particular significance in our present context. In so far as human societies transcend the biological and experience a cultural world, they do so by a process of reification, by what P. Berger and T. Luckmann called 'the social construction of reality'.[46]

The second of Donald's emphases follows on directly from this train of thought. While we construct reality through mimesis and art, we do so above all through language. We not only live in, but we have built, in order to live in it, a 'linguistic universe'. The idea even stands at the heart of religious discourse, in so far as Christ is the 'Word', or creation began with a divine utterance. The idea is, of course, by no means confined to biblical thought.[47]

So far as discourse is concerned, Donald distinguished two main types, narrative and paradigmatic.[48] The latter is to be associated with scientific thought and is a function of modern complex societies. It is largely lacking from traditional societies, where an essentially oral discourse is the norm, even in such cultures as developed writing systems ('external memory-systems')[49] early in their history. It is in the narrative-paradigmatic polarity that we should recognize the difference between traditional and modern cultures. L. Lévy-Bruhl attempted without success to characterize the former as a 'pre-logical mentality'.[50] There was nothing pre-logical about the earlier form of thinking; it was simply that it did so in broadly narrative forms. When narrative was at its most intense, in expressing the sacral values of a community, its most characteristic genre was myth. And myth harnessed to its full potential the symbolic dimension of narrative, in creating imaginary, ideal worlds (such as a typical ancient near eastern cosmology, or a creation-story like Genesis 1) which allowed a coherent encounter with the untidy real world of common experience.[51]

If we may turn to another aspect of the shaping of the human mind, two further studies have much to offer, Boyer (1994) and particularly for present purposes Guthrie (1993). Both argue that the human mind-brain is constructed in such a way that religious ideas are entirely natural.

S. Guthrie has successfully resurrected another somewhat old-fashioned idea, E. Tylor's animism-theory, to a new and useful life, by meticulous analysis of the psychology of perception, and the recognition of the principle of anthropomorphism as a primary category in human experience. Tylor had viewed animism as belonging to a 'primitive' stage in human culture: Guthrie considered it to be a universal feature of the human mind. Experience is actually determined by interpretation, he noted (against Schleiermacher and Otto),[52] and went on to argue that the tendency to perceive human faces and personalities in the external world is innate, and part of an important defensive strategy, which then developed into a meaning-giving strategy.

He cited W. Proudfoot's example of the man who thinks he sees a bear on the forest path.[53] This perception may be false, but it is a better bet to think it may be a bear, and to discover that it is only a boulder, rather than to think the reverse. But even more useful than a bear, or any other dangerous but different creature as a symbol, is the imagining of a human form in the external world. R. Horton had defined religion as 'the extension of the field of people's social relationships beyond the confines of purely human society'.[54] Guthrie glossed this with the comment that 'humans thus model their relations with the world on their relations with other people'. In criticizing Horton, who, he argued, regarded this as simply the idiom rather than the essence of religion, and thus failed to isolate the distinctively religious aspect of this interpretation, Guthrie himself went on to insist that anthropomorphism lies at the very foundation of religion, not merely in an idiomatic sense, but more profoundly, for when it developed into religion a personal relationship was developed with the external anthropomorphic form. Thus the matter of loyalty and social bonding came to lie at the heart of the relationship. While in practical terms the 'idiom' could be switched off at will, as in the development of technology and science, for which it no longer had any useful function, in religion it lay, and remained, at the heart of the experience.[55] We may even think of this as a kind of primitive 'covenant relationship' developing between a community and its gods, who were the developed personifications of these anthropomorphic reflections of the community itself.[56]

The anthropomorphic imperative persists. The characterization of Vedantic thought as non-theistic, or of Buddhist thought as atheistic, as is often done by western commentators, is misleading. Both have attempted a language of transcendence (the noumenal) which goes beyond the personal (the phenomenal, anthropic), but does not deny it. In western religion, attempts to go beyond the personal have been limited to a few metaphysicians, who have introduced the language of paradigmatic thought. For the vast majority, particularly in so far as they experience rather than rationalize religion, and most importantly for the writers of the sacred texts, biblical or qur'anic, which so profoundly influence the mind of all subsequent members of the believing community, the deity is emphatically personal, and even aggressively anthropomorphic. After all, the very attribution of mind to a deity is the transference of a human category. It is only contemporary exegesis, frequently embarrassed by the powerfully corporeal language, that has sought to explain it as purely metaphorical.

The principle of 'patterning', of seeing in the evidence what we expect to see, or want to see, is familiar enough to biblical scholars. It lay at the heart of Kraus' critique of Scandinavian and British scholarship discussed above, just as much as within that scholarship. The principle is best illustrated by the story of the inmate of Friern Barnet hospital who was given some Rorschach tests by his consultant. As the psychiatrist turned the pages in the test book, revealing a succession of abstract blot-designs, the patient, on cue, said what first came into his mind: 'Sex... sex... sex... sex... ' 'Good heavens!' cried the consultant, 'you really *are* obsessed by sex!' 'What do you mean?' was the reply; 'you're the one who's been showing me all the dirty pictures!'

But the anthropomorphizing trait is always with us. It is simply part of the operation of the mind. It becomes a problem only when it continues to misinform the mind beyond the point of usefulness. We see it in the relationship of two disciplines noted above. Theology, as confessional, and operating, as P. Davies has noted, on 'emic' grounds,[57] has tended to remain within the narrative culture described by Donald. The historian of religions will be at odds with theologian-colleagues who see monotheism in every passage in the Hebrew Bible which looks to him like evidence of polytheism, or at the very least henotheism.[58] To the historian of religions, people who write books on Christian ethics based on Iron Age Hebrew ethical stances[59] can seem peculiarly perverse. We all impose a pattern of sorts on the data, of course, depending on where we start from, a phenomenological or a theological perspective, or somewhere in between. But some starting-points have far-reaching consequences. Once the Hebrew Bible is accorded the status of sacred text, 'Scripture', the ideological battle is lost, for canonizing the text (or nowadays accepting the canon of the text) precludes all relativity and comparability, which are arguably essential components of free enquiry, the historian will argue. It can only be on axiomatic grounds, that myth is somehow incompatible with canonical status, that it is ruled out of court as a legitimate biblical category. It is even arguable that this presumption is itself an essentially mythic position. Just as the atheist is accused of adopting a theological position in denying the existence of God,[60] so the anti-mythicist falls into the trap of axiomatic exclusion which intrinsically invalidates his position. It becomes a mere tautology.

I suppose one of the problems besetting this discussion in a biblical context involves the matter of the relationship of revelation to all the issues in hand. If to any attempt at a general approach to mythological thought, which sees continuity between the surrounding cultures of the Near East and 'Israel', the Pavlovian (or Barthian) retort is simply that the principle of divine revelation changes all that, then of course advocates on both sides of the debate will continue to talk past each other. My view here is that a theological concept which, however elevated its motives, so particularizes its subject matter (here the revelation mediated through the Bible) as to cut it off in effect from the mainstream of human consciousness and culture, cannot be a valid position for the historian to take. But it also looks dubious to me as a realistic theological position. Even a revelatory theology speaks of people chosen from the mass, called out from the body of humanity. To make that additional leap, never demanded by the tradition, that is expressed in the axiom that the biblical writers have left common human experience behind, and have gone beyond myth, is to go an axiom too far.

And why be afraid of the category of myth? It vastly enriches our understanding of the narratives and symbolic constructions of the text to see in them localized expressions of universal principles of the structure and working of the human mind. Indeed, it is probably fair to say that if we reject the validity of a comparative approach, we end up not knowing what biblical writers were talking about, because we are cutting them off not only from an ancient comparable world, but also from a modern one.

The Problem of Defining 'Myth'

One of the problems in our subject matter is the sheer polysemy of the term 'myth', as Strenski complained. Not only does every specialist, anthropological, psychological and theological, offer different definitions, but these are often mutually incompatible. We all define the term as we understand it to operate, so that our own position – which our opponents call our prejudice – determines our choice of words, either to conform to our own theory, or to discredit the theories of others.

Quite apart from the technical issues involved in an academic definition, and the objective problems faced by scholars, consider the following: 'The persistence of racial thinking and the myth of racial divergence'. This is the title of a recent article in *American Anthropologist*.[61] The term 'myth' in this title has two clear uses. Firstly it means what 'myth' commonly means in everyday discourse, that is, a story which is patently untrue, a fond belief, or in this case a pernicious one. Racism has no basis in fact, that is, genetic fact, but only in prejudice.[62] 'Urban myths', on the other hand, are an honourable and generally harmless genre, in which the most extraordinary tales travel across huge distances – their speed of transmission now vastly enhanced by the Internet – and of which the ingenuity is matched only by their incredible status. They generally have no particular axe to grind, however, no ideology, and are perhaps an example of the casual misuse of the term even by scholars.

The pernicious example cited, however, has another nuance. It also carries an ideological burden, which has been so powerful in human history that it formed the basis of much early physical anthropology, quite apart from its egregious application in Nazi racial theories. It has operated at a subliminal level in the growth of empires (notably the British Empire), justified countless programmes of genocide, as in the colonization of the Americas, and still controls land-use policy in modern China (that is, Tibet) or the Balkans.[63] This use of 'myth' is so insidious that it forms part of the everyday furniture of our minds and effectively – like all *bona fide* ideologies – blinds us to the logical objections, which are filtered out by the mind as irrelevant. An ideology is simply a system of thought, as regards its structure, which admits of no exceptions to the rule. If no amount of evidence to the contrary convinces the adherent of the falsity of his position, he is in the grip of an ideology.

It is perhaps in part the right use of the term 'myth' in such distasteful contexts as racism which makes it appear to be an unacceptable word in the context of biblical literature and scholarship. But these are not immune to political agendas, ancient and modern, and we certainly should not avoid a useful word simply because we do not like it.

But the ideological dimension of the term is not in any case to be seen as wholly pathological, and nor do I intend to present it in this way, for it is undoubtedly an adaptative strategy, adopted in two main, and commonly interlocking, areas of human experience and interaction, politics and religion. Theology in its classical, dogmatic form as apologia for the faith of a community, is simply ideology.[64] That is, it is a system of thought designed (or developing, for it is largely unconscious in its origins) for the articulation and maintenance of a particular world-view, with a built-in response to all objections. It may parade its myths in the rhetoric of rationalism, but in so far as it demands orthodoxy, and therefore admits no heresy or competing world-view to equal status, it belongs to the thought-world I am trying to characterize. I think this is a fair description of any religion. On the other hand some religions are more ideological than others, because they have built into them explicit intolerance of any opposition and a rejection of pluralism. It is evident from their history that the Judaeo-Christian and Islamic traditions are of this order. Since the three are monotheistic, the question is certainly worth asking as to whether monotheism is in some way intolerant of myth. It is certainly the way some of their exponents wish it to appear (such as Gunkel or Eissfeldt, cited above). But in my view it is a misperception.

Our problem in the field of Biblical Studies arises from the fact that half of us wish to act as theologians – however detached we imagine ourselves to be – and never let objections actually impinge on our belief system, though it may be unconsciously eroded and refined in the process, always with its back to the wall, a kind of heroic defence *à la* Leonidas against the forces of disbelief. We end up writing and reading books on the theology of the Old Testament which owe more to Barth than to any ancient author. The rest of us try to eschew ideology, and certainly a religious ideology, perhaps with varying degrees of success,[65] and to give a history-of-religions account of events and developments. This is admittedly no more objective, for every judgment we make on the antiquity or origins of a ritual, a myth or historiographical composition is indebted to all previous work in a whole galaxy of disciplines; but it may at least be seen as strengthened by its contextualization in a more universal treatment of human behaviour. This endeavour then falls foul of the counter-claim that it errs in over emphasizing the similar, while under rating the distinctive and different.[66] In so far as it avoids value-judgments, this approach is also open to the charge of relativism, though perhaps in view of the results of particularism in world history, this is no bad thing.

At the end of the day, perhaps we can agree to differ. For my part, the difference will be merely one of labels. The anti-mythicist may prefer an expression such as 'the religious imagination'. To my mind, that is synonymous with the mythic mind.

If we have to admit the unlikelihood of any advance from within the disciplines, in which there is fundamental disagreement on matters of literary genre, let me appeal to the broader issue of mental disposition outlined above. We saw that in Donald's view it is narrative as distinct from paradigmatic thought, which distinguishes the mental and cultural processes of traditional societies. We saw that according to Guthrie the propensity to view the external world anthropomorphically is built into the very structure of the human mind. Now unless we concede that the 'Hebrew', 'Israelite' or 'biblical' mind is in some way radically distinct from all other forms of the human mind, which I find an improbable hypothesis, then it follows that these features are also characteristic of these particular manifestations. That is, it seems a reasonable position to adopt that we shall find narrative discourse, and an anthropomorphic world-perception at the heart of the culture under review. And at least as I read the texts, that is precisely what we find.

I am, however, reluctant to offer a precise definition of myth,[67] and especially as a literary genre, because this would naturally tend to exclusivism, as in the common dichotomy between myth, saga, legend and epic, or more particularly between myth and history. Traditional literary forms such as these do not fit neatly into slots, whatever the literary critic may care to say. The genres shade off into each other, and using Donald's broad categorization of narrative and paradigmatic thought, in so far as any of them fits into the narrative mode, myth may be said to be a broad underlying characteristic of all such material, rather than being one exclusive category among others. The kind of discussion we often find as to whether a given biblical narrative constitutes 'historicized myth'[68] or 'mythicized history' seems to me an exercise in futility, predetermined in any case in most instances by a firm intention to preserve a little bit of 'history' at all costs. The opposition of 'myth' and 'history' is not always a useful one. I am inclined to say that all pre-modern history, in the sense of traditional historiography which presents a national narrative, and also the conceptual pattern underlying it, tends to the mythical, because this is to be seen as a certain mind-set, a disposition to impose structure, coherence and meaning on events, which are then systematically expressed in the narrative. If it be objected that this is what the modern academic historian is about as well, the difference surely lies in *his* willingness to revise or even abandon his views in the face of new evidence, while the traditional mode is concerned to preserve a community's sense of identity, which will often lead to the suppression of awkward evidence and uncomfortable truths.[69] If the narrative is about a people's past, we all know how elusive the application of the traditional genres (saga, legend, history) can be, and how one shades off into the other, or how they are combined in a constant reweaving of motifs, shaping this event in the light of that metaphor, even inventing episodes to act out a fiction.

Even modern historiography is not above mythic invention. The substantial revisionism of much historical study associated with famous names such as Michelet or Ranke has been shown by subsequent scholarship to be tendentious, to be in the grip of ideologies. The histories of Israelite religion, we have seen, are not exempt. Von Rad's theology, which attempts to set things within an authentic historical setting, so that historical forms condition the theology, is seen to be the reverse. And nor is this necessarily a bad thing, so long as the cards are on the table.

Myth in the Hebrew Bible

Now before I take the next step, and claim that this is precisely the 'mythic mind' for which I am searching, let me a address a further problem. Not so long ago scholars could open the pages of the *Deuteronomistic History*, for example, and have reasonable confidence that, give or take a few asides by the author(s), we had a fairly reliable history of Israel and Judah down to the exile. Some scholars would still like to maintain this position. But for most of us, such halcyon days are gone for ever, brushed aside without ceremony by the work of the last two decades.

The thrust of much recent work is the firm distinction between the categories 'Israelite' and 'biblical' so far as the witness of the text is concerned. We see not so much a reflection as a critique of Israelite religion in the Bible. Because of its self-conscious removal from the sinfulness of Israel's religious history, and our limitations in being largely bound to the text, all we can hope to achieve is an understanding of the text's position, and not a valid reconstruction of the history lying behind it.

Let us imagine a worst case scenario in our treatment of the Bible, according to which it is *all* late and unreliable as a source for historical study. The only history we can recapture is that of the text itself. We cannot get behind it. Now if it can be shown that the Bible is broadly mythological, in the sense that I wish to maintain, that it is written by people of essentially 'mythic mind', who operate in a world of symbols and narrative just like every surrounding culture, it follows that the (now irrecoverable) historical religion behind the text was all the more so to be characterized, since at some point the texts emerged from people subscribing to this religious tradition.

So how far is the Bible still mythological? Let me briefly summarize my position on this issue with reference to three strands of mythic tradition found at Ugarit, but already of an international nature, and the uses of these traditions in the Hebrew Bible. If it can be argued that the same ideological themes of the earlier material survive, and are even arguably reinforced, in the later, then there is a case to answer that the Hebrew Bible is retaining the tradition precisely because it too is dealing in myth. Indeed the principle should hold true even if there is a measurable reinterpretation or development of an older form, so long as it retains its ideological nature.

The traditions I have in mind are firstly the *Chaoskampf* tradition, occurring in the Ugaritic Baal cycle of myths (KTU 1.1-6) and also widely attested in biblical tradition; secondly the theogony tradition reflected in KTU 1.23 and 1.12 i in particular, and also evident in biblical tradition; and thirdly the narrative referring to Athtar in KTU 1.6 i 43-67. I think that the matter of literary influence is beyond serious dispute for the former two, and in the third instance there is a continuity of theme, though it is significantly modified in the transmission. So the matter at issue (the problem of the presence of myth in the Hebrew Bible) may be confined to the respective meaning of the traditions.

Now my analysis of the *Chaoskampf* tradition[70] leads me to one important conclusion: which is that the ideological basis for this particular myth, as it is to be discerned in the oldest forms thus far recovered, from Eshnunna, Mari and Ugarit, *does* persist. It has nothing to do with any seasonal interpretation, furthermore, but is already from its earliest appearance in the Amorite myths of Tishpak from Eshnunna bound up inextricably with royal ideology. It has to do with social organization and royal authority. This significance persists, in my view, throughout the Marian and Ugaritic tradition, on into the Bible, in both Testaments, and out into the traditions of Perseus and Andromeda and on to George and the dragon, though by this time perhaps the formal ideology is beginning to weaken into folkloric musing on the theme. Even the Arthurian cycle, which is most emphatically ideological in its purpose, is tinged with aspects of the theme.[71]

Within this strong current of tradition, in which the god who fights a marine monster and wins a kingdom latterly becomes a hero[72] who fights a marine monster and wins a kingdom, cuts through Hebrew literary tradition in a great swathe, forming the paradigm of creation (Genesis 1), of redemption from Egypt (Exodus 15), of redemption to come (Isaiah 27.1) and even of redemption made manifest, if traced on into the New Testament (Mark 4.35-41; 6.45-52 and synoptic parallels; John 6.16-21 and cf.

perhaps John 21.1-23).[73] The theme is securely established in the Marian text A1968, concerning royal legitimacy, in which the mythic weapons of the god are ritually delivered into the hand of the king, so that he too may win victories over the forces of chaos. Within the Hebrew literary tradition Psalm 89 in particular relates the granting of royal power to the primaeval battle: it is thanks to Yahweh's victory that the king will rule in security, and as at Mari, the rite is sealed with an anointing.[74]

The theogony traditions of Ugarit, with wide parallels in the ancient Near East, are also echoed in a number of biblical recensions. In earlier studies I have identified Genesis 16–21, 19.30-38, Psalms 8, 19 and 110, Hosea 2, Ezekiel 16 and 23 as being heirs to the tradition.[75] Some of these suggestions have been made by earlier scholars as well.[76] The precise ideological nuance of the Ugaritic material is uncertain. In KTU 1.12 the overall theme, to which the birth episode is merely a prologue, appears to be communal redemption,[77] while in KTU 1.23 Shahar and Shalem, the 'gracious gods', are born to the geminated avatars of Shapsh, Athirat and Rahmay. While there is no consensus on the overall thrust of the text, it is fair to say that in so far as the Dioscuri are probably to be understood as the mythic counterparts of the king, we have the broad theme of the good news that a royal birth brings to a community. It is probably on account of an inherent ideological element in the twinship motif (we may hypothesize the dual nature of the king)[78] that we have so many stories of twins and pairs, such as Ishmael and Isaac, Moab and Ammon (all fathers of nations), or the girls adopted *and then married* by Yahweh, who seem to be transparent reflexes of the geminated goddesses.

The third motif with ancient near eastern antecedents which appears in biblical texts is the deposition myth, which H.R. Page Jr calls 'the myth of cosmic rebellion'.[79] I think that he errs in tracing this disobedience motif back into Ugaritic tradition and discerning there a myth of the same type. What he identifies *is*, however, the antecedent of the type. The narrative of the enthronement and subsequent descent from the throne of Athtar (KTU 1.6 i 56-67) is by no means a deposition, but rather an enthronement narrative, which involves the royal ascent to heaven[80] to receive kingly power and learn the secret wisdom of the gods, followed by a return to earth in order to exercise royal power. The narrative expressly states (ll. 63-65) that

> Athtar the Brilliant came down,
> he came down from the throne of Valiant Baal,
>   and ruled in the earth,
>   god of it all.[81]

This narrative remains somewhat isolated in the context on account of the following gap of some 34 lines in the Ugaritic tablet. What is clear from the surviving material is the ascent of Athtar, his enthronement and subsequent descent. This is the pattern we may discern in a large number of other ancient texts from throughout the Near East. So far as biblical tradition is concerned, we may note the comparable ascent traditions of Moses at Sinai (Exodus 19–24, 32–34). The modified version, which at some point has picked up the additional element of the deposition, appears in the taunt songs addressed to foreign kings in Isaiah 14 and Ezekiel 28.

The texts noted here belong to a wide range of literary types in the Hebrew Bible, prophecy, historiography, and cultic poetry. The themes mentioned are not therefore a few isolated poetic allusions, but motifs which permeate the forms which most characteristically encapsulated the most fundamental convictions of Israel.

Most, if not all, of the elements in the Hebrew Bible which have been recognized by some scholars as having mythic status had antecedents and congeners in the wider near eastern world. It is in the nature of myth that it knows no boundaries, for the power of its symbolic and generally ideological content will tend to have carried weight wherever it went. People 'borrow' myths because they are such effective media for the transmission of cultural and religious values. 'Absorption' may be a better term than 'borrowing', and in the case of a society such as ancient Israel, we do well to consider the very diverse origins of the community, as already mentioned in the tradition, before we try to make a case for the essentially 'foreign' nature of its myths. If the theory of a migration of people from the Hauran to Ugarit[82] is at all cogent, for example, it readily explains the presence in both Ugaritic and biblical tradition of familiarity with the traditions and sacred geography of the region. In such a case Ugarit and Israel are jointly heirs to a common tradition.[83] If there were really Israelites in Egypt, we should expect some elements of Egyptian thought in their later tradition, and if the resulting population of the Levant, whether by conquest, absorption or any other social upheaval, incorporated elements of local populations, who is to claim that this or that enclave is 'foreign' to the true Israel?[84]

The question of whether a given text is strictly mythological in terms of formal literary genre may be ultimately unanswerable, given that such a divergence of views persists with regard to the very definition of myth. Within the more relaxed world of the History of Religions, I believe that every text mentioned would be accepted as at least mythological, if not formally constituting myth. More interestingly there remains the broader question of a type of thinking, which I have attempted to outline above, typically found in myth, however precisely defined, but perhaps to be found more widely in all religious thought. In my view, all religious thought which operates in a dimension other than the purely conceptual (as in modern conceptual systematic theology) is intrinsically mythological. Everyone will be perfectly content to see this assessment made of Buddhist, Hindu, Zoroastrian, Islamic or any other religious world-view, where it would be generally conceived that the entire metaphysical foundation of the given system is at variance with the real world we experience and reify through modern scientific analysis. This is not so far-fetched as it may sound, in view of Guthrie's intriguing claim that 'religion attempts not to explain experience, but to contradict it. Empiricism and logic are not merely irrelevant, but inimical.'[85]

But there is nothing inherently more scientific about the Judaeo-Christian view of the world than in any other religious account. As soon as divine intent, divine creativity, and divine purpose, or indeed any providential, or human purpose, are read into the world of experience, as soon as the certainty of God's presence is perceived in human life, it ceases to be a rational view, in the sense of the historian seeing a chain of events which can be explained in terms of historical causation, the outworking of political strategies or economic cycles, and so forth, and becomes a mythic one. Stories of the beginning and end of the world, and of the resurrection, ascension and second coming of Christ are not in any sense 'historical' narratives, whether past or future in their application. Couched in historiographical form, the narrative of biblical historiography bears the veneer of history, but we know that not only is the facticity of this history largely tendentious, but that introducing Yahweh as the leading character removes it from the cold light of day, and takes it into an interior world of commitment and religious experience. To apply Guthrie's point, this is designed precisely to contradict the drear meaninglessness of the real history through which Israel moved.

I wrote above of the origins of symbols in the development of the early human mind. Symbols in the 'rich' sense of the term (as distinct from the mere synonym of 'signs'), when we consider the human capacity to symbolize, are of various kinds, linguistic and non-linguistic, arbitrary and natural. They allow the concentration in a brief compass, in one image or one metaphor, of complex cultural, moral and religious categories. A national flag carries all the feelings, the ideology, the loyalty, the sense of identity of its nationals. It can even carry all the opposites of such feelings, as when Palestinian protesters burn the American or the Israeli flag. A religious icon performs broadly the same function. But while these, as artefacts, remain mute, a form of words which can encompass all these rich nuances is of immense power. It can be transmitted over the generations, and contain within itself not merely the experience, but the memory of that experience, binding a social, political or religious group in an indissoluble fashion. Indeed it does not merely transmit the memory, but generates it anew for every subsequent participating generation. It need not be a narrative in the strictest sense of a story-line, but it will be narrative in that it carries various levels of meaning capable of verbal explication. A national anthem or song, or even just the music of it, such as strains of *The star-spangled banner* or *Land of hope and glory*, will evoke all the power of the flag, but will also allow a verbal articulation of all the concomitant feelings, and prompt the minds of its hearers to think of the great moments of national 'history', the causes of pride in being a member of the group.

The narration of a religious story, or just reference to chosen words within it, or the strains of a hymn tune, will perform a similar function in the religious dimension. What will be evoked is the whole complex of ideas and above all feelings which are part of membership of the group, which is expressed in most characteristically religious terms as being in a personal relationship not so much with the group, as with the deity, though the emphasis here may vary according to circumstances. This story, whether narrated in full, or merely evoked in stereotyped words, I call myth. The religious group may, just like the national community, think of the great moments of religious community history, the causes of pride in being a member of the group. So a real history, or an imagined history, may just as legitimately belong to this category as an entirely fictitious and symbolic tale. Within the context of memory and narration, there is no essential difference between story and history. Note that I am insisting here as much on the emotional as on the intellectual content of the story.

These observations allow us to identify some of the chief features of myth in its serious sense: it is ideology, and a vehicle for the communication and reinforcement of ideology. It will also contain concentrations of feeling, so hard to analyse in ancient texts, but of great vitality and power in the remembering, narrating and transmitting community. This point should enable us to deal with one of the conundra of contemporary scholarship, voiced in the assertion that 'Canaanite myth' gives way to emancipated forms of thought in the Hebrew experience. If we accept for the sake of argument that there is a discontinuity between the two cultural expressions (which I doubt myself, but that does not matter for the moment), we might claim, for instance, that whatever ideology lay behind the Ugaritic forms of the *Chaoskampf*, such as for example the seasonal interpretation so long championed by de Moor,[86] it has been discarded in the process of the appropriation of the narrative line by the Hebrew tradition. The matter of the appropriation is not in question; what is at issue is the ideological burden. Now according to my characterization of myth as vehicle for ideology, we would have to admit that so long as an ideological message was being communicated in the Hebrew versions of the narrative, then it too remains mythical in the formal sense, quite apart from being mythological in the psychological sense. And we have seen that not merely ideology, but the *same* ideology, is present. Nothing has changed!

So far as the problem of history is concerned, it will now be generally agreed that the 'history' told in the Hebrew Bible is, whatever else it may be, highly ideological in its intent. Even if we concede that it contains 'real history', its telling is ideologically motivated, indeed religiously motivated, and therefore, in conformity with the approach I am taking, is to be classified as myth. Myth and history are not opposing terms. They may to a greater or lesser degree overlap. They may even be synonymous. *Heilsgeschichte* is myth![87]

I see no weakening at all of the ancient power of mythological thinking, which I call 'the mythic mind', in any biblical treatment of earlier myths. This is one reason why I have preferred in this study to write of the 'mythic' rather than the 'mythopoeic' or 'mythopoetic' mind. These two latter terms inevitably carry a historical burden, which is in part the supposition that such thinking is primitive.[88] It is my contention that it is universal, and still an integral part of human thought and experience. Another reason why I have tended to this usage is because, as we have seen, formal definitions of myth are very difficult, in that it is hard to find one that will command general assent. Even my general definition, that it is 'narrative theology' or 'narrative ideology', leaves out of account an important aspect of the broader picture. This is that individual words or phrases from myth, mere allusions which have the power to evoke the whole story, are a ubiquitous feature of Hebrew literature.[89] The whole principle of intertextuality depends on the scholar's recognition that authorial and redactional minds are persistently, whether consciously or unconsciously, drawing on a common fund of tradition in their weaving of new variations on the theme. This is no less true, though in a more intuitive form, no doubt, for the devout reader who reads the text as Scripture.

Apocalyptic Now!

A literary form closely associated with mythological thought is apocalyptic, and so it is appropriate to conclude with some remarks which indicate the bearing of the mythological motifs to which I have drawn attention in this theme, which may also point the way forward to the way in which in Donald's terms narrative thought gave birth in turn to paradigmatic thought. It is worth noting, by way of an aside, that the *a fortiori* argument mentioned above for a mythic dimension to Israelite religion applies here as well. If it is increasingly accepted that apocalyptic literature was not merely some strange excrescence on the fringes of Jewish society, but belonged to the main stream,[90] and exercised the minds of the foremost literary thinkers of the period, then the undoubtedly mythological cast of their literary output reinforces a claim for biblical mythology.

The most characteristic feature of the mythic mind may be said to be its concern with the past, above all with the sacred time which Eliade called *illud tempus*.[91] I believe this to be an obvious function of the enormous importance of memory in the construction and maintenance of a world-view, the ideological foundations of culture. It is very evident in the terminology of orientation, as I have proposed in an earlier study.[92] The evidence adduced there may be supplemented by further examples,[93] so that we can see a clear and widely attested pattern. In the present context I need mention simply the Hebrew instances. The terms *qedem*, *'aḥar*, *s^em'ôl* and *yāmîn* represented respectively aspects of the body, face, back, left and right, and by extension the cardinal points east, west, north and south, on the supposition that 'orientation' was achieved by facing east, towards the rising sun. In addition, the former two terms, by a further extension of meaning, denoted temporal terminology, the past and the future respectively.

Thus in ritual positioning of the self, which always began with setting one's face to the east ('orientation' meant what it said), one looked, as it were, into the past, which was 'before the face' in memory. This provided the paradigms for dealing with the unseen and unknown future, which lay behind the subject. This ancient disposition, which was certainly very widespread if not universal in antiquity, may be seen as appropriate to the authoritative nature of the contents of the narrative mind. This was shaped, and its treatment of all new data and experience was in turn shaped, by the authoritative narrative of the past, the myth.

But religion was also vitally concerned with the future. In a sense it was a strategy for dealing with the future, for decision-making. With regard to this need, ritual techniques were developed to read the signs of the times, the flights of birds, the appearance of animal organs, the flow of the seasons. The practical needs of agriculture and industry required to be addressed, as well as the mechanisms of social control and the emotional sustenance of the community. One significant possibility in this field of experience was an adaptation of the narratives which constituted the paradigms for past and present into the future. Apocalyptic is the logical outcome of this need. The question of immediate crisis or sense of doom need not necessarily arise, but in times of extreme uncertainty, when great power succeeded great power, Persia, Greece, Rome, in the heartless and indifferent management of the Levant for their own economic and strategic benefit, when the ancient kingdom of Israel became a mere plaything of distant emperors, but all-too present armies, the narratives were adapted into tools for addressing the need. And as with all myth, it did not have to explain experience, and in fact systematically contradicted it, displacing the bleak prospect of further taxation and continuing repression with its heavenly journeys, many-headed dragons, miraculous births and heroes emerging from the sea, and the prospect of the final triumph of good. All old friends, all the familiar furniture of the mythic mind.

Postscript and Prescription

Much scholarship is devoted to the demolition of previous positions, all too often without any constructive alternative to the positions under attack. Let me in closing bring together the positive elements in the above discussion, in the hope that it will be of some use in further debate.

The problem with 'myth', we saw, was its ambiguity in common usage; the lie of the common man, it is the sacred word, the archetypal truth, of the phenomenologist of religion. There is no reason why we may not continue to use the term in its second sense, for it is a pity to abandon a useful concept because some prefer to misuse it. Within the disciplines devoted to the study of religion, it is treated with great suspicion by many biblical theologians, because they have tended historically to contrast it with 'history', and we have lived for 200 years in an intellectual climate of historicism, where only the historical is true. Hence the need to establish the historical truth (that is, facticity) of biblical narratives, of the Old and New Covenants, because to call them 'myth' was to impugn their truth. To assuage such fears, I see no problem in an alternative designation being preferred in theological circles, such as 'sacred tradition' (for text) or 'religious imagination' (as above, for mind-set). In my field, however, the History of Religions, the hallmark of the discipline is its refusal to make exclusive truth claims (all religions make them, after all), but to recognize the need for every tradition to hold that its sacred traditions are true. There is a relativity which should inform all our discourse about religions in the plural. We even see an interesting hybrid in some forms of reforming Hinduism which, influenced by the intellectual climate of the west during the British Raj, regard their traditions, which any western observer would classify as myth, as sober history. This is perhaps not dissimilar to the theological assertion that the truth of Judaism, or of Christianity, lies in their historicity.[94] My point is that history in the service of religion is in any case functioning as myth.

It is the need to classify in the first instance, to distinguish myth from history, myth from saga, legend, fairy-tale and any other sub-division beloved of the literary critic, which has led to all the mischief in the first place. B. Otzen's remarks (cited in n. 4) illustrate the difficulties into which the commentator can get in trying to have it both ways, when the matter of strict classification by genre gets in the way. A text is 'mythological', but it is not 'myth'! The flood story echoes virtually every detail of *Atraḫasis* and *Gilgamesh*, and yet somehow is not myth. What kind of useful distinction is really being made in such Jesuitical nit-picking? It can hardly claim to be an instance of clear thinking.

My solution is to cut the Gordian knot, to declare that myth is not a literary genre at all, but a mind-set. While this will sail too close to a Lévy-Bruhlian wind, or to a Bultmannesque one, which blows from another quarter, for some readers, it may be regarded as supported by the insights offered by M. Donald and S. Guthrie. While it represents an archaic element in the development of the human mind, it is in no sense prelogical or otherwise outmoded. Rather is it still emphatically present in all our minds today, as are many other levels of hominid mental development, an ancient substrate on which we draw at every turn, whenever meaning is at issue, or we become emotionally involved in the assessment of our human condition. Whenever we seek to give meaning to life and our experience, and even to 'history', the narrative of our common heritage, we engage in a mythological mode of thought. It is thus almost as broad as the category of religion itself, though it deals specifically with its mental disposition, rather than with the broader framework of behavioural and institutional forms into which religion may also be sub-divided. If this be judged a definition so broad as to evacuate the term of meaning, the same judgment would have to be applied to 'religion'!

Such a reorientation as I have proposed has the added advantage that it removes myth from the literary field altogether, except in so far as it may or may not be present in all literary forms, and no longer requires scholars to decide that a text is or is not myth, or is merely 'mythological' (a problem which evidently taxed B. Otzen). The 'merely' is no longer necessary, because there is no longer any basis for a fear that the label will somehow subvert the truth-value of the religious paradigm in question. No further need to declare that a biblical writer has demythologized the tradition, or that *we* must engage in a demythologizing exercise to present the religious core of a tradition to its believers. This was always a patronizing attitude, in any case. All religious thinking which tells stories (or histories) about 'reality', which narratizes experience in terms of an archetype or paradigm, which uses allusions to such narratives as symbolic short cuts in other contexts, as in cult, meditation or prayer, or even carries such forms across into political thinking, will constitute the activity of the mythic mind, or the mind in myth-mode. Furthermore, all academic analysis which attempts to demythologize will succeed in so doing only at the cost of an illegitimate reductionism.

Some will object to my approach on one of two accounts. The systematic theologian may simply dismiss this as muddled or, worse, as wishful thinking. I am simply not facing reality, and recognizing that ultimately there is only one truth. My response to this kind of argument is that it is precisely a form of mythic thinking, and a pure tautology, to say nothing of a circular argument. It belongs within a self-sustaining system of discourse. The other objection is more substantial. This is that I have departed from normal methodological principles, certainly as regards literary criticism. My response to this is that the thoroughly anarchical pass to which we had come, compounded by the binary division of our disciplines, as outlined by P. Davies, really leaves us with no alternative if we are not to continue the same sterile arguments. If we wish to continue using the term 'myth' to some useful purpose, it is as well to admit that much of the discussion of the last century has not really achieved very much.

Perhaps the alternative approach opened up by the serious advances of the last decade into the prehistory of the human mind will now allow us to advance to more mature forms of analysis.

Endnotes

* First published in *SJOT* 15 (2001): 3-56.

1. My thanks to David Reimer, who discussed a draft of this paper with me, to Laura Yoffe, who as always offered trenchant criticisms, and to Larry Hurtado, who has a gift for discerning wood through the trees. An early form of the paper was delivered to SOTS, University of Nottingham, 20 July 1998, and a revised version to the Edinburgh Biblical Studies Seminar on 25 January 1999. A number of adjustments and additions were consequently made.

2. Strenski 1987: 1-2. These views did not prevent Strenski from adding to the industrial output.

3. E.g. Dulles 1966; Gibbs and Stevenson 1975; Otzen, Gottlieb and Jeppesen 1980 (though B. Otzen's view is ambivalent: see n. 4); Oden 1981; Leach and Aycock 1983 (though this approach undoubtedly horrifies some biblical scholars!); Day 1985; Barker 1991: 178-81; Batto 1993; M.S. Smith 1994a; Epstein 1996; Wyatt 1996b.

4. See the final chapter by H. and H.A. Frankfort in Frankfort and Frankfort 1946; 1949, and the chapter by W.A. Irwin in the former. Note also Clapham 1976. See also Day 1985: 49, for the assertion that Genesis 1 has demythologized the *Chaoskampf*, though he accepted the survival of myth in other passages. Similarly Murray 1992: 11. B. Otzen (Otzen, Gottlieb and Jeppesen 1980: 28-39, extended to Genesis 2–3, p. 45!) also wished to consider Genesis 1 as demythologized: '...what happens to the mythical dimension when it has been accommodated in this system of dry, priestly erudition?' (p. 28). Is myth now a matter of *style*? On p. 39 he wrote 'we can again sense the efforts of the priestly craftsmen to suppress a mythological idea and thus prevent the hearers from wandering into paths of thought which, according to the priestly point of view, lay uncomfortably close to paganism'. On p. 45 he asserted that 'we do not have myths as such in this part of the Old Testament' (i.e. Genesis, and in particular the primaeval history); but immediately afterwards (p. 46) he observed that 'it should hardly surprise us that someone felt compelled to use myth in speaking of these important events'. He appears to have wanted it both ways. Later his judgments are vaguely couched, as though to keep both options open, for on p. 57 he regarded Genesis 4 and 6.1-4 as 'strongly marked with mythological characteristics'; the latter text is described on p. 58 as 'one of the most mythological texts in the Old Testament', and on the same page he wrote of 'the more or less mythologically coloured accounts of the opening chapters of Genesis'. To summarize Otzen's view, Genesis 1 is demythologized because (a) there is no personification of natural phenomena or creatures, (b) there is no deification of natural phenomena or creatures, (c) there is no conflict (but see his own analysis on p. 35!), and (d) it is quasi-conceptual. But this is all along accompanied by some very suspicious perceptions of the 'pagan' material (the term itself gives the game away, in terms of our two disciplines discussed below) and a complete misrepresentation, in my view, of the theology of both Ugaritian and Babylonian texts. Indeed, Otzen's ultimate criterion for his reservations on Genesis appears to have been his *a priori* conception (pp. 59-60) that myth must somehow or other be linked to ritual. It is all handled in a very unsatisfactory manner, but in many respects typifies much of the discussion we shall encounter. Note how the tone changes: H. Gottlieb (p. 69 in the same volume), on the other hand, referred quite naturally to 'the exodus myth'. In Wolff 1974a, the term 'myth' does not even feature in the index, in a book which purported to bring the insights of anthropology into Old Testament studies, but egregiously failed to do anything of the sort. 'Demythologizing', picked up from its comparatively useful employment in New Testament studies, has become a catchword for the thoughtless evacuation from Old Testament narrative of most of its most precious insights. Oden 1992b, 956-57, attributed the antipathy to myth in part to a negative response to D.F. Strauss' *Life of Jesus* (published 1835). This point was also made independently by B. Otzen (Otzen, Gottlieb and Jeppesen 1980: 2). It is a long time for such a hangover to persist!

5. In older studies it was taken more or less for granted that the Hebrew Bible offered a direct insight into historical Israelite religion. Some adjustments were necessary, of course, but by and large a 'history of Israelite religion' could be written, as

offered for example by Oesterley and Robinson 1930; Kraus 1966; Ringgren 1966; Rowley 1967; Fohrer 1973. This is generally no longer considered to be possible, though a further (sophisticated) example has recently appeared: Albertz 1992 and 1994. Such a programme has been in irreversible retreat for some time. But this does at least clear the way for a more realistic history, though it is likely to remain fragmentary.

6. Eilberg-Schwartz 1990: ix.

7. Epstein 1996: 352. He continued (p. 353): 'Liberal reformers and rationalist neoorthodox scholars alike believed that the essence of Judaism should be rational, not mythical or mystical. Most did not even acknowledge that such an entity as Jewish myth existed. Much like contemporary apologists for Christianity, they defensively contended that Judaism needed to cut itself free from the stultifying and the ridiculous fantasies that were embarrassingly present in rabbinic literature. This would require a return to the pristine Hebrew Scriptures, which were deemed to represent the triumph of rational monotheism over the fearful and etiological world of pagan myth...' Thus a common motivation appears to have lain behind the Jewish and Christian rejection of myth. It was part of the attempt to reconcile the belief-systems with the rationalist demands of the Enlightenment. Elements of E. Said's (Said 1978) and K. Whitelam's (Whitelam 1996) strictures also have a bearing on the broad issue of unacknowledged prejudice. I suppose post-modernism is at least to be credited with recognizing the need for deconstruction to be brought to the forefront of discussion. (The virulent *ad hominem* attacks on Whitelam since the publication of his book illustrate all too well the enormous power of the mythic mind even in today's seemingly rational academic community.)

8. Lest it be thought that the situation is merely a prejudice by persons of a particular theological persuasion, Kuper 1988 has identified a broader need among anthropologists to separate 'primitive' societies from modern ones. Part of the unwritten agenda behind such procedures was undoubtedly a desire to justify western colonial control of everywhere in the world beyond Europe. Cf. also the substantival use of the term 'savage' to denote other peoples, usually in a state of colonial dependency. This is the rhetoric of dominance! It is all part of the attitude criticized by Said 1978.

9. Mowinckel 1962. For a recent re-examination of Mowinckel's work see Petersen 1998.

10. Hooke 1933, 1935, 1958.

11. Pedersen 1926, 1940.

12. Kraus 1966: 15.

13. Widengren 1941.

14. Engnell 1943.

15. Both quotations from Kraus 1966: 16.

16. Kirk 1970: 7 remarks that 'there is no one definition of myth. Myths...differ enormously in their morphology and their social function.'

17. See Oden 1992a: 947-48. Eliade 1964: 5, has a similar view: 'Myth...tells how, through the deeds of supernatural beings...' Cf. the view of Spence 1921: 11, which allows *one* such actor: 'A myth is an account of the deeds of a god or supernatural being...' Contrast Kirk 1970: 9: 'The dogma that all myths are about gods can be easily disposed of...' In a penetrating study of Egyptian myth (where some similar prejudices as those discussed above may be found among some scholars), J. Baines himself offers a

minimal definition: 'myth...is a sacred or central narrative' (Baines 1991: 94). His title is revealing, for it recognizes the quasi-mythological nature of iconography, a point also made by Keel and Uehlinger 1992: 13-14 = 1998: 12-13; they acknowledge a debt to Assmann 1982: 13-61; 1983: 54-95. (The close link between visualizing and verbalizing will emerge in our further discussion.)

18. Gunkel 1901b (1964): 15. The section is headed 'Monotheism hostile to myths'. For an analysis of Gunkel's enormous influence on biblical scholarship see Rogerson 1974: 57-65, who noted (p. 59) Gunkel's inconsistency in this matter, since he called Genesis 2–3 myth. (1901a: 4ff.). He explained this (pp. 62-63) in terms of developments in Gunkel's thought not adequately documented in the successive editions of the commentary. He was working with two definitions of myth: (i) stories about gods, and (ii) stories about matters of universal concern.

19. Eissfeldt 1944 (reprinted in 1963: 496): 'For at least two deities, in principle distinguishable from one another, are required for myth, which speaks of the gods'. Cf. *idem* 1965a: 35: '...real myths are not to be found in the Old Testament, at least none which originated in Israel, but only some borrowed from elsewhere. This no doubt is connected with the henotheistic [*sic*: why not 'monotheistic'? henotheism at least concedes the existence of other gods!] nature of Israel's belief in God, which recognises as the really powerful and authoritative deity only the one, Israel's tribal and national God Yahweh. A real myth presupposes at least two gods, the one contesting with the other... For this reason, a real myth could not come into existence in Israel. What the Old Testament offers in the way of myths or allusions to myths has quite clearly come into Israel from outside and has been in large measure at least deprived of its really mythical character.' He goes on to assert that Genesis 1 has demythologized the *Chaoskampf* tradition, 'though in poetic passages like Ps. civ, 6-9; Job xxxviii, 10-11, it has retained clear traces of its original nature' (p. 36). A Zen response to Eissfeldt's remark on conflict might be that 'a myth is the sound of one god fighting'!

20. The point of the controversy raised by R. Bultmann's 1941 essay (see conveniently Bartsch 1972) was precisely that the New Testament was couched in mythological language, and inhabited a mythical world-view, which had to be translated for the modern reader, who allegedly would have no inkling of what the biblical writers were about. This shows just how far removed theologians can be from the real world of their contemporaries! I have met numerous devout people who implicitly accept all the mythological language of the New Testament at face value. (This tendency of the theologian to be seriously out of touch has unfortunately gone on apace.) The striking feature of this debate, however, contrasting strangely with the parallel debate among scholars in Old Testament Studies, was that the latter scholars insisted that the biblical authors had already demythologized. In order to get it all back in place for the New Testament? The scholars are clearly out of touch with each other! The essays in Hick 1977 represented a reassertion of the seriousness of myth in Christian thought, and recognized that the authors were making contentious claims.

21. See in particular G.E. Wright 1950 and 1952. I have touched on the problem of his view in Wyatt 1996b: 382-88.

22. J.B. Curtis showed convincingly that biblical thought, like that of the ancient Near East, was familiar with the concept of cyclical time (Curtis 1963). The Jews of the Hellenistic era were also evidently at home in the principle of the Great Year, widely

attested throughout the Near East and the Indo-Iranian region. On the other hand, apart from Albrektson's incisive observations (Albrektson 1967) it is also clear from Glassner's analysis that Mesopotamian thought was, from the early historical period at least, perfectly at ease with different concepts of time, cyclical and 'linear' (Glassner 1993: 25-26; *idem* 1996; *idem* 2001). (See now further Wyatt 2001a: 323-32.)

23. Von Rad 1962: I, 27. Brief reference may also be made to Westermann 1984. He noted that 'The event which is presented is freed from myth and is an event which concerns human beings and their world... The biblical genealogies describe the history of humankind only and so acquire an importance they could not have in the realm of myth. The uniqueness of what happened before history [*sic*!] or in the primeval period has moved away from the story of the gods to the story of human beings.' This is thus a reiteration of the old Grimm approach. It is difficult to determine why history gives to something an importance that myth cannot give it. Some might argue the contrary, that historical events are ultimately insignificant (as ephemeral, here today and gone tomorrow), while myth grants the event an eternal status. Cf. Church 1975: 39: 'history is one damn thing after another'.

24. Collingwood 1946: 14-18. The section is headed 'Theocratic history and myth'. He called both categories 'quasi-history', but also regarded myth as dealing exclusively with gods.

25. For a broader view, in my opinion altogether more productive, see Kirk 1970.

26. Enunciation of the problem is difficult because of the ambiguity of words like 'history'. Note the wide range of meanings offered in Gibbs and Stevenson 1975. By 'sober history' I mean the 'objective sequence of events' (as far as objectivity here is possible, though *our* subjectivity in apprehending them does not detract from *their* facticity). 'History' as written is best referred to as 'historiography'. It is at this point that subjectivity becomes inescapable. Of course even modern historiography, as pursued in universities, is subject to intellectual fashions and ideologies, as is only too clear from even a cursory study. Marxism, feminism, post-modernism are merely three such contemporary fashions. For a fascinating insight into Soviet 'historiography' (if the use and misuse of photographs in propaganda can be so called), see King 1997.

27. Cf. the typological analysis of Munz 1973, who argued that behind every myth there lies an event, transformed in the telling into a paradigm, and slowly redeveloped into a concept.

28. Some Christian theology offers a hostage to fortune in this respect. While other theologies may quite simply deal in a symbolic structure entirely at odds with phenomenal reality, Christianity is presented as claiming to take account of the real world, to engage with real history, and to transform and redeem them both. This is after all the implication of a theology of the incarnation. (It seems to me that idealistic alternatives betray this principle.) In this respect, Christian theology is obliged to accept the broad principles of historical study, which includes engaging with such problematic issues as the status of the resurrection ('historical fact'? 'myth'?). This is perhaps the *crux*, though for many such other matters as the historicity of events and persons in the Old Testament (e.g. the patriarchs, the exodus) are also troubling. This was the chief concern of the 'biblical theology movement'. The danger is in importing modern historical presuppositions into ancient texts (e.g. rules of evidence into the narrative of the resurrection) and then bringing back the 'proof' into the other field of discourse. But in

our terms, many ancient histories are myths. The real trouble is one of the sociology of knowledge, and the confrontation of conflicting views. On this see Berger and Luckmann 1967: 122-30. Professor Fred Berthold of Dartmouth College defined theology for me as 'the study of insoluble problems'! Perhaps in the final analysis the problem lies in religious claims to 'truth'. If truth is defined in historical terms (see discussion below), then anything non-historical is untrue. But it seems to me that the whole quest of cognitive truth in religious beliefs, though it is particularly common in Christian theology, is misguided. Such a position would force one into the position of rejecting the truths of one tradition because they conflict with those of another. This is not a productive line in academic procedure, whatever theologians want to do with it. For a useful discussion of the issues see Lindbeck 1984: 63-69.

29. The situation is not dissimilar to the issue treated in Albrektson 1967. He demonstrated that biblical commentators were wrong in attributing a historical consciousness solely to Israel. Having shown that it was quite widespread in the ancient world, he then asked just what it was that was distinctive in biblical thought. If the biblical writers did indeed use myths, the question to ask is what was distinctive in their use.

30. As distinct from 'Bible Study' or Theology. A distinction is also to be made between History of Religions (*Religionsgeschichte*) as used fairly narrowly in the context of biblical studies (Hahn 1956: 83-118), and referred to, for example, in Bultmann's essay New Testament and mythology (Bartsch 1972: 14) and the more neutral application of Eliade 1959. My usage is in the latter sense.

31. Canaanite religion and Ugaritian religion are not simply to be equated. For bibliography on the literature distinguishing 'Ugarit' from 'Canaan' see de Moor 1997: 42, n. 5. Of course the confusion is convenient for those who wish to use the 'Canaanite' label, with deuteronomic overtones, to belabour all non-Israelite manifestations of religion. Cf. my comments, Wyatt 1999a: 529-31.

32. A nice example of the matter is provided by Xella 1996a, Zatelli 1998, where Eblaite antecedents to the scapegoat rites of Leviticus 16 are published. It seems that an Ugaritian antecedent is also found in KTU 1.127. On the nature of the two disciplines and the uneasy relationship between them see Davies 1995: 17-55.

33. Cf. W.H. Mills' waspish observation (Mills 1842: II, 9): 'The word *mythus* is a milder as well as a less definite term than delusion or imposture; and though the assertions are perfectly equivalent, it shocks less to be told that Christianity stands on the same footing of mental truth with heathen fables, than to be told, as by the sceptics of a former age, that it is based on falsehood like them'. The kind of prejudice to which Mills here drew attention is the one couched in rather different arguments among biblical scholars, as outlined above. (I do not believe that myth – or any other religious formulation or expression – has any cognitive content, so that the issue of 'truth', which so troubles many, is an irrelevance. This is not to say that such beliefs are false either. The terminology is simply inappropriate.)

34. A number of comparisons may be made between the two disciplines in terms of data and procedures. In both cases the raw data (bones, tools or text) come with no certain context, and only the vaguest 'historical' setting. In both cases the scholar is trying to evoke a complex mental world from extremely sparse data, though the biblical scholar has a head start in that the texts provide a linguistic record. In both cases there is a great deal, relatively speaking, of associated and comparative material, and the

crucial matter is to estimate degrees of 'debt' and independence between any two pieces of evidence. In both cases the overall context is extremely elusive and fluid, and massive paradigm shifts, to say nothing of massive heat in the ongoing debates, characterize the two.

35. Donald 1991: 121, complained that 'the successive cultures of hominid evolution have been reconstructed by archeologists and anthropologists on the best available evidence and constitute an important set of theory and data that has been largely ignored by psychology, presumably because it is not experimental in nature and is therefore seen as speculative'. The same problem besets any historical discipline, because history cannot be repeated or re-experienced. But the History of Religions ought at any rate to be open to revision of previous positions in the light of further evidence. This happens in Theology, too, of course, as any study of the history of Theology will show. But it seems to me that the need to preserve the foundations of commitment ('to keep faith') impedes real freedom of enquiry.

36. In this discussion, every step of the journey is fraught with difficulties, and is likely to be in need of constant revision. A recent cogent account of the origins of symbolizing capacity is found in Deacon 1997: 376-410. He indicated the sheer difficulty which must have obtained at the very beginning, in so far as a symbolic system of communication would not work until there was a sufficient pool of both symbols and symbolically proficient hominids (this is where it begins) for it to function. Symbolic capacity was a strategy achieved at a price. As to location, he placed it within the context of developing reproductive strategies, which in the human context (though not exclusively there!) involve not merely the communication of information between both males and females, and within each gender group, but also the communication of disinformation in the dynamics of courtship and bonding. From this narrow base it would very rapidly broaden out into all social, political and above all ritual spheres of life.

Deacon proposed that it was the use of meat which was a particularly important trigger of symbolic behaviour. Although he did not cite him, this would be entirely in accordance with the theory of Knight 1987: 1991 about blood-symbolism and the correlation between bleeding meat and bleeding women being taboo, and cooked meat and non-menstrual women being accessible. Burkert 1983 has shown the centrality of killing to religious ritual, and it is noteworthy in our present context that meat-production and the sacrificial cult as the primary means of its distribution is the most characteristic feature of ancient near eastern religion, including Israelite religion. Deacon noted the relationship between the long development of hominid tool-making, undoubtedly linked to the increasing use of meat, and the attendant social structuring (long period of child-rearing, advantages in such conditions of strategies for sexual fidelity between bonded pairs) and saw here the genesis of symbolizing, finding its most concentrated form in ritual.

37. Donald 1991: 233, insisted that the capacity to symbolize has already begun independently of the genesis of language (speech).

38. Donald 1991: 35: 'Once some form of verbal communication was in place, a circular interaction between that system and the capacity for thought led to the development of an ability for longer and longer (and presumably more complex) trains of thought and their integral support system, speech'.

39. Donald 1991: 124-26.

40. Donald 1991: 160.

41. Donald's approach is a cumulative process, and rather more sophisticated than the 'successive stage' approaches of some anthropological writing. Cf. Krzak 1993.

42. P. Connerton (Connerton 1989) wrote of 'social memory', which is collective and public, to be distinguished from individual and private memory. He located the former above all in ritual behaviour, seeing in myth an altogether more fluid and dynamic phenomenon; 'it constitutes something more like a reservoir of meanings, which is available for possible use again in other structures' (p. 56). The reapplicability of myth is particularly clear in the Hebrew Bible, where the three types to be discussed below appear to be used in a number of different contexts, and for different immediate purposes. Their fundamental symbolic meaning, however, appears to have remained fairly constant. Another distinction of Connerton is germane to our discussion. On pp. 13-14 he distinguished between the collective enterprise mentioned above and the individual, critical work of the historian, who questions all his evidence. But the ancient historian (e.g. the biblical historian) is in no sense working according to such a scheme. He is more akin to the Assyrian royal analyst, who on the king's behalf lays a historical testimony before Aššur narrating his deeds (in the first person: the king is speaking), as an act of piety. The biblical 'historians' certainly write a critique of events, but it was conceived within a theological and even mythical framework. The 'reservoir of meanings' provided by myth determines the overall shaping of the historiography.

43. Donald 1991: 168.

44. Donald 1991: 173.

45. Eliade 1964.

46. Berger and Luckmann 1971; see also Berger 1973.

47. Divine principles such as Hebrew *ḥokmâ*, 'wisdom', Egyptian *maʿat* ('justice, truth') or Sanskrit *Vāc* ('speech', daughter of Prajāpati the creator-god) express similar conceptions. Conceptual abstractions, as we might call them, appear as goddesses or at least divine hypostases.

48. Donald 1991: 272, citing Bruner 1986. For the latter, the terms 'analytic' and 'logico-scientific' are also suggested. There is a certain irony in the use of the term 'paradigmatic', because in so far as it denotes modern analytical tendencies in thought, its persistent drive may be said to be to break paradigms (as outlined by Kuhn 1970). In practice, of course, something of the mystery-of-the-guild mentality characterizes even scientific communities, and old paradigms take much hard work to overthrow.

49. Dennett 1992 has enlarged on this phenomenon: the growth and the increasing complexity of cultures has been in direct proportion to their development of external memory-systems, which allow the vastly enlarged stores of knowledge necessary for the management of modern industry, medicine, law and government to function effectively. The clay tablet, papyrus and parchment have given way to the printed page and the computer disc. The growth in the power of this process of externalization is exponential.

50. Lévy-Bruhl 1910. See critique in Rogerson 1978: 46-65. Rogerson concedes (p. 65) that much remains to be done in the analysis of mentality.

51. While not 'pre-logical', there is a case to answer that mythological thinking is pre-conscious, though as 'tradition', myth could continue to be productive even in late

periods, as in the rich developments of Hellenistic, early Judaeo-Christian, and Purāṇic thought. On the lateness of consciousness as a factor in human experience see Jaynes 1976. On the pre-analytical aspect of mythic thought, which he treats as a different mode of consciousness, see Lonergan 1957: 542-43: 'Mythic consciousness is the absence of self-knowledge, and myth is a consequence of mythic consciousness as metaphysics is a corollary of self-knowledge. Myth, then, and metaphysics, are opposites. For myth recedes and metaphysics advances in the measure that the counter-positions are rejected, that the attempt to understand things as related to us gives way to the effort to understand them as related to one another, that effective criteria become available for determining the occurrence and the adequacy of understanding. As myth and metaphysics are opposed, so also are they related dialectically. For myth is the product of an untutored desire to understand and formulate the nature of things.'

52. Guthrie 1993: 9: 'Since experience depends on interpretation, it cannot be prior to beliefs and concepts, but is generated partly from them. Schleiermacher and others cannot claim simultaneously that religious emotions are simple, immediate, or unconditioned by belief and that they constitute an experience.'

53. Guthrie 1993: 9, 31, 37; see Proudfoot 1985: 192.

54. Horton 1960: 211, cited by Guthrie 1993: 33. Cf. also Mithen 1996: 164-67, where the author offers a theory on the origins of anthropomorphism and totemism in the Upper Palaeolithic.

55. See Guthrie 1993: 34-36.

56. This in turn lends some new basis for Durkheim's view that in worshipping gods, society essentially worships itself (that is, reifies and authenticates its ontological status).

57. Davies 1995.

58. Perhaps one of the most striking examples of seeing what you think ought to be there is the interpretation of the Aten cult at the time of Amenhotpe IV (Akhhenaten) as monotheistic. That is certainly one possible interpretation, but is scarcely the most probable. It led J. Assmann (Assmann 1972, 1982), followed by J.C. de Moor (de Moor 1990: 42-100), to postulate a 'crisis of polytheism' which allegedly crippled the polytheistic theologies of the Near East in the Late Bronze.

59. Cf. Wyatt 1997: 791-93. What is actually done is that the biblical material is forced into the strait-jacket of contemporary dogmatism. But this is the danger of all commentary carried on for theological motives, and it is that motivation that sells books.

60. Cf. Spengler 1926: 380: 'even atheistic science has religion; modern mechanics exactly reproduces the contemplativeness of faith'. This is an absurd position, based as so often on a half-truth, in this case the fact that the human mind obviously rationalizes and cogitates about any experience within a certain framework, because this is the way the human mind works. To pretend that the scientist is bound by dogma, however, is preposterous, even if this was once the case, as when Galileo fell foul of the Inquisition for failing to conform. There is of course inertia in science, so that a considerable effort may be required to effect a paradigm-shift. See Kuhn 1970. It is also possible that science may be controlled by ideology, as with Soviet psychiatry. But this is a perversion, not the real thing.

61. Keita and Kittles 1997.

62. Since it is so pervasive, we may legitimately ask whether racism is not to be examined in a quasi-biological way. It would stem from the absolute need to preserve the group, thus regarding all outsiders as a potential threat. It is a common feature of ancient cultures and languages that their word for 'man' denoted themselves. Other 'men' were usually denoted by other (non-human) terminology. They might even be assimilated to demons, as with the Sanskrit wordplay on *dāsu*, *dasyu*, for the non-Aryan population of the Punjab. The terms probably denoted originally 'village-dwellers' (i.e. the settled population of the region), but over time came to have the sense of 'demons'. Hebrew thought is by no means immune to this mode of thought. Cf. the almost demonological value of the traditional list of other nations to be dispossessed by Israel, in an early form of ethnic cleansing.

63. Cf. John Carlin's excoriating attack on American (USA) culture in *The Independent on Sunday* (10 May 1998): '...everything is political calculation and ideological abstraction and in so far as the hundreds of thousands who perished in Central America have registered in the national consciousness at all it is in the same way that foreign bad guys do, "communists" and people who look like Arabs, in Arnold Schwarzenegger movies. Or, in the immortal words of the chief US military adviser in El Salvador in 1984 when challenged about a particularly grisly killing carried out by his local charges, "after all, they're only little brown men".' See also Wyatt 1996b: 125.

64. Berger and Luckmann 1967: 141, prefer not to see Christianity in the mediaeval world as ideology, because everybody shared the belief-system. Following the industrial revolution, however, it came to be a bourgeois ideology, over against alternatives developing among the proletariat. I am not clear as to why universal or partial adherence to a world-view in a society determines its ideological status. I am evidently using the term rather more broadly.

65. I suppose that we consciously avoid religious ideology, but may well be caught up in other pervasive currents of thought.

66. Cf. Kraus above, and see also Frankfort 1951.

67. Cf. A. Lang's observation (Lang 1887: I, 22-23): 'All interpretations of myth have been formed in accordance with the ideas prevalent in the time of the interpreters. The early Greek physicists thought that mythopoeic men had been physicists. Aristotle hints that they were (like himself) political philosophers. Neo-platonists sought in the myths for Neo-Platonism; most Christians (like Eusebius) either sided with Euhemerus, or found in myth the inventions of devils, or a tarnished and distorted memory of the biblical revelation.' Myth is like every other human concept in that its precise form has always varied, and been debated, from age to age. It is no worse than any other. In Wyatt 1996b I defined myth as 'narrative theology', but took into account the views expressed in Gibbs and Stevenson 1975 and Tobin 1989.

68. The expression was used by M. Noth (Noth 1928), a paper discussed by Rogerson 1974: 147-48. In so far as the process (if it ever happened) is a naïve development, it hardly contributes to the formation of a real history, but only of a tendentious historiography.

69. The release of government archives, usually after periods of 50 years or so, frequently reveals facts which popular conceptions of a nation's history have conveniently forgotten. Many national 'histories', such as the growth of a free society in the United States, the heroic resistance of wartime France, the provision of a land without a people

for a people without a land in Israel, the uniformly civilizing and enlightened policies of British imperialism, remain serious myths in the societies in question (in the ideological sense) in spite of untimely revelations to the contrary.

70. Wyatt 1996b: 117-218; 1998a.

71. Wyatt 1998a: 872-73. A striking feature of the Eurasian cultural zone is the persistence of a mythic tradition that is arguably from *one* original source (traced back thus far to the Amorite myth of Tishpak in Eshnunna). Cf. also Chapter 12.

72. Or an angel: Michael in Revelation 12.7-9. Michael also serves in Christian iconography as the latter-day transformation of a deity: the mediaeval motif of the weighing of souls or sins (as at Autun, Bourges, Chartres, Santo Domingo de Silos, Torcello etc.) may be traced back to the role of Thoth at the weighing of the heart in the Egyptian Book of the Dead. Thoth was identified by the Greeks with Hermes, he in turn with Mercury and Lug, and ancient shrines of Lug became Christian sanctuaries dedicated to St Michael. This is a western parallel to the East Mediterranean development of Khidr and St George out of Baal.

73. See Heil 1981; Madden 1997; Aus 1998: 51-133. While the Jesus narratives are consciously modelled on the narratives concerning Moses, the old *Chaoskampf* tradition still shines through, and the disciples' question on the nature of the one who commands the wind and the sea in Mark 4.41b presupposes a divine, not a human, antecedent.

74. On the widespread use of rites of unction see Fleming 1998.

75. Wyatt 1994a; 1994b; 1995a; 1996b: 219-82. (Cf. Wyatt 1990f for discussion of Genesis 34, related to KTU 1.24.)

76. See Porter 1978 (KTU 1.23 and Genesis 19.30-38), Ginsberg 1936 and Astour 1967: 86-87 (KTU 1.12 and Genesis 16).

77. Cf. Wyatt 1976; 2002a: 162.

78. See Wyatt 1987.

79. Page 1996.

80. This too is developed independently in the late literature, as the type of the prophetic ascent. See Himmelfarb 1993.

81. Translation from Wyatt 2002a: 132-33.

82. Cf. Margalit 1989: 473-75.

83. Cf. Day 1994. He draws a number of parallels between Ugaritic and biblical material, such as the nature and abode of El, the number of his sons, aspects of Athirat associated with Asherah, echoes of Baal's dying and rising in Hosea, of the *Chaoskampf* and the cosmic significance of Saphon, titles of Baal, mention and evident familiarity in the Hebrew Bible (and consequently the antecedent historical Israel) with other members of the Ugaritic pantheon. At the same time he notes a number of differences (e.g. no child-sacrifice at Ugarit) and some issues on which certainty is elusive (e.g. the matter of cult-prostitution). His conclusion, though couched in cautious terms, is that 'there was considerable continuity between the Canaanite mythology and religion at Ugarit and that presupposed by the Bible'.

84. The claim can only be made by a religious community which seeks to isolate itself from neighbours. Labels such as 'Canaanite', 'Amorite' etc. serve such an excluding function in biblical narrative. If we as modern scholars bring in religious values (i.e. prejudices) to determine the answer to this question, we have left dispassionate scholarship behind.

85. Guthrie 1993: 13.

86. See de Moor 1971; 1987.

87. Cf. Grabbe 1998: 15: '...myth is not just an interpretation of history but it also served *to shape* history...' (his emphasis).

88. Oden 1992a: 951, 954.

89. See Wyatt 1996b: 405-406, where I draw attention to the usefulness of Tobin's category of 'mythotheology'. (See also Tobin 1989: xii [introduction by Bonnel] and 61.) My only quarrel with the author would be his incautious separation of Egyptian thought from logical thought. What is at issue is rather conscious and deliberative, or unconscious and intuitive thought.

90. Käsemann 1960, cited and discussed in Koch 1972: 14.

91. Eliade 1958: 378; 1964: 75-91; 1974, *passim*. For analysis see Rennie 1996: 77-87.

92. Chapter 9. Here I have listed just the Ugaritic and Hebrew vocabulary.

93. See Wyatt 2001a: 33-52. Here I have added Akkadian, Arabic, Greek, Latin, Sumerian, Egyptian and Sanskrit terminology, which entirely corroborate the findings from Ugaritic and Hebrew.

94. This point was well-criticized by T.L. Thompson (Thompson 1974: 326-30).

Chapter 12

‘Water, water everywhere...’: Musings on the Aqueous Myths of the Near East*

Water, water everywhere,
Nor any drop to drink.
Samuel Taylor Coleridge

And sense the solving emptiness
that lies just under all we do.
Philip Larkin

1. *Introduction*

Scholars who work in some of the disciplines which make up the field of Near Eastern studies are generally inclined to emphasize the distinctive nature of its various parts, rather than to discern and discuss the broad similarities which may link ideas across cultural boundaries. This is an admirable stance, especially as the disciplines emerge as independent subjects of study. Autonomy is not only an academic desideratum, but is seen as a cultural and historical virtue. But this tendency is paralleled by a similar tendency to isolationism between different disciplines which might benefit from cross-fertilization.

Those who are afraid to make mistakes will usually contribute little to the sum of human knowledge. They will play safe, never stepping out of line from the current view, never challenging the paradigm. Many volumes are published each year in which all that has been achieved is a slight rearrangement of the pieces on the board. Consensus is the order of the day. Real contributions are commonly made by those who are prepared to take the risk, and not only to challenge the consensus and rattle the bars of the paradigm-cage, but also to speculate and ask new questions about an old problem, and even identify new ones.

For we have come of age, as a new millennium dawns! There is no reason to fear the similar, or to argue that the barriers that have been half-consciously erected must be manned at all costs, to preserve the integrity of the disciplines. It is increasingly difficult to see them as anything more than conveniences, useful up to a point, but able to be called into question when larger patterns can be discerned. Patterns, and 'patternism', are the bane of some scholars. Certainly, if used in an uncritical way, glossing over significant differences, and over-emphasizing as fundamental those similarities which are to be judged rather as superficial, claims to see broader connections between apparently quite distinct phenomena are to be treated with the utmost caution. But caution is not to be confused with narrow-mindedness.[1] The fact remains that the human mind works by the detection in or imposition on all it experiences of patterns of recognition, seeking to incorporate the new and unknown into the framework of previous experience.[2]

In this paper I shall present a survey of comparative points generally conceded, or at least recognized as viable options among a range of possibilities, and assess the case for the recognition of specific events in prehistory as the cause of the composition of some of the most widespread mythic themes of Eurasia. I must first acknowledge that much of the ground-work has been done by others, and part of the exercise is drawing attention to work that may have escaped the attention of colleagues. But on top of the debt which will immediately be obvious to my readers, I believe that there is now reason to erect the superstructure which I shall propose, for which I do not claim all the credit. At least it should serve as a topic for further discussion.

2. *The Nomenclature of the Ocean*

The cosmic sea, imagined as encircling the world, is known by a number of names in the ancient world. The following list, giving some of the most typical, contains some of which the etymology is either self-evident, or past reconstruction, while others have given rise to interesting speculations, ancient and modern, and others have taken on more restricted meanings.

	Sumerian[3]	*Akkadian*[3]	*Ugaritic*	*Hebrew*	*Greek*
Sea	AB, A.AB.BA	*aiabba, iamu,*[4] *marratu*[5]	*yammu*	*yām* (*sûp*)	θαλασσα
Dragon		*mušḫuššu*	*litanu*[6]	*l*^{e}*wiyātān*	(Λαδων)
River			*naharu*	*nahar*	Αχερων Ληθη Στυξ[7]
Water				*māyîm*	
Lion, Monster		*labbu*		*rāhāb*[8]	

sweet water	AB.ZU[9]	*apsû*	*apsu*	(*'epes*)	'Αβυσσος
Salt water	*tâmtu,* *têmtu,* *ti'amat*[10]		*tihamatu*	*t^ehôm*	
Varia				*Giḥôn*	'Ωκεανος[11]

Table 1. *Terms for Cosmic Waters*

	Waters above	*Waters around*	*Waters below*
Sumerian	AB.ZU	AB.ZU	AB.ZU
Akkadian	*apsû*[12]	*marratu, tâmtu, têmtu*	*tâmtu, têmtu, ti'amat*
Ugaritic	*thmt*[13]	*tihamu*[14]	*thmt*
Hebrew	*hammāyîm 'ašer mêʿal lārāqîaʿ*	*yām sûp*	*t^ehôm, hammāyîm 'ašer mittaḥat lārāqîaʿ*
Greek		'Ωκεanoς	'Ωγενια
Egyptian	*Nwt*	*wg-wr*	*Nw(n)*

Table 2. *Location of the Waters, Where Specified*

The general features of this vocabulary may be relegated to the footnotes and later discussion. What perhaps deserves mention here is the draconian aspect which is sometimes apparent in the Near Eastern material. The *mušḫuššu* appearing in the third millennium texts from Eshnunna, and overcome by Tishpak, appears to have been a dragon of extravagant length; the *labbu* also encountered in a number of texts, which I have suggested may also be lurking in an Ugaritic passage,[15] even rears its ugly head(s) in *Ahiqar* 34. As **labbu tâmti* was 'the lion of the deep', so the serpent appearing in *Gilgamesh* 11.313, which stole the plant of rejuvenation from the hero, was called *labbu irṣiti*, 'lion of the earth (or, underworld)'. A number of Mesopotamian artifacts portray serpentine figures with seven heads being attacked by deities:[16] these may plausibly be interpreted as representations of the various *Chaoskampf* stories in which Tishpak, Adad, Baal, Ashur, Enlil or Marduk fought the powers of chaos. I have dealt with the *Chaoskampf* motif at length,[17] and need not repeat the discussion here, beyond noting its wide variations, and the extreme longevity of the tradition, which in literary terms spans the period from the mid-third millennium BCE to the fifteenth century CE (the *Golden Legend*). The length of its preliterate, and thus prehistoric, transmission, is an unknown quantity. We shall revert below to various matters touched on here.

An early attempt at explanation of the Greek term 'Ωκεανος was offered by Bérard.[18] He cited the Semitic forms *ḥwq*, *ḥyq*, 'hollow, breast, bay' and *hyn*, 'riches, means of sustenance', and postulated the compound **ḥwq-hwn*, vocalized as *ḥok-ewan*. He took this, in his view the direct source of ʾΩκεανος, to be a translation of *Kolpos Ploutonios, Sinus Lucrinus*, that is, the Gulf of Lucre, which he identified as the original 'ocean'. This bay lies to the north of Pozzuoli, near Naples, and was the location of the traditional entry into the Underworld described in *Aeneid* 6.236-42. It is the very specificity of this explanation, anchoring the form to a location on the west coast of Italy, which creates problems for Bérard's explanation, as he himself conceded. He responded to this by pointing out that Ocean came to mean the Atlantic, and that the Moroccan Atlantic coast was known to the Greeks as *Kolpos Emporikos*, which had the same sense as the Neapolitan toponym, and, furthermore, had Phoenician trading posts.[19] Thus the western location of the name reflects an eastern cultural source, namely the Phoenicians. The western location, however, makes it an improbable genuine etymology for the term, and weakens rather than strengthens Bérard's case, though it would conceivably have developed as a folk-etymology after the fact in polyglot seafaring circles.

D. Neiman offered an interesting discussion in which he identified the Hebrew term *Gîḥôn* as the source of the Greek *Okeanos*.[20] His argument, in a nutshell, ran as follows. He suggested that the names of the last two rivers of Paradise in Genesis 2.10-14, the Pishon and the Gihon, were to be explained on the basis of a serpentine imagery. Pishon (*pîšôn*) he linked with the Hebrew form *peten*, 'serpent',[21] a term to which we shall return. He related the Gihon (*gîḥôn*) to Hebrew *gāḥôn*, 'the belly of a serpent'. At Genesis 3.14, where Yahweh-Elohim curses the serpent, he says *ʿal gᵉḥōnᵉkā tēlēk*, 'On your belly you shall crawl'.[22] Neiman's reasoning ran thus: the name of the cosmic ocean which surrounds the world is, in Greek, ʾΩκεανος. The *Odyssey* speaks (1.22-23) of the Ethiopians who dwell in a far-off land in the south, on the shore of this ocean. (The name of Abyssinia – 'Land of the Abyss', ʾΑβυσσ[ος] + ινια – confirms the symbolism of the end of the world which Abyssinia had for the Greeks.)[23] The parallel with Genesis 2.13, 'this surrounds the entire land of Cush', is striking.

Neiman suggested that the name *Giḥôn* may have been the source of the Greek name *Okeanos*. He argued that if *Giḥôn* were heard by the early Greeks and represented graphically as they heard it, it would appear approximately as γηαν. 'The *Giḥôn* would appear as ΟΓΗΑΝ (ὁ γηαν, with article) and later as ΟΚΕΑΝ (which does not carry an article).

He envisaged the following phonological sequence, somewhat telescoped: ὁ γηαν > ὀκεαν > ʾΩκεανος.[24] He then observed that

> the name ʾΩγενια is the *epiklesis* of Styx, a universal stream in Greek mythology that corresponds in nature to *Okeanos*. *Ogenia* is the other-worldly counterpart to *Okeanos*.[25]

But since Neiman's explanation, in intra-Hebrew etymological terms, actually explains the form by reference to *gāḥôn*, 'the belly of a serpent', the formal link (apart from assonance) between the two Hebrew terms remains unexplained as well, unless it be conceded that *Gîḥôn* and *gāḥôn* are in fact etymologically identical.

In fact there is probably no connection between them, beyond the convenient phonetic similarity, and the fact that a serpentine link makes excellent sense in terms of the broad conceptualization of the cosmic sea as serpentine in nature. The form *Gîḥôn*, however, requires an etymology independently of *gāḥôn*, since the vowel-shift is not readily explicable on intra-Hebrew terms, except as a clever play on words, which however has no etymological validity, and is itself perhaps to be explained as derived from some other form.

The etymology commonly proposed for *Gîḥôn*, √ *gyḥ*, *gwḥ*, given by BDB (161b) and *HALOT* (I, 189ab), which has the sense 'burst forth', 'gush' (thus *Gîḥôn* meaning 'the Gusher'), is an adequate explanation of the term without recourse to an anterior source. Whatever its origin, we may of course have a lexeme which contributed, by way of popular rather than scientific etymology, to the developing mythological form of the referent of the name, since in Job 38.8 this verb is used in the description of the birth of the sea at creation (a suitably cosmogonic context):

wayyāśep bidl ātayim yām	(Who) confined Sea behind the double doors
b^e^gîḥô mēreḥem yēṣē'	when he burst forth[26] from the womb?

Here we may imagine the primaeval amniotic waters of the chaotic womb of all being burst forth as the universe comes to birth. It is an interesting parallel in Semitic mythology to the origins of various creator-deities in Egypt, such as Amun, Atum, Ptah and Thoth, who are variously described as emerging from Nu (himself, with his pair Nut, a scarcely defined androgyne) or as being identical with him.

In his treatment of the philological problem, Neiman made no reference to the spring flowing beneath Jerusalem, also called Gihon ('Gusher'), confining himself to the cosmic sea bounding the world, and flowing round the Land of Cush (Genesis 2.13). But the two must surely be related, and any explanation of the name must take into account the significance of the stream and its name in both contexts, at the centre of the world, and at its end. Such a link is made the more inescapable once the identity of the Garden of Eden with Jerusalem, or a part of it, is conceded.[27] Were this not the location, the name of this particular river would remain unexplained, unless it be taken as a later popular etymology superimposed on the older real one. The cosmic waters, surrounding the end of the world ('the well at the world's end') were ritually tapped and harnessed to human needs at the life-giving city-spring, which provided Jerusalem's water-supply. It was in turn replicated for ritual purposes in the great bronze sea in the Jerusalem temple, which had its counterparts elsewhere, such as that at Hierapolis.[28] So far as the Gihon is concerned, in terms of purely historical probability, it seems more likely that a local stream would, in assuming cosmic significance as the life-giving waters of an important royal shrine, have lent its name in an extended sense to the cosmic ocean, than that the reverse should have happened. Perhaps the residual problem with this explanation is the lack of attestation so far of other West Semitic cognates.

West noted the Aramaic terms *'ôgānâ*, 'basin' and *'ôgen*, 'rim', as 'the least implausible etymology'[29] for ᾿Ωκεανος. This would fit the temple basins of Hierapolis (Lucian, *De Dea Syria* 13) and Jerusalem (1 Kings 7.23-26), which replicated the ocean, and the 'four rims' which surrounded the earth in a number of Mesopotamian royal inscriptions.[30] The expression 'the four parts (of the world)' (or 'four quarters...', 'four rims...' or 'the universe', according to translator), is the formula *kibrāt arba'im*, variant *kibrāt erbettim*. The term *kibru* (singular of *kibrāt*[*u*]) means a bank of a river, or the shore of the sea. So the four rims seem to have represented the cardinal points,[31] and the sense is of the furthest limits of the world, bounded by the ocean (*Apsû*). On this explanation, then, we have the macrocosmic application of the technical name of the microcosmic cult-vessel.

M. Astour also offered an intriguing alternative etymology for ᾿Ωκεανος. According to him it was an adaptation to Greek form of Sumerian A.KI.AN.A(K),[32] 'the water of heaven and earth'. This form would make an excellent alternative to Neiman's account in the explanation of *Gîḥôn*, though the final element AK remains unaccounted for. Unfortunately, in a gracious reply to a recent enquiry, Astour wrote the following to me:

> My good friend and former graduate student, Prof. David Owen, has a good memory. I made, in passing, a remark about the possible Sumerian derivation of Okeanos in class, some time between 1963 and 1965, but I gave it no further thought after I checked the evidence and found that the sequence *ki-an* never occurs; it is only *an-ki*.[33]

Noegel also mentioned Egyptian *wg3*, meaning 'a type of water or flood', and cited M. Bernal.[34] Bernal in turn also linked Og, Ogygos and Ogygia with the Semitic √ʿ*wg*, 'to draw a circle'.

It is evident from this survey that a number of possibilities, some perhaps stronger than others, are available as explanations. But as so often in such cases, any or all of them may have been local midrashic treatments of altogether older, and more opaque terminology.

3. *Conceptions of the Ocean*

Mesopotamian sources give a number of pieces of information concerning the cosmic sea. The vocabulary given above provides the main evidence. There was a dualistic view, of the cosmic waters consisting of two opposed yet complementary principles, the fresh water above, *apsû*, a masculine term, and personified as the primordial father-god Apsû; and the salt water below, *tāmtum, temtum*, personified as the goddess Ti'amat. The androgynous nature found so commonly among Egyptian and Syrian creator-gods does not seem to have been present in Mesopotamian thought, where these two primordial principles appear to have been coeval. There may be a hint of their common origin in *Enuma Elish* 1.5, where the waters of the two were mingled, presumably before differentiation into two bodies. But whether this represented a primordial unity, or just a primordial coitus, remains unclear. Be that as it may, the physical, spatial relationship of the two appears to be the paradigm for the *hieros gamos*, which produced generations of *Urgötter*, as described in the sequel.

A remarkable document from the first millennium is the Babylonian world map (BM 92687).[35] The map, which is now rather damaged, consists of two concentric circles scored with compasses on a clay tablet. The inner circle is bisected by two lines, defining the River Euphrates. This is in turn bridged by a rectangle above the centre denoting Babylon, and further lines below demarcating a swamp, a channel, and Susa. Various other geographical features are marked in a ring just inside the inner circle. The two circles mark the inner and outer confines of ^{id}*mar-ra-tum*, the salt sea, that is, the ocean, namely the Persian Gulf. This was probably imagined to be contiguous with the 'Upper Sea', the eastern Mediterranean reached nearly two millennia earlier by Sargon of Akkad. Beyond it lie a number of triangular shapes called *na-gu-ú*, 'regions'. Five are indicated, but the bottom of the tablet having broken away, and the surviving text alluding to 'the eighth region' (rev. l. 24), it is a reasonable supposition to conclude that eight were originally shown. It appears from the text that these regions served as convenient locations for various rare things heard of in Babylonia, but not actually encountered. The ring-shaped form of the salt sea almost evokes the idea of a river, so that the image of Okeanos, the cosmic river (distinguished by West from the salt sea, above n. 11) is explicable. But its label *marratum*[36] on the map, meaning 'bitter', emphasizes that if there were two different conceptions, as West argued for Greek thought, and is suggested by the designation *apsû-ti'amat* in Mesopotamia, the convenient distinction could probably be maintained concurrently with their recognition as *one* body of water. That is, the kind of exclusive logic we tend to apply today ('it cannot be this and that at the same time') was not applicable.

Ugaritic material is sparse, when compared to the more voluminous material in neighbouring regions. There are three main elements. Firstly, we have a description of El's dwelling-place at the world centre:

idk ly/ttn pnm ʿm il	Then (various deities set their) face indeed towards El
mbk nhrm	at the source of the rivers,
qrb apq thmtm	amidst the springs of the two deeps.[37]

The number of rivers may be variously computed, the actual form *nhrm* being indeterminate. It may be read as a plural, indicating four rivers flowing from the centre of the world, as in Genesis 2.10-14.[38] Alternatively, it may be read as dual (thus many translators), thus balancing the two deeps (*thmtm* is dual) of the following colon, providing a strict synthetic parallelism, the same two bodies of water (cf. *apsû* and *tāmtum*) being now riverine, now oceanic. It may even, conceivably, be singular with enclitic, the two deeps of the following colon being the common sources of the one riverine ocean.

An interesting feature emerges from this allusion, which goes on to describe the questing deities' arrival at El's cosmic tent, which is evidently located at the centre of the world. For in KTU 1.1 iii 21-22 the arrival at El's tent is preceded by this account of a journey:

idk	Then
yt [n pnm]	he (Kothar) set [his face]
[ʿm ltpn] il dpid	[towards the Wise], the perceptive god,[39]
tk hrš [n]	towards (his) moun[tain],
[ǵr ks[40]*]*	[Mount Throne].[41]

As I have argued previously, this double anticipation of the arrival at El's tent requires that the two locations, the junction of the Deeps and the throne mountain, be identified.[42] It sounds very like the tradition preserved in Ezekiel 28.2. Some discussion by Wensinck[43] is also germane to our understanding of the cosmology involved here. For he noted that the concept of the omphalos was not confined to an earthly, territorial centre, but could be located elsewhere. He drew attention to *Qur'ān* Sura 11.9, where

God's throne was upon the waters at the time of creation, and showed how Muslim speculation saw this as anticipating the 'navel of the earth' and thus constituting a 'navel of the ocean'. That this was not merely a late invention was shown, he argued, by *Odyssey* 1.52, where in mentioning Ogygia, Homer called it ὀμφαλὸς...θαλασσης, 'the navel of the sea'. This would also be a fine description of Tyre! The oceanic waters also came together in the heavens, where a further omphalos could be found, called 'the navel of heaven'.[44] But these were not in reality three navels, an oxymoron, but one reality, perceived in different idioms, as though all three orders of reality merged at the ontological centre. It is reasonable to see the same kind of thinking, or perhaps *intuition*, in Late Bronze Ugarit.

The second piece of Ugaritian evidence is provided by the whole cosmological presupposition of the Baal cycle of texts, KTU 1.1-2, in which the water-god, Yam-Nahar, appears to have represented the cosmic ocean, now perhaps as its controller (he is enthroned as king of the gods at KTU 1.1 iv 9-29), at other times as its personification, even divided into constituent powers, KTU 1.3 iii 38-46, or embodied in the primordial dragon, Litanu (Leviathan), in KTU 1.5 i 1-3. Even if the various personages listed in these passages have a kind of independence, they are ultimately all aspects of the power of the sea.

The third piece of Ugaritic evidence is the setting of KTU 1.23, now at the cult-centre, where the king and queen were apparently present at the rites (l. 7), now at the end of the world, on the shore of the ocean (*gp thm*),[45] where El performed the *hieros gamos* with his daughter-wives (l. 30). Given the similarity of vocabulary which is evident from the present discussion, and the readiness of one area to provide at least echoes of the conceptions of other regions, it is fair to say that the Ugaritian conception of the world was very similar to that obtaining elsewhere, and particularly to both Israel[46] and Greece. We shall meet other features of Ugaritian thought as we continue with further discussion.

The Israelite view of the cosmic ocean is best illustrated by the use of the expression *yam-sûp*, occurring a number of times in biblical literature,[47] and particularly during the exodus narrative. LXX translated the formula 19 times by ἐρυθρα θαλασσα or with the same words in reverse order.[48] This expression is naturally to be translated as 'the Red Sea', but this usage proves nothing either on the historical or the geographical plane, except the fact that at the time of the translation of the LXX, the translators believed that in these 19 cases it was this sea that *yam-sûp* denoted.

Two passages in LXX are of relevance to a consideration of the cosmological use of the term *yam-sûp*. In 1 Kings 9.26, the text is certainly dealing with the Red Sea, since the narrative speaks of Solomon's fleet which was based at Ezion-Geber in the Gulf of Aqaba. The Hebrew reads *yam-sûp*, but LXX reads της ̓εσχατης θαλασσης, that is, 'the Last Sea'. This suggests that the sea in question was understood to be at the end of the world. It is still probable that the translators had the Red Sea in mind, but by using this form of words they were alluding to its cosmological rather than purely geographical nature.

In Psalm 106.9 (LXX 105.9), MT reads thus:

> *wayyigʿar b^{e}yam-sûp wayyeḥ^{e}rāb*
> *wayyôlîkēm batt^{e}hōmôt kammidbār*
> And he rebuked *Yam-Sûp* and it dried up,
> and he brought them out of [49] the depths as (though from) the desert.

Arguing that this texts betrays redundant elements, I have proposed that the following *Vorlage*[50] can be reconstructed:

yam-sûp yeḥ^{e}rāb	*Yam-Sûp* he smote, (or: *yaḥ^{a}rîb*: 'he dried up')
wayyôlîkēm batt^{e}hōmôt	and he brought them out of the depths.
	Psalm 106.9 (LXX 105.9) putative *Vorlage*

In this reconstructed original text we see even more clearly the close parallel between *yam-sûp* and *t^{e}hōmôt*. This parallel imposes an exegetical condition. The two words being complementary, *yam-sûp* evidently signifies the same reality as *t^{e}hōmôt*, that is, the sea at the end of the world. LXX translated *t^{e}hōmôt* by ̓εν ἀβυσσω, thus corroborating my interpretation.

The same parallel is found, for instance, in Exodus 15.4-5:

mark^{e} bōt parʿô w^{e} ḥêlô	The chariotry of Pharaoh and his army
yārâ bayyām	he cast into the sea,
ûmib ḥar šālîšāyw	and the choicest of his charioteers
Tubbeʿû b^{e}yam-sûp	were submerged in the Sea of Extinction.
t^{e} hōmōt y^{e}kasyumû	The deeps covered them:
yār^{e}dû bim^{e} ṣôlōt k^{e}mô-ʾāben	they went down into the depths like a stone.

Snaith observed of this passage that

> in verse 5 with its references to the Deeps and the depths we have passed into the realm of the great Creation-myth, that story of the fight against the monster of Chaos which is interwoven with the story of God's rescue of the people from bondage in Egypt and in Babylon... The word *t^{e}hôm* does not refer to the depths of any natural sea...[51]

But to what does *yam-sûp* refer? The key word is *sûp*. The identification with the Red Sea (thus LXX and modern versions) is secondary, and it has nothing to do with the idea of redness. The broad consensus nowadays is that it is to be explained with reference to the Egyptian word *ṯwfy*, 'reed'.

Thus the common translation as 'the Reed Sea' or 'the Sea of Reeds'. The word *ṯwfy* is attested as a loanword in Hebrew, as witnessed by Isaiah 19.6, where the reed-beds of the Delta are in Hebrew *qāneh wāsûp*. Similarly with the reeds of the river bank in Exodus 2.3. This etymology is all the more seductive for the reader of Exodus because it lends a gloss of historicity and geographical reality to the event. But we must begin with philology rather than with putative history. It may well be history, but that is another problem. Besides, a sea of reeds can hardly be harmonized with the Red Sea.

Montgomery suggested that the root of the word is rather *swp* 'to come to an end' (verb *sûp*, substantive *sôp*), so that the sense of *yam-sûp* is 'the last sea' (*ultimum mare*), the ocean at the end of the world.[52] He was followed in this by Snaith, Batto, and myself.[53] I have taken it in the metaphorical sense of an allusion to death, whence my translation 'the sea of extinction'.[54] Snaith preferred to read it as the substantive form (*sôp*)[55] while others retained the verbal form *sûp*, since the infinitive can also have a substantival use. This cosmological ocean could well be identified by various writers as the Red Sea (as for example at 1 Kings 9.26) or even as the Mediterranean Sea (Jonah 2.5), for these seas bounded the known world. Beyond them there was no more world.[56] Or rather, there *was* a 'beyond', but it was the world of the dead. This was the view of the Mesopotamian evidence, where Gilgamesh, for example, spoke with Utnapishtim on the far side of the sea.

I proposed[57] that the reason the narrative of the exodus spoke of *yam-sûp* was as follows: for the Hebrew mind Egypt signified death. It was a country of funerary monuments of stupendous dimensions. Whatever may be the historical status of a sojourn in Egypt, for the pentateuchal tradition it was rather a symbol of the exile, signifying the death of a people. One always 'goes down' to Egypt, a curious expression if it is to be understood in a neutral, geographical sense. It is found with no other crossing of frontiers. The expression *yārad b^emiṣrayim* recalls the formula *yārad bā'āreṣ*, 'to go down into the earth', and was arguably intended to evoke it.

Greek allusions to the world-surrounding ocean are evidently from the same conceptual background as the Mesopotamian material, perhaps with an admixture of Egyptian and West Semitic thought. The derivation of the technical terms from Akkadian or Sumerian (below) is further evidence of a close cultural relationship with the first region.

Let us now pursue another line of enquiry. The Hebrew term *'epes* (cognate with Ugaritic *aps*), meaning 'end', or 'extremity', as in *'apsê 'ereṣ*, 'the ends of the earth',[58] has been linked etymologically with Akkadian *apsû*, Sumerian AB.ZU, by Pope[59] and Reymond.[60] *HALOT* cites these references as possible explanations for *'epes*.[61] Let us examine the usage to see whether it provides any firm evidence in support.

The Ugaritic term appears once in KTU 1.6 i (59-) 61 in the account of Athtar's enthronement:

pʿnh ltmǵyn hdm	His feet did not reach the footstool;
rišh lymǵy apsh	his head did not come to its top.[62]

This gives us no immediate clue as to the cosmological burden of the term, till we recognize that this is confidently to be seen as an allusion to the same image that occurs in Isaiah 66.1:

haššāmayîm kis'î	The heavens are my throne
w^{e}hā'āreṣ h^{a}dōm raglāy	and the *'ereṣ* is my footstool.

Here the throne of the deity served as the *axis mundi*, penetrating on a vertical axis the underworld beneath and the firmament above.[63] The latter, in biblical as well as in Ugaritian cosmology, was the abode of supra-firmamental waters corresponding to the Akkadian conception of the *apsû* (Sumerian AB.ZU) and 'mystically present', as it were, in the very form *haššāmayîm*. Thus the upper limit to which Athtar's head does not reach, is in distinction from Baal's head, the aqueous location of which is so graphically described below. So while we may concede that the lexical meaning of Ugaritic *aps* (probably vocalized *apsu*, like the Akkadian *apsû*) quite possibly does mean no more than 'end', its actual usage clearly preserves the overtones of its source, retaining a cosmological nuance. The top of the throne touches the *apsû*.

The remarkable passage in KTU 1.101.5-8,[64] a hymn to Baal as cosmic ruler, confirms our analysis:

rišh tply	His head is magnificent,
ṯly bn ʿnh	His brow is dew-drenched.
uzrʿt tmll išdh	his feet are eloquent in (his) wrath.
qrn[*h*] [*rm*]*tʿlh*	[His] horn is [exal]ted;
rišh bglṯ bšm[*m*]	his head is in the snows in heaven,
[*ʿm*] *il ṯr*	[with] the god there is abounding water.[65]

As I interpret this, Baal's head as it were bursts through the firmament, he acting, in what is almost his identification with the mountain (cf. descriptions of Yahweh as *ṣûr*), as a divine *axis mundi*.[66]

The Hebrew term is similarly used. A particularly instructive expression is Isaiah 41.17:

kol-haggôyim kᵉ'ayin negdô	All the nations are as nothing before him;
mê'epes wātôhû neḥšᵉbû-lô	as far as he is concerned they are (as) utter waste.

The expression *mê'epes wātôhû* is surely pregnant with resonances. The initial *mê* is best explained not as the Hebrew preposition *mᵉ*, 'from', but possibly as analogous to the Egyptian *m* of predication, but even more probably, as the noun *māyîm* in construct form. *mê'epes* would then be taken to mean something such as 'the waters of the end (of the earth)'.[67] While *'epes* and *tôhû* have standard meanings in Hebrew, the latter term undoubtedly carried for the poet echoes of *tᵉhôm*, 'abyss',[68] which in turn invites the recognition of the cosmological overtones of *'epes*. We may even conjecture that *'ayin*, 'nothing', has been selected because it evokes the phonetically similar *ʿayin*, 'spring, well'. It is perhaps going too far to say that these are here the primary meanings, but the poet surely evokes nonentity less in abstract, conceptual terms as in spatial terms: reality is that which is contained within the bounds of the universe, and all is bounded by water. If we wished to be perhaps a little over-bold, we might even offer the following as grasping at the meaning implied:

*kol-haggôyim *kᵉʿayin negdô*	All the nations are as well-water before him;
**mê 'epes *wātᵉhôm neḥšᵉbû-lô*	as far as he is concerned they are the upper and lower seas.

Here the expression 'the upper and lower seas' would more literally, on this hypothesis, be rendered 'the waters of the end (of the earth) (or of the *apsû*) and the deep', and imply that people are reducible to their original raw material, the primaeval waters. We may compare the view of West, who, speaking in the Hesiodic context, compared the primordial pair Oceanos and Tethis with the Babylonian Apsu-Ti'amat, who 'were originally united, the chthonic water and the brine, and their children were created inside them'.[69]

It seems that *'epes* does indeed invite a cosmological sense, and this I consider confirmed in the passages discussed.

A consideration of the significance of *'epes* also invites us to look at *Iliad* 18.399, *Odyssey* 20.65, and *Theogony* 776, where we read of ἀψορροος Ὠκεανος, supposedly meaning something like 'back-flowing Ocean'. LSJ offered 'back-flowing, refluent', explaining the term as 'a stream *encircling* the earth and *flowing back* into itself' (my emphasis); Evelyn-White observed that 'Oceanus is here regarded as a continuous stream enclosing the earth and the seas, and so as flowing back upon himself'.[70] Unless this is supposed to mean flowing round continuously, as water swirling round in a bowl, a kind of whirl-pool *cum* river, it can only be described as devoid of sense. At the very least the commentator is having some difficulty in expressing himself unambiguously. But our consideration of Semitic terminology suggests a much better possibility. I propose that we recognize in the first element ἀψος a Hellenized form of Akkadian *apsû*, Ugaritic *aps* (= *apsu*), which in the compound form ἀψορροος, to be understood with a sense such as 'flowing *apsû*', is a conscious borrowing which then became glossed with the explanatory Ὠκεανος, which simply attempted to provide a Greek equivalent, subsequently understood on a pseudo-etymological basis. It thus means, in a redundant fashion, 'the sea-flowing ocean'.[71]

A number of Greek authors had interesting things to say about the Ocean. While of course they were writing with a Greek readership in mind, it is increasingly recognized that many of their ideas stretched back into a pre-Greek (or at least pre-Hellenic) antiquity, and Semitic antecedents are often cited for many of these ideas.[72]

Hesiod, just cited alongside Homer, also made further reference to the Ocean.

> At the ends of the earth... along the shore of deep and tumultuous Ocean...
> (*Works and Days* 168-71)

The first part of this (ἐς πειρατα γαιης) is a remarkable echo of the Hebrew term *'apsê 'ereṣ* discussed above, and perhaps has a bearing on its particular application in cosmological terms.

The Homeric Hymns followed in the same tradition:

> By the streams of Ocean, at the end of the earth (ἐπι πειρατα γαιης)
> (*Hymn to Aphrodite* 227)

and

> Over Ocean's stream and the furthest bounds of Earth (και πειρατα γαιης)
> (*The Cypria* 8)[73]

Herodotus also made a number of interesting observations. He was at pains to pass on information he picked up during his travels, frequently giving a number of opinions on a topic. He stated, for instance (*Histories* 2.21),[74] as the second of three opinions, the extraordinary view, which he himself rejected, that

> It [the Nile] flows from the Ocean, which flows all round the world.[75]

A little later (*Histories* 2.23) he went on to aver that

> I know no river of Ocean, and I suppose that Homer or some other poet invented the name and brought it into his poetry.

Toponyms are frequently obstinate pieces of information that are not inventions, contrary to Herodotus' view, but preserve otherwise lost records of ancient habitation and past ethnic presences. Writing later on Greek cosmology, he stated (*Histories* 4.8) that

> as for the Ocean, the Greeks say that it flows from the sun's rising round the whole world, but they cannot prove that this is so...

And he referred (*Histories* 4.36) to ill-informed cartographers who

> draw the world as round as if fashioned by compasses, encircled by the river of Ocean, and Asia and Europe of a big likeness.

This last allusion to an exactly drawn circle reads almost like a commentary on the Babylonian cosmic map discussed above. Dating from no earlier than the ninth century, and possibly the late period, it was perhaps drawn at no great distance in time from Herodotus himself.

Herodotus' scepticism was in any event untimely. The Babylonian map may be the ultimate inspiration, not only of those Greek maps he scorned, but of a host of early maps right down into the Mediaeval period, including the earliest printed map, the so-called 'TO map' (from its circular design, with rivers shown as a 'T'). Other shapes, notably rectangles and mandorlas, also occur in later cartography.[76]

Another passage in Herodotus (*Histories* 3.23) is also remarkable in view of our general enquiry, and perhaps offers a clue to one of the more general problems I am addressing, concerning the relationship of the centre and the end of the world with regard to the waters of life. The occasion was the embassy of Cambyses to the Ethiopians. The fish-eaters, who acted as the king's mediators, asked the latter about their great longevity. The Ethiopian spokesman then stated that most of his compatriots lived to

> 120 years, and some to even more; their food was roast meat and their drink milk. The spies showed wonder at the tale of years; whereon he led them, it is said, to a spring, by washing wherein they grew sleeker, as though it were of oil; and it smelt as it were of violets. So frail (ἀσθενες), the spies said, was this water, that nothing could float on it, neither wood nor anything lighter than wood, but all sank to the bottom. If this water be truly such as they say, it is likely that their constant use of it makes the people long-lived.

Pindar, in *Pythian Odes* 4.251, made an interesting allusion to Ocean, describing it thus:

ἐν τ' ᾿Ωκεανου πελαγεσσι μιγεν	And they reached the streams of Ocean
ποντω τ'ερυθρῳ	and the Red Sea.[77]

Here we see the identification of the cosmic sea with the Red Sea which is apparent at times in biblical usage.

The Greek references as a whole are of interest, for they echo biblical idiom (that is, the two literary contexts betray familiarity with the same tradition).

4. *The Denizens of the Ocean*

The terms used for the primordial sea, noted above, when treated mythologically, vary considerably in ancient literature. Thus we find the Akkadian forms *ti'amat, têmtum,* and *tâmtum,* corresponding to Hebrew *t^ehôm*. Ugaritic *yammu,* corresponding to Hebrew *yām,* and *naharu,* corresponding to *nahar,* are frequently used in parallel. Akkadian also used *mušḫuššu,* and rather strangely, at first glance, *labbu,* as we noted above. The Sumerian AB.ZU became in turn Akkadian *apsû,* Ugaritic *aps* (vocalized *apsu*), Greek *'Αβυσσος* and Hebrew *'epes,* where in the last instance the meaning has shifted to 'extremity, furthest part'.

The use of the Akkadian term *labbu* ('lion') to denote 'sea-monster' in some contexts prompts the question whether under the guise of various biblical lions, referred to by various terms, there do not lurk similar allusions to sea-monsters, dragons, and other serpentine denizens of chaos.

I believe that a case can be made for two passages, though they are disguised by the use of terms other than *l^ebî,* such as *'aryê, šaḥal* or *k^epîr* for 'lion'. Let us consider, for instance, the following curious bicolon in Deuteronomy 33.22:

Dān gûr 'aryê	Dan, the whelp of a lion
y^ezannēq min-habbāšān	springs forth from Bashan.

This verse has already been noted by Noegel.[78] The second word in MT, *gûr,* 'whelp', is sometimes emended to *gar,* 'dwells' (*BHS* app.). The same phrase is also used of Judah in Genesis 49.9. There is no need for any change to MT, though we may suspect that the imagery associated with *l^ebî* (cognate with *labbu*) has been transferred to the present use of *'aryê*.[79] The reasons for this proposal are as follows. Firstly we may note the allusion to Bashan, which we find to have serpentine connections. Secondly, the term *zānaq* in the second colon, in the Piel form, has in NH an aqueous sense, 'cause to spring, spurt' (BDB 276). It may of course be used in a metaphorical sense of a lion leaping, but equally possibly, it suggests that an aqueous aspect should be recognized in the 'lion'. Perhaps the sense 'sea-monster' is not too far-fetched. This conjecture is strengthened if we recall that Dan was one of the tribes associated with the movements of the Sea Peoples, and its maritime past was well-known to biblical tradition, as narrated in Judges 5.17, where Dan remained with its ships, while Asher remained in its maritime ports.[80] Thirdly, Dan is actually called a 'serpent' (*nāhāš* || *šᵉpîpôn*) in Genesis 49.17.

The link with Bashan is curious, if the term be accorded its usual geographic sense, since Dan is linked with the sea (above) and also with the Shephelah (its original settlement, bordering the sea) and the northern Galilee (to which it migrated). Does Bashan perhaps retain here its older serpentine sense as discerned by del Olmo?[81] Let me suggest the following translation for our bicolon, which now gains an inner consistency, previously lacking:

Dān gûr 'aryê	Dan, the whelp of a sea-monster
yᵉzannēq min-habbāšān	springs forth from the Serpent.

This now interprets Dan's origin as *ab initio*, a typical claim for an autochthonous people, which is particularly justified by Dan's evident pre-Israelite origin. In the case of Judah (since we must obviously give a convincing explanation for both passages, though the one has arguably borrowed the figure from the other) it may have the same autochthonous implication, which is odd only if we forget that it was the northern tribes which developed the early exodus and settlement tradition. An alternative original sense for the Dan allusion might arguably be the invasions of the Sea Peoples. In this case, its adoption by Judah would suggest an alternative, perhaps an autochthonous, understanding.

The other passage which deserves further consideration is Psalm 91.13. This is undoubtedly a royal psalm, addressed to the king, who 'is enthroned in the hidden place of Elyon, and dwells in the shadow of Shaddai' (v. 1), an allusion to his enthronement in the sanctuary. Even in the thick of battle, as his hosts fall around him in their thousands, their ten thousands (v. 7), he will remain inviolate. The promise of angelic protection in vv. 11-12 was given a messianic gloss (or rather, its royal application was recognized) in its application in Matthew 4.6 and Luke 4.10-11. So when we encounter v. 13, also, incidentally, recognized as messianic (see previous comment) in Luke 10.19, we may reasonably have our suspicions of its ideological content. The verse reads as follows:

ʿal šaḥal wᵉpeten tidrōk	On lion and serpent you shall walk;
tirmōs kᵉpîr wᵉtannîn	you shall trample lion-cub and dragon.

Once the royal dimension is recognized in this psalm, it is evident that the present verse belongs in the context of the ideological application to the king of the *Chaoskampf* motif.[82] The future triumph of the king over cosmic monsters (*alias* the enemy), and his anticipated trampling on their cadavers, is guaranteed by his possession of the divine weapons given him at his enthronement.[83] The lion here parallels the serpent, because it too echoes the old imagery of *labbu* as a maritime beast. In each colon, the terms 'lion and serpent' || 'lion-cub and dragon' are a hendiadys, naming the Chaos-monster in binomial fashion.

5. *Heroes of the Flood*

The earliest named hero was probably the Sumerian Ziusudra (Xisuthros, Sisuthrus, 'Life of lengthened days'),[84] who attracted the sobriquets Utnapishtim ('He saw life') and Atrahasis ('Supremely wise'), as the tale circulated in Akkadian versions. The tradition appears to be slightly ambivalent about whether or not he was a king.[85] Thus in the Sumerian flood tradition he was a king of Shuruppak,[86] but two views of him appear to have prevailed in the Akkadian tradition, though his royal function appears to be predominant.[87] The narratives concerning Atrahasis and Utnapishtim never identify the hero as a king, in Davila's estimate.[88] In view of the emphasis on the hero's wisdom, alluded to in his sobriquet, this is perhaps surprising, since wisdom was so often a particular quality of kings, and indeed a necessary gift. And in view of this reticence in the texts, it is perhaps ironic (that is, an irony on the part of the writer) that Utnapishtim should narrate his experience to a king, Gilgamesh.

But there is one passage in *Gilgamesh* which may in fact suppose that Utnapishtim was a king, for the hero tells of the divine instruction given him by Ea:

> Man of Shuruppak, son of Ubara-Tutu,
> dismantle your house; build a boat.
>
> (*Gilgamesh* 11.23-24)

The expression 'man of TN' (LU, *awîlu* TN) can, like its West Semitic equivalent '*mt* (*mētu*) TN', may have the nuance 'ruler of TN',[89] and while it may not be conclusive, is at least susceptible of a royal sense, perhaps reinforced in the present context by the patronymic reference. It appears to be a deliberate allusion to the older tradition, and to its ideology. Nor need such a passing allusion occasion any puzzlement. When myths are narratives,[90] they naturally live and function in a context of familiarity with a tradition, and may explicitly state common knowledge, or just as well presuppose it without making direct reference. So the lack of explicit reference to a theme does not necessarily mean that the theme is absent.

Noah, hero of the biblical flood, is the subject of two traditions. Quite independent of the flood-story, evidently indebted ultimately to the

Mesopotamian tradition, which circulated widely in the Near East,[91] there is a story of Noah as culture hero, and as the discoverer of the benefits of the vine (Genesis 9.20-27). It is on account of this narrative that he received the name Noah, meaning 'Consolation' (Genesis 5.29).

Noah is nowhere said to be a king, and nor are any of his ancestors, though commentators have often drawn attention to similarities in the antediluvian king-lists and that of the patriarchs (e.g. Enoch and Enmeduranki). But one important element in the story suggests that he at least had an aura of royalty. It is *as though* he were a king. This element is contained in his ritual functions, firstly offering sacrifice on emerging from the ark (a feature shared with other flood heroes, and a priestly function often performed by kings, and particularly on portentous occasions), and more strikingly, his making of a covenant with the deity in Genesis 9.1-17.[92] This is written against the background of Genesis 1; Noah is thus presented as a primal man, like Adam before him, initiating a new human history. While treaties in the ancient world obviously addressed the concerns of whole societies, they were invariably made between kings. So as the recipient of this covenantal overture from Elohim, Noah cannot have had any lesser status. We may compare this episode with the Horeb-Sinai covenant in Exodus 19–24, 32–34, where Moses is never once called a king, and yet is so represented in a number of obvious ways, such as his horns (a sign of divinity), his speaking directly to the deity, without intermediaries, his 'royal' ascent, and his return with documents from the deity which have been compared with the tablets of destiny.[93] Only some of these features are present with Noah, yet the occasion is explicitly a covenant (vv. 9, 11, 12, 13, 15, 16, 17: seven times!). Abydenus, incidentally, cited by Eusebius in his account of flood stories (*Praeparatio Evangelica* 9.11-12), also states that Xisuthros (that is, Ziusudra) ruled as a king, among a series of unnamed monarchs.

Deucalion[94] (in Apollodorus, *The Library*, 1.7.2), variously the son of Prometheus or Minos, is said to have been a king of Phthia in Thessaly; and he also was renowned (Lucian, *De Dea Syria*, 12-13) for wisdom and piety. Ovid's treatments of Deucalion and Cerambus (*Metamorphoses* 1.177-189, 262-415; 7.353-56) tell us nothing of their status. These late versions of the tradition have largely lost their ideological content, and so we should not expect any particularly perceptive treatment.

6. *The Problem of Og King of Bashan, Last of the Rephaim*

Noegel wrote an interesting study, already cited,[95] concerning Ogygos, a legendary king of Thebes in Boeotia, and his possible connections with Og, king of Bashan. Ogygos was the hero of a flood narrative, the survivor of a cataclysm, who subsequently founded the city of Thebes. According to Fontenrose, he was the flood itself, a king of the Titans, subsequently banished by Zeus to Tartessus (this reads almost as an allegory of the formation of the Atlantic Ocean, kept beyond the bounds of the known world); he was also a doublet of Ophion, indicating his serpentine and oceanic nature.[96] The Thebans would thus have seen their city as founded by an antediluvian hero, at once royal and divine.

It is the possibility of links between Ogygos and Og that is particularly tantalizing.[97] I shall not repeat here all of Noegel's points, but pursue other materials which may have something to offer to the discussion.

Since the first discoveries were made at Tell Ras Shamra, ancient Ugarit, scholars have drawn attention to similarities between features of the literature from Ugarit and the Hebrew Bible. Not least among the connections sought or asserted are a number of geographical allusions. Some of the connections made have not stood up well to continuing scrutiny.[98] Others have remained remarkably persistent, however, and are worthy of further discussion.

Perhaps the most intriguing passages for our present discussion concern the region of the Hauran, which includes the Golan plateau south west of Damascus, referred to in the Bible as Bashan.[99] This area is persistently linked with the mysterious figure of Og, who with Sihon represented enemy kings overcome by Joshua in his *Blitzkrieg* assault on Palestine.

The passages from the Bible which are of interest are the following: Og is not mentioned in Genesis 14.5, but we read there of Chedorlaomer and his allies conquering, among others, the Rephaim in Ashteroth-Qarnaim. In Numbers 21.33 Moses and his party are met by Og, king of Bashan,[100] joining battle at Edrei; in Numbers 32.33, presumably following an Israelite victory, the conquered territory is distributed among various tribes. The victory is mentioned in Deuteronomy 1.4, where Og is said to have lived or reigned (√*yšb*) in Ashtaroth and Edrei. The battle and its aftermath are also treated in 3.1-13, while 4.47 outlines the territory of Og's erstwhile kingdom:

> And they took possession of [Sihon's] territory and of the territory of Og king of Bashan, the two kings of the Amorites from east of the Jordan, from Aroer on the edge of the Wadi Arnon to Sirion,[101] that is, Hermon.

Various passages in Joshua mention Og's (and Sihon's) defeat without comment as a precursor of the conquest to come; 12.4-5, however, give another broad summary, stating for the first time Og's own membership of the group of the Rephaim:

And the frontier of (the territory of) Og king of Bashan, the last of the Rephaim, who reigned in Ashtaroth and Edrei, who ruled from Mount Hermon and Salecah and all Bashan to the frontier of the Geshurites and the Maacathites...

Some poetic texts mention the Rephaim in passing, and deserve a brief mention. In Isaiah 14, a taunt against the Assyrian or Babylonian king, the Rephaim are envisaged in v. 9 rising from their thrones in the underworld to greet and mock the newcomer into their midst. In 26.14 and 19 their continued, but impotent, presence in the underworld is accepted.

Job 26.5 is particularly interesting, since it links the Rephaim with water:

hār^{e}pā'îm y^{e}ḥôlelû mittaḥat	The Rephaim below trembled,
mayim w^{e}šōknêhem	the waters and their denizens.

This is highly allusive. But what precisely does it mean? Why should the Rephaim be specifically linked with waters, and why, evidently, the subterranean waters? The answer to this question lies in the information to be gleaned from Psalm 68.15-16, 23 (EV 14-15, 22).

b^{e}porēś šadday m^{e}lākîm bâh
tašlēg b^{e}ṣalmôn
har-'^{e}lōhîm har bāšān
har gabnunnîm har bāšān
...
'āmar '^{a}dōnāy
mibbāšān 'āšîb
'āšîb mimm^{e}ṣṣ ulôt yām

When Shaddai stretched out[102] kings upon it,
snow fell on Salmon.[103]
Mountain of God, mountain of Bashan!
Many-summited mountain, mountain of Bashan!
...
The Lord said, 'From Bashan I shall bring back,[104]
I shall bring back, from the depths, Sea'.

By any assessment, this is somewhat cryptic material. It appears that in the first excerpt Bashan is a mountain, while in the second it is a name of the sea, as required by the parallelism. Let us deal firstly with the sense that this is an anomaly, expressed by J. Day.[105] He has rightly dealt fairly briskly with the considerable number of scholars who have resorted to textual emendation, often of an excessively adventurous kind, in order to solve the puzzle. Not that textual emendation is a bad thing; but it must be a necessary thing, and result in a better (and more plausible) reading than MT. It seems to me that MT stands fairly well without amendment.

In v. 15 (EV 14), the term *ṣalmôn*, 'the Black Mountain', is commonly identified with a hill near Shechem (mentioned in Judges 9.48), and in the present case, perhaps with Jebel Druze,[106] or some other prominence in the Hauran (= Bashan). The apparent doubling may be explained by the psalm identifying a specific sacred mountain (which in its multiple summits is perhaps to be compared with Saphon, Lebanon – with Anti-Lebanon, Parnassus, etc.) with Bashan as a whole. Similarly, 'the Land of Moriah' of Genesis 22.2 became 'Mount Moriah' when assimilated to the temple mountain in 1 Chronicles 3.1. So the image is *totus pro parte*, in terms of size of the territory envisaged, but the reverse in terms of importance. Similarly, of course, 'Zion' frequently represents all Judah or 'Israel' (the theological construct), as *pars pro toto*. Besides, the construct form *har bāšān* confirms that the mountain is the sacred representation of the land. Thus the expressions 'mountain of God' and 'many-summited mountain' actually refer back to Salmon, not directly to Bashan. In any event, there is no compelling reason to identify any site here with Hermon, as proposed by J. Day,[107] though of course Hermon should be considered as a possible candidate. But to conclude that it alone fits the data, simply because it is the highest peak in the region and has a suggestive name (√*ḥrm*), will not do. The region is littered with sacred mountains (Tabor, Ebal, Gerizim, Jebel Druze, Lebanon and Anti-Lebanon, Saphon, Tyre, Carmel, Nebo, Baal Saphon near Pelusium, and no doubt further undocumented ones), from some of which Hermon is visible on a clear day. And 'highest' can be a theological rather than geographical term, as in the case of Zion.

J. Day was also unhappy with the identification of Bashan as serpentine on the basis of the equation *bṯn* = *bāšān*, on the grounds that the equation *bṯn* = *peten* is more secure, and we should not expect two such conflicting etymologies in Hebrew.[108] This can be answered on two grounds. Firstly, the example of the development of *apsû* in Greek (n. 71 above) shows that a common source can lead to two ulterior forms. Secondly, who is to say that *bāšān* is Hebrew? To fob it off on the grounds that it is not as some evidently propose 'a more Canaanitizing form' merely confuses the issue. We should rather look to the language spoken by King Og! But short of finding Bronze Age archives in the region, this is never going to be resolved. The safest thing that can be said is that there is no reason to look for Hebrew here. *Bāšān* is a foreign loan-word, taken from the region so named, and used only for purposes of identifying localities. A link with Ugaritic *bṯn* is entirely plausible, and especially so since Ugaritic literature is evidently familiar with this local geography.

The reason for the mention of Bashan in the first place in Psalm 68 is to record the interesting theological point that its sacred mountain, which had evidently featured in local cosmology, was now being usurped by the greater theological claims, not, surprisingly, of Zion, but of Sinai (vv. 15-24, EV 14-23; see especially v. 17, EV 16). But it is in fact a case of the mystical assimilation of Sinai to Zion, the temple mount, in view of the explicit cultic language of vv. 17bc, 25-27 (EV 16bc, 24-26), and in particular v. 18 (EV 17). The reason for these theological claims is, on the surface, the ideological counterpart to the narratives of conquest noted above, in which Og's kingdom was seized by the Israelites. What concerns us at present is that it now supersedes the sacral traditions of Bashan in favour of higher claims, but by way of specific allusion to Bashan's own claims. These, it is no surprise to discover, closely parallel those of other sacred mountains. We can almost speak of a 'sacred mountain template', which is imposed on any locality that becomes religiously significant.

In the present instance the template contains predictable elements. Firstly, we have the possible *Chaoskampf* allusion in v. 15 (EV 14), though not, in my view, v. 23 (EV 22), as explained in n. 103. I am happy to concede the provisional nature of this assessment, since it is unclear how the 'kings' are to be explained. One possibility is that this is an example of a historical battle which, like all ancient warfare, was assimilated to the *Chaoskampf* ideology.[109] It is even possible that Og and Sihon are to be supposed to be among their number. Another is to see in 'kings' (*m*ᵉ*lākîm*) an allusion to the god Rapiu (see below), who was linked with the region, and with Milku (the 'Molech' of the Bible) who according to KTU 1.100.41 was associated with Athtarat,[110] the Ashtaroth of the biblical tradition. The Ammonite form of the divine name, Milkom, may explain the apparent plural of the psalm.

The other verse here, v. 23 (EV 22) brings us back to our overall theme of water:

> The Lord said,
> 'From Bashan I shall bring back,
> I shall bring back, from the depths, Sea.'[111]

As I construe this, it is a rather surprising allusion to a sort of reversal of the ancient combat. In view of our later discussion, we can frame this in the following terms: it is a foretelling of a flood to come, which undoes the work of creation. It seems to me that this is not only the most obvious sense of a straight reading of the text, but all the more surprising in that no one has read the text correctly, even when leaving it unamended.[112] This is on account of the general failure to recognize the aqueous reference of the passage. As to whether this quasi-oracular pronouncement dealt with an event in future time from the psalmist's perspective, or represented some past event (in the future when the passage was composed), we cannot say.

The juxtaposition of sea and mountain, Bashan representing both, may be regarded as an embarrassment.[113] But it is on the contrary precisely the kind of cosmological nexus we should expect with a sacred mountain. First of all, the sea itself, 'killed' as the divine opponent of the victorious god, becomes the mountain, and is 'frozen' into a transformed reality.[114] Secondly, the mountain is itself the source of flowing, life-giving water, as shown in a widespread iconographic tradition ('the vase with flowing streams' motif),[115] in a cosmological tradition, as witnessed by Genesis 2.10-14, and is a natural aspect of mountains, the source of rivers. Furthermore, Jerusalem lies over the Gihon, which we have seen above to have significance precisely as a local manifestation of the *Tᵉhôm*, also implicit in Hierapolis in that the flood was drained off through the omphalos. So that Bashan should be both aqueous and serpentine on the one hand, and mountainous on the other, is no accident.

In the passage just discussed, 'Bashan' is strictly parallel not with 'Sea', but with 'the depths'. This itself is a further confirmation, if my analysis is correct, of the watery, and therefore potentially serpentine, nature of Bashan. For the depths, *mᵉṣulôt*, are a specific feature of the underworld. Tromp has drawn attention to, and well analysed, the associations of the underworld and water.[116] This chthonian aspect leads to our next observation.

Og, king of Bashan was, we have noted, the last of the Rephaim, reigning in Ashtaroth and Edrei. We cannot dissociate this tradition from the remarkable parallel in KTU 1.108:

[ ]*n yšt rpu mlk ʿlm*	May Rapiu, King of Eternity, drink [wi]ne,
wyšt [*il*] *gṯr wyqr*	yea, may he drink, the powerful and noble [god],
il yṯb bʿṯtrt	the god enthroned in Athtarat,
*il ṯpẓ bi*ˈ*dry*	the god who reigns in Edrei...[117]

There is no need to reiterate here the complex discussion raised by this hymn, and associated materials.[118] In my estimate Rapiu is probably to be seen as a collective, the eponym and patron of the *rpum*, themselves selected and perhaps legendary rather than historical dead kings of Ugarit.[119] This is probably the majority view. They live in the underworld, as KTU 1.161 implies, their representatives being invoked along with recently deceased kings to meet Niqmaddu III-IV in the threshold of his tomb (KTU 1.161). He (Rapiu) is also here formally identified with the god Milku,[120] and his chthonian, and indeed mortuary, function is perhaps nicely encapsulated in the epithet *ʿlm*. I wonder, indeed, if 'eternity' is really the best translation for this term in the context. Perhaps Rapiu is 'King of the Hereafter'.

What is striking here is that the Ugaritian evidence itself points to the Hauran, and to the same tradition that underlies the biblical material.[121] Here too, if we go further afield than the allusions to Og, the Rephaim are evidently former kings, who come to the threshold of the underworld to greet the newly-deceased king, in Isaiah 14.9-11. This reads almost as a parody of KTU 1.161. It is meaningless unless recognized as having the same cultic presuppositions, however much the prophet may be attempting to ridicule them.

We are now in a position to explain the strange bicolon in Job 26.5:

> The Rephaim below trembled,
> the waters and their denizens.

It draws on the two strands of imagery we have discussed, the local aspect of the chthonian Rephaim, and the associations of the underworld with water.

So we have been able to discover that Ugarit and Israel both preserved literary traditions concerning the Hauran, and that both traditions invested the region with a peculiar importance, seeing in it, apparently, a region particularly associated with the underworld, and perhaps having specific points of access to it. One obvious reason for this may have been the volcanic nature of the region, peppered with old craters and lava flows in one of the most impressive (extinct) volcanic zones on earth. Simply by way of comparison, without wishing to make further connections, we may compare Virgil's description of the entrance to Hades just north of Naples, at modern Pozzuoli, noted above, another volcanic region where the earth even today heaves with activity. Other volcanoes, Etna, Vesuvius, and the islands of Stromboli and Volcano also have chthonian associations, with cyclopean forges, and entrances to Tartarus.

The fate of King Og long captivated Hebrew thought. In the Talmud, he is represented as surviving the flood, by clinging to the roof of Noah's ark! Noegel cited the sources and allusions.[122]

This sounds rather like claiming sanctuary by clinging to the altar, as Joab tried vainly to do (1 Kings 2.28-34), and I suspect that the parallel has some substance. We shall see below that the character of the ark, as a floating sanctuary, supports this idea. It also indicates an interesting undercurrent in Jewish thought, evidently flourishing in Talmudic times, which perhaps discerned theological mileage to be made out of this seeming symbol of the autochthonous opposition to the incoming Israelites.

Was Og an antediluvian king? Can we construct the list? Such questions can remain only rhetorical, but they deserve asking, because in Og we may have the tip of a local iceberg (if such things are to be found in volcanic regions!) in which ancient lists of antediluvian kings and heroes, Rephaim, *Rpum*, *Apkallû*, Titans and so forth, trace human culture back as far as may be imagined. If we wished to speculate, we might also ask whether 'Og king of Bashan', remembering that his Greek counterpart Ogygos was a personification of the flood according to Fontenrose, above, was not himself a personification of the flood, and lord of the flood, as the royal title suggests ('king of [the] serpent'), who was subsequently cast in the guise of a quasi-historical figure. His destruction according to one strand of tradition would thus reflect the theme of a complete break with the past, as befits a flood tradition with its hint at a new creation; and at the same time that lingering connection with the past, as suggested by his survival as a stowaway, which was implicitly celebrated in continuing water-rites in temples, where the Chaos waters were tapped for their life-giving properties.

7. *The Saving Ark*

Astour drew attention to the name of the Boeotian city founded by Ogygos, and its interesting symbolic aspects. An early, Homeric, form of Thebes (Θηβαι) was Θηβα,[123] a transcription into Greek of West Semitic *tēbâ*, meaning 'ark', and the term used in Genesis for Noah's ark; and Greek θηβα and κιβωτον were considered to be synonyms (thus the 'ark' in *Genesis* 6.14 is *tēbâ* in MT, and κιβωτον in LXX: see table), the latter term also denoting the ritual vessel 'the ark of the covenant'.[124] Usage is as follows, which also serves to hint at Moses also being a virtual flood-hero, an element to which we shall animadvert.

		Hebrew	*Greek*
Noah's Ark	Genesis 6.14	*tēbâ*	κιβωτον
Moses' Basket of Bulrushes	Exodus 2.3	*tēbâ*	θιβις
The Ark of the Covenant	Exodus 25.10	*'ārôn*	κιβωτον

Table 3. *Hebrew Terms for the Ark*

Holloway wrote a suggestive study comparing the ideas presupposed in the stories of Noah's flood in Genesis and Utnapishtim's in *Gilgamesh* 11.[125] He proceeded by way of a number of propositions. These were as follows:

i. 'the temple is the architectural embodiment of the cosmic mountain;
ii. 'the cosmic mountain represents the primordial hillock...';

iia. 'the temple is often associated with the waters of life which flow forth from a spring within the building itself...the temple is...built upon such a spring... The temple is founded upon the chaos waters...the temple and its ritual guard against the eruption of the waters';

iib. 'the world is recreated every year by agency of the temple, whose activities serve to define the primordial and liturgical New Year';

iii. 'the plan and measurements of the temple are revealed by God to the king...';

iv. 'the temple is associated with abundance and prosperity...[it] is a sanctuary, a haven from the powers of chaos...';

v. 'the destruction...of the temple is...calamitous...the sentence of divine judgment';

vi. 'the temple is the place where human beings relate...to the divine by means of sacrifice'.

Much of this is uncontentious, and may almost be stated as the theoretical principles of any sanctuary in the ancient world. Apart from the evidence Holloway himself adduced, evidence in support could be multiplied over a wide cultural and geographical area.

Holloway then went on to draw attention to features of Utnapishtim's ark in *Gilgamesh* which suggested that it represented a temple, and made a similar claim for Noah's ark. Mallowan had already drawn attention to the fact that *Gilgamesh* once actually calls Utnapishtim's ship 'a temple' (*ekallu* 11.96).[126] Holloway argued that the vessel is described as cuboid, in the sense not that it was a cube, but that its overall dimensions conformed to a cube, since length, breadth and height were identical (11.29-30). It could be quasi-pyramidal in structure, which would allow for the six roofs that were mentioned, as Holloway understood it (11.60-61), seven tiers of diminishing size rising one above the other, like a seven-levelled ziggurat.

When the raven failed to return (11.153-55) we must suppose, Holloway argued, that the ship still had Utnapishtim on board at the point where he celebrated by offering sacrifice on top of the 'ziggurat of the mountain' (11.157).[127] This description, he opined, denoted not the mountain top (thus others) but the vessel, already called a 'temple', as we have seen. In circumstantial terms, the similarity of the loading of the ship to a temple inventory (11.80-85) supported the theory.[128]

The apparent three-deck structure of Noah's ark (Genesis 6.16) seems to have mirrored the three-level structure of Solomon's temple (1 Kings 6.6), both conforming to the three levels of the Israelite cosmos; the beginning of the receding of the flood-waters was given as the first day of the first month (Genesis 8.13), and the wilderness sanctuary was dedicated on the same day (Exodus 40.1-15), while Solomon's temple was dedicated at the New Year festival[129] in the autumn (the month of Ethanim, 1 Kings 8.2). The same symbolism was thus applied to all three.

Hendel responded to this study by pointing out that *Gilgamesh* 11.58 computes the area of the top ('roof') of Utnapishtim's ship as 'ten NINDA square' (= 60 × 60 = 3,600 square 'double-cubits'). That is, Holloway was misconstruing the meaning the text was attempting to communicate. The problem lay with the precise sense of *muḫḫu*, taken by Holloway to mean 'deck', but in reality meaning skull, 'top of head', and by extension 'top side, upper part'. 'On any ordinary reading of *muḫḫīša* in line 58, the shape of Utnapishtim's ark is that of a cube.'[130] But Hendel's objection was on a matter of a technicality, and he readily conceded the overall significance of the ark, by citing Bottéro:

> There is, at least in the 'seven stages', a subtle reference to the proper arrangement of the universe, according to the conception current at the time: three heavens superimposed above, the same number of underworld levels below, and between them, the ark of humankind. One might well consider the ark to be a floating *microcosm*.[131]

The use of the terms *ekallu* and *ziqqurat* he left uncommented.

Holloway responded in turn, seemingly playing down the excerpt from Bottéro, drawing attention to further aspects of temple symbolism, and reiterating his former observations on temple elements in the narrative, pointing out that however individual problems in the text be resolved, there was a deliberate attempt by the literary author(s) of *Gilgamesh* to evoke the temple as a locus of salvation, realized in the ship.

The points at issue here are not trivial, but are evidently conducive, according to both scholars, to the recognition that in some sense we are to understand the Babylonian ship to have at least associations with the temple theology.

8. *Sourcing the Flood*

There have always been people very anxious to locate the flood (specifically Noah's Flood) within the early history of the Near East. Their primary motivation has undoubtedly been the confirmation of the 'truth', by which is generally meant the historical truth (or perhaps rather accuracy), of the biblical narrative. While this search for history is natural enough in an era largely beset by historicism, and was even vindicated in spectacular fashion by Schliemann in his discovery of Troy, it is generally ignored today by all but the most conservative biblical scholars. I certainly hold no brief for such a position as crucial to our understanding of the tradition. But if we are to be open-minded about such issues, then we have every right to ask questions about the origin, or at least the antecedents, of any surviving narrative. And one possibility that must always be open is that a narrative, now fantastic in its depiction of giants and monsters, flying heroes and virgin goddesses who yet give birth, actually had some initial inspiration in 'fact', that is, in an actual event, be it historical or prehistoric. At least it will be conceded that it was the experience of floods of various kinds, rising sea levels, rivers bursting their banks, and so forth, which gave rise to the literary motif of floods as divine punishment.

As much was recognized by Munz, in his study of the nature of myth.[132] He proposed a typology of myth, by which he meant that we can consider a number of versions of a tradition, which, moving forward in time, lead us to its 'conceptual form', but working backwards in time, lead us back to the event that triggered the narrative in the first instance.

> The very earliest or unspecific version of the myth differs from a recital of a natural event only in formal details. It diverges from a report of a natural event or occurrence, perhaps, only because some slightly incredible feature has been introduced; and at times, when an incredible feature is lacking, it may differ from a report of a natural occurrence by nothing more than an opening line, 'Once upon a time...', which indicates that it is remembered although, unlike natural occurrences, it cannot be located to have taken place (*sic*) at any one particular or precise point in time.[133]

While I do not think that this is a necessary starting point for a myth, it certainly cannot be ruled out as a possible starting point. It is by no means inherently unreasonable to ask about the status of the flood (or floods) which gave rise to the story of Noah, or of Atrahasis, or Utnapishtim, or Deucalion, or Ziusudra, or Manu, or any number of flood-heroes.[134] But while I think it pretty implausible to mount a well-funded expedition to Mount Ararat to find the alleged timbers of Noah's ark, my doubt in this matter springs more from what I suspect as being the real motive of the expeditors (viz. biblical inerrancy) than from the feeling that such largesse could be better spent (such as towards the costs of my own research).

A recent study by Ryan and Pitman[135] provides an intriguing possibility concerning a prehistoric cataclysm that may have given rise to the flood story. I shall not enquire too closely into their motives, which, to be sure, they nowhere state. Good research may emerge from a bad prejudice, and in any case, they are to be judged primarily on their oceanographic, rather than ancient Near Eastern or biblical skills.

The beauty of their hypothesis lies in the fact that it answers a number of questions about the dispersal of various cultural forms and technologies, may have an explanatory part to play in the development of languages, and would also, if accepted, offer a plausible account of how two important mythic themes in Eurasian culture diverged from a common source. Whether the sheer comprehensive scale of the hypothesis is finally substantiated, I leave to others to determine. It will require the concerted efforts of a considerable range of scholarship to speak authoritatively on such diverse matters as the genetic evidence for population movements.[136]

The last Ice Age, which began to come to an end c.10,000 BCE, caused a mean rise in Sea Level. After a 'cold snap' at the end of the seventh millennium, the melting continued until, in about 5,600 BCE, the rising waters broke through the natural barrier formed by the Bosphorus, and flooded the basin of the Black Sea, in which there was a fresh-water lake, replenished by the main rivers of the basin, the Danube, the Dnieper and the Dniester, whose surface lay some 100 metres below the surface of the Aegean.[137] This was the genesis of the Black Sea as a body of saline water. The area would already have been occupied by lakeside dwellers, and those who were not cut off and drowned by the catastrophe would have fled in all directions, to gain higher ground. In Ryan and Pitman's estimation, the filling of the basin to its present level probably took about ten months.[138]

This catastrophe, in the view of Ryan and Pitman, gives a satisfactory account of how the flood myth arose: it recalled, and gave symbolic meaning to an event that devastated the lives of many, and changed the lives of others for ever. As people dispersed, they took with them the awful account of what had happened, and by way of explanation of how they came to be where they now were, it took on the power of myth. That is, it combined narrative power with the prevailing religious viewpoint characterizing all archaic cultures, and became a story of human corruption and divine wrath and justice. A moral cast overlay the whole.

One of the problems regarding the flood-story as it occurred in ancient Near Eastern cultures was how the dispersal was to be explained. Was it through the dissemination of one story, passed on, always subsequent to any hypothetical event, so that the further the story travelled from its homeland, the more secondary or even tertiary the forms it adopted? Thus a common assessment of the biblical flood narrative is that it was essentially derivative from Mesopotamian tradition. And while this may be conceded on literary and stylistic grounds, it constitutes no proof that the entire idea of a flood was itself derived from this source. This would merely be the medium, or the transmission route, whereby a narrative of older and more remote provenance, would reach Israel. The trouble with this sort of approach is that it tends to allow only one original version, whereas what we have in the surviving tradition may be not diverging versions, but rather converging ones, from many originals, whereby originally quite distinct accounts of the event, based on different local experiences, may have to some extent coalesced through literary influences.

Reactions to Ryan and Pitman's hypothesis, implicitly reinforced by Ballard's claimed discoveries on the floor of the Black Sea,[139] have been varied, and perhaps predictable. Scholars are entirely cautious, and rightly so. The issue here is perhaps the degree of caution, and to what extent we should run with it at least in hypothetical terms, conceding from the start that it is scarcely the kind of claim that is ever likely to be proved. We shall return to this issue below. More entertaining, and entirely predictable, is the response of the evangelical opposition, whom we might expect to leap to the defence of the Ryan–Pitman hypothesis, as lending scientific credence to their position. But this end of the spectrum does not have one single position. I once watched a television programme of excruciating banality, in which a camera team accompanied an American 'archaeologist' (for so he called himself) on his quest for the remains of Noah's ark on Mount Ararat. The highlight for me occurred when a rival crew was encountered at several thousand feet (hundreds of metres) above sea level heading in the opposite direction, on the same quest! There are now a number of fundamentalist and creationist websites,[140] where we might expect some enthusiastic support for a claim (as they interpret it) to have demonstrated the historicity of the event. Objections seem to follow two lines of argument. Firstly, because the Black Sea flood was demonstrably local, it cannot be the biblical flood because that was universal. Thus biblical inerrancy provides the norm for all assessments. Secondly, it cannot have taken place in c. 5600 BCE, because according to Archbishop Ussher's chronology, which they appear to accept implicitly, the world was not created for a further 1,200 years! Other such sites simply peddle a conservative line as old as Darwinism.

9. *On the Longevity of Oral Tradition*

Stephanie Dalley raised a number of detailed objections from an Assyriological perspective to the Pitman and Ryan hypothesis.[141] These obviously weaken individual parts of their argument, and I would not wish to defend them on these. But what is perhaps her most substantial argument, that it is difficult to credit an oral tradition surviving for 4,000 years (that is, from c. 5600 BCE down to the earliest written form of *Atrahasis*, c. 1700 BCE), is more difficult to take seriously without some qualification. Before the invention of writing, all human traditions, that is, cultural forms, were carried down by three means, oral transmission (anything taking the form of words: stories, 'history', 'law' and genealogies), art and artefacts (plastic and pictorial arts, painting, sculpture, and so on, in addition to lithic and later metal tools), and mimesis (anything taking the form of action: all social mores, ritual and technology). Let me give one or two examples. They do not have to be taken from the ancient Near East, my main concern, since what is at issue here is a principle.

The most general one is language itself. Of course, language changes down the generations (as do traditions), but there is a recognizable continuity. Furthermore, given the huge weight of tradition as observed in the ancient world, the further back we go, the more conservative do we find cultural forms. While some languages have changed rapidly in history (English being a good example, where the language of 500 years ago is incomprehensible to the average native-speaker), others, notably Arabic and Chinese, have evolved altogether more slowly. The Upper Palaeolithic cave art of Europe covers a period of some 25,000 years, according to Clottes and Courtin;[142] even on the most conservative span the distance from Gargas, c. 27,000 BP, Chauvet, c. 21,000 BP, and Cosquer, c. 19,000 BP, to Lascaux c. 17,000 BP, Altamira, c. 14,000 BP and Niaux c. 13,000 BP is a minimum of 14,000 years. Stone tools, which we can view with hindsight as developing in various well-documented ways, actually persisted virtually unchanged over hundreds of thousands of years. Of course these physical artefacts are not so fragile and inherently ephemeral as language, but we have no reason to insist on the latter's rapid development, or the unstable nature of its primitive literary expressions, at all times in prehistory.

It is well known that toponyms tend to be very conservative, many surviving substantial cultural changes and linguistic identities, and even if these be recorded in writing by administrators and historians, so far as a local population is concerned, the persistence of the name is essentially an oral tradition. Thus Basseda[143] listed considerable numbers of pre-Roman or pre-Indo-European toponyms in the region of the Roussillon. Toponyms of Basque formation in the western Pyrenees may well have a prehistory lasting into Upper Palaeolithic times, the Basques being perhaps survivors of the early Cro-Magnon peoples of Western Europe. While toponyms are only fragments of tradition, there is no reason in principle why longer strings of material, particularly myths and other traditional tales carrying memetic and authoritative information, should not be relatively stable, adaptation resulting from the need to address changing political or environmental circumstances. The matter of oral versus written tradition, in terms of their relative stability down the generations, is in any case an entirely irrelevant matter. The stability or changeability of a given tradition depends entirely on the stability or changeability of the social, political and ideological circumstances attending it. And any author in the ancient world evidently felt entirely free to modify and corrupt tradition as he saw fit!

One of Dalley's substantive objections to the Ryan and Pitman hypothesis is that the reconstruction of the inundation they described is simply incommensurate with the flood accounts from the ancient Near East. But this, at first sight, reasonable objection is perhaps rather weakened if we acknowledge that the biblical narrative in Genesis 6–8 itself gives two entirely incompatible accounts of events: the J strand deals with 40 days of rain, that is, a naturalistic account of an entirely plausible kind, while the P material describes an irruption from above and below of the waters of the cosmic deeps, in a formal reversal of the supernatural events of creation. What has happened is that the miraculous and cosmological aspects have been greatly enhanced, and yet apparently, to judge from the conflated product, concurrently with the survival of the naturalistic account.[144] Thus formal differences between accounts do not necessarily require that they are dealing with different kinds of events (real or imagined). Again, the Indian forms of the tradition have departed in entirely new directions, with their adaptation to nascent Hindu cosmology.[145] Yet their organic links with the Mesopotamian source material is not in question. It is fair to say that whatever the local variations on the theme which develop, a relatively constant theological basis is maintained in all the versions, with moral or environmental tweakings here and there.

It is perhaps too early to say that Ryan and Pitman have established that the Black Sea inundation is the source of all the Old World flood stories. The debate is still in its infancy. But I think that they have made a case that has some merit, not least in its account of the general dispersal of cultural elements in the region. The main problem lies in the fact that every aspect of matter, linguistic, cultural, historical, is beset with problems. Perhaps a grand theory has something to be said for it, and at least as a serious, intellectually-developed, theory it is open to verification or falsifiability on grounds of evidence rather than dogma.

10. *The Conflict Myth, an Analogous Mythic Tradition*

The account given above offers a possible explanation of how the flood traditions of Eurasia originated. Now flood traditions are manifestly accounts of an attempt by the gods to destroy the world, a plan which always fails, because, if the idiom be permitted, the secret is leaked. In some versions it allows a soteriological development, in that a deity comes to one wise and pious individual, a priest or devotee of the deity, and warns him of the approaching catastrophe, so that, prepared for it, he and his family escape.

But apart from this exclusion clause, as it were, the tradition is primarily an eschatological one, for it tells of the destruction of the world, and its subsequent renewal.

I think that a case can be made for regarding this eschatological motif as closely relating to a corresponding cosmogonic one. The new beginning which follows the flood is in any case itself a cosmogony of sorts, as is generally recognized by the traditions, which all emphasize the primordial nature of the surviving humans, who are the parents of all subsequent humanity.

One obvious candidate suggests itself as the cosmogonic counterpart of the flood tradition: this is the *Chaoskampf* myth, which, perhaps significantly, has more or less the same geographical dispersal as the flood story. It is even, in some instances at least, consciously linked to the flood story by individual tradition. A good example of this is the accounts of creation in Genesis 1, and of the flood, followed by its new creation and the institution of the Noachic covenant in Genesis 6–9. Two passages in particular seem intended to draw attention to the link.

Genesis 1.28-29	*Genesis 6–8*	*Genesis 9.1-4*
Now God blessed them; and he said to them, 'be fruitful, increase, and fill the earth.	intervening flood narrative	Now God blessed Noah and his sons; and he said to them, 'be fruitful, increase, and fill the earth.
And subdue it, and have dominion over the fish in the sea, and the birds in the sky, and every living animal on earth.'	two recensions, J and P,	And let fear and dread of you be upon every living thing on earth, and upon every bird in the sky, of everything crawling on the ground, and upon all the fish in the sea: they are delivered into your hands.
And God said,		
'Look, I have given you every seed-bearing plant in all the earth and every seed-bearing tree: these shall be your food.'	conflated	Every animal which lives shall be food for you, just as green plants. I give everything to you.
		However, meat with its life – that is, its blood – in it you must not eat.'

Table 4. *Creation, Flood and Recreation in Genesis*

The second passage goes on to narrate Elohim's covenant with Noah and all other living things. In the present passages this idea is already implicit, since it governs the relationship between men and other life-forms. The pattern is the vassal-treaty texts of the ancient near East, in which conditions are imposed on the subordinate contracting party. But this formal link serves to regard the events of Genesis 9 as a new creation, so that the flood now forms a transition from one world-order to the next. This pattern, of a repeated cycle of events, also characterizes the Indian versions of the tradition.

Wensinck had already drawn attention to a pattern repeated, often in the most allusive form, in the biblical tradition.[146] He observed that

> This reign of Chaos which in the cosmogonic stories is identical with the reign of the ocean, has not only its place in the cosmogony, but, according to the Old Testament, it occurs several times in history in a series of events always following the same order. A period of chaos is succeeded by the creative act of God; then a covenant is made with man and a new time begins, a time of new relations between man and nature, a golden age in the land of paradise.
>
> It is evident that this series of events as it is described in the story of the creation and of paradise, has its counterpart in the story of the deluge. The cosmos is destroyed by the ocean; the reign of chaos is the reign of Tehom. When the waters have disappeared God makes a new covenant with Noah...

Before we proceed with the biblical aspect of these observations, it is worth noting that if Wensinck was correct in his analysis, as I believe him to have been, then it has an interesting implication for the Ugaritic tradition. Since the pattern to which he pointed is substantially that occurring in Mesopotamian literature,[147] and since Ugarit was evidently familiar with the *Atrahasis* (fragment, RS 22.421) and *Gilgamesh* (fragment found in 1994) narratives, it is probably not going too far to discern an echo of the triumph of the flood in the coronation scene of KTU 1.1 iv, in which Yam is consecrated as king of the gods. Subsequently his opponent Baal is bound[148] and placed as his prisoner beneath his footstool:

'[ ]
[ ]
[ ] I cannot drive out.
If I see? [ ]
    and with Yam is the sieve of destruction.
By Yam I shall be worm-eaten [ ]
    [and thanks to] Nahar (devoured by) maggots.
There with a sword I shall be destroyed;

(my) [hou]se shall be knocked down?.
Into the netherworld will fall my strength,
and into the dust my power.'
[From] his mouth his speech barely went forth,
from his lips his word,
and he gave forth his voice in groaning
beneath the throne of Prince Yam.
And Kothar-and-Hasis spoke:
'Indeed I say to you, O Prince Baal,
I repeat, O Charioteer of the Clouds,
now your foe, Baal,
now your foe you must smite;
now you must destroy your adversary!
Take your everlasting kingdom,
your eternal dominion!'[149]

The opening sequence here remains entirely opaque. It appears that Baal then anticipates his immediate descent into the underworld (a type of his later descent into Mot's jaws), and predicts that there the conflict will resume. At this juncture, in his darkest moment, Kothar brings the divine weapons, with which his victory is now assured. We have here, in the much-damaged material of KTU 1.1-2, the merest echo of the tradition expanded on in Mesopotamian and Hebrew literature. Even on a minimalist approach, we would have to concede that Ugarit was not entirely ignorant of the flood tradition.

The pattern he discerned in the biblical tradition was therefore, Wensinck claimed, a typological reiteration of the same literary nexus throughout the tradition, canonical and non-canonical. His treatment is rather allusive than detailed, but it may be tabulated as follows (selecting representative verses alluding to these themes):

	Chaos (flood)	*Creation (exodus)*	*Covenant*
Genesis	Genesis 1.2	Genesis 1.3-25	Genesis 1.26-31
Genesis	Genesis 7.17–8.9	Genesis 8.10-19	Genesis 8.20–9.17
Exodus	Exodus 1.22, 2.3-5[150]	Exodus 14–15	Exodus 19–24, 32–34
Deutero-Isaiah	Isaiah 43.2,[151] 48.10, 54.7-9	Isaiah 40,[152] 41.18, 43.19, 48.6-8, 50.2, 51.9-11, 51.15	Isaiah 51.3, 52.7-12, 54 *passim*, 55 *passim* (esp. v. 3)
Pseudepigrapha[153]	*Jubilees* 5.20–6.3, *T. Naphtali* 6.1-10, *1 Enoch* 65-66, 83, 89.1-9	*4 Ezra* 13.1-13 *1 Enoch* 89.10-40 *2 Enoch* 24-30	*Jubilees* 6.4-16

Gospels	John 1.1-5, 14-16	*Baptism:* Matthew 3, Mark 1.3-8, Luke 3.2-17, John 1.6-8, 19-28 *Stilling storm:* Matthew 8.18, 23-27; Mark 4.35-41, Luke 8.22-25, *Walking on sea:* Matthew 14.22-33, Mark 6.47-52, John 6.15-21, (21.1-14) Revelation 12.7-9, 21.1–22.5	Matthew 5–7

Table 5. *Typology in Biblical Tradition*

The striking feature of this pattern is that while its reiterated form is not found to the same degree elsewhere as in the biblical literature, the basic structure is in fact a constant of all flood stories. It is indeed the very essence of flood stories. In two instances in particular from the biblical milieu, Moses passing through the sea in Exodus 14–15, and the Man emerging from the Sea in *4 Ezra* 13, it is probably fair to say that the tradition is as conscious of a Noah Redivivus in both narratives as it is of a king re-enacting the *Chaoskampf*. In the cases of Noah and Moses, both narratives were given their definitive shape in the context of exile, in a world that had been destroyed, and was now being reconstructed in the post-exilic Jewish community. This reconstruction, with the reiterated use of the old motifs in a number of new ways, permeated all subsequent Jewish and early Christian literature.

So far as our broader discussion is concerned, the recognition in the conflict myth of the mirror image of the flood story has one interesting implication. Given that the two themes tend to appear together in various cultures (that is, if one is to be found, the other is not far away), any historical conclusions concerning one would have implications for the other. One of the conclusions I reached in my extended study of the former tradition[154] was that elements in its ritual performance (for here is a myth closely related to a ritual pattern) can be traced back to weapon-hoards and deposits stretching back into the Neolithic. I am not going to be so egregious as to try to pinpoint the prehistoric origin of the myth. But it is possible that it concentrates in some literary and ritual nexus fairly typical experiences of early social life, at the interface of the hunter-gatherer and agricultural lifestyles. It implies the conceptions of property and territory, power and prestige, as they became essential parts of the transformed world of the first settlers.

Endnotes

* First published in D.A. González Blanco, J.P. Vita and J.A. Zamora (eds.), *De la Tablilla a la Inteligencia Artificial. Homenaje al Prof. Jesús Luis Cunchillos en su 65 aniversario* (Próximo Oriente Antiguo, Insituto de Estudios Islámicos y del Oriente Próximo: Zaragoza, 2004): 211-59.

1. *Mutatis mutandis*, cf. the useful observation of Whitelam 1989: 136: 'The emphasis of much previous biblical scholarship has been upon the uniqueness of Israelite kingship and its leading representatives. There is now a need for a comparative study of the dynamics and processes of monarchic society as a whole which can only come from the risks, and, hopefully, rewards of interdisciplinary research.' To some extent, this applies to every branch of Biblical Studies. Of course, the stricture implied here is not likely to apply to scholars specializing in Ugaritian and other ancient Near Eastern branches of scholarship! In these, a comparative dimension is of the essence. But in Biblical Studies there are pockets of isolationism to this day.

2. A fine example of this, not irrelevant to religious experience and cosmology, is the predisposition to seeing human faces in the natural world. See Guthrie 1993. More generally see Blackmore 1999.

3. For discussion of the Sumerian and Akkadian terms for the sea and ocean, much simplified here, see Horowitz 1998: 301-17.

4. The Akkadian terms *aiabba* and *iamu* are derivatives respectively from Sumerian and West Semitic.

5. The first millennium term *marratu* in Akkadian is probably an Aramaic loanword.

6. Cf. the River Litani in the Lebanon. Greek Λαδων, below, is the name of the dragon guarding the golden apples of the Hesperides. These being at the entrance to the Atlantic Ocean, it is likely that the epithet, presumably Phoenician in origin, has been transferred. The Ugaritic Litanu is called *šlyṭ*, 'Encircler', in KTU 1.5 i 3, no doubt with reference to his serpentine coils; cf. Akkadian *mu-gam-mir-tú*, 'encloser', an epithet of the sea cited by Horowitz 1998: 305 (following von Soden). Note also the river Ladon in Greece, a tributary of the Alpheus in Arcadia. J.A. Fontenrose 1980: 236, 370, noted that the poet Dionysios called this river 'Ogygian', that is, relating to Ogygos, on whom see further below. He also noted (p. 236) that 'Hesiod calls Ogygian the waters of Styx, Ocean's daughter' (*Theogony* 806).

7. Specifically the crossing from life to death; ᾿Αχερων ('Last', from West Semitic *'aḥarôn*); Ληθη ('Forgetting'); Στυξ ('Abhorrent'). To Ληθη cf. ἀληθεια, 'truth' ('not-forgetting'), to be compared with AB.ZU, 'waters of knowing' (n. 9).

8. Explained as possibly a derivative of *labbu* by K. Spronk 1995: col. 1292 (= 1999, 685). He cited Lambert 1986: 55, n. 1.

9. 'The waters of knowing'.

10. Variants, *tâmtum, têmtum* generally restricted to common usage, while Ti'amat was the goddess (consort of Apsû). In discussing Tethis (Tethys) in Hesiod's *Theogony*, 136, M.L. West 1966: 204, noted her original role with Okeanos as parent of the gods, and suggested that the pair *Okeanos-Tethis* were a reflex of the Mesopotamian pair *Apsû-Ti'amat* ; 'but by Hesiod's time the myth may have been almost forgotten, and Tethis remembered only as the name of Oceanus' wife'.

11. West 1966: 201 observed that *Okeanos* is 'the great river that flows round the rim of the world... He is father of all other rivers and springs...and must therefore be himself a fresh-water stream, quite distinct from the sea, though later equated with it.' (*Tethis* being the salt sea.) The pair *Apsû-Ti'amat* were similarly the fresh and salt waters respectively, though *apsû* was often used apparently indiscriminately of the entire cosmic ocean, around, above and below. We might extend this in relation to the Ugaritian water-deity, commonly identified as *zbl ym, ṯpṭ nhr*, 'Prince Sea, Ruler River' (KTU 1.1.2 iii 16 etc.). But in this context there is no reason to suppose that the Mesopotamian differentiation is operative. It is rather the conception of the cosmic sea now as oceanic, now as riverine, which I suspect is the point of the Greek language, whatever the antecedents may have been.

12. Horowitz 1998: 306, cited *a-ru-ru* as a synonym for *apsû*. Is this to be taken as throwing light on the toponym *arr* in KTU 1.10 iii 29-30? In that context, it appears to be part of the Saphon massif, in that Anat passes through or by it on her way to the summit (Wyatt 2002a: 160). But locating a cosmic sea near the sacred mountain, while bizarre by our understanding, made perfect sense for the ancients. The mountain lay over the sea in West Semitic cosmology, as in Jerusalem or Hierapolis, where the flood was swallowed up by the sacred rock. Cf. Psalm 29.10 cited below. In Ezekiel 28.13-14 the sacred mountain lies at the heart of the Garden of Eden, a feature long felt to be at odds with the description of Eden in Genesis 2. A suggestion of C.H. Gordon (Gordon 1955: 62) may offer a solution. Starting with the expression *hdm id* in KTU 1.4 iii 34, which he explained, on the basis of Cretan cultural influence, as 'an Idaean or Cretan footstool', by reference to Mount Ida, he went on to propose that the *'ēd* rising up in the Garden of Eden in Genesis 2.6, commonly construed as a mist or some such, on the basis of ^{d}Id, a Marian river-god, or Sumero-Akkadian *edû*, 'flood' (thus Reymond 1958: 169, citing Albright and Speiser), was rather a mountain. This makes excellent sense, and at least deserves serious attention, for this immediately gives a strong confirmation of the four streams which flowed out of Eden (and implicitly *down*, as down from a mountain source). Mountain gods holding vases with flowing streams, appearing widely in iconography, point to a strong tradition in this respect. See van Buren 1933.

13. The Ugaritic *thmtm* is dual, and therefore evidently denoted two bodies of water, meeting beneath El's throne. Whether the two were respectively upper and lower (cf. *Apsû* and *Ti'amat*) is not entirely clear, but is consonant with the drift of much of the imagery. See further below, and cf. Psalm 42.8. A strange passage in the *Qur'an*, Sura 18.61-62 has Moses say to his servant, 'I will not give up until I reach the meeting of the two seas, though I go on for many years' (Arberry 1964: 295-96). They then arrive at the point in question, but 'forget their fish', which makes its way off through the waters. Is the place Jerusalem, or Mecca, or somewhere indeterminate?

14. KTU 1.23.30 uses *gp thm*, evidently to be distinguished from *thmt*(*m*), as parallel to *gp ym* (or read *ḫp ym*, *ḫp thm*? Wyatt 2002a: 330, n. 29) in a horizontal sense, of waters at the end of the land.

15. Wyatt 2002a: 116, n. 11, *ad* KTU 1.5 i 14-16.

16. See *ANEP* §§670 (Maltaya: Hittite, Illuyankas myth; the number of heads is lost through a break in the relief) and 671 (shell plaque of unknown provenance; deity and seven-headed flaming dragon). The tradition lived on into Revelation 12, and even mediaeval iconography kept it alive (see *inter alia* illustrations in the *Beatus* Apocalypse

series, and the Anger Apocalypse Tapestry, a pictorial commentary on Revelation). Ti'amat sometimes features on *Kudurru* stones, encircling the base, or reaching from bottom to top, as though the *Kudurru* were a microcosm. See Seidl 1989: figs. 4, 7, 11, 13, 14, 16, 22, 23; pll. 8, 18a, 20a, 22a, 28c, 29ab.

17. Wyatt 1998a. See also, for the texts from Eshnunna, Lewis 1996; for the Marian material, Durand 1993; for Ugarit Bordreuil and Pardee 1993; and more generally Fontenrose 1980; Wakeman 1973; Wyatt 1996b: 117-218. J. Day 1985, compares the Ugaritic and biblical traditions.

18. Bérard 1902-1903: II, 316.

19. Strabo 17.3.2.

20. Neiman 1977.

21. In this context it is worth also mentioning Bashan, the south Syrian toponym, which del Olmo 1988 associated with Ugaritic *bṯn*, 'serpent', and which as a location of the Underworld is a further point of access to the Ocean. We shall revert to this below.

22. Lit. 'go'.

23. In Rendsberg 2000 the author has correctly pointed out the falsity of this equation: 'The term Abyssinia does not derive from Greek ἀβυσσος, but rather from *ḥbšt*, one of the two South Arabian tribes which comprised the kingdom of Aksum... In fact, the term Abyssinia does not appear in ancient Greek sources.' He refers his readers to W. Pape and G. Bensler, *Wörterbuch der griechischen Eigennanme* (Braunschweig 1875^{3}) and acknowledges the assistance of Saul Levin with this reference. While I am happy to accept this correction, it looks suspiciously as though familiarity with the Greek term ἀβυσσος has nevertheless shaped the Greek (and Latin) form of the name, if only with regard to the vowels. So perhaps I am 25 percent right! (This matter has a bearing on n. 71 below.)

24. In the final stage the initial *omikron* has shifted to *omega* and the aspiration has been lost (Ὁ > Ὠ).

25. Neiman 1977: 327. See also discussion at Wyatt 1996b: 99-101. On Ὠγενια see also below, and LS 2030.

26. The *yēṣē'* is surely superfluous here, perhaps glossing *b*^{e}*gîḥô* as an obscure, recherché term. This supports the idea of it being a scholarly loanword. See Pope 1973: 293 for general comments, though he does not raise this one. V. 9 continues the birth imagery:

b^{e} *sûmî* ^{c} *ānān l*^{e} *bušô*	when I made clouds its clothing,
wa^{ca}*rāpel ḥ*^{a}*tullātô*	and a thick darkness its swaddling-band.

The conceptual similarity to Genesis 1.2 is clear, although in that passage the filial nature of Yam is not evoked. Who were Yam's parents? The question is unanswerable, except that El, the androgynous father *and mother* of the goddess(es) in KTU 1.23, addresses Yam as 'my son' in the enthronement at KTU 1.1 iv 14; cf. l. 29. Some might insist that this was merely a legal formulation (as in Psalm 2.7), but the context is wholly mythological.

27. For the connection see Wyatt 1990b. See also del Olmo 1986 for discussion of the Ugaritic *gn*, used in similar royal ideological contexts as the biblical *gan hammelek*, which seems to have denoted the royal burial ground inside the city. A similar royal necropolis evidently lay within the palace complex at Ugarit. See also Wyatt 1999b.

28. Lucian, *De Dea Syria* 13.

29. M.L. West 1971: 50. He also noted ᾿Ωγηνος, mentioned by Pherecydes (*idem*, 50). Cf. also Akkadian *akūnu*, Hebrew *'aggān*, Aramaic *'gn*, tentatively suggested as loaned from Egyptian *ikn*: Muchiki 1999: 63. He could also have included Ugaritic *agn*.

30. E.g. Hammurabi's code, v. 12: Richardson 2000: 41.

31. On these see Chapter 10; also Wyatt 2001a: §1.

32. Noegel 1998: 413, n. 11. To this expression may be compared Sumerian A.KI-TA.K, 'the water of below'. This would correspond more directly to Akkadian *têmtum*, *ti'amat*, Ugaritic *thm*, Hebrew *t^ehôm*, that is, the subterranean, but not the supra-firmamental, waters.

33. Letter dated March 9, 2001. Professor Astour is also to be congratulated on *his* memory!

34. Bernal 1991 (1993): II, 83-85. Bernal's work might perhaps be usefully included in the list in n. 72, were it not for the fact that his stimulating insights are all too frequently vitiated by his uncritical adoption of an afrocentric perspective. See the balanced comments of Ray 1997.

35. See now Horowitz 1998: 21-42. See also Wyatt 2001a: 81-82 (§2 [24]).

36. An Aramaic loan-word into Akkadian: Horowitz 1998: 304-305.

37. KTU 1.2 iii 4, 1.3 v 5-7, 1.4 iv 20-22 (Wyatt 2002a: 52, 84, 99).

38. Thus Wyatt 2002a: 52, n. 63.

39. This designation of El (Wyatt 2002a: *passim*), as opposed to 'the Compassionate, god of mercy' of Wyatt 1998c, *passim*, results from applying the analysis offered by Healey 1998. On p. 350 he allowed 'sharp-sighted, acute, one who understands mysteries' for *lṭpn*, and 'the percipient one' for *dpid*. This new approach is supported by Watson's account of *rḫnt* in KTU 1.4 v 5: Watson 2001.

40. The expression *ǵr ks* may be confidently restored on the basis of KTU 1.1 iii 12. On its reference see Chapter 9.

41. Wyatt 2002a: 46.

42. Wyatt 1999b: 876.

43. Wensinck 1918. Discussion 7-13.

44. Wensinck cited his earlier monograph, 1916: 45ff.

45. See n. 14 above.

46. See my earlier sketch of Ugaritian and Israelite conceptions in Chapter 5.

47. See Montgomery 1938; Snaith 1965; Batto 1983; Wyatt 1990c; *idem* 1996b: 84-89. A more general treatment of the sea and its symbolism was offered by Kaiser 1959.

48. Judges 11.16 A reads ἐρυθρα θαλασσα, but B reads θαλασση Σιφ *(that is, Sûp)*. Exodus 10.19 and Jeremiah 30.15 (= MT 49.21) read θαλασσα; Deuteronomy 1.1 reads ἐρυθρας.

49. The particle *b^e* can have the sense of 'from', 'out of', in Ugaritic, and at times appears to have the same sense in Hebrew. See Gordon 1965: 92, §10. 1, and Dahood 1965-70: III, 391-93; on the Ugaritic particle see now Tropper 2000: 756, §82.11.

50. Wyatt 1996b: 85-86.

51. Snaith 1965: 397.

52. Montgomery 1938.

53. References in n. 46.

54. Wyatt 1990c: 70; *idem* 1996b: 87-88.

55. Cf. the name of God in rabbinic tradition: *'en sôp*: '(The One) Without End'.

56. Of course, it will be objected, the world at least to the Atlantic was known by the sixth century BCE, and specifically by Phoenician exploration. But this would probably not detract from the *poetic* image of the great unknown into which departing ships sailed. And Israelites are not simply to be equated with Phoenicians. For the latter, the sea was a lifeline. For the former, a real fear was present in Jonah, and nicely summed up in the (Christianized) aspiration that come the Eschaton, 'there would be no more sea' (Revelation 21.1). See also Reymond 1958: 163.

57. Wyatt 1990c: 72.

58. Cf. Hesiod's phrase ἐς πειρατα γαιης cited above.

59. Pope 1955: 72.

60. Reymond 1958: 170-71.

61. *HALOT* 1.79. The matter had already been raised by Wensinck 1918: 21.

62. Wyatt 2002a: 132.

63. Yahweh in the Isaianic corpus is identified as El (Isaiah 40.18, 42.5, 43.12, 46.9, etc.); in KTU 1.1-6 one throne, El's, is at issue throughout: Wyatt 1996c; *idem* 1996b: 35-48. The present allusion undoubtedly draws on the same cosmological presuppositions.

64. Wyatt 2002a: 389.

65. Parts of this are conjectural. See Wyatt 2002a: 389, nn. 8-12 for text and interpretation adopted. For a recent alternative approach see Xella 1996b.

66. It is no accident that the king sits on his throne, since he seems to act the role of *axis mundi* himself, which explains the common representation of kings as trees, and especially as the cosmic tree at the centre of the world. The throne may be seen as an analogue of the world tree: Ellis-Davidson 1964: 192 and n. 1, noted that Odin's throne sat on the top of Yggdrasill, the *axis mundi*, and that this in turn was assimilated to the cosmic mountain. The righteous king in the present context, however, is not as extensive as the deity as he represents, as we see in the case of Athtar in KTU 1.6 i 59-61.

67. We might conjecture that *mê'epes wātôhû* could even be construed as 'the waters of the Apsu and Tiamat', making the distinction, familiar from the *Enuma Elish*, between sweet and salt waters. But this would require the restoration of final *m* to *tôhû* to give **t^ehôm*, as conjectured for KTU 1.5 i 15 (Wyatt 2002a: 116, n. 11).

68. Cf. the discussion in Wensinck 1918: 41, 49-50, acknowledging that *thm* and *thw* were distinct roots, yet recognizing a poetic association, citing *T. Hagiga* 12a: '*Tohu* is the green cord that surrounds the whole earth and from which darkness springs'. On p. 53 he observed, '*thw* (*sic*) is the technical term for chaos and the ocean as chaos. *thw* is also a designation of the desert and the desert as chaos.'

69. West 1971: 205-206.

70. Evelyn-White 1914: 135, n. 1. Cf. West's attempt at solving the issue, suggesting that there was a Heraclitean element, West 1971: 122-23: 'circulation of elements up and down: Heraclitus' river: Oceanus'.

71. Cf. also the toponym Abyssinia above (and note n. 22a). The divergence of **apsû* into both ἀψο- and ἀβσυ- forms is not an insuperable problem, if they had a different history of development. (Cf. the different histories of English and French *frail* and *frêle*, and *fragile*, from Latin *fragilis*, one developing through Norman French, the other a neologism in the sixteenth century.) We may even suggest that *apsû* became firstly ἀπσος, then ἀβσος as the initial plosive became voiced in conjunction with unvoiced σ

(cf. the different pronunciation of -bs- in French and English), the combination -βσ- finally becoming the syllable -βυσσ- for euphony. Thus the sequences would be: i) *apsû* >* ἄπσος > ἀψο-; and ii) *apsû* > * ἄπσος > * ἄβσος > ἄβυσσος.

(It was only after the submission of the original paper that I had access to West 1997: 148, where the author also links the Greek term ἀψορροος with Akkadian *apsû*.)

72. Note in particular Walcot 1966; Astour 1967; Kerstein 1968; West 1971; *idem* 1997; Hoffner 1973; Mondi 1990; Burkert 1992; Penglase 1994; Duchemin 1995; Feldman 1996; Marblestone 1996.

73. Passages from Hesiod and the Homeric Hymns are taken from Evelyn-White, *Hesiod*.

74. Passages from Herodotus are taken from Godley 1921–31.

75. This is particularly intriguing in view of the fact that it is from Herodotus (*Histories* 4.42) that we learn of a Phoenician voyage round Africa, sailing clockwise, and lasting about three years. As Godley noted, Herodotus' own remark, whose significance he obviously could not appreciate, that 'in sailing round Libya they had the sun on their right hand', confirms the fact that they had passed into the southern hemisphere.

76. See the map based on the cosmology of Pomponius Mela (c. 44 CE) in Schoff 1912: 100. For the TO map see Larner 1999: pl. 2. Numerous mediaeval examples of world maps are given in Bagrow 1964. The notion of the encircling sea is also well-expressed in the so-called ascent of Alexander (Pseudo-Callisthenes, *The Greek Alexander Romance* 2.41: Stoneman 1991: 123). He met a heavenly being, who told him to look down. 'I looked down...and saw...a great snake curled up, and in the middle of the snake a tiny circle like a threshing floor.' His companion then said, 'that is the world. The snake is the sea that surrounds the world.' The Egyptian Uroboros motif expressed much the same conception.

77. Sandys 1946.

78. Noegel 1998: 422.

79. The toponym Laish, taken by the Danites on arrival in the north, also means 'lion'.

80. Cf. Genesis 49.13, where Zebulun (in the thick of battle in Judges 5.18) dwells by the sea and serves on board ship.

81. Del Olmo 1988: note especially p. 56; cf. also M.J. Dahood 1965–70: II, 145.

82. Dahood noted the parallel in the use of *peten* || *tannîn* with KTU 1.3 iii 40-41, which suggests an organic link with the Ugaritic tradition: Dahood 1965–70: II, 333. Another late example, perhaps, is 1QH 5.9b-10a (Stanza C), where *kpyrym* (for *lby'ym*?) is parallel to *tnynym*, as with the internal parallelism in the second colon above.

83. Wyatt 1998a, *passim*.

84. Thus Glassner 1993: 244, n. 24.

85. Davila 1995.

86. Nippur fragment, *ANET* 44. The Sumerian king-list however gives only one king of Shuruppak, Ubar-Tutu, who reigned for 18,600 years, until the flood (*ANET* 265). Glassner (1993) in his analysis of the synoptic tradition, based on a number of fragments, 71, introduces Ziusudra as a son of Ubar-Tutu (school exercise: Finkelstein 1963: 40; and again as son of Shuruppak son of Ubar-Tutu (OB list from Sippar, Langdon 1923: pl. VIb). Thus Davila 1995: 201. As Davila points out, following Jacobsen's analysis, the 'Primaeval King List' was originally independent of the Sumerian King list,

to which it has been subsequently attached. It was probably also independent of the flood narrative, which has become its closure. Ziusudra was added to the list at the time of the connection of genealogy and event.

87. Davila 1995: 199, citing Finkelstein 1963: 49.

88. Davila 1995: 204.

89. *CAD* A ii 57b, *amilu* §4d, citing LÚ *bābili*... 'the ruler of Babylon...'.

90. A good account of myth is given by Glassner 1993: 70: 'that intellectual instrument which in a form at once symbolic and concrete articulates the conceptual system enabling political and social norms to be thought, validates institutions, practices and customs by means of its powers of verbalization and organization'. He treated myth as a literary genre, however, a common categorization with which I am not particularly happy myself. Cf. Chapter 8 above, and also the view of Mondi, Greek and near eastern myth, cited with approval by Noegel 1998: 412, and see chapter 11.

91. A fragment of *Atrahasis* (RS 22.421) was found in Ugarit in 1959, and a fragment of *Gilgamesh*, which if complete would have given another account, was found there in 1994, in addition to a fragment at Megiddo. Other fragments have been found at Hattusa, the Hittite capital, from Assyrian sites, and from Emar on the central Euphrates.

92. Cf. Holloway 1991: 353. He wrote that Noah's kingship was deliberately 'factored out'.

93. See Wyatt 1999b: 871-73; *idem* 1986a. My point here is perhaps a matter of some exegetical importance. That which we are seeking (here, the royal status of a hero) may not be stated in so many words. But it is absurd to demand the presence of a particular form of words ('so and so is a king'), and to ignore other evidence such as all the accompanying paraphernalia of kingship. Here is the difference between the minimalist and the medialist approach. I do not advocate a maximalist approach! But we must at times hypothesize, or our research makes no advances. Hunches are often proved right by subsequent discoveries. If not, then we have learned from the mistake. Noegel 1998: 411-12, cites the following useful observation of Burkert 1992: 8: 'My emphasis is deliberately on providing evidence for correspondences and for the likelihood of borrowings. If in certain cases the materials themselves do not provide incontrovertible evidence of cultural transfer, the establishment of similarities will still be of value, as it serves to free both Greek and the oriental phenomena from their isolation and to create an arena of possible comparisons.' The possibility that Tartessos and Tartaros are to be related, being respectively the end-of-the-world and underworld limits of the conceptualized universe, is an intriguing possibility. See Annus 1999: 23, citing C. Müllerus, *Fragmenta Historicorum Graecorum*, Paris 1883: III, 517-18. The majority of the Titans were consigned to Tartarus after their rebellion, while Atlas was sent to the edge of the ocean named after him. In the fragment of Thallos which Müllerus cited, Ogygos is equated with Kronos, king of the Titans.

94. Graves 1960: II, 141 (§38 n. 3) interpreted the PN Deucalion as δευκος + ἁλιευς ('new wine sailor'), noting the parallel with Noah.

95. Noegel 1998.

96. Fontenrose 1980: 237 and n. 27. Cf. Bernal 1987–91: II, 83: '...Alalkomena or Alkomena was supposed to have been one of the three daughters of Ogygos, the legendary first ruler of Boiotia. Pausanias also reported that Ogygos was also the father of Eleusis – in Attica. Ogygia was the name of Kalypso's far-off island in the *Odyssey*.

Linking the insular, the Boiotian and the Attic connotations of the name is the idea that all come from a primal flood. The German ancient historian Eduard Meyer specifically linked Ogygos with the flooding of Kopais...'

97. Gog and Magog, quasi-mythical representatives of peoples at the remotest confines of the known world, are also possible reflexes of the tradition, though not recognized as such by Lust 1999a; *idem* 1999b.

98. For instance Virolleaud's views of Southern Palestinian references in *Keret,* Virolleaud 1936: 19-20; cf. also de Langhe's Galilean identiates for toponyms in de Langhe 1958; B. Margalit and his 'Kinneret hypothesis' and associated locations, Margalit 1989: 410-22.

99. Lake Hule features (as *ṯmq*) in KTU 1.10 ii 9, 12, probably not to be identified with *ṯmk* of KTU 1.22 i 17. See Wyatt 2002a: 156, n. 4.

100. 'Bashan' generally carries the article in Hebrew: *habbāšān,* though not in Joshua 12.5 above. The title may be descriptive.

101. Corrected according to Syriac: MT *ṣî'ōn,* LXX Σηαν.

102. Or, as most have it, 'scattered'. I have translated as above, supposing that we have in the first two verses an allusion to the *Chaoskampf,* as a result of which El, here evidently the victor, stretched out the corpse of Sea. This is a theme common to biblical, Ugaritic, Mesopotamian and Indian versions of the myth. See for instance Habel 1972; see also Chapter 9.

103. 'The Black Mountain'. See further below.

104. Some translations (e.g. RSV) introduce 'them', supposedly the 'enemies' of v. 22 (EV 21). This is not a necessary interpretation. Note also Dahood's translation (1965-70: II, 131):

> 'I stifled the Serpent,
> muzzled the Deep Sea.'

He himself confesses, rather surprisingly, on p. 145, that 'stifled' is 'a doubtful translation of consonantal *'šyb...',* which he vocalizes *'aššīb.* The important feature is that he regards the bicolon as an allusion to the *Chaoskampf.* My translation takes it to be an allusion to a forthcoming flood, by way of recalling (the supposedly dead) Yam from the depths.

105. Day 1985: 113-19.

106. Dahood 1965-70: II, 142.

107. Day 1985: 115-17, citing Lipiński 1971, and Vlaardingbroek 1973: 75.

108. Day 1985: 113-14.

109. See discussion in Wyatt 1998a.

110. Wyatt 2002a: 383.

111. In terms of prosodic structure, and bearing in mind that there is no pronominal object as in many translations, it seems that *yām* is to be construed in the accusative, as object of *'āšîb,* though this entails not taking it as genitive following construct *m*ᵉ*ṣulôt,* the usual interpretation. This would leave the transitive verb with no object. Taking the first words as anacrusis, I take the bicolon to be in the form *ab.bac* (or *abc.cbd* including the anacrusis), a simple form of staircase parallelism, incorporating a chiasmus, giving some sense of anticipation before the object is mentioned as a closure.

112. Construal of the text as proposed here may also cast new light on the mysterious windows episode of KTU 1.4 v-vi. If the *Chaoskampf* and flood traditions are closely related not merely thematically, but as a literary pair, as proposed below, then it is unsurprising to find in Baal's anxiety a fear that all too soon the chaotic waters will return, to overwhelm his microcosmic temple.

113. As for Day 1985: 115. He therefore construes v. 23 (EV 22) as antithetical parallelism.

114. Cf. Kloos 1986: 136-37 (√*qpy* = 'congeal').

115. Van Buren 1933.

116. Tromp 1969: 54-66. See also Wyatt 1996b: 80-101.

117. Translation from Wyatt 2002a: 395, slightly adapted.

118. A selection of important discussion would include Caquot 1960; *idem* 1976; de Moor 1969b; *idem* 1976; Margulis (= Margalit) 1970; Parker 1972; L'Heureux 1974; *idem* 1979; Pope 1977; Healey 1978; Pitard 1978; *idem* 1987; *idem* 1992; *idem* 1999; Ribichini and Xella 1979; Dietrich and Loretz 1980; Bordreuil and Pardee 1982; Levine and de Tarragon 1984; Good 1980; *idem* 1991; Schmidt 1994; Wyatt 2002a: 210, n. 152; 212, n. 156; 250, n. 5; 314-23; 395-98; 423-25; 430-41.

119. None of the historical kings of Ugarit is so identified. Keret, a literary figure, is proleptically included among their number in KTU 1.15 iii [3], 14, the divine blessing given him by El. Though I have treated Danel's title *mt rpi* differently in Wyatt 1998c: 250, n. 5, (first edition) there is the possibility that he too is to be numbered among them. See now Wyatt 2002a: 250, n. 5. Cf. also the Greek formula μεροπης ἀνθρωποι, noted by Annus 1999: 17, 21. *Rpum* attend the funeral of Niqmaddu III-IV in KTU 1.161. They come to some indeterminate cultic assembly in KTU 1.20-22. Given the context of our discussion, the divine arrival from Sinai with thousands of chariots (Psalm 68.18, EV 17) may perhaps be seen as evoking the imagery of these latter texts.

120. Del Olmo 1999, notes that Og may also be reflected in this deity.

121. The fact that there is geography, and specifically sacred territory, common to both the Ugaritic and biblical literatures, implying a considerable overlap of tradition at the point of Israelite settlement, is an important, and often understated, argument in favour of the use of the former for the interpretation of the latter. So we should not take refuge in accounts of 'similarity' or 'parallels', but recognize frankly that we are talking of the *same* tradition.

122. Noegel 1998: 414, n. 21: *Midrash Bereshit Rabba* 31.13; *Bavli Sanhedrin* 108b; *Targum Pseudo-Jonathan Deuteronomy* 2.11, 3.10; *Yalkut Reubeni* on Genesis 7.22; *Zebaḥim* 113b. The last of these, and *Niddah* 61b, are the most useful. (See also *Hadar* 59a, *Daʿat Huqqat* 18a, cited Graves and Patai 1965: 115, n. 5.)

123. *Iliad* 4.406.

124. Astour 1967: 158 and n. 2; and 212-13, where he also noted that Ogygos' wife was called Thebe (Θηβη). Dalley 1991: 7, drew attention to Apamea Kibotos, a city in the Konya Plain, where a local promontory was identified as 'Mount Ararat'. The element Kibotos (κιβωτος) is obviously epithetal from κιβωτον.

125. Holloway 1991. This drew a response from Hendel, Hendel 1995; and this in turn one in Holloway 1998.

126. Mallowan 1964: 64.

127. Holloway 1991: 343-44: *ziq-qur-rat* KUR-*i*, commonly translated as 'the peak of the mountain', most recently by George 1999: 94. I have cited line numbers as given by George, and by Parpola 1997.

128. Holloway 1991: 346: 'I am suspicious that, at this point, the storyteller's yarn about a sea-going ziggurat has given way to the mundane facts of Mesopotamian temple economy'.

129. Holloway's expression! Many scholars regard the search for the New Year festival to be something of a futile exercise.

130. Hendel 1995: 129.

131. Bottéro 1986: 80, cited (and translated), Hendel 1995: 129. This symmetrical arrangement of the seven layers above and below the habitable world was in some narratives expanded to denote seven heavens above, or seven layers of the underworld below (as in *the Descent of Ishtar* or *Inanna*). The image of Noah's Ark as a type of the Church is common in mediaeval iconography, as well as finding expression in the architectural term 'nave'.

132. Munz 1973.

133. Munz 1973: 40. Cited in Wyatt 1996b: 399-407, where I discussed Munz's general theory.

134. See Mallowan 1964.

135. Ryan and Pitman 1999.

136. Ryan and Pitman 1999: 212-16, refer to the important work of Cavalli-Sforza on genetic drift and human migration. See Cavalli-Sforza and Cavalli-Sforza 1995.

137. Ryan and Pitman 1999: 161: 350 feet.

138. Ryan and Pitman 1999: 263: 'at least three hundred days'. Their figure of 'half a foot per day' (p. 163), however, would give a period of 700 days (2 × 350)

139. For Ballard see www.npr.org/programs/re/archives/991122.blacksea.html, www.npr.org/programs/re/archives/991122.blacksea.html, etc.

140. Here is a short selection:

www.christiananswers.net provides an outline of a number of creationist solutions to various detail problems in the flood narrative. It also thoughtfully provides a 'kids' coloring page', presumably because of its educational value in the Tennessee junior school teaching programme! (postal address: Christian Answers Network, 1832 S. Macdonald Suite 101, Mesa AZ 85210, USA.)

www.geocities.com/truedino and www.cadvision.com/aska/noah have the same home page, and evidently address the common problem (creationism *versus* evolution and Noah's flood as evidence) from slightly different perspectives. The second site was inaccessible and may be discontinued. The first offers a 12-chapter book on Genesis, the flood and the fulfilment of prophecy in Christ, from a creationist perspective. The following charming account (from chapter one) of how fossil mammals occur in the northern tundra is typical: 'The fossils they find in the northern Arctic show evidence of death due to very unusual circumstances. From Siberia to Alaska they have found mammoths, camels, sheep, bisons (*sic*), horses, lions and sabertooth tigers frozen in the ice and mud with their stomach contents still intact. They are found in tangled masses, many torn apart, interspersed with uprooted trees and other vegetation. From their very apparent drowning in water laden sediments they were instantly frozen. The pre-flood canopy model to the post flood adjustment stages account for the physical evidence quite easily. The flood with the collapse of the canopy would account for rapid drowning then rapid freezing due to extreme climatic change.'

www.tagnet.org/anotherviewpoint/ offers a Noachic perspective starting from the geological evidence of the Grand Canyon. The theme is summarized in the opening statement: 'Are you fed up with the pervasive propaganda from the religious philosophy of Evolutionism? Are you tired of constantly telling your kids that the signs and the guides are wrong? We are not the end result of evolution of millions of years. The land is the way it is not because of millions of years of erosion and deposition, but because of Noah's flood catastrophe.'

www.angelfire.com/ca/DeafPreterist/noah.html is a detailed account of the Genesis narrative, judged to be a real historical event, written from a pre-modern perspective.

www.infidels.org/library/modern/frank_zindler/morris-zindler.html is billed as 'The question of Noah's flood: a debate between John D. Morris, of the Institute For Creation Research and Frank R. Zindler, of the Ohio Chapter of American Atheists, broadcast 13 February, 1989 on "AM Indiana", The Dick Wolfsie Show, Channel 13 TV, Indianapolis, Indiana'. It is a splendid example of the non-meeting of minds. 'Debate' is probably too optimistic a term.

These are just a few examples trawled through the Google search engine.

141. Report in the *New York Times* 9 February 2001. Dr Dalley obligingly sent me a transcript of her observations, for which I am grateful.

142. Clottes and Courtin 1994: 166.

143. Basseda 1990.

144. A similar process of elaboration can be discerned in the narrative of the plagues of Egypt in Exodus 7–12. The P version greatly develops the supernatural dimension.

145. The saving of Manu, *Śatapatha Brāḥmaṇa* 1.8.1-16, *Mahābhārata* 3.185; the Avatar of Matsya, *Matsya Purāṇa* 1.11-34, 2.1-19, *Mahābhārata* 12.300, *Agni Purāṇa* 2, *Garuḍa Purāṇa* 1, *Kālikā Purāṇa* 33-34, *Padma Purāṇa* 5.4, 5.73, *Viṣṇu Purāṇa* 9 etc. To be linked to this tradition is the 'Churning of the Ocean', which retrieves items lost in the flood: *Padma Purāṇa* 3.8-10, *Matsya Purāṇa* 249-51, *Mahābhārata* 1.15.5-13, 1.16.1-40, 1.17.1-30, 5.100.1-13, *Bhāgavata Purāṇa* 8.6-12, etc.

146. Wensinck 1918: 50-55.

147. Note too how Sennacherib presented his destruction of Babylon in terms of the flood: 'I arranged it so that the water level of my destruction surpassed that left by the Flood', cited Glassner 1993: 43; Glassner also noted, 70-73, that this is part of the political rhetoric of Mesopotamia, indicating that the mythic basis under discussion here was also present there. The fundamental division of Mesopotamian historiography (followed in turn by biblical historiography), dividing those kings from before the flood from those who followed, reflects the same consciousness.

148. The fragmentary allusion to a binding at KTU 1.1 iv 22 most plausibly refers to Baal. See Wyatt 2002a: 51, n. 59. The context is extremely fragmentary, and how the apparent binding here (perhaps already anticipated at KTU 1.1 ii 7?) and the subsequent humiliation of Baal in the passage above is to be reconciled with the very active Baal of KTU 1.2 i remains obscure. Note that the weapons given to Baal in the present passage are apparently already mentioned at KTU 1.2 i 5-7. As Yam was enthroned above Baal in the passages alluded to, so we may assume that Baal in turn was en-

throned over Yam upon his victory. This would seem to be the implication of Psalm 29.10, in which the very Baal-like Yahweh is said to be enthroned on the flood (*yhwh lammabûl yāšāb*).

149. KTU 1.2 iv 1-10, Wyatt 2002a: 63-65, slightly modified.

150. Note that the same term, *tēbâ,* is used of both Noah's ark and Moses' basket, as indicated in Table 3 above. This is a further interesting link between the flood and *Chaoskampf* traditions, since in some versions of the tradition (e.g. Moses, Perseus), the hero who is to grow up to kill the dragon has himself been cast out to sea in a box or basket. The motif of Sargon cast adrift on the river, who is later to wash his weapons in the sea (i.e. to reenact in his wars the *Chaoskampf*) reflects the same literary nexus.

151. The skilful wording here may refer to exodus or flood, or perhaps both. This suggests that the exodus narrative itself has a diluvian quality. 'The exile is the time of chaos', remarked Wensinck 1918: 51.

152. Isaiah 40.3-11 echoes the wilderness-wandering; 40.12-17, with aqueous allusions, speaks of cosmogony; 40.22 implies the *Chaoskampf* victory, following which the corpse of the chaos-monster is stretched out as the canopy of heaven (echoed in 42.5, 44.24, 45.12, 48.13, this is evidently a *Leitmotif* in Deutero-Isaiah). The figure also appears in Job 9.8, and Psalms 18.10-22, 104.2-3 and 104.5-7.

153. The pseudepigraphical treatment of the themes is not tightly constructed in the way that they are dealt with in the Pentateuch and *Deutero-Isaiah,* where the relationship of the three motifs is most tightly correlated.

154. Wyatt 1998a.

Chapter 13

Androgyny in the Levantine World*

Introduction

A number of colleagues have reacted adversely to my characterization in recent studies on the Ugaritic texts of the deity El as androgynous. It was in response to this criticism that I wrote the first draft of the present paper for a *Festschrift* in honour of Yitzhak Avishur in the summer of 2002. The present version has broadened it a little, and alluded to, but not merely repeated, other elements that I have already published, as well as adding new material, in order to address more directly than in the first draft some of the biblical passages which I shall maintain have a connection with the theme. This in turn will provide at least circumstantial evidence in support of my interpretation of the Ugaritic matieral.

By 'androgyny' in the ensuing discussion I mean not merely 'bisexuality' (as with an aphid or other invertebrate life-forms) or 'hermaphroditism', as having both male and female genitalia, and therefore a monster both in reality and in symbolism (as representing chaos), but rather a widespread metaphor, which has its origin in ancient conceptions of sexuality, concerning primordial deities and primordial men, who contain within themselves an archetype, later to be reified in the separated genders.

Such figures, divine or human, are essentially prototypical, and this mode of their being belongs to the primordial time of the foundation of the world. It follows from their wholly conceptual imagining, that is, as having no actual reality in the world of experience, that they represent a 'theoretical reality', which in Platonic terms would be called an Idea. There is no reason to assume that Platonic modes of thought were invented by Plato. In all probability he was heir to an ancient tradition, and as regards the theme of androgyny, he himself is credited with a version of the concept in mythic form, of Hermaphroditus the offspring of the love of Hermes and Aphrodite. This figure was, however, bisexual rather than androgynous in the sense espoused here, and in any event was hardly a primal figure. In a pre-scientific (even formally pre-philosophical) world, the concept is generally expressed in a rather unsophisticated way by positing a single parent, who performs the roles of both father and mother of divine or human offspring. That is, the image has its origin in a simpler, bisexual expression, but which is striving through the metaphor to articulate something more complex, and which is consequently filled out with symbolic potential over and above the original sense.

This initial act sets in train a new order, perhaps to be seen rather broadly as 'creation', though strictly confined in practice to those subsets we classify as theogony or anthropogony, that is, those conceptual forms which attempt to describe a derivative order which is 'of one substance with the father'. The androgynous state is thus *ipso facto* transformed, as in the Ugaritic example below, in which henceforth the creator deity who is at first male *and* female becomes simply male, for purposes of the initiation of the next generation, thus distinguishing the further levels of the pantheon. That is, the androgynous condition does not persist, but is itself a primordial phase in a developmental process, though the period of initial development may be prolonged, if we assess the Egyptian examples correctly.

The once separated genders, particularly when dealing with human examples, are often regarded as deficient until reunited, as perhaps hinted at in Genesis 2.24, which also offers a clue to the correct overall interpretation of the metaphor. An associated notion which we have no time to develop here is the Aristotelian idea that there was only *one* gender, the conventional 'male' and 'female' manifestations of it being 'perfect' and 'imperfect'.[1]

In his essay *The Two and the One*, Eliade subsumed the concept of androgyny under the more philosophical term *Coincidentia Oppositorum*, the sexual nature of the androgyne being thus one of a range of metaphors for the expression of the totality of the concept.[2] Eliade evidently considered androgyny to be a sexual metaphor for the philosophical ontological issue involved in the ultimate being, namely the oppositions of '*esse* and *non esse*'.[3] This comes out rather nicely in the developing metaphysics of late Vedism, where Prajāpati, an androgynonus creator and prototype of Brahmā, was the personification of Brahman, which was developed in the later *Upaniṣads* on two levels, as *sat* ('being') and *asat* or *bhava* ('not being', 'becoming'). There is no evidence of such thought in the ancient Near East, and yet it *may* already have been intuited by the mythographers. Without explicit clues, we are often at some loss as to the precise meaning of what they wrote. The primacy of the androgyne may be explained in terms of the importance of anthropomorphism in human consciousness (and the unconscious) from hominid times.[4] If some of the Vedic insights just mentioned be regarded as falling foul of E. Johnson's critique of the implicit sexism of much male discourse on this subject (see below), this may be explained frankly in the context of what W.D. O'Flaherty has called the 'virulent misogyny' of much Hindu thought.[5] But the Indian androgyne is not anti-female; it is anti-gender, in its insistence on the phenomenality of all dualities.

The chief importance of androgyny as a religious symbol lies in its offering a counter to the relentlessly analytical nature of human thought, which so readily and persistently splits hairs into ever finer strands, inventing differentiations where none were perceived before, and essentially fragments the universe and human experience into disparate and opposed orders of reality. To this schizoid trend in human culture, androgyny proposes a countervailing primordial oneness, a wholeness from which the fragments emerged, and to which they may periodically return. Cult offers some realization of this aspiration, theology affirms it in seeking a higher synthesis of reality, and as we shall see, it lies deeply within sexual consciousness, and in the longing of lovers to be one, and in the biblical concept of marriage as enunciated in poetic form in Genesis 2.24.

Examples of the motif are well known from around the ancient world, notably in Egypt and India, but also in Greece, Iran, Asia Minor and Mesopotamia. I am going to deal here with evidence from Egypt, Ugarit, and Israel.

Egypt

Within the ancient Near East the idea is perhaps most explicitly developed in Egypt.[6] I shall give a few examples. Their distribution indicates that we have a pan-Egyptian conception here, probably with its roots deeply embedded in African culture, which found particular expression in the local theologies of the cities lying along the Nile.

One of the striking features of Egyptian cosmology, in its various and varied manifestations, is a fundamental dualism. Everything splits into two, and sets of two principles in opposition represent, in merismic fashion, every aspect of reality. To take the most obvious example, the geography of the country: Egypt was always known as 'The Two Lands', a usage preserved in the Hebrew *Miṣra'îm* (a dual form), divided at Memphis between the Delta ('Lower Egypt') and the Nile Valley ('Upper Egypt'). At the same time, another opposition existed, between agricultural land in the valley ('The Black Land') and the desert to east and west ('The Red Land'). This particular opposition easily assumed other oppositions, between life and death, and good and evil, and was represented mythologically in the perpetual opposition of Horus and Seth. These gods also came to symbolize north and south, and so religion articulated, through narrative and cult, the basic realities and antinomies of life in Egypt.

But this opposition, though fundamental, was not *ab origine*. The two gods formed part of the great Ennead of Heliopolis, Seth in the earlier period, a later modified form excluding Seth, and replacing him with Horus:

Earlier Ennead of Heliopolis

Atum *itm*

š(3)w	Shu	Tefnut	*tfnt*
qb	Geb	Nut	*nwt*
wsir	Osiris	Isis	*3st*
stẖ	Seth	Nephthys	*nbt ḥt*

Later Ennead of Heliopolis

Atum

	Shu	Tefnut	Atum was early identified
	Geb	Nut	with Ra, in the triad Khepri-
	Osiris	Isis	Ra-Atum (the sun at his ris-
ḥrw	Horus	Nephthys	ing, zenith and setting)

This structure suggests, given a formal illogicality in the latter form (Horus was never husband to Nephthys), that there was felt to be some sort of identity between the two gods, who were brothers in some versions of the myth of their conflict. In some way they were complementary, so that one could readily replace the other. And this is entirely borne out by their mythology and iconography, in which while in perpetual opposition, each was necessary to the other's being.

The Ennead as set out in these tables shows another pertinent feature: apart from the primordial figure of Atum, all the deities are paired off sexually, in terms of husband and wife (with the exception of Horus and Nephthys mentioned). But this sexual differentiation is *secondary* in the system. This is most clearly represented in the similar

Ennead of Hermopolis

Thoth *ḏḥwty*

nwn	Nun	Naunet	*nwnt*
ḥḥ	Huh	Hauhet	*ḥwḥt*
kk	Kuk	Kauket	*kwkt*
imn	Amun	Amaunet	*imnt*

Though probably originating as a pentad (Thoth and the four figures on the left), the arrangement here is often referred to as the Ogdoad, a concept going back into early Pharaonic times, if not earlier, since the ancient name of Hermopolis was *Ḫmnw*, 'Eight', preserved in the modern Arabic name of the city, *Ashumein*, 'Eight Town'. In this instance, the 'female' elements are merely the feminine forms of the nouns in the left-hand column, themselves all cosmological abstractions, respectively 'Primordial Ocean', 'Infinitude', 'Darkness', and 'Invisibility', the last more familiar to us in his Theban manifestation (a paradox!) of Amun. More to the point, these elements now differentiated by gender and sex are essentially hypostases, phenomenological outworkings, of their source, Thoth. Thoth therefore contained the potential for sexual differentiation, which suggests that he (she!) was conceptualized androgynously, and if the pentadic theory be correct, so were his four evolutes. At this stage we cannot perhaps prove this, but shall see that parallel forms such as the following indicate it. I think that we are to see the Ogdoad with its oppositions as developing rather than perpetuating the potential within Thoth himself, and whether we should accept Peter Schäfer's characterization of the Aeons of the Gnostic systems[7] (he writes of 'androgynous pairs of two', an oxymoron!), so that he can refer to the aeons as androgynous, remains uncertain: it seems to me that the mental differentiation which gives rise to the Aeons, especially when they acquire sexual distinction (as in the Ogdoad perhaps developing from a Pentad) is already a move from an ideal androgyny to a real sexual distinction. We shall detect a similar confusion in some of the modern biblical discussion below.

If we now revert to the Heliopolitan Ennead, we see that the hint we have noted is to be found clearly expressed. Here are some versions of the Heliopolitan cosmogonic myth:

> Atum evolved (*ḫpr*) growing ithyphallic, in Heliopolis.
> He put his penis in his grasp
> that he might make orgasm with it,
> and the two siblings were born – Shu and Tefnut.
>
> (PT 1248: *CS* i 7)

Atum KhepRer!
When you became high, as the high ground,
when you rose, as the benben (*bnbn*)
in the Phoenix (*bnw*) enclosure in Heliopolis,
you sneezed (*išš*) Shu (*šw*),
you spat (*tfn*) Tefnut (*tfnt*),
and you put your arms about them, as the arms of *Ka*,
that your *Ka* might be in them.

(PT 1652-53a: *CS* i 7)

These two narratives give alternative accounts of the cosmogonic process, involving different body fluids. The two metaphors are combined synthetically in this later text:

I (Atum) became united with my members.
They came forth from my very self
after I had played the husband with my fist.
The seed which fell from my hand
I sneezed from my mouth (*išš*) as Shu,
I expectorated (*tfn*) as Tefnut.
I became three gods from one god...

(P. Nes-Min)

A Coffin Text spell explicitly claims androgyny for Atum in these terms:

I am Atum who created (*qm3*) the great ones. I am he who gave birth (*ms*) to Shu. I am the He-She (*pn tn*).

(CT II 160g-161a: cit. Troy, *PQ* 16)

The Ennead of Memphis was probably constructed as follows, though it is nowhere listed in full, so that certainty is not possible. But the Shabaqo stone, which contains the text of the so-called 'Memphite theology' mentions the following in the narrative.

Ennead of Memphis

Ptah *ptḥ*

	Nun	Naunet
	Shu	Tefnut
	Horus	Isis
was Atum a member?	Thoth	Nephthys (?)
was Geb a member?		
Osiris not mentioned in surviving text		

The text also seems to make a deliberate attempt to supersede the older Heliopolitan tradition, by subsuming it, as can be seen from the following excerpts:

> There was evolution (*ḫprw*) into Atum's image through both the heart and the tongue. And great and important is Ptah, who gave life to all the [gods] and their kas as well through this heart and this tongue, as which Horus and Thoth have both evolved (*ḫpr*) by means of Ptah...
>
> His (Ptah's) Ennead is before him, in teeth and lips – that seed and those hands of Atum: for Atum's Ennead evolv[ed] through his seed and his fingers, but the Ennead is teeth and lips in this mouth that pronounced the identity of everything, and from which Shu and Tefnut emerged and gave birth to the Ennead....
>
> *So were all the gods born*, Atum and his Ennead as well...
>
> It has evolved (*ḫpr*) that Ptah is called 'He who made totality and caused the gods to evolve,' since he is Ta-tenen, *who gave birth to the gods*, from whom everything has emerged...
>
> (Shabaqo Stone: *CS* i 22-23)

Ptah was thus taken to be the author in every sense, as father and mother, of the gods (among whom, of course, the king was to be numbered).

If we consider Egyptian iconography, we see something of the elements of the symbolism I have discussed so far, particularly in the ithyphallic representations of divinity. There are numerous examples:

Nut often overarches an ithyphallic Geb in representations of the cosmos. Min and associated figures, notably Amenapet of Thebes, are ithyphallic. Numerous examples appear in relief at Karnak. Two predynastic colossi of Min are in the Ashmolean Museum in Oxford. The Khonsu temple at Karnak even has an ithyphallic Sekhmet, while in the Ptolemaic BD P. Haremheb, a two-headed Min-dwarf, a three-headed ithyphallic (!) winged goddess, another dwarf (= Bes?), the *S3-T3* serpent, and two winged Wadjet-Eyes in procession illustrate BD 163, 164.

We see here a number of deities, Geb, the old earth god of the Heliopolitan Ennead, Min, primaeval god of Coptos who was early identified with Amun, and a form of Amun called Amenapet ('Amun of Luxor') who also assumed a serpentine form, and periodically every tenth year died and regenerated himself. The first of these is curious, because his posture, beneath Nut, his celestial consort, clearly demonstrates a sexual differentiation, though his father Shu, who separates the couple, has also been seen as implicitly androgynous. With Min and Amenapet the situation is clearer, and particularly with the former, since he is shown grasping his phallus, like Atum in the mythic texts. He thus performs a single-handed parenting act. In the royal cultus, a number of mysterious and unseen rituals were performed at Thebes, in which the king and queen participated, in which the queen took the title 'the god's hand', hinting at some sexual activity akin to the iconography seen here. If the present theology is a guide here, the king was represented as androgynous, albeit acting through the agency of his queen.

The final two examples, of Sekhmet (consort of the androgynous Ptah, and apparently here echoing his nature) and a Ptolemaic goddess, with male characteristics, demonstrate at once the paradox of this symbolic language, and the inadequacy of simply regarding the ithyphallic male deities as indelicate art: it is essentially attempting to represent a metaphysical reality through an all-too-physical outer form.

What we have discerned so far, then, is a primordial figure who begets divine offspring as their father and mother. To carry the androgyny from here on into the subsequent generations is problematic. While the sexual differentiation in these subsequent generations (as, most graphically, in the Hermopolitan evidence) is itself evidently merismic, the fact remains that their conceptualization is as pairs, complementary yet distinct. With the primordial father–mother figure, Atum, Thoth or Ptah, the complementarity is contained within the one person, and it is this that constitutes androgyny.

With Sekhmet, consort of Ptah, the paradox is heightened. The idea of a *god* with a phallus is no problem. What is very striking, and disturbing, is the portrayal of an ithyphallic *goddess*.

What is this iconography attempting to express? Perhaps it is similar in conception to the portrayal of Hathor as the outgoing energy and rage of the somewhat reclusive Ra; in this case, Sekhmet is the life-force of a god – Ptah – who is generally represented as mummiform, thus as 'dead', until energized in his consort. Perhaps she is essentially his androgynous dimension.

A number of important Egyptian triads were closely linked with the person of the king.

City	*Father*	*Mother*	*Son (= the king)*
Heliopolis	Ra (= Atum)	Hathor	Horus
Buto, Abydos	Osiris	Isis	Horus
Thebes	Amun	Mut (= Amaunet)	Khonsu
Memphis	Ptah	Sekhmet	Nefertem

The only example here not so far dealt with is the Osirian, and Plutarch relates, in conformity with tradition, that Osiris and Isis, twins, 'consorted while yet in the womb'. This seems to be an attempt to express the principle of the androgyne while at the same time flagging up their sexual differentiation.

Ugarit

Let us now turn to the Ugaritic evidence which triggered this whole enterprise. I remarked above on the rejection of my interpretation of what follows by a number of colleagues.[8] I have animadverted to this on a number of occasions.[9] This evidence is strictly limited to one clear textual passage, but other texts appear to assume the sense which I claim for it, and its implications seem incontrovertible to me. At any rate, no one else has so far made any observations on the issue which might offer a satisfactory alternative explanation, so that even if I am wrong, the dialectic of scholarship may lead on to a better explanation of the material. It has yet to catch up.

The text is KTU 1.23, also known as 'The Gracious Gods'. It is set in a temple at Ugarit, begins with a ritual, premarital circumcision of the deity El, and then narrates his erotic encounter with two wives,[10] who are the goddesses Athirat and Rahmay, avatars of the Ugaritian sun-goddess Shapsh. It was recently characterized by Dennis Pardee as a relatively unimportant myth, involving secondary goddesses.[11] I have challenged this in a review article, since the goddesses in question are consorts of El, the high god, the king and queen are both present at the ritual at which the poem is narrated, and its theme is a royal birth. Indeed, I have elsewhere argued that this text underlies a number of important biblical narratives and liturgical texts.

In the course of the erotic play between the aged god and his partners, they cry out in their ecstasy, using three different forms of address.

The passages are as follows:

hlh tṣḥ ad ad *whlh tṣḥ um um*	Lo, one cried: 'Father! father!' and lo, the other cried: 'Mother! mother! (KTU 1.23.32-33, *RTU* 330)
hm aṯtm tṣhn *ymt mt nḥtm ḫṭk* *mmnnm mṭ ydk*	Lo, the two wives cried out: 'O husband, husband! Lowered is your staff, drooping the rod in your hand!' (KTU 1.23.39-40, 47-48, *RTU* 331-32)
hm aṯtm tṣhn *ad ad nḥtm ḫṭky* *mmnnm mṭ ydk*	And lo, the two wives cried out: 'O father, father! Lowered is your staff, drooping the rod in your hand!' (KTU 1.23.42-44, *RTU* 330)

In addition, this double formula also occurs:

btm bt il *bt il wʿlmh*	The two daughters are the daughters of El, the daughters of El, and forever. (KTU 1.23.45-46, *RTU* 330)
aṯtm aṯt il *aṯt il wʿlmh*	The two wives are the wive[s of El], the wives of El, and forever. (KTU 1.23.48-49 *RTU*, 330)

The following passage also belongs to the present concern, though its form is one used of other deities too, so that at first glance it appears to show no more than El's 'general paternity' of the rest of the pantheon. It is by comparison with the passages cited above that it is seen to point to the more specific picture of androgyny which I am attempting to trace here. These words are addressed by Anat to Shapsh:

tḥm ṯr il abk *hwt lṭpn ḥtkk*	'Message of Bull El, your father, word of the Wise One, your sire. (KTU 1.6 iv 10-11, *RTU* 138-39)

As others have observed and I have argued elsewhere,[12] we are to recognize in this theogonic narrative and its congener in KTU 1.12 i the *Vorlage* of such biblical narratives as the conception and birth of Ishmael (Genesis 16, now separated from its other half, the birth of Isaac), the daughters of Lot and the birth of Moab and Ammon (Genesis 19.30-38), and the traditions of Hosea 1–2, and Ezekiel 16 and 23. In addition, it is the mythic framework for the understanding of the royal Psalms 8, 19 and 110, and demonstrates the hitherto unrecognized royal status of the first two. While Yahweh is the deity involved in most of these contexts, his cognate relationship with El is patent or at least latent.

But the birth of the divine offspring of El and his partners is not the original theogony in this tradition, but a secondary one, following the earlier generation by El, acting the parts of both father and mother, of a goddess or two goddesses (the pair being avatars of the one, as Athirat and Rahmay are hypostases of Shapsh in KTU 1.23). That is why they address him in both terms, as is evident from the quotations above. It is not on account of any future role, however ambiguous, that he may fulfil, but because of what he has already achieved. Herein lies his androgynous nature. It is perhaps significant that no myth from the Semitic world actually narrates this prior event. It is as though it is taken as an axiom from which the stories that are told derive *their* significance: it provides their theological context. The ineffable is passed over in silence.

It might be possible for an analysis hostile to this interpretation to find some alternative explication of the texts just cited, were it not the case, firstly, that there are a number of similar representations of creator-deities in the ancient world as androgynous, as we have already seen to be the case in Egypt, and secondly, were there not so many interesting references in Hebrew literature which are evidently familiar with this way of thinking, and are happy to use it without apology or indeed explanation. For none is needed: writer and reader are agreed on the force of the axiom. Indeed, it is almost a *natural* means of expression in the circumstances. It is ourselves, hedged about by modern philosophical presuppositions and a long tradition of exegesis largely conditioned by the misogyny which so debases western thought,[13] which has led to our incomprehension of the metaphor.

What can we say of the Ugaritic example? It appears that as in Egypt, we have a striking metaphor, but one drawn from the depths of the human psychic constitution, so often veiled in the subconscious. It hints at a primordial oneness underlying the inevitable duality posed by sexual generation. Perhaps it also attempts, in the only way possible in a language with a dearth of abstract forms, to express the abstract through the concrete, and to use the physical form to explore moral and metaphysical possibilities. Indeed, my hesitancy in going further than this points to a critique which I think should be directed at some forms of biblical exegesis, where the language remains in the same way essentially physical, and yet in no way appears to embarrass theologians bent on discerning the most abstract concepts in the text. Since this material from Ugarit is isolated, we cannot really say much more without going beyond the evidence. However, it is without doubt cognate with the biblical material, as the passages cited indicate, and is thus amenable to further analysis by way of adjunct to the more extended exploration of the motif in Hebrew thought. If abstraction in biblical hermeneutics is acceptable, perhaps we should try the same approach here.

Israel-Judah

One area where we might not expect the theme of androgyny is in the Bible. Yet it is here that are to be seen the antecedents of those much-discussed themes of Philo of Alexandria, some early Christian thought, and gnosticism. These are to be seen not as strange aberrations from a biblical norm, but perfectly legitimate outworkings of the potential of the text. Let us introduce this area of our discussion with a lovely rhetorical question which Yahweh puts to Job:

> Does the rain have a father (*'āb*)?
> Or who begot (*hôlîd*) the dewdrops ?
> From whose womb did the ice come forth ?
> and who brought forth (*ye lādô*) the hoarfrost of heaven ?
> (Job 38.28-29)

An equally bold figure occurs in Job 38.8-9:

> (Who) confined Sea behind the double doors
> when he burst forth from the womb?
> when I made clouds his clothing,
> and a thick darkness his swaddling-band. [14]

This is more striking than the first passage, since it clearly draws on the same mythological narrative tradition as the Ugaritic material.

While it cannot be asserted that Job is a monotheistic composition, there is no warrant for supposing these passage to refer to two parents. It is rather the same deity, Yahweh himself, identified with the El Shaddai of the bulk of the poem, who here adopts both paternal and maternal roles in the production of the natural world. In the second passage, though it does not spell it out, there is only one possible womb that could gestate and give birth to the sea, that of Yahweh-El Shaddai himself.

This language in itself is bold enough, and should warn the unwary that we are in the world of metaphor, a perspective all too easily forgotten when the other ancient Near Eastern religions resort to the same idiom. But the passages also specifically represent the deity as androgynous. It may be countered that there is a world of difference between the implicit pantheism of the Egyptian texts and the present instances, but no such charge could be levelled against the Ugaritic material. And all three worlds, Egyptian, Ugaritic and Israelite, are all evidently at ease with the same metaphor.

A number of passages in Deutero- and Trito-Isaiah are also implicitly androgynous in their import: Isaiah 42.14, 49.15a and 66.12-13.[15]

These passages all fulfil our expectations based on the definitional observations offered above, that the image belongs in the context of cosmogony and anthropogony. The Joban passages deal with the origin of the natural world in terms of a birthing metaphor; those in Deutero- and Trito-Isaiah treat the origins of a people, but more particularly, their fashioning in the context of the new creation (the new victorious outcome of the recapitulated *Chaoskampf*) envisaged in such passages as Isaiah 43.16-21 and 51.9-10. The primordial criterion is thus honoured.

The following is perhaps the chief biblical passage, in terms of its historical doctrinal impact.

Genesis 1.26a, 27

> Then God said
> 'Let us make man in our image,
>   according to our likeness...'
> ...
> And God created man in his image;
>   in the image of God he created him;
>   male and female he created them.

The text may be ambiguous concerning the androgynous or unisexual nature of the *'ādām* here, a point to which we shall return immediately, but for present purposes it is evident that the text sees the full range of human sexual identity as constituting the 'divine image'. That is, it points to the incorporation of *both* elements in the nature of the deity. Perhaps the difficulty some modern commentators have had with this lies in the kind of conception of the deity found in the following excerpt from W.F. Albright:[16]

> If...the term 'monotheist' means one who teaches the existence of only one God, the creator of everything, the source of justice, who is equally powerful in Egypt, in the desert, and in Palestine, who has no sexuality and no mythology, who is human in form but cannot be seen by human eye and cannot be represented in any form – then the founder of Yahwism was certainly a monotheist.

M. Smith, who cites this passage in his recent study on monotheism, points out that Albright's conception here is synthetic, and would require citations from very diverse parts of the record to sustain what is in effect a composite picture. That is, it is not in its entirety supported by any single text. More to the point, from our present perspective, the assertion that a monotheistic god has no sexuality flies in the face of the primary evidence for just that perception, quoted above from Genesis 1. The non-sexual view of the deity is a non-biblical one. It belongs rather to the field of philosophy of religion, and perhaps owes something to the misconception of Canaanite religion, and thus of the relationship of Yahwism to it, as a perverse, depraved and overwhelmingly orgiastic 'fertility cult', which the Israelites at their best eschewed. Such a view is no longer tenable. And as Margalit demonstrated,[17] the sexual imagery of so many prophetic diatribes speaks not against the 'foreign' orgiastic cults so dear to the modern commentator, but rather against the true marriage relationship between Israel and Yahweh. That is, the root of this sexual metaphor lies in a sexual conception of Yahweh's relationship with his people, an idea some evidently find a hard one to swallow, even when it is recognized as symbolic and mythological in nature.

I have also argued elsewhere against the non-mythological conception of Yahweh entertained by many biblical scholars.[18] But to make assertions of this kind does not mean that we are stuck with an unreflective conception of the deity. The conscious human mind, and perhaps the unconscious mind too, working in what I have called 'myth-mode', uses elements of the real world (of human experience, including sexuality) as a means of postulating an ideal world. So we are not, if we wish to penetrate the ideal world, obliged to remain hung up on the metaphor (which I suspect is one reason why some biblical theologians are distinctly uncomfortable with it). In fact, I think that the metaphor of sexuality is a profound one, and evokes perhaps the widest possible range of emotional and moral dimensions of human experience: it is in short by far the richest metaphoric field that can be used.

This passage from Genesis 1 was discussed in a perceptive article by E. Johnson.[19] Writing in the earlier days of feminist scholarship on the Bible, she noted the inadequacy of two modes of discussing the divine nature which dominated the male-dominated scholarship of the time, and set an unbalanced agenda, reinforcing various social stereotypes, and misrepresenting the inclusive message of the Bible. The Bible itself is hardly without prejudice in such matters, of course, but has moments of great insight which, she argued, were being systematically misinterpreted. Her starting point in the part of the discussion which concerns us here is the incomprehensibility of God.

(It is this tendency to go way beyond the letter of the text, while purporting to express, and possibly succeeding in legitimately so doing, the meaning of the author, that I was suggesting above was perhaps too bold an approach to ancient texts. My starting point is a case in point, since I was criticized precisely for attempting to get behind the letter to discern the spirit in the Ugaritic material.) However, let us remain with Johnson.

Before proceeding to her preferred exposition, she describes two inadequate forms of exegesis; the first, characteristically in the work of male theologians, recognizes feminine traits in the biblical portrayal of the divine, but does so almost consciously as a patronizing concession which merely reinforces the implicit sexism;[20] the second seeks, as she puts it, 'a more ontological footing for the existence of the feminine in God',[21] yet still concludes that the spiritual, transcendent aspect of the deity is masculine, while the material and immanent aspect is feminine, with just a hint of its subordinate status. Her option is 'the image of God male and female',[22] in which paradox she discerns an attempt to express the incomprehensibility of God: 'God is not a person as anyone else we know, but the language of person evokes in a unique way the mysteriousness, nonmanipulability, and freedom of action associated with God'.[23] By and large I find this a reasonable position, particularly as it is elaborated in her further discussion. However, I think that this perception is to some extent in tension with the materials to which I now wish to turn, so that it requires some qualification within a larger framework.

Many years ago I was speaking with a late friend of mine, Abe Sirton. 'I always think of Anthropology as the best kind of Theology', I remarked. Quick as a flash he retorted, 'Anthropology is the only kind of Theology!'

He spoke as a confirmed atheist. But I find myself in sympathy with his perspective whenever I find myself among theologians! And I think that we have to turn to the anthropology of the Hebrew Bible to set things in a proper balance.

We have spoken thus far of androgyny as peculiar to creator deities, and belonging to primordial time. But there is one interesting exception. This relates to the person of the king. The tradition so dear to Hollywood of the irrepressible incest of the Egyptian royal family may be explained on two counts. First, it may relate to the legal conventions of matrilineal descent, in which the king must marry all women who are actual or potential channels of the legal possession of the kingdom, represented mythologically by their identification with Isis. But secondly, or alternatively, it may be explained on the ground that the king must marry all those women of whom he is the father, just as the creator god did *in illo tempore*. The king would thus impersonate and act out in his life the cosmogony. This is the more plausible in that in the other, martial tradition, which begins with the myth of divine victory of the Chaos-monster, the king is given divine weapons at his coronation, so that he may re-enact the *Chaoskampf* in his own battles.[24] Of all the kings of Egypt, one stands out as most clearly representing this second theme. Amenhotpe IV, better known as Akhenaten, is often credited with the invention of monotheism. He abolished the Theban cult of Amun-Ra in favour of that of the Aten, the sun-disc. This issue is immeasurably complex, and need not detain us. One of the features of Akhenaten's reign was the abandonment of the idealizing conventions of Egyptian art, in favour of contorted forms often represented as a kind of realism, warts and all.

The king himself is shown in statues and reliefs with the most extraordinary body, which has led to all kinds of theory as to which particular glandular or hormonal dysfunction he was subject. A far simpler explanation is that he is deliberately represented as androgynous. He is father and mother to his people. R.E. Freed, for instance, among those scholars recognizing this aspect, observes

> In other ways these statues [of the king] are quite traditional... Those with double crowns may represent Atum, the androgynous god, identified with the sun...those with feather crowns...evoke Shu, his firstborn son, and those with tall crowns recall Tefnut, Shu's female twin...[25]

To return to the Genesis tradition. The second account of the creation of Man, Genesis 2.4-7, 18, 21-24, generally credited to the Yahwist, is no less clear with regard to the theme of androgyny. So far as the actual narrative is concerned, however, the androgyny is this time specifically implied only of the *'ādām* figure, in contrast to (but obviously complementing and echoing) the explicit androgyny of the deity in Genesis 1 above:

> On the day when Yahweh-God made earth and heaven,
> before any plant of the steppe was on the earth,
> or any herb of the steppe had sprouted;
> for Yahweh-God[26] had not yet caused it to rain upon the earth,
> and there was no Man to till the soil,
> a mist[27] was rising up from the underworld
> and watered the whole surface of the ground.
> Then Yahweh-God fashioned man from dust from the ground,
> and he breathed into his nostrils the breath of life,
> and the Man became a living being.
> ...
> And Yahweh-God said, 'It is not good for the Man to be alone. I shall make him a helper suitable for him.'
> ...
> Then Yahweh-God caused a deep sleep to fall on the man, and he slept. And he took one of his ribs, and closed up the flesh in its place. And Yahweh-God turned the rib which he had taken from the Man into a Woman, and he brought her to the man.
> Then the Man said:
> 'At last!
> Bone from my bone,
> flesh from my flesh;
> this shall be called "Woman",
> for from Man was this taken.'
> Therefore a man leaves his father and his mother and cleaves to his wife, and they are one flesh.

This charming narrative, part-poetic in construction, as I have suggested in my layout of the text, is a nice, if surprising, example of the application of the theory of androgyny to the real world of experience, and incidentally to the newly-developed idea of monotheism. There is an intriguing twist: in the older tradition, surviving elsewhere in the Bible, daughters are parented by the deity. Now at first glance it is a son. But this son is androgynous. His female part is locked up inside him until released by the removal of the rib. In fact another mother lurks in the background, as the following pattern demonstrates:

> Earth (*ʾădāmâ*) gives birth to man (*ʾādām*);
> Man (*ʾîš*) gives birth to Woman (*ʾiššâ*)

The man is mother to the woman. Perhaps this makes more sense once we recognize the often overlooked ideological element in the Eden narrative, for the Man is not simply Everyman; rather is he prototypical Man, as embodied in the king. The androgynous dimension is thus an ideological feature. This may be compared with the iconography of the Egyptian royal tradition. To be divine – as all kings are according to the ideology – means to be the image, that is the visible form, of one's divine parent. The parent of the West Semitic king is El himself. The parent of the king of Judah is Yahweh.

It is the presentation of the Adam-figure in Genesis 2, in combination with the erotic interplay of the lovers in the Song of Songs, whose attribution, remember, is a king, Solomon, which leads me to consider whether we should not see in such language precisely the *anthropology* of which Abe Sirton and I spoke. That is, what is really incomprehensible, and requires teasing out through the paradoxes of theological construction, is the true and transcendent nature of man. Born of earth and the divine breath, his very flesh, that most ephemeral of dimensions, for 'all flesh is grass', yearns for oneness with being, and this is achieved in that most magnificent of estimates of the man–woman relationship which I cited above: the becoming one flesh… By this I think I mean – I am still puzzling this out – that the image is one of individuation, of the achievement of psychic maturity, of true adulthood.

Endnotes

* An earlier version of this paper was published in M. Heltzer and M. Malul (eds.), *Teshûrôt LaAvishur. Studies in the Bible and the Ancient Near East, in Hebrew and Semitic Languages. Festschrift Presented to Prof. Yitzhak Avishur on the Occasion of his 65th Birthday* (Tel Aviv: Archaeological Center Publications, 2004): 191*-98*.

1. Van der Horst 1990.
2. Eliade 1962: particularly 78-124; cf. *idem* 1958: 420-25.
3. Eliade 1958: 421.
4. Guthrie 1993.
5. See O'Flaherty 1997: 170.
6. My student Richard McCrea wrote a fine account of the Egyptian evidence: McCrea 2001. See also Zandee 1988; Westendorf 1977.

7. Schäfer 2002: 74.

8. E.g. H. Niehr 2001: 310; J.-M. de Tarragon 2001: 424. Cf. also M.S. Smith 2000: 669; *idem* 2001: 90 and 247-48, n. 41, and Rendsberg 2000: 195, for a rejection of my interpretation of Psalm 19, which involves the implicit androgyny of Asherah's father and husband, and thus extends the androgyny to Yahweh, whom I understand to be in origin a hypostasis of El.

9. Wyatt 1998a: 330, n. 33; *idem* 1999a: 542-43.

10. The term *aṯt* in ll. 39 etc. is better translated 'wives' than 'women' (thus, for instance, Gray 1956: 123; for a more nuanced approach see Pardee 1997: 280-81), which prejudges their status, implicitly precluding a divine nature.

11. Pardee 2000: 56.

12. Wyatt 1994a; 1994b; 1996b: 219-91 (219-356), all with references to earlier discussion.

13. For the pervasive nature of this see Coakley 1997, and my review, Wyatt 1998b.

14. The problems of this passage are discussed in Chapter 12, n. 25.

15. I leave out of the account as ambiguous for this present discussion such passages as Isaiah 44.2a; 44.21, 24; 46.3b; 49.1b and 49.5a. All these draw on the idiom of divine parentage of the king, in which a distinct female figure (the queen, be she divine or human) plays a role alongside Yahweh. Cf. Eve in Genesis 4.1.

16. Albright 1946: 271; cited for discussion by M.S. Smith 2001: 150.

17. Margalit 1990.

18. See Wyatt 1996b *passim* and Chapter 11.

19. Johnson 1984.

20. Johnson 1984: 454-56.

21. Johnson 1984: 457 (457-60).

22. Johnson 1984: 460-63.

23. Johnson 1984: 460.

24. See 1998a.

25. Freed 1999: 113.

26. Or perhaps 'Lord of the gods': Wyatt Chapter 11, n. 1.

27. Or perhaps 'a mountain'. See Gordon 1955: 62, linking *'ēd* with Greek Ida, and Chapter 12, n. 12

Bibliography

Aberbach, M., and L. Smolar

1967 'Aaron, Jeroboam and the Golden Calves', *JBL* 86: 129-40.

Ackroyd, P.R.

1968 *Exile and Restoration* (OTL; London: SCM Press).

Ahlström, G.W.

1963 *Aspects of Syncretism in Israelite Religion* (Horae Söderblomianae, 5; Lund: C.W.K. Gleerup).

Aimé-Giron, N.

1941 'Baʿal Saphon et les dieux de Tahpanhês dans un nouveau papyrus phénicien', *ASAE* 40: 433-60.

Aitken, K.

1990 *The Aqhat Narrative* (JSSMS, 13; Manchester: University of Manchester).

Albertz, R.

1994 *A History of Israelite Religion in the Old Testament Period* (2 vols.; London: SCM Press); ET of *Religionsgeschichte Israels in alttestamentlicher Zeit* (2 vols.; ATD Ergänzungs-reihe, 8; Göttingen: Vandenhoeck & Ruprecht).

Albrektson, B.

1967 *History and the Gods* (Horae Soderblomianae, 5; Lund: C.W.K. Gleerup).

1968 'On the Syntax of אֶהְיֶה אֲשֶׁר אֶהְיֶה', in P.R. Ackroyd (ed.), *Words and Meanings: Essays Presented to David Winton Thomas on his Retirement from the Regius Chair of Hebrew in the University of Cambridge* (Cambridge: Cambridge University Press): 15-28.

Albright, W.F.

1926 'The Jordan Valley in the Bronze Age', *AASOR* 6 (1924–25): 13-74.

1934 'The North Canaanite Poems of Al'eyan Baʿal', *JPOS* 14: 101-40.

1936 'The Song of Deborah in the Light of Archeology', *BASOR* 62: 26-31.

1940 *From the Stone Age to Christianity* (Baltimore: The Johns Hopkins University Press).

1941 'Anath and the Dragon', *BASOR* 84: 14-17.

1946 *From the Stone Age to Christianity: Monotheism and the Historical Process* (Baltimore: The Johns Hopkins University Press, 2nd edn [1940]).

1950 'Baal-Zephon', in W. Baumgartner (ed.), *Festschrift für Alfred Bertholet* (Tubingen: Mohr): 1-14.

1950–51 'A Catalogue of Early Hebrew Lyric Poems (Psalm lxviii)', *HUCA* 23: 1-39.

1957 'Recent Books', *BASOR* 146: 34-35.

1965 *Archeology and the Religion of Israel* (Garden City, NY: Doubleday, 5th edn).

1968 *Yahweh and the Gods of Canaan* (London: Athlone Press).

1972 'Ašerah', in *EJ* iii: 700-704.

Allan, R.

1999 'Now that Summer's Gone; Understanding *qẓ* in KTU 1.24', *SEL* 16: 19-25.

Allard, M.

1957 'Note sur la formule *Ehyeh ašer Ehyeh*', *RSR* 45: 79-86.

Allegro, J.M.

1955 'Uses of the Demonstrative *z* in Hebrew', *VT* 5: 309-12.

Alt, A.

1929 *Der Gott der Väter* (BWANT, 3.12; Stuttgart: W. Kohlhammer); ET 'The God of the Fathers', in Alt 1966: 1-77.

1934 *Die Ursprünge des israelitischen Rechts* (*BVSAWL* Philologisch-Historische Klasse, 86.1; Leipzig: S. Hirzel); ET 'The Origins of Israelite Law', in Alt 1966: 79-132.

1966 *Essays in Old Testament History and Religion* (Oxford: Basil Blackwell).

Andersen, F.I., and D.N. Freedman

1980 *Hosea* (AB, 24; Garden City, NY: Doubleday).

Anderson, B.W.

1962 'Exodus Typology in Second Isaiah', in B.W. Anderson and W. Harrelson (eds.), *Israel's Prophetic Heritage: Essays in Honor of James Muilenburg* (New York: Fortress Press; London: SCM Press): 177-95.

Anderson, K.T.

1962 'Der Gott meines Vaters', *ST* 16: 170-88.

Annus, A.

1999 'Are there Greek Rephaim? On the etymology of Greek Meropes and Titanes', *UF* 31: 13-30.

d'Aquili, E.G., and C.D. Laughlin

1979 'The Neurobiology of Myth and Ritual', in E.G. d'Aquili and C.D. Laughlin (eds.), *The Spectrum of Ritual* (New York: Columbia University Press): 152-82.

Arberry, A.J.

1964 *The Koran Interpreted* (London: Oxford University Press).

Ardrey, R.

1969 *The Territorial Imperative* (London: Collins [1967]).

Arnold, W.R.

1905 'The Divine Name in Exodus III 14', *JBL* 24: 107-65.

Assmann, J.

1972 '"Die Häresie" des Echnaton: Aspekte der Amarna-Religion', *Saeculum* 23: 109-26.

1982 'Die Zeugung des Sohnes: Bild, Spiel, Erzählunge und das Problem des ägyptischen Mythos', in J. Assmann, W. Burkert and F. Stolz (eds.), *Funktionen und Leistungen des Mythos: drei altorientalische Beispiele* (OBO, 48; Fribourg: Fribourg University Press; Göttingen: Vandenhoeck & Ruprecht): 13-61.

1983 *Re und Amun: die Krise des polytheistischen Weltbilds im Ägypten der 18.–20. Dynastie* (OBO, 51; Fribourg: Fribourg University Press; Göttingen: Vandenhoeck & Ruprecht); ET *Egyptian Solar Religion in the New Kingdom: Re, Amun and the Crisis of Polytheism* (London: Routledge, 1995).

Astour, M.C.

1967 *Hellenosemitica* (Leiden: E.J. Brill, 2nd edn).

1975 'Place Names §89: *Spn*', in Fisher 1975–81: II, 318-24.

Aus, R.D.

1998 *Caught in the Act, Walking on the Sea, and the Release of Barabbas Revisited* (SFSHJ, 157; Atlanta GA: Scholars Press).

Bagrow, L.
1964 *History of Cartography* (London: Watts).
Bailey, L.R.
1971 'The Golden Calf', *HUCA* 42: 97-115.
Baines, J.
1991 'Egyptian Myth and Discourse: Myth, Gods, and the Early Written and Iconographic Record', *JNES* 50: 81-105.
Barker, M.
1991 *The Gate of Heaven* (London: SPCK).
Barr, J.
1957–58 'The Problem of Israelite Monotheism', *TGUOS* 17: 52-62.
1961 *The Semantics of Biblical Language* (Oxford: Oxford University Press).
Bartsch, H.-W. (ed.)
1972 *Kerygma and Myth* (London: SPCK, 2nd edn); ET of *Kerygma und Mythos* (Hamburg: Reich, 1948–1955).
Basseda, L.
1990 *Toponymie Historique de Catalunya Nord* (Prades: Terra Nostra).
Batto, B.F.
1983 'The Reed Sea: *Requiescat in Pace*', *JBL* 102: 27-35.
1984 'Red Sea or Reed Sea?', *BAR* 10: 57-63.
1993 *Slaying the Dragon* (Louisville, KY: Westminster/John Knox Press).
Beal, T.K.
2002 *Religion and its Monsters* (New York; London: Routledge).
Bérard, V.
1902–03 *Les Phéniciens et l'Odyssée* (2 vols.; Paris: Armand Colin).
Berger, P.
1973 *The Social Reality of Religion* (Harmondsworth: Penguin); orig., *The Sacred Canopy* (London: Faber, 1967).
Berger, P., and T. Luckmann
1971 *The Social Construction of Reality* (Harmondsworth: Penguin [London: Allen Lane, 1967]).
Bernal, M.
1987–91 *Black Athena: The Afro-Asiatic Roots of Classical Civilization* (2 vols.; London: Free Association Press; New York: Rutgers University Press). (Reference to Rutgers University Press third printing 1993.)
Betz, H.D. (ed.)
1986 *The Greek Magical Papyri*, I (Chicago: University of Chicago Press).
Beyerlin, W.
1978 *Near Eastern Religious Texts Relating to the Old Testament* (London: SCM Press).
Bič, M.
1949 'Bet'el – le sanctuaire du roi', *ArOr* 17: 49-63.
Binger, T.
1997 *Asherah: Goddesses in Ugarit, Israel and the Old Testament* (JSOTSup, 232; CIS, 2; Sheffield: Sheffield Academic Press).
Blackmore, S.
1999 *The Meme Machine* (Oxford: Oxford University Press).
Blythin, I.
1962 'A Note on Genesis i 2', *VT* 12: 121.

Boman, T.

1960 *Hebrew Thought Compared with Greek* (London: SCM Press); ET of *Das hebräische Denken im Vergleich mit dem Griechischen* (Göttingen: Vandenhoeck & Ruprecht, 2nd edn, 1954).

Bonnet, H.

1952 *Reallexikon der Ägyptischen Religionsgeschichte* (Berlin: W. de Gruyter).

Bordreuil, P.

1989a 'A propos de la topographie économique de l'Ougarit: jardins du midi et pâturages du nord', *Syria* 66: 263-74.

1989b 'La citadelle sainte du Mont Nanou', *Syria* 66: 275-79.

1990 'La déesse ʿAnat et les sources du Sapon', in *Techniques et Pratiques Hydro-agricoles Traditionelles en Domaine Irrigué, Approches Pluridisciplinaires des Modes de Culture avant la Motorisation en Syrie. Actes du Colloque de Damas 27 Juin–1er Juillet 1987* (supervised by Bernard Geyer; BAH, 136; Paris: Geuthner): 257-69.

Bordreuil, P., and D. Pardee

1982 'Le rituel funéraire ougaritique', RS 34: 126; *Syria* 59: 121-28.

1993 'Le combat de Baʿlu avec Yammu d'après les textes ougaritiques', *MARI* 7: 63-70.

Bottéro, J.

1986 'La première Arche de Noé', *L'Histoire* 94: 80ff.

Bourke, M.M.

1958 'Yahweh, the Divine Name', *The Bridge* 3: 271-87.

Bowman, R.A.

1944 'Yahweh the Speaker', *JNES* 3: 1-8.

Boyce, M.

1975 *A History of Zoroastrianism*, I (Leiden: E.J. Brill).

Boyer, P.

1994 *The Naturalness of Religious Ideas: A Cognitive Theory of Religion* (Berkeley: University of California Press).

Brandon, S.G.F.

1963 *Creation Legends of the Ancient Near East* (London: Hodder & Stoughton).

Brekelmans, C.H.W.

1954 'Exodus xviii and the Origins of Yahwism in Israel', *OTS* 10: 215-24.

Briggs, C.A., and E.G. Briggs

1907 *Psalms* (2 vols.; ICC, Edinburgh: T. & T. Clark).

Brillant, M., and R. Aigrain

1953–57 *Histoire des Religions* (4 vols.; Paris: Bloud & Gay).

Brooke, G.J., A.H.W. Curtis and J.F. Healey (eds.)

1994 *Ugarit and the Bible: Proceedings of the International Symposium on Ugarit and the Bible. Manchester, September 1992* (UBL, 11; Münster: Ugarit-Verlag).

Brown, C.H.

1983 'Where Do Cardinal Direction Terms Come from?', *AL* 25: 121-61.

Brown, W.N.

1942 'Creation in the Rig Veda', *JAOS* 62: 85-98.

Brueggemann, W.

1972 'From Dust to Kingship', *ZAW* 84: 1-18.

Bruner, J.

1986 *Actual Minds, Possible Worlds* (Cambridge, MA: Harvard University Press).

Budde, K.
1895 'The Nomadic Ideal in the Old Testament', *NW* 4: 726-45 (Das nomadische Ideal im Alten Testament, *PJ* 1896).
van Buren, E.D.
1933 *The God with Vase and Flowing Streams* (Berlin: Schoetz).
Burkert, W.
1983 *Homo Necans: The Anthropology of Ancient Greek Sacrificial Ritual and Myth* (Berkeley: University of California Press); ET of *Homo Necans* (Berlin: W. de Gruyter, 1972).
1992 *The Orientalizing Revolution* (Cambridge, MA: Harvard University Press).
Campbell, J.F.
1911 *The Celtic Dragon Myth* (ET G. Henderson; Edinburgh, 1911).
Caquot, A.
1960 'Les Rephaim ougaritiques', *Syria* 37: 75-93.
1976 La tablette RS 24: 252 et la question des Rephaïm ougaritiques, *Syria* 53: 295-304.
Caquot, A., and M. Sznycer
1980 *Ugaritic Religion* (Iconography of Religions, 15.8; Leiden: E.J. Brill).
Caquot, A., M. Sznycer and A. Herdner
1974 *Textes Ougaritiques i: Mythes et Légendes* (LAPO, 7; Paris: Cerf).
Cassuto, U.
1971 *The Goddess Anath* (Jerusalem: Magnes Press).
Cavalli-Sforza, L.L., and F. Cavalli-Sforza
1995 *The Great Human Diasporas: The History of Diversity and Evolution* (Reading, MA: Addison Wesley).
Changeux, R.
1985 *Neuronal Man* (Oxford: Oxford University Press); ET of *L'Homme Neuronal* (Paris: Fayard, 1983).
Charlesworth, J.H. (ed.)
1985 *The Old Testament Pseudepigrapha* (2 vols.; New York: Doubleday).
Chelhod, J.
1973 'Contribution au problème de la préeminence de la droite, d'après le témoignage arabe', *Anthropos* 59 (1964): 529-45; ET in Needham 1973: 239-62.
Childs, B.S.
1974 *Exodus* (OTL, London: SCM Press).
Christen, E.J., and H.E. Hazelton (eds.)
1969 *Monotheism and Moses* (Lexington, MA: Heath).
Church, C.D.
1975 'Myth and History as Complementary Modes of Consciousness', in Gibbs and Stevenson 1975: 35-55
Clapham, L.
1976 'Mythopoeic Antecedents of the Biblical World-View and their Transformation in Early Israelite Thought', in F.M. Cross, W.E. Lemke and P.D. Miller (eds.), *Magnalia Dei, the Mighty Acts of God: Essays on the Bible and Archaeology in Memory of G.E. Wright* (Garden City, NY: Doubleday): 108-19.
Clear, J.
1976 *Ugaritic Texts in Translation* (Seattle, 2nd edn).
Clifford, R.J.
1972 *The Cosmic Mountain in Canaan and the Old Testament* (HSM, 4; Cambridge, MA: Harvard University Press).

Clines, D.J.A.
1978 *The Theme of the Pentateuch* (Sheffield: Sheffield Academic Press).
Clottes, J., and J. Courtin
1994 *La Grotte Cosquer: Peintures et Gravures de la Grotte Engloutie* (Paris: Seuil).
Coakley, S. (ed.)
1997 *Religion and the Body* (CSRT, 8; Cambridge: Cambridge University Press).
Collingwood, R.G.
1946 *The Idea of History* (Oxford: Oxford University Press).
Connerton, P.
1989 *How Societies Remember* (Cambridge: Cambridge University Press).
de Contenson, H.
1992 *Préhistoire de Ras Shamra* (RSO, VIII; 2 vols.; Paris: ERC).
Coogan, M.D.
1978 *Stories from Ancient Canaan* (Philadelphia: Westminster Press).
Cook, R.
1974 *The Tree of Life* (London: Thames & Hudson).
Cross, F.M.
1973 *Canaanite Myth and Hebrew Epic* (Cambridge, MA: Harvard University Press).
Curtis, J.B.
1963 'A Suggested Interpretation of the Biblical Philosophy of History', *HUCA* 34: 115-23.
Cutler, B., and J. Macdonald
1982 'On the origin of the Ugaritic text KTU 1.23', *UF* 14: 33-50.
Dahood, M.J.
1965-70 *Psalms I-III* (3 vols.; AB, 16-17a; Garden City, NY: Doubleday).
Dalley, S.
1991 *Myths from Mesopotamia* (Oxford: Oxford University Press).
Danielus, E.
1967–68 'The Sins of Jeroboam ben-Nebat', *JQR* 58: 95-114.
Danthine, E.
1961 'Creation et séparation', *Le Muséon* 74: 441-51.
Danthine, H.
1937 *Le Palmier-Dattier et les Arbres Sacrés dans l'Iconographie de l'Asie Occidentale Ancienne* (BAH, 25; Paris: Geuthner).
Davies, D.
1977 'An Interpretation of Sacrifice in Leviticus', *ZAW* 8: 387-99.
Davies, P.R.
1995 *Whose Bible Is It Anyway?* (JSOTSup, 204; Sheffield: Sheffield Academic Press).
Davila, J.
1995 'The Flood Hero as King and Priest', *JNES* 54: 199-214.
Day, J.
1985 *God's Conflict with the Dragon and the Sea* (UCOP, 35; Cambridge: Cambridge University Press).
1989 *Molech: A God of Human Sacrifice in the Old Testament* (UCOP, 42; Cambridge: Cambridge University Press).
1994 'Ugarit and the Bible: Do They Presuppose the Same Canaanite Mythology and Religion?', in Brooke, Curtis and Healey 1994: 35-52

Deacon, T.
1997 *The Symbolic Species. The Co-Evolution of Language and the Human Brain* (Harmondsworth: Penguin Books).
Delitzsch, F.
1888 *The Psalms* (3 vols.; London: Hodder & Stoughton).
Denison, S.
1995 'From Modern Apes to Human Origins', *British Archaeology* (October 1995): 8-9.
Dennett, D.C.
1992 *Consciousness Explained* (London: Viking; repr. Harmondsworth: Penguin Books, 1993).
Dhorme, E.
1926 *Le Livre de Job* (Paris).
Dietrich, M., and O. Loretz
1980 '*Baal Rpu* in KTU 1.108; 1.113 und nach 1.17 vi 25-33', *UF* 12: 171-82.
1990 'Ugaritisch *ṣrrt ṣpn, ṣrry* und hebräisch *yrkty ṣpwn*', *UF* 22: 79-86.
Dijkstra, M.
1991 'The Weather-God on Two Mountains', *UF* 23: 127-40.
Dijkstra, M., and J.C.De Moor
1975 'Problematic Passages in the Legend of Aqhatu', *UF* 7: 171-215.
Dimond, S.J., and J.G. Beaumont
1974 *Hemisphere Function in the Human Brain* (London: Elek).
Donald, M.
1991 *Origins of the Modern Mind* (Cambridge, MA: Harvard University Press).
Donner, H.
1973 'Hier sind deine Götter, Israel!', in H. Gese and H.P. Ruger (eds.) *Wort und Geschichte (FS K. Elliger)* (AOAT, 18; Neukirchen-Vluyn: Neukirchener Verlag).
Dougherty, J.J.
1955 'The Origins of Hebrew Religion, a Study in Method', *CBQ* 17: 258-76.
Douglas, M.
1970 *Purity and Danger* (Harmondsworth: Penguin Books [London, 1966]).
1972 'Deciphering a Meal', *Daedalus* 101: 61-81; later in *Natural Symbols* (London: Harmondsworth, 2nd edn, 1975): 249-75.
Drinkard, J.H.
1992 'Direction and Orientation', *ABD*: II, 204.
Driver, G.R.
1955 'Birds in the Old Testament', *PEQ* 87: 129-40.
1956 *Canaanite Myths and Legends* (Edinburgh: T. & T. Clark).
Dubarle, A.M.
1951 'La signification du nom de Iahweh', *RSPT* 85: 3-21.
Duchemin, J.
1995 *Mythes Grecs et Sources Orientales* (Paris: Les Belles Lettres).
Dulles, A.
1966 'Symbol, Myth and Biblical Revelation', *TS* 27: 1-26.
Dumermuth, F.
1958 'Zur deuteronomistischen Kulttheologie und ihren Voraussetz-ungen', *ZAW* 70: 59-98.
Dumézil, G.
1934 *Ouranos-Váruna* (Paris: Maisonneuve).

Dunbar, R.I.M.
1993 ‘Coevolution of Neocortical Size, Group Size and Language in Humans’, *BBS* 16: 681-735.

Durand, J.-M.
1984 ‘A propos du nom de la hache à Mari’, *MARI* 3: 279.
1993 ‘Le mythologème du combat entre le dieu de l’orage et la mer en Mésopotamie’, *MARI* 7: 41-61.

Dus, J.
1968 ‘Die Stierbilder von Bethel und Dan und das Problem der “Moseschar” ’, *AION* 18: 105-37.

Edwards, I.E.S, *et al.* (eds.)
1970-75 *Cambridge Ancient History (*vols. I.1, I.2, II.1 and II.2; London: Cambridge University Press, 3rd edn).

Eichrodt, W.
1970 *Ezekiel* (OTL; London: SCM Press).

Eilberg-Schwartz, H.
1990 *The Savage in Judaism: An Anthropology of Israelite Religion and Ancient Judaism* (Bloomington, IN: Indiana University Press).

Eissfeldt, O.
1932 *Baal Zaphon, Zeus Kasios, und der Durchzug der Israeliten durchs Meer* (BRA, 1; Halle: Niemeyer).
1963 ‘Mythus und Sage in den Ras-Schamra-Texten’, in *Kleine Schriften* (Tübingen: Mohr): II, 489-501; reprint of article in *Beiträge zur Arabistik, Semitistik und Islamwissenschaft* (1944): 267-83.
1965a *The Old Testament, an Introduction* (Oxford: Basil Blackwell); ET of *Einleitung in das Alte Testament* (Tübingen: Siebeck, 3rd edn, 1934).
1965b ‘ ’Äheyäh ’ašär ’äheyäh und ’El ʿOlam’, *FuF* 39: 298-300.
1966 ‘Baʿal Saphon von Ugarit und Amon von Agypten’, *FuF* 36: 338-40; also published as *Kleine Schriften* (Tübingen: Mohr): IV, 53-57.

Eliade, M.
1958 *Patterns in Comparative Religion* (London: Sheed & Ward); ET of *Traité d’Histoire des Religions* (Paris: Payot, 1949).
1959 ‘Some Methodological Remarks on the Study of Religious Symbolism’, in M. Eliade and J. Kitagawa (eds.), *History of Religions: Problems of Methodology* (Chicago: University of Chicago Press): 86-107
1964 *Myth and Reality* (London: Allen & Unwin).
1965 *The Two and the One* (trans. J.M. Cohen; London: Harvill Press).
1974 *The Myth of the Eternal Return: Or, Cosmos and History* (New York: Bollingen [1954]); ET of *Le mythe de l’éternel retour: archétypes et répétition* (Paris: Gallimard, 1949).

Ellis-Davidson, H.R.
1964 *Gods and Myths of Northern Europe* (Harmondsworth: Penguin Books).

Emerton, J.A.
1972 ‘A Difficult Part of Mot’s Message to Baal in the Ugaritic Texts’, *AJBA* 1: 50-71.
1982 ‘Leviathan and *ltn*: The Vocalization of the Ugaritic Word for the Dragon’, *VT* 32: 327-31.

Engnell, I.
1943 *Studies in Divine Kingship in the Ancient Near East* (Uppsala: Almqvist & Wiksells).
Epstein, M.M.
1996 'Harnessing the Dragon: A Mythos Transformed in Medieval Jewish Literature and Art', in L.L. Patton and W. Doniger (eds.), *Myth and Method* (Charlottesville; London: University Press of Virginia): 352-89.
Evelyn-White, H.G.
1914 *Hesiod, the Homeric Hymns and Homerica* (LCL; New York: Harvard University Press; London: Heinemann).
Fairman, H.W.
1935 'The Myth of Horus at Edfu I', *JEA* 21: 26-36.
Faulkner, R.O.
1937 'The Bremner-Rhind Papyrus, III', *JEA* 23: 166-85.
1938 'The Bremner-Rhind Papyrus, IV', *JEA* 24: 41-53.
Fauth, W.
1990 'Das Kasion-Gebirge und Zeus Kasios', *UF* 22: 105-18.
Feldman, L.H.
1996 'Homer and the Near East: The Rise of the Greek Genius', *BA* 59: 13-21.
Finkelstein, J.J.
1963 'The Antediluvian Kings: A University of California Tablet', *JCS* 17: 39-51.
Fishbane, M.
1971 'Jeremiah iv 23-26 and Job iii 3-13: A Recovered Use of the Creation Pattern', *VT* 21: 151-67.
Fisher, L.R. *et al.* (eds.)
1972–81 *Ras Shamra Parallels*, III (ed. S. Rummel; 3 vols.; AnOr, 49-51; Rome: Pontifical Biblical Institute).
Fleming, D.
1998 'The Biblical Tradition of Anointing Priests', *JBL* 117: 401-14.
Flight, J.W.
1923 'The Nomadic Idea and Ideal', *JBL* 42: 158-226.
Fohrer, G.
1973 *History of Israelite Religion* (London: SPCK); ET of *Geschichte der israelitischen Religion* (Berlin: W. de Gruyter, 1968).
Fontenrose, J.
1980 *Python: A Study of Delphic Myth and its Origins* (Berkeley: University of California Press [1959]).
Forsyth, N.
1987 *The Old Enemy* (Princeton, NJ: Princeton University Press).
Frankfort, H.
1939 *Cylinder Seals, a Documentary Essay on the Art and Religion of the Ancient Near East* (London: Macmillan).
1951 *The Problem of Similarity in Ancient Near Eastern Religions* (Oxford: Clarendon Press).
Frankfort, H., and H.A. Frankfort (eds.)
1946 *The Intellectual Adventure of Ancient Man*; republished minus Chapters 8–11 as W.A. Irwin, *Before Philosophy* (Harmondsworth: Penguin Books, 1949).
Freed, R.E.
1999 'Art in the Service of Religion and the State', in R.E. Freed, Y.J. Markovitz and

S.H. d'Auria (eds.), *Pharaohs of the Sun: Akhenaten, Nefertiti, Tutankhamun* (Boston: Museum of Fine Arts): 110-29.

Fronzaroli, P.
1965 'Studi sul lessico comune semitico', *Accademia Nazionale dei Lincei* (Scienze morale Ser. VIII): XX, fasc. 5-6, 246-269; §5, 'L'orientamento': 255-59.

Frost, H.
1991 'Anchors Sacred and Profane', in M. Yon (ed.), *Arts et Industries de la Pierre* (RSO, 6; Paris: ERC): 355-410.

Gardner, H.
1975 *The Shattered Mind: The Person after Brain Damage* (London: Routledge & Kegan Paul).

Gaster, T.H.
1950 *Thespis* (New York: Schumann, 2nd edn, 1966).
1969 *Myth, Legend and Custom in the Old Testament* (London: Gerald Duckworth).

George, A.R.
1999 *The Epic of Gilgamesh: A New Translation* (New York: Barnes & Noble).

Gibbs, L.W., and W.T. Stevenson (eds.)
1975 *Myth and the Crisis of Historical Consciousness* (Missoula, MT: Scholars Press).

Gibson, J.C.L.
1978 *Canaanite Myths and Legends* (Edinburgh: T. & T. Clark).
1984 'The Theology of the Ugaritic Baal Cycle', *Orientalia* 53: 202-19.

Ginsberg, H.L.
1936 'Baʿlu and his Brethren', *JPOS* 16:138-49.
1938 'A Ugaritic Parallel to 2 Samuel 1.23', *JBL* 57: 209-13.
1941 'Did Anath Fight the Dragon?', *BASOR* 84: 12-14.

Glassner, J.-J.
1993 *Chroniques Mésopotamiennes* (Paris: Les Belles Lettres); ET in preparation (Atlanta: Scholars Press).
1996 'Les temps de l'histoire en Mésopotamie', in A. Pury *et al.* (eds.), *Israël construit son histoire* (Le Monde de la Bible; Geneva: Labor et Fides): 167-89.
2001 'Le devin historien en Mésopotamie', in T. Abusch (ed.), *Proceedings of the XLV Rencontre Assyriologique Internationale: Historiography in the Cuneiform World*, I (Bethesda, MD: CDL Press); ET *Mesopotamian Chronicles* (SBLWAW, 19; Atlanta, GA: SBL, 2004).

Godley, A.D.
1921–31 *Herodotus* (4 vols.; LCL; Cambridge, MA: Harvard University Press; London: Heinemann).

Goetze, A.
1941 'The City Khalbi and the Habiru People', *BASOR* 79: 32-34.

Good, R.M.
1980 'Supplementary Remarks on the Ugaritic Funerary Text RS 34.126', *BASOR* 239: 41-42.
1991 'On RS 24.252', *UF* 23: 155-60.

Goodenough, E.R.
1954 *Jewish Symbols in the Graeco-Roman Period* (12 vols.; New York: Pantheon).

Gordon, C.H.
1949 *Ugaritic Literature* (Rome: Pontifical Biblical Institute).
1955 'Homer and the Bible, the Origin and Character of East Mediterranean Literature', *HUCA* 26: 43-108.

1965 *Ugaritic Textbook* (AnOr, 38; Rome: Pontifical Biblical Institute).
1966 'Leviathan: Symbol of Evil', in A. Altmann (ed.), *Biblical Motifs* (Cambridge, MA: Harvard University Press): 1-9.
1969 'Vergil and the Near East', *Ugaritica* 6: 267-88.
1977 'Poetic Legends and Myths from Ugarit', *Berytus* 25: 5-133.

Grabbe, L.L. (ed.)
1998 *Leading Captivity Captive: The 'Exile' as History and Ideology* (JSOTSup, 278; ESHM, 2; Sheffield: Sheffield Academic Press).

Graetz, H.
1874–92 *Geschichte der Juden* (4 vols.; Leipzig: Leiner).

Grave, C.
1980 'The Etymology of Northwest Semitic *ṣapanu*', *UF* 12: 221-29.
1982 'Northwest Semitic *ṣapanu* in a Break-up of an Egyptian Stereotype Phrase in *EA* 147', *Orientalia* 51: 161-82.

Graves, R.
1960 *The Greek Myths* (2 vols.; Harmondsworth: Penguin Books, 3rd edn).

Graves, R., and R. Patai
1965 *Hebrew Myths: The Book of Genesis* (London: Cassell, 2nd edn).

Gray, J.
1949 'The Desert God ᶜAṯtr in the Literature and Religion of Canaan', *JNES* 8: 72-83.
1956 *Canaanite Myths and Legends* (OTS, 3; Edinburgh: T. & T. Clark).
1964 *I and II Kings* (OTL; London: SCM Press).
1965 *The Legacy of Canaan* (SVT, 9; Leiden: E.J. Brill; 2nd edn).

Grimme, H.
1896 'Abriß der biblisch-hebräischen Metrik', *ZDMG* 50: 529ff.

Gunkel, H.
1901a *Genesis* (Göttingen: Vandenhoek & Ruprecht; 3rd edn 1910, 6th edn 1964); ET *Genesis* (Macon, GA: Mercer University Press, 1997).
1901b *The Legends of Genesis: The Biblical Saga and History* (New York: Schocken Books, 1964 reprint); ET of first section of 1901a.

Guthrie, S.E.
1993 *Faces in the Clouds: A New Theory of Religion* (Oxford: Oxford University Press).

Habel, N.
1965 'The Form and Significance of the Call Narratives', *ZAW* 77: 297-303.
1972 'He Who Stretches out the Heavens', *CBQ* 34: 417-30.

Hahn, H.
1956 *The Old Testament in Modern Research* (London: SCM Press; 2nd edn).

Haldar, A.
1950 'The Notion of the Desert in Sumero-Accadian and West-Semitic Religions', *UUÅ* 1950: 3.

Hall, E.H.
1966 *The Hidden Dimension* (Garden City, NY: Doubleday).

Hay, L.S.
1964 'What Really Happened at the Sea of Reeds?', *JBL* 83: 397-403.

Hayman, A.P.
1986 'Some Observations on Sefer Yesira: (2) The Temple at the Centre of the Universe', *JJS* 37: 176-82.

Healey, J.F.
1978 'Ritual Text KTU 1.161 – Translation and Notes', *UF* 10: 83-91.
1998 'The Kindly and Merciful God', in M. Dietrich and I. Kottsieper (eds.), *'Und Mose schrieb dieses Lied auf...' Studien zum Alten Testament und zum alten Testament. FS O. Loretz* (AOAT, 250; Münster: Ugarit-Verlag): 349-56.

Heider, G.C.
1985 *The Cult of Molek* (JSOTSup, 43; Sheffield: Sheffield Academic Press).

Heil, J.
1981 *Jesus Walking on the Sea: Meaning and Gospel Functions of Matt 14.22-33, Mark 6.45-52 and John 6.15b-21* (AnBib, 87; Rome: Pontifical Biblical Institute).

Heller, J.
1958 'Der Name Eva', *ArOr* 26: 636-56.

Hendel, R.S.
1995 'The Shape of Utnapishtim's Ark', *ZAW* 107: 128-29.

Hertz, J.
1960 *Death and the Right Hand* (Aberdeen: Cohen & West).
1973 'La préeminence de la main droite: étude sur la polarité religieuse', *RP* 68 (1909), 553-80; reprinted in *Mélanges de sociologie religieuse et folklore* (1928): 99-129; ET in Hertz 1960, and in Needham 1973: 3-31.

L'Heureux, C.
1974 'The Ugaritic and Biblical Rephaim', *HTR* 67: 265-74.
1979 *Rank among the Canaanite Gods: El, Baʿal and the Repha'îm* (HSM, 21; Missoula, MT: Scholars Press).

Hick, J. (ed.)
1977 *The Myth of God Incarnate* (London: SCM Press).

Himmelfarb, M.
1993 *Ascent to Heaven in Jewish and Christian Apocalypses* (Oxford: Oxford University Press).

Hoffner, H.A.
1990 *Hittite Myths* (SBLWAW, 2; Atlanta, GA: Scholars Press).

Hoffner, H.A. (ed.)
1973 *Orient and Occident FS C.H. Gordon* (AOAT, 22; Neukirchen-Vluyn: Neukirchener Verlag; Kevelaer: Verlag Butzon and Bercker).

Höfner, M.
1965 'Südarabien (Saba', Qatabān u. a.)', in H.W. Haussig (ed.), *Wörterbuch der Mythologie*. I. *Götter und Mythen im Vorderen Orient* (Stuttgart: E. Klett) 483-552.

Holloway, S.W.
1991 'What Ship Goes There: The Flood Narratives in the Gilgamesh Epic and Genesis Considered in Light of Ancient Near Eastern Temple Ideology', *ZAW* 103: 328-55.
1998 'The Shape of Utnapishtim's Ark: A Rejoinder', *ZAW* 110: 617-26.

Holt, J.M.
1964 *The Patriarchs of Israel* (Nashville: Vanderbilt University Press).

Hooke, S.H. (ed.)
1933 *Myth and Ritual: Essays on the Myth and Ritual of the Hebrews in Relation to the Culture Pattern of the Ancient East* (London: Oxford University Press).
1935 *The Labyrinth: Further Studies in the Relation between Myth and Ritual in the Ancient World* (London: SPCK).

1958 *Myth, Ritual and Kingship: Essays on the Theory and Practice of Kingship in the Ancient Near East and in Israel* (Oxford: Clarendon Press).

1962 *Genesis In the Beginning* (Oxford: Clarendon Press, 2nd edn).

Hopkins, W.D., K.A. Bard, A. Jones, and S.L. Bales

1993 'Chimpanzee Hand Preference in Throwing and Infant Cradling: Implications for the Origin of Human Handedness', *CA* 34: 786-90.

Horowitz, W.

1998 *Babylonian Cosmic Geography* (Mesopotamian Civilizations, 8; Winona Lake IN: Eisenbrauns).

van der Horst, P.W.

1990 'Sarah's Seminal Emission: Hebrews 11.11 in the Light of Ancient Embryology', in D.L. Balch, E. Ferguson and W.A. Meeks (eds.), *Greeks, Romans and Christians: Essays in Honor of Abraham J. Malherbe* (Minneapolis: Fortress Press).

Horton, R.

1960 'A Definition of Religion, and its Uses', *JRAI* 90: 201-26.

Husser, J.-M.

1997 'Shapash psychopompe et le pseudo-hymne au soleil (KTU 1.6 vi 42-53)', *UF* 29: 227-44.

Hyatt, J.P.

1967 'Was Yahweh Originally a Creator Deity?', *JBL* 86: 369-77.

1971 *Exodus* (NCB; London: Oliphants).

Irwin, W.A.

1939 'Exodus iii 14', *AJSL* 56: 297-98.

Jagersma, H.

1982 *A History of Israel in the Old Testament Period* (London: SCM Press).

Jamme, F.

1947 'Le panthéon sud-arabe préislamique d'après les sources épigraphiques', *Le Muséon* 60: 57-147.

1948 'D. Nielsen et le panthéon sud-arabe préislamique', *RB* 55: 227-44.

Jaynes, J.

1976 *The Origin of Consciousness in the Breakdown of the Bicameral Mind* (Boston: Houghton Mifflin).

Jenson, R.P.

1983 'The Praying Animal', *Zygon* 18: 311-25.

Jirku, A.

1962 *Kanaanäische Mythen und Epen aus Ras Schamra-Ugarit* (Gütersloh: Mohn).

Johnson, E.A.

1984 'The Incomprehensibility of God and the Image of God Male and Female', *TS* 45: 441-65.

Jones, G.H.

1984 *1 and 2 Kings* (NCB; Grand Rapids MI: Eerdmans).

Jung, C.G.

1969 *Psychology and Religion: West and East* (Collected Works, 11; Princeton, NJ: Princeton University Press, 2nd edn).

Kaiser, O.

1959 *Die mythische Bedeutung des Meeres* (BZAW, 78; Berlin: W. de Gruyter).

1974 *Isaiah 13–39* (OTL; London: SCM Press; ET of *ATD* 18, 1973).

Kapelrud, A.S.

1969 *The Violent Goddess* (Oslo: Universitets Forlaget).

Kaplan, L.
1981 '"And the Lord Sought to Kill Him" (Exod 4.24) Yet Again', *HAR* 5: 65-74.

Käsemann, E.
1960 'Die Anfänge christlicher Theologie', *ZTK* 57: 162-85; reprinted in *Exegetische Versuche und Besinnungen* (2 vols.; Göttingen: Vandenhoeck & Ruprecht, 2nd edn 1965): II, 82-104; ET 'The Beginnings of Christian Theology', in *idem*, *New Testament Questions of Today* (London: SCM Press, 1969): 82-107.

Kaye, A.S. (ed.)
1991 *Semitic Studies in Honor of Wolf Leslau on the Occasion of his Eighty-Fifth Birthday, November 14th, 1991* (2 vols.; Wiesbaden: Harrassowitz).

Keel, O.
1978 *The Symbolism of the Biblical World* (London: SPCK).

Keel, O., and C. Uehlinger
1992 *Göttinen, Götter und Gottessymbole. Neue Erkenntnisse zur religionsgeschichte Kanaans und Israels aufgrund bislang unerschlossener ikonographische Quellen* (QD, 134; Freiburg: Herder); ET *Gods, Goddesses and Images of God in Ancient Israel* (trans. Thomas H. Trapp; Edinburgh: T. & T. Clark, 1998).

Keita, S.O.Y., and R.A. Kittles
1997 'The Persistence of Racial Thinking and the Myth of Racial Divergence', *AA* 99: 534-44.

Kemp, B.
1989 *Ancient Egypt: Anatomy of a Civilization* (London: Routledge).

Kerstein, G. *et al.* (eds.)
1968 *Oriens-Occidens. Ausgewählte Schriften zur Wissenschafts- und Kulturgeschichte. Festschrift für Willy Hartner zum 60. Geburtstag* (Collectanea, 3; Hildesheim: Georg Olms Verlagsbuchhandlung).

Key, A.F.
1965 'Traces of the Worship of the Moon-god Sin among the Early Israelites', *JBL* 84: 20-26.

Kiessling, N.K.
1970 'Antecedents of the Mediaeval Dragon in Sacred History', *JBL* 89: 167-77.

Kikawada, I.M.
1972 'Two Notes on Eve', *JBL* 91: 33-37.

Kilian, R.
1966 'Gen. i 2 und die Urgötter von Hermopolis', *VT* 16: 420-38.

King, D.
1997 *The Commissar Vanishes: The Falsification of Photographs and Art in Stalin's Russia* (Edinburgh: Canongate).

Kinsbourne, M.
1978a 'Biological Determinants of Functional Bisymmetry and Assymetry', in *idem* (ed.), *Assymetrical Function of the Brain* (Cambridge: Cambridge University Press): 3-13.
1978b 'Evolution of Language in Relation to Lateral Action', in *idem* (ed.), *Assymetrical Function of the Brain* (Cambridge: Cambridge University Press): 553-65.

Kirk, G.S.
1970 *Myth: Its Meaning and Functions in Ancient and Other Cultures* (Cambridge: Cambridge University Press).

Klein, R.W.
1979 *Israel in Exile* (Philadelphia: Fortress Press).

Kloos, C.
1986 *Yhwh's Combat with the Sea* (Leiden: E.J. Brill).
Knight, C.
1987 'The Lunar Analogue and the Origins of Culture', *Cosmos* 3: 72-106.
1991 *Blood Relations: Menstruation and the Origins of Culture* (New Haven: Yale University Press).
Koch, K.
1972 *The Rediscovery of Apocalyptic* (London: SCM Press); ET of *Ratlos vor der Apokalyptik* (Gütersloh: Mohn, 1970).
Kraus, H.-J.
1966 *Worship in Israel* (Oxford: Basil Blackwell); ET from second edition, 1962 of *Gottesdienst in Israel* (Munich: Kaiser Verlag, [1954]).
Krzak, Z.
1993 'From Panshamanism to Panrationalism: An Outline of Evolution of Human Thought from the Stone Age to the Twentieth Century', *AP* 38: 51-73.
Kselman, J.S.
1978 'The Recovery of Poetic Fragments from the Pentateuchal Priestly Source', *JBL* 97: 161-73.
Kuhn, T.
1970 *The Structure of Scientific Revolutions* (Chicago: University of Chicago Press).
Kuiper, F.B.J.
1975–76 'The Basic Concept of Vedic Religion', *HR* 15: 107-20.
Kuper, A.
1988 *The Invention of Primitive Society: Transformations of an Illusion* (London: Routledge).
Lack, R.
1962 'Les origines de Elyon, le Très-Haut, dans la tradition cultuelle d'Israël', *CBQ* 24: 44-64.
Lambert, W.G.
1986 'Ninurta Mythology in the Babylonian Epic of Creation', in K. Hecker and W. Sommerfeld (eds.), *Keilschrifliche Literaturen: Ausgewählte Vorträge der X. Rencontre Assyriologique Internationale* (Berlin: Dietrich Reimer): 55-60.
Landy F.
1983 *Paradoxes of Paradise* (Sheffield: Almond Press).
Lane, W.R.
1963 'The Initiation of Creation', *VT* 13: 63-73.
Lang, A.
1887 *Myth, Ritual and Religion* (2 vols.; London: Longmans, Green).
Langdon, S.
1923 *The H. Weld-Blundell Collection in the Ashmolean Museum* (*OECT*, 2; Oxford: Clarendon Press).
de Langhe, R.
1945 *Les Textes de Ras Shamra-Ugarit et leurs Rapports avec le Milieu Biblique de'Ancien Testament* (2 vols.; Paris: Desclée de Brouwer).
1958 'Myth, Ritual and Kingship in the Ras Shamra Tablets', in S.H. Hooke (ed.), *Myth, Ritual and Kingship* (Oxford: Oxford University Press): 122-48.
Larner, J.
1999 *Marco Polo and the Discovery of the World* (London and New Haven, CT: Yale University Press).

Leach, E., and A. Aycock

1983 *Structuralist Interpretations of Biblical Myth* (Cambridge: Cambridge University Press).

Leibovitch, J.

1948 'Un nouveau dieu égypto-cananéen', *ASAE* 48: 435-44.

Levine, B.A., and J.-M. de Tarragon

1984 'Dead Kings and Rephaim: The Patrons of the Ugaritic Dynasty', *JAOS* 104: 649-59.

Lévi-Strauss, C.

1977 'The Structural Study of Myth', in *Structural Anthropology* (Harmondsworth: Penguin Books), I, 206-31.

Lévy-Bruhl, L.

1910 *Les fonctions mentales dans les sociétés inférieures* (Paris: Bibliothèque de Philosophie Contemporaine).

Lewis, T.H.

1996 '*CT* 13: 33-34 and Ezekiel 32: Lion-Dragon Myths', *JAOS* 116: 28-47.

Lewy, H.

1895 *Die semitischen Fremdwörter im Griechischen* (Berlin: Gaertners).

Lewy, I.

1956 'The Beginnings of the Worship of Yahweh: Conflicting Biblical Views', *VT* 6: 429-35.

Lewy, J.

1934 'Les textes paléo-assyriens et l'Ancien Testament', *RHR* 110: 29-65.

1945–46 'The Late Assyro-Babylonian Cult of the Moon and its Culmination in the Time of Nabonidus', *HUCA* 19: 405-89.

Lex, B.

1979 'Neurobiology of Ritual Trance', in d'Aquili and Laughlin 1979: 117-51.

Lindbeck, G.A.

1984 *The Nature of Doctrine: Religion and Theology in a Postliberal Age* (Philadelphia: Westminster Press).

Lipiński, E.

1967 'Juges 5. 4-5 et Psaume 68. 8-11', *Biblica* 48: 185-206.

1971 'El's Abode: Mythological Traditions Related to Mount Hermon and to the Mountains of Armenia', *OLP* 2: 13-69.

1972 'The Goddess Aṯirat in Ancient Arabia, in Babylon, and in Ugarit', *OLP* 3: 101-19.

Littleton, C.S.

1982 *The New Comparative Mythology* (Berkeley: University of California Press, 3rd edn).

Lods, A.

1932 *Israel, from its Beginnings to the Middle of the Eighth Century* (London: Routledge & Kegan Paul).

Loehr, M.

1936 *A History of Religion in the Old Testament* (London: Ivor Nicholson & Watson).

Loewe, M., and C. Blacker (eds.)

1975 *Divination and Oracles* (London: Allen & Unwin).

Lonergan, B.J.F.

1957 *Insight: A study of Human Understanding* (London: Longmans, Green).

Lust, J.

1999a 'Gog', in *DDD*, 2nd edn: 373-75.

1999b 'Magog', in *DDD*, 2nd edn: 535-37.

Luysten, R.

1978 'Myth and History in Exodus', *Religion* 8: 155-70.

Lyle, E.

1990 *Archaic Cosmos* (Edinburgh: Polygon).

Macdonell, A.A.

1974 *A Practical Sanskrit Dictionary* (Oxford: Oxford University Press; [Longman, Green, 1893]).

Maclean, P.D.

1982 'Evolution of the Psychencephalon', *Zygon* 17: 187-211.

Madden, P.

1997 *Jesus' Walking on the Sea: An Investigation of the Origin of the Narrative Account* (BZNW, 81; Berlin: W. de Gruyter).

Malamat, A.

1989 *Mari and the Early Israelite Experience* (Schweich Lectures; Oxford: British Academy).

Mallowan, M.E.L.

1964 'Noah's Flood Reconsidered', *Iraq* 26: 62-82.

Manning, J.T., and A.T. Chamberlain

1990 'The Left-Side Cradling Preference in Apes', *AB* 39: 1224-226.

Marais, E.,

1973 *The Soul of the Ape* (Harmondsworth: Penguin, 1970).

Marblestone, H.A.

1996 '"Mediterranean Synthesis": Professor Cyrus H. Gordon's Contributions to the Classics', *BA* 59: 22-30.

Marc, O.

1977 *Psychology of the House* (London: Thames & Hudson).

Margalit, B.

1970 (as B. Margulis), 'A Ugaritic Psalm (RŠ 24.252)', *JBL* 89: 293-304.

1989 *The Ugaritic Poem of Aqht* (BZAW, 182; Berlin: W. de Gruyter).

1990 The Meaning and Significance of Asherah, *VT* 40: 264-97.

1996 'Ugaritic *ʿṯtr.ʿrẓ* and DAPT (I 14) *šgr.wʿštr*', in Wyatt, Watson and Lloyd, 1996: 179-203

Margulis, B. – see B. Margalit

May, H.G.

1941 'The God of my Father – a Study of Patriarchal Religion', *JBR* 9: 155-58, 199-200.

Mayani, Z.

1935 *L'arbre sacré et le rite de l'alliance chez les anciens Sémites. Etude comparée des religions de l'Orient Classique* (Paris: Geuthner).

Mayer, W.R.

1989 'Akkadische Lexicographie: *CAD* Q III Babylonisch', *Orientalia* 58: 267-75.

Mayrhofer, M.

1966 *Die Indo-Arier im alten Vorderasien* (Wiesbaden: Harrassowitz).

Mazar, B.

1969 'The Historical Background to the Book of Genesis', *JNES* 28: 73-83.

McCrea, R.G.
2001 'Androgyny as a Cosmogonical Motif in Ancient Egyptian Religion' (MA dissertation, Department of Archaeology, University of Edinburgh).

McCurley, F.R., Jr
1974 'The Home of Deuteronomy Revisited: A Methodological Analysis of the Northern Theory', in H.N. Bream *et al.* (eds.), *A Light unto my Path* (Philadelphia: Temple University Press): 295-317.

Meek, T.J.
1920–21 'Some Religious Origins of the Hebrews', *AJSL* 37: 101-31.
1950 *Hebrew Origins* (New York: Harper, 2nd edn [1936]).

Meier, S.
1986 'Baal's Fight with Yam (KTU 1.2.I,IV)', *UF* 18: 241-54.

Merlat, P.
1951 'Observations sur les Castores dolichéniens', *Syria* 28: 229-49.

Millard, A.R.
1984 'The Etymology of Eden', *VT* 34: 103-106.

Miller, P.D.
1981 'Ugarit and the History of Religions', *JNSL* 9: 119-28.

Mills, W.H.
1842 *Observations on the Attempted Application of Pantheistic Principles to the Theory and Historical Criticism of the Gospel* (2 vols.; Cambridge: Deighton, Bell).

Minette de Tillesse, G.
1962 'Sections "tu" et sections "vous" dans le Deutéronome', *VT* 12: 29-87.

Mithen, S.
1996 *The Prehistory of the Mind: A Search for the Origins of Art, Religion and Science* (London: Thames & Hudson).

Mol, H.
1976 *Identity and the Sacred* (Oxford: Basil Blackwell).

Mondi, R.
1990 'Greek and Near Eastern Mythology', in L. Edmunds (ed.), *Approaches to Greek Myth* (Baltimore: The Johns Hopkins University Press): 140-98.

Monier-Williams, M.
1899 *A Sanskrit–English Dictionary* (Oxford: Oxford University Press).

Montgomery, J.A.
1938 '*Yam sup.* ("The Red Sea") = *Ultimum Mare?*', *JAOS* 58: 131-32.
1951 *Kings* (ICC; Edinburgh: T. & T. Clark).

de Moor, J.C.
1969a 'Review of Gröndahl *PTU*', *BiOr* 26: 106-107.
1969b 'RS 24.252', *UF* 1: 175-79.
1971 *The Seasonal Pattern in the Ugaritic Poem of Baʿlu According to the Version of Ilimilku* (AOAT, 16; Neukirchen-Vluyn: Neukirchener Verlag; Kevelaer: Verlag Butzon & Bercker).
1976 'Rāpi'ūma – Rephaim', *ZAW* 88: 323-45.
1987 *An Anthology of Religious Texts from Ugarit* (Nisaba, 16; Leiden: E.J. Brill).
1990 *The Rise of Yahwism: The Roots of Israelite Monotheism* (Leuven: Leuven University Press; Peeters).
1998 'The Duality in God and Man: Gen. 1.26-7 as P's Interpretation of the Yahwistic Creation Account', in J.C. de Moor (ed.), *Intertextuality in Ugarit*

and Israel: Papers Read at the Tenth Joint Meeting of the Society for Old Testament Study and Het Oudtestamentisch Werkgezelschap in Nederland en Belgie, Held at Oxford 1997 (*OTS*, 40; Leiden: E.J. Brill): 112-25.

Moran, W.L.
1987 *Les lettres d'El Armana* (LAPO, 13; Paris: PUF).

Morgenstern, J.
1920–21 'The Elohist Narrative in Exodus 3 1-15', *AJSL* 37: 242-62.

Motzki, H.
1975 'Ein Beitrag zum Problem des Stierkultes in den Religionsgeschichte Israels', *VT* 25: 470-85.

Mowinckel, S.
1962 *The Psalms in Israel's Worship* (2 vols.; Oxford: Basil Blackwell, repr. 1982); ET of *Offersang og sangoffer* (Oslo: Aschehoug, 1951).

Muchiki, Y.
1999 *Egyptian Proper Names and Loan-Words in North-West Semitic* (SBLDS, 173; Atlanta GA: Society of Biblical Literature).

Mullen, H.P.
1980 *The Divine Council in Canaanite and Early Hebrew Literature* (HSM, 24; Chico, CA: Scholars Press).

Munz, P.
1973 *When the Gold Bough Breaks: Structuralism or Typology?* (London: Routledge and Kegan Paul).

Murray, R.
1992 *The Cosmic Covenant* (Heythrop Monographs; London: Sheed & Ward).

Naccache, A.
1996 'El's Abode in his Land', in Wyatt, Watson and Lloyd, 1996: 249-72.

Needham, R. (ed.)
1973 *Right and Left: Essays on Dual Symbolic Classification* (Chicago: University of Chicago Press).

Neiman, D.
1977 'Gihôn and Pishôn: Mythological Antecedents of the Two Enigmatic Rivers of Eden', in A. Shinan (ed.), *Proceedings of the 6th Congress of Jewish Studies* (Jerusalem: World Congress of Jewish Studies): 321-28.

Nicholson, E.W.
1973 *Exodus and Sinai in History and Tradition* (Oxford: Basil Blackwell).

Niehr, H.
1990 *Der Höchste Gott* (BZAW, 190; Berlin: W. de Gruyter).
1997 'Zur Semantik von nordwestsmeitisch *ʿlm* als "Unterwelt" und "Grab"', in B. Pongratz-Leisten, H. Kühne and P. Xella (eds.), *Ana šadî Labnāni lū allik: Beiträge zu altorientalischen und mittelmeerischen Kulturen. FS für Wolfgang Röllig* (AOAT, 247; Neukirchen-Vluyn: Neukirchener Verlag; Kevelaer: Verlag Butzon and Bercker): 295-305.
2001 'Review of *HUS*', *JSS* 46: 309-10.

Nielsen, D.
1927 *Handbuch der altarabischer Altertumskunde I* (Paris, Copenhagen, Leipzig: Busck).
1936 'Ras-Šamra-Mythologie und biblische Theologie', *AKM* 214: 1-69.

Noegel, S.
1998 'The Aegean Ogygos of Boeotia and the Biblical Og of Bashan: Reflections of the Same Myth', *ZAW* 110: 411-26.

Noth, M.
1928 'Die Historisierung des Mythus im Alten Testament', *CW* 4: 265-72, 301-309; Reprinted in *Gesammelte Studien zum Alten Testament II* (Munich: Kaiser, 1969).
1960 *History of Israel* (London: A. & C. Black, 2nd edn).
1962 *Exodus* (OTL; London: SCM Press).
1968 *Numbers* (OTL; London: SCM Press).
1981 *The Deuteronomistic History* (JSOTSup, 15; Sheffield: Sheffield Academic Press); originally *Überlieferungsgeschichtliche Studien* (Tübingen: M. Niemeyer, 2nd edn, 1957).

Nougayrol, J.
1956 *Le Palais Royal d'Ugarit IV: Textes accadiens des archives sud* (Paris: Imprimerie Nationale; Klinksieck).

Nyberg, H. S.
1935–36 *Studien zum Hoseabuch* (UUÅ, 6; Uppsala: Almquist & Wiksells).
1938 'Studien zum Religionskampf im Alten Testament', *ARW* 35: 329-87.

Obbink, W.
1929 'Jahwebilder', *ZAW* 47: 264-74.

O'Connor, M.
1991 'Cardinal-Direction Terms in Biblical Hebrew', in Kaye 1991: II, 1140-157.

Oden, R.A.
1979 'The Contendings of Horus and Seth (Chester Beatty P 1): A Structural Interpretation', *HR* 18: 352-69.
1981 'Transformations in Near Eastern Myths: Genesis 1–11 and the Old Babylonian Epic of Atrahasis', *Religion* 11: 21-37.
1992a 'Mythology', *ABD*: IV, 946-56.
1992b 'Myth in the Old Testament', *ABD*: IV, 956-60.

Oesterley, W.O.E., and T.H. Robinson
1930 *Hebrew Religion: Its Origin and Development* (London: SPCK).
1942 'Egypt and Israel', in S.R.K. Glanville (ed.), *The Legacy of Egypt* (Oxford: Oxford University Press): 218-48.

O'Flaherty, W.D.
1975 *Hindu Myths* (Harmondsworth: Penguin Books).
1980 *Sexual Metaphors and Animal Symbols in Indian Mythology* (Delhi: Motilal Banarsidass).
1981 *The Rig Veda* (Harmondsworth: Penguin Books).
1997 'The Body in Hindu Texts', in S. Coakley (ed.), *Religion and the Body* (CSRT, 8; Cambridge: Cambridge University Press): 167-84.

Oldenburg, U.
1969 *The Conflict between El and Baal in Canaanite Religion* (Numen Supplements, Second Series, 3; Leiden: E.J. Brill).

del Olmo Lete, G.
1975 'Notes on Ugaritic Semantics I', *UF* 7: 89-102.
1981 *Mitos y Leyendas de Canaan* (Madrid: Cristiandad).
1986 'GN, el cemetario regio de Ugarit', *SEL* 3: 62-64.
1988 'Bašan o el "infierno" cananeo', in P. Xella (ed.), *Cananea Selecta. Festschrift für Oswald Loretz zum 60. Geburtstag*; originally *SEL* 5: 51-60.
1999 'Og', in *DDD*, 2nd edn: 638-40.

Ornstein, R.
1986 *The Psychology of Consciousness* (Harmondsworth: Penguin Books; 2nd edn).

Östborn, G.
1955 *Yahweh and Baal* (LUÅ, 51.6; Lund: C.W.K. Gleerup).
Otzen, B., H. Gottlieb and K. Jeppesen
1980 *Myths in the Old Testament* (London: SCM Press); ET of *Myter i det gamle Testamente* (Copenhagen: Gad, 1976).
Page, H.R., Jr
1996 *The Myth of Cosmic Rebellion: A Study of its Reflexes in Ugaritic and Biblical Literature* (SVT, 65; Leiden: E.J. Brill).
Pardee, D.
1988 *Les Textes Paramythologiques de la 24ᵉ Campagne (1961)* (RSO, 4; Paris: ERC).
1997 'West Semitic Canonical Compositions', in W. Hallo (ed.), *The Context of Scripture*. I. *Canonical Compositions of the Biblical World* (Leiden: E.J. Brill): 239-375.
2000 *Les Textes Rituels* (RSO, 12; 2 vols.; Paris: ERC).
Parker, S.B.
1972 'The Ugaritic Deity Rāpi'u', *UF* 4: 97-104.
Parpola, S.
1997 *The Standard Babylonian Epic of Gilgamesh* (SAACT, 1; Helsinki: The Neo-Assyrian Text Corpus Project).
Paton, L.B.
1894 'Did Amos Approve the Calf-Worship at Bethel?', *JBL* 13: 80-90.
Pedersen, J.
1926–40 *Israel, its Life and Culture* (vols. I-II; Copenhagen: Branner; London: Humphrey Milford, Oxford University Press, 1926; vols. III-IV; Copenhagen: Branner og Koch; London: Geoffrey Cumberlege, Oxford University Press, 1940). ET of *Israel*. I-II. *Sjæleliv og samsfundsliv;* III–IV. *Hellighed og guddomelighed* (Copenhagen, 1920–34).
Penfield, W., and T. Rasmussen
1950 *The Cerebral Cortex of Man* (New York: Macmillan).
Penglase, C.
1994 *Greek Myth and Mesopotamia* (London: Routledge).
Perrot, N.
1937 'Les representations de l'arbre sacré sur les monuments de Mésopotamie et d'Elam', *Babyloniaca* 17: 5-144.
Peter, R.
1975 *Pr* et *šwr*: note de léxique hébraique, *VT* 25: 486-96, 691.
Petersen, A.R.
1998 *The Royal God: Enthronement Festivals in Ancient Ugarit and Israel?* (JSOTSup, 259; CIS, 5; Sheffield: Sheffield Academic Press).
Petersen, D.L., and M. Woodward
1977 'Northwest Semitic Religion: A Study of Relational Structures', *UF* 9: 237-43.
Pfeiffer, R.H.
1926 'Images of Yahweh', *JBL* 45: 211-22.
1961 *Religion in the Old Testament* (New York: Harper).
Pitard, W.T.
1978 'The Ugaritic Funerary Text RS 34.126', *BASOR* 232: 65-75.
1987 'RS 34.126: Notes on the Text', *Maarav* 4: 75-86, 111-55.
1992 'A New Edition of the '*Rāpi'ūma*' Texts: KTU 1.20-22', *BASOR* 285: 33-77.

1994 'The "Libation" Installations of the Tombs at Ugarit', *BA* 57: 20-37.
1999 'The Rpum Texts', in W.G.E. Watson and N. Wyatt (eds.), *Handbook of Ugaritic Studies* (HdO, Abteilung 1: Der Nahe und der Mittlere Osten, 39; Leiden: E.J. Brill): 259-69.

Pope, M.H.
1955 *El in the Ugaritic Texts* (SVT, 2; Leiden: E.J. Brill).
1973 *Job* (AB, 15; Garden City, NY: Doubleday).
1977 'Notes on the Rephaim Texts from Ugarit', in M. de Jong Ellis (ed.), *Essays on the Ancient Near East in Memory of J.J. Finkelstein* (MCAAS, 19; Hamden CT: Archon): 163-82.
1987 'The Status of El at Ugarit', *UF* 19: 219-30.

Porten, B., and U. Rappoport
1971 'Poetic Structure in Genesis ix 7', *VT* 21: 363-69.

Porter, J.R.
1978 'The Daughters of Lot', *Folklore* 89: 127-41.

Proudfoot, W.
1985 *Religious Experience* (Berkeley: University of California Press).

Pugh G.E.
1978 *The Biological Origins of Human Values* (London: CMS).

von Rad, G.
1962–66 *Old Testament Theology* (2 vols.; Edinburgh: Oliver & Boyd); ET of *Theologie des Alten Testaments* (Munich: Kaiser Verlag, 1957–60).
1963 *Genesis* (OTL; London: SCM Press; 2nd edn).
1966a *Deuteronomy* (OTL, London: SCM Press); originally *Das fünfte Buch Mose: Deuteronomium* (Göttingen: Vandenhoeck & Ruprecht, 1964).
1966b *The Problem of the Hexateuch and Other Essays* (Edinburgh: Oliver & Boyd).

Ramsey, G.W.
1982 *The Quest for the Historical Israel* (London: SCM Press).

Ray, J.
1997 'How Black Was Socrates? The roots of European Civilization and the Dangers of Afrocentrism', *TLS* (February 14, 1997): 3-4.

Rendsberg, G.A.
2000 'Review of W.G.E. Watson and N. Wyatt (eds.) *Handbook of Ugaritic Studies*, (HdO, I.39; Leiden: E.J. Brill, 1999)', *JQR* 91: 191-96.

Rendtorff, R.
1954 'Die theologische Stellung des Schöpferglaubens bei Deutero-jesaja', *ZTK* 51: 3-13.

Rennie, B.S.
1996 *Reconstructing Eliade: Making Sense of Religion* (Albany, NY: State University of New York Press).

Reymond, P.
1958 *L'Eau, sa Vie et sa Signification dans l'Ancien Testament* (SVT, 6; Leiden: E.J. Brill).

Ribichini, S., and P. Xella
1979 'MilkʿAštart, mlk(m) e la traduzione siropalestinese sui Refaim', *RSF* 7: 145-58.

Richardson, M.E.J.
2000 *Hammurabi's Law: Text, Translation and Glossary* (BS, 73; STS, 2; Sheffield: Seffield Academic Press).

Ringgren, H.
1966 *Israelite Religion* (London: SPCK); ET of *Israelitische Religion* (Stuttgart: W. Kohlhammer Verlag, 1963).
Roberts, J.J.M.
1975 '*Saphôn* in Job 26.7', *Biblica* 56: 555.
Robinson, A.
1974 'Zion and Saphon in Ps. 48.3', *VT* 24: 118-23.
Rogerson, J.W.
1974 *Myth in Old Testament Interpretation* (BZAW, 134; Berlin: W. de Gruyter).
1978 *Anthropology and the Old Testament* (Oxford: Basil Blackwell).
Rosén, H.B.
1991 'Some Thoughts on the System of Designation of the Cardinal Points in Ancient Semitic Languages', in Kaye 1991: II, 1337-344.
Rowley, H.H.
1967 *Worship in Ancient Israel: Its Forms and Meaning* (London: SPCK).
Ryan, W., and W. Pitman
1999 *Noah's Flood: The New Scientific Discoveries about the Event that Changed History* (London: Simon & Schuster).
Ryckmans, G.
1947 'Les religions arabes préislamiques', in M. Gorce and R. Mortier (eds.), *Histoire générale des religions* (Paris: Quillet): IV, 307-32.
Said, E.W.
1978 *Orientalism* (London: Routledge & Kegan Paul; repr. Harmondsworth: Penguin Books, 1985).
Sandys, J.
1946 *The Odes of Pindar* (LCL; Cambridge, MA: Harvard University Press; London: Heinemann).
Sanmartín, J.
1978 'Glossen zum ugaritischen Lexikon II', *UF* 10: 349-56.
Sasson, J.M.
1968 'The Bovine Symbolism in Exodus', *VT* 18: 380-87.
1971 'The Worship of the Golden Calf', in H.A. Hoffner (ed.), *Orient and Occident (FS C.H. Gordon)* (AOAT, 22; Neukirchen-Vluyn: Neukirchener Verlag): 151-59.
de Savignac, J.
1953 'Note sur le sens du terme *Sâphôn* dans quelques passage de la Bible', *VT* 3: 95-96.
1984 'Le sens du terme Sâphôn', *UF* 16: 273-78.
Schaeffer, C.F.A.
1966 'Nouveaux témoignages du culte de El et de Baal a Ras Shamra et ailleurs en Syrie-Palestine', *Syria* 43: 1-19.
Schäfer, P.
2002 *Mirror of his Beauty: Feminine Images of God from the Bible to the Early Kabbalah* (Princeton, NJ: Princeton University Press).
Schick, K.D., and N. Toth
1993 *Making Silent Stones Speak* (London: Weidenfeld & Nicolson).
Schild, E.
1954 'On Exodus iii 14 "I am that I am"', *VT* 4: 296-302.

Schmidt, B.B.

1994 *Israel's Beneficent Dead: Ancestor Cult and Necromancy in Ancient Israelite Religion and Tradition* (FAT, 11; Tübingen: Mohr).

Schoff, W.H. (ed.)

1912 *The Periplus of the Erythraean Sea: Travel and Trade in the Indian Ocean by a Merchant of the First Century* (London: Longmans, Green).

Seidl, U.

1989 *Die Babylonischen Kudurru-Reliefs: Symbole Mesopotamische Gottheiten* (OBO, 87; Fribourg: Fribourg University Press; Göttingen: Vandenhoeck & Ruprecht).

van Seters, J.

1972a 'The Terms "Amorite" and "Hittite" in the Old Testament', *VT* 22: 64-68.

1972b 'Confessional Reformulation in the Exilic Period', *VT* 22: 448-59.

1975 *Abraham in History and Tradition* (New Haven: Yale University Press).

1983 *In Search of History: Historiography in the Ancient World and the Origins of Biblical History* (New Haven: Yale University Press).

1992 *Prologue to History: The Yahwist as Historian in Genesis* (Louisville, KY: Westminster/John Knox Press).

Sethe, K.

1929 *Amun und die acht Urgötter von Hermopolis* (Berlin: W. de Gruyter).

Skinner, J.

1910 *A Critical and Exegetical Commentary on Genesis* (ICC; Edinburgh: T. & T. Clark).

Smith, M.

1987 *Palestinian Parties and Politics that Shaped the Old Testament* (London: SCM Press, 2nd edn).

Smith, M.S.

1990 *The Early History of God* (San Francisco: Harper & Row).

1994a 'Mythology and Myth-making in Ugaritic and Israelite Literature', in Brooke, Curtis and Healey 1994: 293-341.

1994b *The Ugaritic Baal Cycle*, I (SVT, 55; Leiden: E.J. Brill).

2000 'Review of *HUS*', *JAOS* 120: 667-69.

2001 *The Origins of Biblical Monotheism: Israel's Polytheistic Background and the Ugaritic Texts* (New York: Oxford University Press).

2001 *The Origins of Biblical Monotheism: Israel's Polytheistic Background and the Ugaritic Texts* (Oxford: Oxford University Press).

Smith, P.J.

1980 'A Semiotactical Approach to the Meaning of the Term *ruaḥ 'ělōhîm* in *Genesis* 1.2', *JNSL* 8: 99-104.

Smith, W.R.

1927 *The Religion of the Semites* (London: A. & C. Black, 3rd edn).

Snaith, N.H.

1963–65 'The Advent of Monotheism in Israel', *ALUOS* 5: 100-13.

1965 'ים סוף: The Sea of Reeds: The Red Sea', *VT* 15: 395-98.

Spence, L.

1921 *An Introduction to Mythology* (London: Harrap).

Spengler, O.

1926–28 *The Decline of the West* (2 vols.; New York: Knopf).

Spronk, K.
1995 'Rahab', *DDD*: cols. 1292-95; *DDD*, 2nd edn, 1999: 684-86.

Staal, F.
1975 *Exploring Mysticism* (Harmondsworth: Penguin Books).

Stadelmann, H.I.J.
1970 *The Hebrew Conception of the World* (AnBib, 39; Rome: Pontifical Biblical Institute).

Stadelmann, R.
1967 *Syrisch-Palästinensische Gottheiten in Agypten* (Leiden: E.J. Brill).

Stalker, D.M.G.
1962 'Exodus', in M. Black and H.H. Rowley (eds.), *Peake's Commentary on the Bible* (London: Nelson): 208-40

Stoneman, R.
1991 *The Greek Alexander Romance* (Harmondsworth: Penguin Books).

Strenski, I.
1987 *Four Theories of Myth in Twentieth-Century History* (London: Macmillan).

Stuhlmueller, C.
1970 *Creative Redemption in Deutero-Isaiah* (Rome: Pontifical Biblical Institute).

Talmon, S.
1966 'The "Desert Motif" in the Bible and in Qumran Literature', in A. Altmann (ed.), *Biblical Motifs* (Cambridge, MA: Harvard University Press): 31-63.

de Tarragon, J.-M.
2001 'Review of *RTU*', *RB* 108: 422-27.

Taylor, J.G.
1993 *Yahweh and the Sun* (JSOTSup, 111; Sheffield: Sheffield Academic Press).

Terrien, S.
1970 'The Omphalos Myth and Hebrew Religion', *VT* 20: 315-38.

Thompson, T.L.
1974 *The Historicity of the Patriarchal Narratives: The Quest for the Historical Abraham* (BZAW, 133; Berlin: W. de Gruyter).

Tobin, V.A.
1989 *Theological Principles of Egyptian Religion* (AUS, 7.59; New York: Peter Lang).

Tournay, R.
1957 'Le nom du "buisson ardent"', *VT* 7: 410-13.

Towers, J.R.
1959 'The Red Sea', *JNES* 18: 150-53.

Trigger, B.G. *et al.* (eds.)
1983 *Ancient Egypt: A Social History* (Cambridge: Cambridge University Press).

Tromp, N.J.
1969 *Primitive Conceptions of Death and the Nether World in the Old Testament* (BibOr, 21; Rome: Pontifical Biblical Institute).

Tropper, J.
2000 *Ugaritische Grammatik* (AOAT, 273; Münster: Ugarit-Verlag).

Tsumura, D.T.
1978 'A Problem of Myth and Ritual Relationship – *CTA* 23 (*UT* 52): 56-57 Reconsidered', *UF* 10: 387-95.
1989 *The Earth and the Waters in Genesis 1 and 2* (JSOTSup, 33; Sheffield: Sheffield Academic Press).

Tucker, G.M.
1966 'The Legal Background of Genesis 23', *JBL* 85: 77-84.

Turner, V.
1983 'Body, Brain and Culture', *Zygon* 18: 221-45.

Tur-Sinai, H.
1964 'אָבִיר, אֱבִיר', in *EBB* (*Encyclopaedia Biblica of the Bialik Institute*) (Jerusalem: sumptibus Instituti Bialik): I, 31-33.

Ullendorf, E.
1962 'Ugaritic Marginalia II', *JSS* 7: 339-51.

de Vaux, R.
1943 'Le schisme religieux de Jeroboam', *Angelicum* 43: 77-91.
1965 *Ancient Israel* (London: Darton, Longman & Todd, 2nd edn); originally *Les institutions de l'ancien Israel* (Paris, 1958–60).
1969 'Sur l'origine kénite ou madianite du Yahvisme', *EI* 9: 28-32.
1971 *Histoire ancienne d'Israël* (2 vols.; Paris: Lecoffre).

te Velde, H.
1977 *Seth, God of Confusion* (Probleme der Ägyptologie, 6; Leiden: E.J. Brill; 2nd edn).

Vermeylen, J.
1985 'L'affaire du veau d'or (Ex. 32-34)', *ZAW* 97: 1-23.

Virolleaud, C.
1936 *La Légende de Keret, Roi des Sidoniens* (MRS 1; BAH 21; Paris: Geuthner).
1938 *La déesse ʿAnat* (MRS 4; BAH, 28; Paris: Geuthner).

Vlaardingbroek, J.
1973 'Psalm 68' (Amsterdam: Free University dissertation).

de Vries, S.J.
1985 *I Kings* (WBC, 12; Waco, TX: Word Books).

Wakeman, M.K.
1973 *God's Battle with the Monster* (Leiden: E.J. Brill).

Walcot, P.
1966 *Hesiod and the Near East* (Cardiff: University of Wales Press).

Ward, W.H.
1910 *The Cylinder Seals of Western Asia* (Washington, DC: Carnegie Institution).

Wasserstrom, S.
1998 'Uses of the Androgyne in the History of Religions', *SR* 27: 437-53.

Watson, W.G.E.
1977 'Ugaritic and Mesopotamian Literary Texts', *UF* 9: 273-84.
1983 'The Nature of Ugaritic Poetry', *JNSL* 11: 157-69.
1986 *Classical Hebrew Poetry* (JSOTSup, 26; Sheffield: Sheffield Academic Press).
1993 '*Aṯrt ym*: Yet Another Proposal', *UF* 25: 431-34.
2001 'El's Erudition', *AuOr* 19: 138-42.

Weber, M.
1952 *Ancient Judaism* (Glencoe, IL: Free Press; London: George Allen & Unwin).

Weippert, M.
1961 'Gott und Stier', *ZDPV* 77: 93-117.
1971 *The Settlement of the Israelite Tribes in Palestine* (SBT, 2.21; London: SCM Press).

Weiser, A.
1962 *Psalms* (OTL; London: SCM Press).

Wenham, G.J.
1987 *Genesis 1–15* (WBC, 1; Waco TX: Word Books).

Wensinck, A.J.
1916 *The Ideas of the Western Semites Concerning the Navel of the Earth* (VKAWA, NS xvii, 1; Amsterdam: J. Müller).
1918 *The Ocean in the Literature of the Western Semites* (VKAWA, NS xix, 2; Amsterdam: J. Müller).

West, M.L.
1966 *Hesiod: Theogony* (Oxford: Oxford University Press).
1971 *Early Greek Philosophy and the Orient* (Oxford: Oxford University Press).
1997 *The East Face of Helicon: West Asiatic Elements in Greek Poetry and Myth* (Oxford: Oxford University Press).

Westendorf, W.
1977 'Götter, Androgyne', in *Lexikon der Agyptologie* (Wiesbaden: Harrassowitz): II, 633-35.

Westergaard, G.C.
1995 'The Stone-Tool Technology of Capuchin Monkeys: Possible Implications for the Evolution of Symbolic Communication in Hominids', *WA* 27: 1-9.

Westermann, C.
1984 *Genesis 1–11, a Commentary* (London: SPCK); ET of *Genesis* (BKAT; Neukirchen-Vluyn: Neukirchener Verlag, 2nd edn [1976]).

Wheeler, M.
1968 *The Indus Civilization* (Cambridge: Cambridge University Press; 3rd edn).

Whitelam, K.
1989 'Israelite Kingship: The Royal Ideology and its Opponents', in R.E. Clements (ed.), *The World of Ancient Israel* (Cambridge: Cambridge University Press): 119-39.
1996 *The Invention of Ancient Israel: The Silencing of Palestinian History* (London: Routledge).

Whitley, C.F.
1963 'Covenant and Commandment in Israel', *JNES* 22: 37-48.

Widengren, G.
1941 'Psalm 110 och det sakrala kungadömet i Israel', in *UUÅ* 1941: 7.1.
1950 'The Ascension of the Apostle and the Heavenly Book', in *UUÅ* 1950: 7.
1951 'The King and the Tree of Life in Ancient Near Eastern Religion', in *UUÅ* 1951: 4.

Wifall, W.
1980 'The Sea of Reeds as Sheol', *ZAW* 92: 325-32.

Wilkinson, R.H.
1991 'The Representation of the Bow in the Art of Egypt and the Ancient Near East', *JANES* 20: 83-99.

Winnett, F.V.
1965 'Re-Examining the Foundations', *JBL* 84: 1-19.

Wirgin, W.
1962 'The Menorah as Symbol of Judaism', *IEJ* 12: 140-42.

Wolff, H.W.
1974a *Anthropology of the Old Testament* (London: SCM Press); ET of *Anthropologie des Alten Testaments* (Munich: Kaiser Verlag, 1973).
1974b *Hosea* (Hermeneia, Philadelphia: Fortress); originally *Dodekapropheten 1 Hosea* (Neukirchen-Vluyn: Neukirchener Verlag, 2nd edn [1965]).

Wright, G.E.

1950 *The Old Testament against its Environment* (SBT, 2; London: SCM Press).

1952 *God Who Acts* (SBT, 8; London: SCM Press).

Wright, G.R.H.

1970 'The Mythology of Pre-Israelite Shechem', *VT* 20: 75-82.

Würthwein, E.

1977 *Das erste Buch der Könige* (ATD, 11.1; Göttingen: Vandenhoek & Ruprecht).

Wyatt, N.

1973–74 'ʿAṯtar and the Devil', *TGUOS* 25: 85-97.

1976 'Atonement Theology in Ugarit and Israel', *UF* 8: 415-30.

1977 'The Identity of *Mt-w-Šr*', *UF* 9: 379-81.

1981 'Interpreting the Creation and Fall Story in Genesis 2–3', *ZAW* 93: 10-21.

1983 'The Stela of the Seated God from Ugarit', *UF* 15: 271-77.

1984 'The ʿAnat Stela from Ugarit and its Ramifications', *UF* 16: 327-37.

1985a '"Jedidiah" and Cognate Forms as a Title of Royal Legitimation', *Biblica* 66: 112-25.

1985b 'Killing and Cosmogony in Canaanite and Biblical Thought', UF 17: 375-81.

1985c 'Possible Indo-European Influences in Ugaritic Thought', *UF* 17: 371-74.

1985d '"Araunah the Jebusite" and the Throne of David', *ST* 39: 39-53.

1986a 'The Hollow Crown: Ambivalent Elements in West Semitic Royal Ideology', *UF* 18: 421-36.

1986b 'Devas and Asuras in Early Indian Religious Thought', *SJRS* 7: 61-77.

1986c 'The Significance of the Burning Bush', *VT* 36: 361-65.

1986d 'The AB Cycle and Kingship in Ugaritic Thought', *Cosmos* 2: 136-42.

1986e 'Cain's Wife', *Folklore* 7: 88-95, 232.

1987 'Echoes of the King and his Ka: An Ideological Motif in the Story of Solomon's Birth', *UF* 19: 399-404.

1988a 'The Source of the Ugaritic Myth of the Conflict of Baal and Yam', *UF* 20: 375-85 (Loretz FS).

1988b 'When Adam Delved: The Meaning of Genesis III 23', *VT* 38: 117-22.

1989 'Near Eastern Echoes of Aryan Tradition', *SMSR* 55 (NS 13): 5-29.

1990a 'The Story of Dinah and Shechem', *UF* 22: 434-58.

1990b '"Supposing Him To Be the Gardener" (John 20, 15): A Study of the Paradise Motif in John', *ZNW* 25: 21-38.

1990c 'There and Back Again: The Significance of Movement in the Priestly Work', *SJOT* (1990.1): 61-80.

1990d 'The Expression *bᵉkôr māwet* in Job xviii 13 and its Mythological Background', *VT* 40: 207-16.

1990e 'A Further Weapon for Baal?', *UF* 22: 459-66.

1990f 'The Story of Dinah and Shechem', *UF* 22: 434-58.

1992 'The Pruning of the Vine in KTU 1.23', *UF* 24: 425-27.

1994a 'The Theogony Motif in Ugarit and the Bible', in Brooke, Curtis and Healey 1994: 395-419.

1994b 'The Meaning of *El Roi* and the Mythological Dimension of Genesis 16', *SJOT* 8: 141-51.

1995a 'The Liturgical Context of Psalm 19 and its Mythical and Ritual Origins', *UF* 27: 559-96.

1995b 'Calf', in K. van der Toorn, B. Becking and P.W. van der Horst (eds.), *Dictionary of Deities and Demons in the Bible* (Leiden: E.J. Brill): cols. 344-81; (2nd edn, 1999): 180-82.

1995c 'Jonathan's Adventure and a Philological Conundrum', *PEQ* 995: 62-69.
1996a 'The Vocabulary and Neurology of Orientation: The Ugaritic and Biblical Evidence', in Wyatt, Watson and Lloyd 1996: 351-80 = Chapter 10.
1996b *Myths of Power: A Study of Royal Myth and Ideology in Ugaritic and Biblical Tradition* (UBL, 13; Münster: Ugarit-Verlag).
1996c 'Le centre du monde dans les littératures d'Ougarit et d'Israël', *JNSL* 21: 123-42.
1997 'Ilimilku's Ideological Programme: Ugaritic Royal Propaganda, and a Biblical Postscript', *UF* 29: 773-96.
1998a 'Arms and the King: The Earliest Allusions to the *Chaoskampf* Motif and their Implications for the Interpretation of the Ugaritic and Biblical Traditions', in M. Dietrich and I. Kottsieper (eds.), *'Und Mose schrieb dieses Lied auf...'. Festschrift O. Loretz* (AOAT, 250; Münster: Ugarit-Verlag): 833-82.
1998b 'Review of Coakley 1997', *ERTR/SWC* 4: 269-73.
1998c *Religious Texts from Ugarit: The Words of Ilimilku and his Colleagues* (The Biblical Seminar, 53; Sheffield: Sheffield Academic Press, 2nd edn, 2002).
1999a The Religion of Ugarit: An Overview', in W.G.E. Watson and N. Wyatt (eds.), *Handbook of Ugaritic Studies* (HdO, I.39; Leiden: E.J. Brill): 529-85.
1999b 'Degrees of Divinity: Mythical and Ritual Aspects of West Semitic Kingship', *UF* 31: 853-87.
2001a *Space and Time in the Religious Life of the Ancient Near East* (BS, 85; Sheffield: Sheffield Academic Press).
2001b 'Dennis Pardee, *Les Textes Rituels* (RSO 12, Paris 2000), an Appraisal', *UF* 33: 697-706.
2001c 'The Mythic Mind', *SJOT* 15: 3-56.
2002a *Religious Texts from Ugarit* (BS, 53; London: Continuum, 2nd edn).
2002b 'Ilimilku the Theologian: The Ideological Roles of Athtar and Baal in KTU 1.1 and 1.6', in O. Loretz, K. Metzler and H. Schaudig (eds.), *Exod. Mesopotamia et Syria Lux. Festschrift für Manfried Dietrich zu seinem 65. Geburtstag am 6.11.2000...* (AOAT, 281; Münster: Ugarit-Verlag): 845-56.
2003 'Review of T.K. Beal, *Religion and its Monsters*', *ERTR/SWT* 9: 128-34.
2004 '"Water, water everywhere...": Musings on the Aqueous Myths of the Near East', in D.A. González Blanco and J.P. Vita (eds.), *De la Tablilla a la Inteligencia Artificial. Homenaje al Prof. Jesús Luis Cunchillos en su 65 aniversario* (CD-ROM publication and WWW Site, Madrid): 61-110 = Chapter 12.

Wyatt, N., W.G.E. Watson and J.B. Lloyd (eds.)
1996 *Ugarit, Religion and Culture: Proceedings of the International Colloquium on Ugarit, Religion and Culture, Edinburgh, July 1994. Essays Presented in Honour of Professor John C.L. Gibson* (UBL, 12; Münster: Ugarit-Verlag).

Xella, P.
1981 *I Testi Rituali di Ugarit* (SS, 24; Rome: Istituto di Studi del Vicino Oriente).
1996a 'Il «capro espiatorio» a Ebla. Sulle origini storiche di un antico rito mediterraneo', *SMSR* (FS D. Sabbatucci) 62: 677-84. (Late publication in 1998).
1996b 'Les pouvoirs du dieu ʿAṯtar. Morphologie d'un dieu du panthéon ugaritique', in Wyatt, Watson and Lloyd 1996: 381-404.

Yadin, Y.
1961 *Hazor* III-IV (Jerusalem: Magnes Press).
1972 *Hazor* (Schweich Lectures; Oxford: British Academy).

Yon, M.
1990 'Ougarit et ses dieux', in P. Matthiae, M. van Loon and H. Weiss (eds.), *Resurrecting the Past* (FS A. Bounni; Istanbul: Nederlands Historisch-Archaeologisch Instituut te Istanbul): 325-43.
1992 'The End of the Kingdom of Ugarit', in W.A. Ward and M.S. Joukowsky (eds.), *The Crisis Years: The 12th century* B.C. (Dubuque, IA: Kendall, Hunt): 111-22.

Zandee, J.
1963 'Seth als Sturmgott', *ZÄS* 90: 144-56.
1988 'Der androgyne Gott in Ägypten', in M. Görg (ed.), *Religion im Erbe Ägyptens: Beiträge zur spätantiken Religionsgeschichte zu Ehren von Alexander Böhlig* (ÄAT, 14; Wiesbaden: Otto Harrassowitz): 240-78.

Zatelli, I.
1998 'The Origin of the Biblical Scapegoat Ritual: The Evidence of Two Eblaite Texts', *VT* 48: 254-63.

van Zijl, P.J.
1972 *Baal* (AOAT, 10; Neukirchen-Vluyn: Neukirchener Verlag).

Index

Index of References

Bible

Genesis

1 60, 96, 99, 101, 161, 168, 178, 180, 222, 250, 251, 253
1.1 42, 50, 93-95
1.1-9 101
1.1–2.4 60, 70, 92
1.2 93-96, 98-101, 224, 228
1.3 96
1.3-25 224
1.4 95
1.5 101
1.10 100, 101
1.11 69
1.12 69
1.16 101
1.20 101
1.21 69
1.22 101
1.24 69
1.25 69
1.26 250
1.26-31 224
1.27 100, 101, 250
1.28-29 222
2 227, 254
2–3 178, 180
2.2-3 59
2.4-7 253
2.6 227
2.8 128
2.10-14 192, 196, 212
2.13 192, 193
2.18 253
2.21-24 253
2.23 100
2.24 240
3.14 192
3.14-15 100
3.16 100
3.17-19 100
4 10, 86, 178
4.1 82, 86, 255
4.6-7 100
4.16 86
4.23-24 100
4.26 82, 86
5.29 207
6–8 221, 222
6–9 222
6.1-4 178
6.14 214
6.16 215
6.20 69
7.14 69
7.17–8.9 224
8.10-19 224
8.13 215
8.20–9.17 224
9 223
9.1-4 222
9.1-17 207
9.9 207
9.11 207
9.12 207
9.13 207
9.15 207
9.16 207
9.17 207
9.20-27 207
12.7-8 82
14.5 208
14.15 149
15 60
16 187, 247
16–21 169
16.1 64
17 60, 63
17.14 60
17.24 63
17.25 63
19.8 89
19.25 89
19.30-38 64, 169, 187, 247
21.2 63
21.4 63
21.8 64
22.2 210
24.5-8 38
25.28 91
26.3 89
26.4 89
26.24 2
27.28 3
28.13 2
28.17 3

28.22 3
31.4-9 4
31.5 2, 4
31.8-9 4
31.13 3
31.29 2
31.42 2
31.53 2
32.10 2
32.31 3
34 61, 62
35.1 3, 90
35.3 3, 90
35.21 3
37.25 38, 91
37.28 91
37.35 38, 92
42.38 38
43.23 2
44.23 38
44.26 38
44.31 38
46.1 2
46.3 3
49.9 204
49.13 231
49.17 205
49.25 1-4, 11, 112
50.17 2

Exodus
1.22 224
2 14
2.1-23 16
2.3 199, 214
2.3-5 224
2.15 16
2.16 87
2.18 87
2.21 87
2.22 16, 86
3 6, 10, 12-14, 82, 83
3.1 6, 8, 14, 82, 87
3.2 6, 11, 13
3.3 6, 13
3.4 6, 8, 13
3.5 6, 13
3.6 2, 6-8, 83
3.7 2, 6, 11
3.7-8 13
3.8 6, 9
3.9 2, 8
3.9-15 6
3.10 8
3.11 8
3.12 8
3.13 2, 6
3.13-15 6, 8, 11, 83
3.14 6, 7, 11
3.15 2, 6, 7
3.16 2, 9
3.16-18 6, 13
3.17 9
3.19 8
3.19-22 6
3.20 8
3.21-22 8
4.5 2
4.18 87
4.24-26 61, 63
4.25-26 62
6 82
6.2 82, 88
6.2-3 5
6.28 82
7–12 236
7.14 11
7.14-25 11
7.15 11
7.16 11
7.17 11
7.18 11
7.19 11
7.20 11
7.21 11
7.22 11
7.24 11
7.25 11
7.28 11
10.1-2 8
10.19 38, 229
12.43-49 63
12.48 61
13.17 38
14 170
14–15 38, 224, 225
14.1 103
14.2 121
14.9 121
14.11 38
15 124, 168
15.4 38
15.4-5 198
15.17 117
17.15-16 122
17.16 110
18 86, 87
18.1 87
18.8-11 87
18.10-11 87
19–24 170, 207, 224
20 58-60
20.8-11 58
23.12 57, 59
25.10 214
25.31-40 15
31.12 60
31.12-17 60
31.13 60
31.15 60
31.16-17 60
32 72, 75, 78, 79, 86
32–34 76, 91, 170, 207, 224
32.4 79-81, 89
32.8 79-81
34 58, 60
34.21 58, 59
35.1-2 59
37.17-24 15
40.1-15 215

Leviticus
5.2 65
7.21 65
11 65-67
11.3-8 67
11.8 69
11.11 69
11.13-19 68
11.14 69

Leviticus (cont.)
11.15 69
11.16 69
11.16-47 67
11.22 69
11.24 69
11.24-25 65
11.29 69
11.31 69
11.39 69
11.45 67
12.3 61
17.15 65
18.27 89

Numbers
6.6-11 65
8.1-4 15
10.29 87
14.2-3 38
15.32-36 59
19.11-16 65
21.33 208
23.10 127
23.22 9, 83, 90
24.8 9, 83, 90
32.33 208
33.7 121

Deuteronomy
1.1 229
1.4 208
1.37 15
3.1-13 208
3.26 15
4.11 96
4.42 89
4.47 208
5 58, 60
5.12-15 58
5.23 96
7.22 89
9.18-20 15
10.10 15
12 75
14 66, 67
14.3 64, 66
14.4 67
14.4-20 64
14.4-21 64
14.5 67
14.6-8 67
14.8 69
14.12-18 68
14.13 69
14.14 69
14.15 69
14.18 69
14.21 64, 66, 67
17.16 38
19.11 89
24.1-4 65
25.13-16 65
32.15 124
33.2 142
33.13 112
33.22 204

Joshua
5 61, 62
5.2 61
5.5 61
5.9 61
12.4-5 208

Judges
1.16 87
4.11 87
5.3 142
5.5 89
5.17 205
5.18 231
5.21 148
6.25-28 16
7.12 91
8.22-24 91
8.26 91
9.48 210
11.16 229
13.2-7 66
17.6 73

1 Samuel
2.8 93
4.5-8 74
5.1-3 74
7.6-12 105
7.13 105
11.8 73
11.12-15 73
13.1 73
17.1-54 73
17.19 73
18.17-19 88
18.25 61
18.27 74
26.19 52
28.13 92

2 Samuel
1.21 123
2.7 73
2.23 127
5.6-12 74
5.17-25 74
8.1-14 74
10.1–11.27 74
12.8 88
12.25 45
12.26-31 74
15–18 74
20.1-2 74
22.12 95

1 Kings
2.28-34 213
4.7–5.3 75
5.13 75
5.27 75
6.6 215
7.23-26 194
7.49 15
8 67, 143
8.2 216
8.11-14 142
8.12-13 142
8.13 123
8.30 142
8.39 123
8.43 123
8.49 123
8.53 142, 150
9.15-24 75
9.22 75
9.26 38, 197, 199
11.28 75

12 76, 79
12.1-15 75
12.16 75
12.20 75
12.26-27 75
12.26-33 72, 75
12.28 78, 79, 81, 82
14.24 65

2 Kings
4.23 58
5.17 52
10.15-27 87
11.5 58
23.6 16

1 Chronicles
2.55 87
3.1 210
20.8 89
28.5 116
29.23 116

2 Chronicles
6.2 123
6.30 123
6.33 123
6.39 123
34.3-4 16

Nehemiah
9.18 79, 89

Job
3.8 35
4.23 92
7.12 35
9.8 114, 121, 237
15.25 1
15.29 92
21.14-15 1
23.8-9 133
23.9 148
26.5 209, 213
26.7 98, 99, 103-105
38.7 82
38.8 193
38.8-9 249
38.10-11 180
38.28-29 249
40.25 35

Psalms
2.7 228
3.3 90
3.4 90
3.42 90
3.43 90
6.5 52
6.6 52
8 169, 247
18.10-22 237
18.11 95
18.12 95, 99
19 169, 247, 255
19.1-6 99
19.2-7 99
29 111
29.6 90
29.9 90
29.10 227, 237
33.13-14 124
42.8 227
43.8 40
48 104
48.2 40
48.3 103, 141, 142
62.7 90
62.8 90
68 210
68.8 89
68.9 89
68.14 210, 211
68.14-15 209
68.14-23 211
68.15 210, 211
68.15-16 209
68.15-24 211
68.16 211
68.17 211, 234
68.18 211, 234
68.22 209, 211, 234
68.23 209, 211, 234
68.24-26 211
68.25-27 211
71.20 92
72.8 53
74.13-17 35
77.18 93
77.19 93
86.16 45
88.4 92
88.5 92, 100
88.6 100
89 169
89.10-12 35
89.11 93
89.11-13 35
89.12 93, 99, 113
89.13 99, 113
89.25 53
89.26 53, 124
89.27 124
91.1 205
91.7 205
91.11-12 205
91.13 205
104.2-3 114, 121, 237
104.5-7 237
104.6-9 180
104.26 35
105.9 198
106.7 84
106.9 198
106.19-22 9, 84
110 169, 247
110.1 117, 131
116.16 45
139.7 52
139.8 52
143.6 92

Ecclesiastes
6.12 127

Song of Songs
3.6 48

Isaiah
7.14 45
14 116, 209
14.7-21 105
14.9 209
14.9-11 213
14.12 92
14.13 40, 105, 124
16.9 230
19.6 199
19.13 120
21.1-10 49
21.5 113
21.9-10 49
26.14 209
26.19 209
27.1 35, 107, 168
30.2 38
34.11 98
40 224
40.3-11 237
40.12-17 237
40.18 230
40.22 121, 237
40.25-26 11
41.4 11
41.17 200
41.18 224
41.23 35, 42
42.5 121, 230, 237
42.8 11
42.14 249
43.1-2 39
43.2 224
43.5-7 39
43.11 11
43.12 230
43.16-21 39, 249
43.19 224
44.2 255
44.6 11
44.21 255
44.24 121, 237, 255
44.27 39
45.7 35, 42
45.12 121, 237
46.3 255
48.6-8 224
48.10 224
48.13 237
49.1 255
49.5 255
49.15 249
50.2 39, 224
51.3 224
51.9-10 35, 249
51.9-11 39, 224
51.13 121
51.15 224
52.7-12 224
54 224
54.7-9 224
55 224
55.3 224
66.1 200
66.12-13 249

Jeremiah
1.13-15 135
2.16 120
4.6 135
4.23 98
6.1 135
10.12 121
30.15 229
35.1-11 87
42.19 38
43.7-9 120
44.1 120
46.19 120
49.21 229
51.15 121

Lamentations
2.15 121

Ezekiel
4.9 66
4.14 66, 68
8.16 143
8.16-17 143
8.16-18 142
16 169, 247
20.12-13 60
23 169, 247
28 116, 170
28.2 120, 196
28.12 120
28.14 120
28.16 124
30.14-19 120
38.12 120
47.10 69

Hosea
1–2 247
2 169
2.13 58
2.18 77
7.16 84, 85
8.1-3 90
8.3 90
8.4 90
8.4-6 84
8.5 91
8.5-6 35
8.6 84, 91
9.3 38
9.3-4 66
9.6 120
10.5 85
11.1 48, 49, 91
11.5 38
11.7 85
12.1 85

Joel
2.3 49

Amos
8.5 58

Jonah
2.5 199

Habakkuk
3.3 142

Zechariah
4.1-14 15
12.1 121

Matthew
1.21 45
1.23 45
3 225
4.6 205

5–7 225
8.18 225
8.23-27 225
14.22-33 225

Mark
1.3-8 225
4.35-41 168, 225
4.41 187
6.45-52 168
6.47-52 225

Luke
2.7 52
2.12 52
3.2-17 225
4.10-11 205
4.13 205
8.22-25 225
10.19 205

John
1.1-5 225
1.6-8 225
1.14-16 225
1.19-28 225
6.15-21 225
6.16-21 168
21.1-14 225
21.1-23 169

Acts
15.20 69
15.29 69

Revelation
12 227
12.7-9 187, 225
21.1 230
21.1–22.5 225

OTHER ANCIENT TEXTS

Pseudepigrapha
1 Enoch
65-66 224
83 224
89.1-9 224
89.10-40 224

2 Enoch
24–30 224

4 Ezra
13 225
13.1-13 224

Jubilees
5.20–6.3 224
6.4-16 224

Testament of Naphtali
6.1-10 224

Qumran
1QH
5.9-10 231

Targums
Targum Pseudo-Jonathan
2.11 234
3.10 234

Talmuds
T. Hagiga
12 230

Midrash
Bereshit Rabba
31.13 234

Classical Authors
Apollodorus
1.6.3 107

The Library
1.7.2 207

Eusebius
Praeparatio Evangelica
1.10.11 34
9.11-12 207

Ezekiel the Tragedian
Exagoge
68–76 123

Herodotus
Histories
2.21 202
2.23 202
3.23 203
4.8 203
4.36 203

Hesiod
Theogony
304 107, 121
306-307 121
776 201
806 226
820-22 121
820-68 99

Works and Days
168-71 202

Homer
Iliad
2.781-83 121
4.406 234
18.399 201

Odyssey
1.22-23 192
1.52 197
20.65 201

Homeric Hymns
Hymn to Aphrodite
227 202

Hymn to Apollo
305-57 121

The Cypria
8 202

Lucian
De Dea Syria
12–13 207
13 194, 229

Ovid
Metamorphoses
1.177-189 207
1.262-415 207
7.353-56 207

Pindar
Pythian Odes
4.251 203

Pseudo-Callisthenes
The Greek Alexander Romance
2.41 231

Strabo
Geography
13.4.6 121
16.2 121
16.7 121
16.2.7 121

Virgil
Aeneid
6.236-42 192

Other References

ANET
4–6 36
6–7 33
44 231
66–67 33, 358
137 35
265 231
533-34 119

Agni Purāṇa
2 236

Ahiqar
34 191

CS
i 7 242, 243
i 22-23 244

CT
II 160-161 243

Enuma Elish
1.5 195
4.104-106 114
4.128-46 114

Garuḍa Purāṇa
3 236

Epic of Gilgamesh
6.117-162 90
11 214
11.23-24 206
11.29-30 215
11.58 216
11.60-61 215
11.80-85 215
11.96 215
11.153-55 215
11.157 215
11.313 191

KTU
1.1-2 111, 197, 224
1.1-6 27, 108, 149, 168, 230
1.1.2 iii 16 227
1.1 ii 7 236
1.1 iii 12 108-10, 229
1.1 iii 21-22 196
1.1 iii 23-24 122
1.1 iii 26 90
1.1 iv 9-29 197
1.1 iv 12-32 108
1.1 iv 14 52, 228
1.1 iv 15 45
1.1 iv 17 45
1.1 iv 19 45
1.1 iv 22 236
1.1 iv 29 45
1.1 iv 223
1.2 108
1.2 i 5-7 236
1.2 i 20-21 124
1.2 i 30 126
1.2 i 39-40 131
1.2 i 40 132
1.2 iii 4 229
1.2 iii 12 44
1.2 iii 12-25 26
1.2 iii 18 44
1.2 iii 19-20 36
1.2 iv 1-10 237
1.2 iv 11 45
1.2 iv 11-26 131
1.2 iv 18 45
1.2 iv 27-28 21, 22
1.3.5-7 229
1.3.10-12 122
1.3 ii 8 149
1.3 iii 29-31 117
1.3 iii 31 111
1.3 iii 32 21
1.3 iii 38-46 197
1.3 iii 40 21
1.3 iii 40-41 231
1.3 iv 19-20 117
1.3 iv 41-42 127
1.3 vi 4-5 34
1.3 vi 8-9 34
1.3 vi 9 120
1.4.5 229
1.4.44 126
1.4 ii 3-4 130
1.4 ii 31 18
1.4 iii 23-24 126
1.4 iii 34 227
1.4 iv 20-22 229
1.4 v-vi 234
1.4 v 45-46 127
1.4 v 46-48 131
1.4 vii 31-34 128
1.4 vii 40 128
1.4 vii 40-41 130
1.4 viii 1 46
1.4 viii 7-9 92
1.5 i 1 22, 35

1.5 i 1-3	21, 197
1.5 i 2	107
1.5 i 3	226
1.5 i 14-16	227
1.5 i 15	230
1.5 v 1-25	89
1.5 v 12	46
1.5 v 15-16	92
1.5 v 17-23	47
1.5 v 18-23	48
1.5 v 19	46
1.5 vi 4	46
1.5 vi 11	37
1.6 i 14-31	116
1.6 i 43-67	168
1.6 i 56-65	26
1.6 i 56-67	169
1.6 i 59-61	200, 230
1.6 i 63-64	116
1.6 i 63-65	169
1.6 i 65	36, 53
1.6 ii 19	46
1.6 iv 10-11	247
1.6 vi 12-33	116
1.6 vi 43-53	51
1.6 vi 45-52	19
1.6 vi 51	34
1.10 ii 12	233
1.10 ii 6-7	130
1.10 ii 9	233
1.10 iii 11-14	111, 117
1.10 iii 29-30	227
1.10 iii 29-31	111, 117
1.12	44, 45, 47, 64, 169, 187
1.12.8	128
1.12 i	43, 168, 247
1.12 i 14-29	42
1.12 i 15-16	45
1.12 i 28-29	45
1.12 i 34-37	42
1.13.32	45
1.14 ii 3	45
1.14 ii 13-15	130
1.14 iii 25	45
1.14 iv 32-33	126, 149
1.14 iv 38-39	18
1.14 iv 46	126
1.15.5-7	128
1.15.18	149
1.15.18-99	149
1.15 ii 16-18	130
1.15 ii 25	45
1.15 ii 26-27	45
1.15 iii 3	234
1.15 iii 14	234
1.15 iii 18-19	105
1.15 iv 21-23	128
1.16 i 6-9	111
1.16 i 8	122
1.16 ii 44-47	111
1.16 ii 46	122
1.16 iii 3-4	46
1.17.31-33	121
1.17 vi 35	127
1.17 vi 36-37	122
1.19 i 44-45	123
1.19 iii 49	127
1.19 iii 56	127
1.19 iv 7	127
1.20-22	234
1.22 i 17	233
1.23	43-47, 49, 64, 168, 169, 187, 197, 228, 246, 247
1.23.4	43
1.23.30	43, 227
1.23.32-33	246
1.23.33-35	43
1.23.39-40	246
1.23.42-44	246
1.23.45-46	247
1.23.47-48	246
1.23.48-49	247
1.23.60-68	43
1.23.63-64	132
1.23.64	133
1.24	44, 187
1.25.21	37
1.47	98
1.54.3	36
1.59	45
1.61	45
1.92.8-9	132
1.100.41	211
1.100.62	128
1.101	112
1.101.1	112
1.101.1-3	117
1.101.5-8	200
1.108	212
1.109.26-27	132
1.113	129
1.127	182
1.161	34, 129, 212, 213, 234
4 vii 40-41	131
7.88.7	37
8.20.17	36
10.31.6	36
10.70.10	37
16 i 56-59	116

Kālikā Purāṇa

33–34	236

Mahābhārata

1.15.5-13	236
1.17.1-30	236
3.185	236
5.9.3-22	37
5.100.1-13	236
12.300	236

Matsya Purāṇa

1.11-34	236
2.1-19	236
249-51	236

Niddah

61	234

PT

1248	242
1652-53	243

Padma Purāṇa

3.8-10	236
5.4	236
5.73	236

Qur'ān

Sura

11.9	196
18.61-62	227

Ṛgveda
1.24.14 36
1.32 106
1.174.1 37
2.12.5 37
3.38.4 37
4.17.4 37
5.10.2 36
6.20.2 37
6.36.1 37
7.2.3 36
8.42.1 36
9.73.1 36
9.99.1 36
10.10.2 36
10.11.6 36
10.73.10 37
10.81-82 29, 36
10.82.5 36
10.90 29, 36
10.120 37
10.121 29, 36
10.129 29, 36
10.129.2 37
10.129.3 29

Śatapatha Brāḥmaṇa
1.6.3.9 37, 107
1.8.1-16 236
3.7.4.1-3 37
3.8.1.15-16 37

Viṣṇu Purāṇa
9 236

Zebaḥim
113 234

INDEX OF NAMES AND PLACES

Aberbach, M. 76, 88, 89
Abner 74
Abraham 2, 7, 10, 11, 63
Absalom 74
Abydenus 207
Abydos 128, 146, 245
Abyssinia 228, 230
Acheron 126
Ackroyd, P.R. 60
Adad 77, 81, 191
Adityas 31
Aegean 218
Aesir 36
Ahlström, G.W. 53
Aigrain, R. 36
Aimé-Giron, N. 119-21
Aitken, K. 127
Akhenaten 185, 252
Aksum 228
Alalkomena 232
Albertz, R. 179
Albrektson, B. 11, 146, 148, 181, 182
Albright, W.F. 18, 19, 23, 33-35, 52, 77, 89, 103, 109, 119-22, 227, 250, 254
Alexandria 78
Alkomena 232
Allan, R. 63
Allard, M. 11
Allegro, J.M. 89
Alpheus 226
Alt, A. 2, 5, 57, 83, 90
Altamira 220
Amalek 122
Amalekites 73
Amanus 113
Amaunet 96, 242, 245
Amenapet 244
Amenhotpe IV 185, 252
Ammon 74, 169, 247
Amun 96, 193, 242, 244
Amun-Ra 252
Anat 18, 21, 23-27, 32, 45, 47, 48, 77, 126, 131, 227, 247
Andersen, F.I. 90
Anderson, B.W. 51
Anderson, K.T. 5, 9, 11, 91
Andromeda 106, 168
Annus, A. 232, 234
Anunaki 36
Apamea Kibotos 234
Apepi 19, 33, 51
Aphrodite 238
Apis 78
Apollodorus 107, 207
Apsu 50, 195, 226, 230
Apsu-Ti'amat 201, 227
Aqaba 87
d'Aquili, E.G. 140
Aram 74
Ararat 217, 219, 234
Arcadia 226
Ardrey, R. 56
Aristotle 186
Arnold, W.R. 11
Aroer 208
Arsh 34, 35
Arthur 168
Aruru 111
Asher 205
Asherah 81, 187, 254
Ashtaroth 208, 209, 211, 212
Ashteroth-Qarnaim 208
Ashumein 242
Ashurd 191
Ashurites 74
Asia Minor 240

Assmann, J. 180, 185
Assyria 66
Astour, M.C. 33-35, 64, 99, 101, 107, 109, 114, 115, 121-23, 126, 187, 194, 214, 229, 231, 234
Asuras 29-31, 36, 106
Atargatis 78
Aten 252
Athena 107
Athirat 18, 21, 23-26, 31-33, 42, 45, 81, 130, 169, 187, 246
Athtar 26-28, 32, 44, 45, 47, 116, 122, 168-70, 200, 230
Athtarat 211, 212
Athtart 131, 132
Atik 35
Atlas 232
Atrahasis 206, 217
Attica 232
Atum 193, 241, 243-45
Aus, R.D. 187
Autun 187
Aycock, A. 178

Baal 18-33, 35, 37, 43-48, 51, 72, 77, 81, 82, 86, 99, 103, 106-109, 111, 113-16, 119, 121-23, 126, 130, 131, 141, 143, 144, 149, 168, 169, 187, 191, 197, 200, 223, 224, 236, 237
Babylon 40, 42, 49, 55, 56, 68, 69, 195, 198, 236
Bagrow, L. 231
Bailey, L.R. 89
Baines, J. 179, 180
Balaam 83, 147
Bales, S.L. 136
Ballard, R. 219, 235
Bard, K.A. 136
Barker, M. 178
Barr, J. 11, 148
Barth, K. 165
Bartsch, H.-W. 180, 182
Bashan 204, 205, 207-12, 214, 228, 233
Basileos 108
Basseda 220, 236
Batto, B.F. 51, 90, 178, 199, 229
Be 33
Beal, T.K. 36
Beaumont, J.G. 137
Benjamin 74
Bensler, G. 228
Bérard, V. 191, 192, 228
Berger, P. 52, 146, 160, 182, 184, 186
Bernal, M. 194, 229, 232
Beth Shean 107, 144
Bethel 3
Betz, H.D. 51
Beyerlin, W. 53
Bič, M. 89
Binger, T. 33
Black Sea 218, 219, 221
Blacker, C. 150
Blackmore, S. 226
Blythin, I. 101
Boeotia 108, 149, 207, 214
Boiotia 232
Boman, T. 125, 148
Bonnel, R.G. 188
Bonnet, H. 101
Bordreuil, P. 111, 112, 122, 228, 234
Bosphorus 218
Bottéro, J. 216, 235
Bourges 187
Bourke, M.M. 11
Bowman, R.A. 11
Boyce, M. 37
Boyer, P. 161
Brahma 239
Brahman 239
Brandon, S.G.F. 101
Brekelmans, C.H.W. 87, 91
Briggs, C.A. 120
Briggs, E.G. 120
Brillant, M. 36
Brown, C.H. 125
Brown, W.N. 29, 31, 36, 37
Brueggemann, W. 51
Bruner, J. 184
Budde, K. 53, 120
Bultmann, R. 153, 176, 180, 182
van Buren, E.D. 227, 234
Burkert, W. 183, 231, 232
Buto 245

Cambyses 203
Cain 86, 91
Campbell, J.F. 121

Caquot, A. 35, 89, 108, 122, 131, 149, 234
Carlin, J. 186
Carmel 210
Cassuto, U. 34, 35, 85, 91
Cavilli-Sforza, F. 235
Cavilli-Sforza, L.L. 235
Cerambus 207
Chamberlain, A.T. 136
Changeux, R. 137
Charlesworth, J.H. 123
Chartres 187
Chauvet 220
Chedorlaomer 208
Chelhod, J. 125, 132, 138, 141
Childs, B.S. 15
Christen, E.J. 11
Church, C.D. 181
Clapham, L. 178
Clear, J. 149
Clifford, R.J. 109, 115, 120, 122-24
Clines, D.J.A. 67
Clottes, J. 220, 236
Coakley, S. 254
Coleridge, S.T. 189
Collingwood, R.G. 148, 154, 181
Connerton, P. 184
de Contenson, H. 141
Cook, R. 15
Coptos 244
Cosquer 220
Courtin, J. 220, 236
Cross, F.M. 35, 148
Curtis, J.B. 180
Cush 192, 193
Cutler, B. 52

Dagan 115, 141, 143, 144
Dahood, M.J. 5, 35, 89-93, 100, 120, 130, 229, 231, 233
Dalley, S. 219, 221, 234, 236
Damascus 208
Dan 204, 205
Danavas 31
Danel 234
Danelius, E. 78, 89
Danites 231
Danthine, E. 15, 123
Danube 218
David 73-75, 83, 88, 116
Davies, D. 15, 41, 52, 56
Davies, P.R. 162, 177, 182, 185
Davila, J. 206, 231, 232
Day, J. 33, 35, 51, 52, 88, 96, 101, 120, 121, 178, 187, 209, 228, 233, 234
Deacon, T. 183
Delitzsch, F. 120
Denison, S. 138
Dennett, D.C. 140, 149, 184
Deucalion 207, 217
Devas 29-31, 106
Dhorme, E. 148
Dietrich, M. 119, 123, 234
Dijkstra, M. 121, 127
Dimond, S.J. 137
Dionysios 226
Dioscuri 169
Dnieper 218
Dniester 218
Donald, M. 137, 138, 158-60, 162, 166, 176, 183, 184
Donner, H. 89, 90
Dougherty, J.J. 5
Douglas, M. 67-69
Drinkard, J.H. 125
Driver, G.R. 35, 68, 123, 149
Dubarle, A.M. 11
Duchemin, J. 231
Dulles, A. 178
Dumermuth, F. 89
Dumézil, G. 37
Dunbar, R.I.M. 158
Durand, J.-M. 128, 228
Durkheim, E. 185
Dus, J. 89
Dyaus 29

Ebla 144
Eblaite 182
Echidna 107, 121
Eden 227
Edom 74
Edrei 208, 209, 212
Eichrodt, W. 120
Eilberg-Schwartz, H. 151, 179
Eissfeldt, O. 11, 90, 115, 119, 123, 153, 155, 165, 180
El Elyon 84

El Salvador 186
El Shaddai 1, 78, 88, 249
Eleusis 232
Eliade, M. 15, 145, 160, 174, 179, 182, 184, 188, 239, 254
Ellis-Davidson, H.R. 230
Elohim 3, 192, 207, 223
Elyon 205
Emerton, J.A. 35
Engnell, I. 152, 179
Enlil 191
Enmeduranki 207
Ennead 241-44
Enoch 207
Enosh 86
Ephraim 74
Epstein, M.M. 152, 178, 179
Eshnunna 168, 187, 191
Ethanim 216
Etna 107, 213
Euhemerus 186
Euphrates 195
Eusebius 20, 34, 186, 207
Evelyn-White, H.G. 201, 230, 231
Ezekiel 143, 144
Ezion-Geber 198

Fairman, H.W. 33
Faulkner, R.O. 33
Fauth, W. 109, 122
Feldman, L.H. 231
Finkelstein, J.J. 231, 232
Fishbane, M. 101
Fisher, L.R. 119, 122, 123, 130, 133
Fleming, D. 187
Flight, J.W. 53
Fohrer, G. 7, 11, 57, 179
Fontenrose, J. 36, 101, 106, 107, 121, 208, 214, 226, 228, 232
Forsyth, N. 121
France 186
Frankfort, H. 16, 146, 154, 155, 178, 186
Frankfort, H.A. 146, 178
Freed, R.E. 252, 254
Freedman, D.N. 90, 91
Fronzaroli, P. 144
Frost, H. 123

Galilee 205
Galileo 185
Gardner, H. 137
Gargas 220
Gaster, T.H. 34-37, 91
Ge 121
Geb 241, 243, 244
George, St 168, 187
George, A.R. 235
Gerizim 149
Geshurites 74
de Geus, C.H.J. 10
Gibbs, L.W. 148, 178, 181, 186
Gibson, J.C.L. 34-37, 52, 53, 120, 126, 127, 149
Gihon 192-94, 212
Gilead 74
Gilgal 61
Gilgamesh 199, 206
Ginsberg, H.L. 35, 123, 149, 187
Glassner, J.-J. 181, 231, 232, 236
Godley, A.D. 231
Goetze, A. 109, 122
Gog 233
Golan 208
Golf of Lucre 192
Goliath 73
Gonzalez Blanco, D.A. 226
Good, R.M. 234
Goodenough, E.R. 15, 17
Gordon, C.H. 35, 36, 53, 91, 101, 132, 227, 229, 254
Gottlieb, H. 178
Grabbe, L.L. 188
Graetz, H. 78, 89
Grave, C. 104, 119, 120, 123
Graves, R. 232, 234
Gray, J. 33, 35, 89, 254
Greece 175, 240
Grimm, J. 153
Grimm, W. 153
Grimme, H. 89
Gulf of Aqaba 38, 198
Gulf of Suez 38
Gunkel, H. 153, 165, 180
Guthrie, S.E. 161, 166, 171, 176, 185, 188, 226, 254

Habel, N. 15, 98, 101, 105, 121, 233
Hadad 22
Hahn, H. 119, 182
Haldar, A. 15, 53

Hall, E.H. 41, 51, 146
Hamath 87
Hasis 20, 34, 126, 224
Hathor 78, 81, 245
Hauhet 242
Hauran 208, 210, 213
Hay, L.S. 51
Hayin 121
Hayman, A.P. 51
Hazelton H.E. 11
Hazor 77, 81, 89, 144
Hazzi 51, 108
Healey, J.F. 229, 234
Hebron 74
Heider, G.C. 90
Heil, J. 187
Heliopolis 241-45
Heller, J. 91
Heltzer, M. 254
Hendel, R.S. 216, 234, 235
Hera 107, 121
Heraclitus 230
Herdner, A. 35, 108, 122
Hermaphroditus 238
Hermes 187, 238
Hermon 111, 113, 149, 208-210
Hermopolis 242
Herodotus 202, 203, 231
Hertz, J. 138, 142
Hesiod 202, 226, 230, 231
Hesperides 226
L'Heureux, C. 91, 234
Hick, J. 180
Hierapolis 104, 212
Himmelfarb, M. 187
Hiraṇyakṣa 106
Hittite 107
Hivites 62
Hobab 87
Hoffner, H.A. 121, 231
Höfner, M. 33
Holloway, S.W. 214-16, 232, 234, 235
Holt, J.M. 11
Homer 107, 202
Hooke, S.H. 5, 152, 179
Hopkins, W.D. 136
Horeb 11, 60
Horeb-Sinai 207
Horowitz, W. 226, 227, 229
van der Horst, P.W. 254
Horton, R. 161, 185
Horus 20, 33, 44, 45, 81, 133, 241, 243-45
Huh 242
Hule 233
Hurrians 61, 62
Husser, J.-M. 51
Hyatt, J.P. 7, 11, 15

Iau-bidi 87
Ida 227, 254
Igigi 36
Inbubu 111
India 240
Indra 29-31, 34
Iran 240
Irwin, W.A. 11, 178
Isaac 2, 7, 10, 45, 63, 169, 247
Ishbaal 74
Ishmael 64, 169, 247
Ishmaelites 91
Isis 78, 81, 241, 243, 245
Italy 192

Jabesh Gilead 73
Jacob 2-4, 7, 10, 38, 45, 63
Jacobsen 231
Jagersma, H. 89
Jamme, F. 33, 36, 89
Jaynes, J. 137, 140, 141, 145, 146, 150
Jebel Druze 210
Jebel el Aqra 51, 111, 114, 140, 141, 144, 149
Jenson, R.P. 150
Jeppesen, K. 178
Jeroboam 72, 75-79, 81, 82
Jerusalem 40, 42, 74, 75, 105, 143, 149, 193, 194, 212, 227
Jethro 86, 87
Jezreel 74
Jirku, A. 35
Joab 213
Job-stone 103, 120
Johnson, E.A. 240, 251, 254
Jones, A. 136
Jones, G.H. 89
Jordan 61, 62
Josephus 78
Joshua 208
Jung, C.G. 26, 36

Kadmos 108
Kaiser, O. 35, 229
Kalypso 232
Kapelrud, A.S. 21, 35
Kaplan, L. 62
Karnak 244
Kas 108
Käsemann, E. 188
Kasion 107, 108, 113
Kasios 51
Kassab 111
Kauket 96, 101, 242
Keel, O. 51, 53, 59, 180
Keita, S.O.Y. 185
Kemp, B. 121
Kenites 10, 86, 87, 91
Kennedy, C.A. 90
Kenyon, K. 119
Keret 45, 234
Kerstein, G. 231
Key, A.F. 89
Khazzi 109
Khepri 20
Khepri-Ra-Atum 241
Khidr 187
Khnum 53
Khonsu 45, 245
Kiessling, N.K. 24, 35, 36
Kikawada, I.M. 91
Kilian, R. 101
King, D. 181
Kinsbourne, M. 140, 141, 149
Kirk, G.S. 179, 181
Kittles, R.A. 185
Klein, R.W. 55
Kloos, C. 51, 54, 88, 234
Knight, C. 183
Koch, K. 188
Kothar 20, 21, 34, 45, 108, 121, 126, 131, 196, 224
Kraus, H.-J.57, 59, 152-154, 162, 179, 186
Krzak, Z. 184
Kselman, J.S. 101
Kuhn, T. 184, 185
Kuiper, F.B.J. 30-32, 36, 37
Kuk 96, 101, 242
Kuper, A. 179

Lachish 144
Lack, R. 91
Ladon 226
Laish 231
Lambert, W.G. 226
Landy, F. 128
Lane, W.R. 101
Lang, A. 186
Langdon, S. 231
de Langhe, R. 113, 123, 233
Larkin, P. 189
Larner, J. 231
Lascaux 220
Laughlin, C.D. 140
Leach, E. 178
Lebanon 111, 149
Leibovitch, J. 34
Leonidas 165
Levi 62
Lévi-Strauss, C. 101, 145
Levine, B.A. 234
Lévy-Bruhl, L. 160, 176, 184
Lewis, T.H. 228
Lewy, H. 126
Lewy, I. 90, 91
Lewy, J. 1, 5, 78, 86, 89, 91
Lex, B. 137
Libya 231
Lindbeck, G.A. 182
Lipiński, E. 33, 89, 103, 119, 120, 122, 149, 233
Litan 22
Litani 226
Litanu 197
Littleton, C.S. 37
Lloyd, J.B. 147, 149
Lods, A. 5
Loehr, M. 5
Loewe, M. 150
Lonergan, B.J.F. 185
Loretz, O. 119, 123, 234
Lot 64, 247
Lucian 194, 207, 229
Luckmann, T. 52, 160, 182, 184, 186
Lug 187
Lust, J. 233
Luysten, R. 51, R.
Lyle, E. 125

Macdonald, J. 52
Macdonell, A.A. 37

Maclean, P.D. 140
Madden, P. 187
Magog 233
Mahanaim 74
Malamat, A. 125, 133, 147, 148
Mallowan, M.E.L. 215, 234, 235
Malul, M. 254
Mami Stela 103, 113, 120,
Manasseh 56
Manning, J.T. 136
Manoah 66
Manu 217, 236
Marais, E. 146
Marblestone, H.A. 231
Marc, O. 52
Marduk 19, 191
Margalit, B. 127, 147, 149, 187, 233, 254
Margulis, B. 234
Mari 147, 168, 169
May, H.G. 2, 5, 11, 90
Mayani, Z. 15
Mayer, W.R. 128
Mayes, A.D.H. 10
Mayrhofer, M. 121
Mazar, B. 5
McCrea, R.G. 254
McCurley, F.R., Jr 89
Mecca 227
Mediterranean sea 199
Meek, T.J. 5, 10, 91
Megiddo 144
Meier, S. 149
Memphis 34, 36, 104, 120, 121, 240, 243, 245
Merab 88
Mercury 187
Mesopotamia 236, 240
Meyer, E. 233
Michael 187
Michal 74
Michelet 167
Midian 9, 14, 15, 42, 82, 87, 91
Milkom 211
Milku 211, 212
Millard, A.R. 53
Miller, P.D. 119, 124
Mills, W.H. 182
Min 244
Minat el Beida 115
Minette de Tillesse, G. 58
Minos 207
Mithen, S. 185
Moab 74, 169, 247
Mol, H. 54, 56
Molech 211
Mondi, R. 231
Monier-Williams, M. 37
Montgomery, J.A. 51, 77, 89, 90, 229
de Moor, J.C. 34, 36, 53, 112, 120-23, 126-28, 148, 173, 182, 185, 188, 234
Moran, W.L. 104, 120
Morgenstern, J. 7, 11, 87, 91
Moriah 210
Moses 2, 6, 7, 38, 42, 62, 78, 82, 83, 86, 116, 122, 170, 214, 225, 227, 237
Mot 19-22, 24-28, 31, 32, 35, 37, 53, 99, 116, 224
Motzki, H. 90
Mowinckel, S. 152, 179
Mullen, H.P 120
Müllerus, C. 232
Munz, P. 181, 217, 235
Murray, R. 178
Mut 245

Naccache, A. 149
Nahar 35, 223
Nanu 111
Naples 192, 213
Nathan 88
Naunet 242, 243
Nebo 210
Nefertem 245
Negev 49, 73, 87
Neiman, D. 192-94, 228
Nephthys 241, 243
Niaux 220
Nicholson, E.W. 89
Niehr, H. 254
Nielsen, D. 33, 36
Nile 11, 33, 78, 133, 202, 240
Niqmaddu III-IV 212, 234
Noah 206, 207, 213-17, 219, 222, 223, 225, 232, 235, 237
Noegel, S. 194, 204, 207, 208, 213, 229, 231, 232, 234
Noth, M. 6, 9, 11, 15, 67, 90, 91, 186
Nougayrol, J. 119

Nu 193
Nun 242, 243
Nut 193, 241, 244
Nyberg, H.S. 85, 91
Nysa 107

Obbink, W. 89
O'Connor, M. 125, 133, 134, 149
Ocean 190-95, 201-204, 226, 228
Oceanus 226, 227
Oceanus and Tethis 201
Oden, R.A. 133, 148, 178, 179, 188
Odin 230
Oesterley, W.O.E. 5, 78, 89, 179
O'Flaherty, W.D. 29, 36, 37, 121, 240, 254
Og 194, 207, 208, 210-14, 234
Ogdoad 242
Ogygia 194, 197, 232
Ogygos 194, 207, 208, 214, 226, 232, 234
Oldenburg, U. 34, 91, 107, 121
del Olmo Lete, G. 34, 35, 52, 53, 120, 124, 126, 127, 149, 205, 228, 231, 234
Ophion 208
Ornstein, R. 137
Orontes 107, 121
Osiris 33, 45, 78, 86, 241, 243, 245
Ostborn, G. 72, 77, 88, 89
Otto 161
Otzen, B. 176, 178
Ovid 207

Page, H.R., Jr 169, 187
Palestine 39, 62, 69, 73, 79, 87, 88, 113, 208, 250,
Pape, W. 228
Pardee, D. 112, 122, 128, 149, 228, 234, 246, 254
Parker, S.B. 234
Parpola, S. 235
Patai 234
Paton, L.B. 89
Pausanias 232
Pedersen, J. 15, 52, 152, 179
Penfield, W. 137
Penglase, C. 231
Peniel 3
Perrot, N. 15
Perseus 106, 168, 237
Persia 175
Peter, R. 90
Petersen, A.R. 179
Petersen, D.L. 25, 32, 35, 36, 53
Peterson, H. 37
Pfeiffer, R.H. 78, 89
Philistines 61, 73, 74
Philo 20, 248
Phthia 207
Pindar 203
Pishon 192
Pitard, W.T. 53, 234
Pitman, W. 217-19, 221, 235
Plato 238
Plutarch 245
Pomponius Mela 231
Pope, M.H. 35, 91, 122, 148, 200, 228, 230, 234
Porten, B. 101
Porter, J.R. 64, 187
Pozzuoli 192, 213
Prajapati 239
Prometheus 207
Proudfoot, W. 161, 185
Pṛthivi 29
Pseudo-Callisthenes 231
Ptah 21, 34, 105, 193, 244, 245
Pugh, G.E. 137

Ra 19-21, 51, 81, 241, 245
von Rad, G. 5, 51, 65, 89, 154, 167, 181
Rahmay 169, 246
Rameses II 129
Ramsey, G.W. 89
Ranke 167
Rapiu 211-13
Rappoport, U. 101
Ras shamra 103, 114, 208
Rasmussen, T. 137
Ray, J. 229
Rechabites 47, 86, 87
Red Sea 38, 197-99, 204
Reed Sea 199
Rehoboam 75
Remus 86
Rendsberg, G.A. 228, 254
Rendtorff, R. 51, 59
Rennie, B.S. 188

Rephaim 207-209, 212-14
Reuel 87
Reymond, P. 200, 227, 230
Ribichini, S. 234
Richardson, M.E.J. 229
Ringgren, H. 179
Roberts, J.J.M. 120
Robertson, R.G. 123
Robinson, A. 121
Robinson, T.H. 5, 179
Rogerson, J.W. 180, 184, 186
Rome 175
Romulus 86
Rosén, H.B. 125, 134, 144, 149
Rowley, H.H. 179
Ryan, W. 217-19, 221, 235
Ryckmans, G. 36

Said, E.W. 179
Salecah 209
Salmon 210
Sama'l 132
Samaria 90
Samson 66
Sandys, J. 231
Sanmartín, J. 34, 120
Sante Domingo de Silos 187
Sapan 103
Saphon 51, 98, 102, 104, 105, 109, 114, 121, 122, 140-142, 144, 187, 210, 227
Sapunu 107-109, 111, 116, 117
Sargon 195, 237
Sasson, J.M. 78, 89
Saul 73, 74, 88
de Savignac, J. 119
Schaeffer, C.F.A. 79, 89, 90
Schäfer, P. 242, 254
Schick, K.D. 138
Schild, E. 11
Schleiermacher, F. 161, 185
Schliemann, H. 216
Schmidt, B.B. 234
Schoff, W.H. 231
Seidl, U. 228
Sekhmet 244, 245
Sennacherib 236
van Seters, J. 5, 9, 11, 60, 146
Seth 33, 44, 86, 103, 121, 133, 241
Sethe 101
Seti 129
Seti I 128, 146
Shabaka stone 36
Shabaqo stone 243, 244
Shahar 44, 132, 169
Shalem 44, 132, 169
Shapsh 19, 20, 34, 37, 51, 52, 81, 169, 246, 247
Sheba 74, 75
Shechem 62, 75, 144, 149, 210
Shephelah 205
Shu 241-44
Shuruppak 206, 231
Sihon 208, 211
Simeon 62
Sin 78, 79
Sinai 14, 48, 60, 78, 86, 116, 149, 170, 211, 234
Sirion 208
Siryon 111
Sisuthrus 206
Skinner, J. 5
Smith, M. 90
Smith, M.S. 11, 36, 88, 89, 120, 149, 178, 250, 255
Smith, P.J. 101
Smith, W. 145
Smith, W.R. 16
Smolar, L. 76, 88, 89
Snaith, N.H. 11, 51, 90, 199, 229
Socoth 73
von Soden,W. 226
van Soldt, W. 124
Solomon 74, 75, 88, 116, 142, 143, 198, 215, 254
Speiser, E.A. 227
Spence, L. 179
Spengler, O. 185
Spronk, K. 226
Staal, F. 52
Stadelmann, R. 120, 125, 144
Stalker, D.M.G. 6, 11
Stevenson, W.T. 148, 178, 181, 186
Stoneman, R. 231
Strabo 107, 121, 228
Strauss, D.F. 178
Strenski, I. 151, 163, 177
Stromboli 213

Stuhlmueller, C. 35, 51, 59
Styx 226
Suez Canal 38
Susa 195
Syria 78
Sznycer, M. 35, 89, 108, 122, 131

Ta-tenen 244
Tabor 113, 149, 210
Tahpanhes 120, 121
Talmon, S. 15, 47, 48, 53, 54
de Tarragon, J.-M. 234, 254
Tartaros 232
Tartarus 213, 232
Tartessos 232
Tartessus 208
Taylor, J.G. 142, 143, 150
Tefnut 241-44
Tehom 223
Teman 51, 142
Terrien, S. 51
Tethis 226, 227
Thebe 234
Thebes 108, 207, 208, 214, 244, 245
Thessaly 207
Thompson, T.L. 5, 11, 124, 146, 188
Thoth 187, 193, 242, 243, 245
Thrace 107
Thronos 110, 111
Ti'amat 19, 31, 50, 195, 226, 228, 230
Tishpak 168, 187, 191
Titan 107, 208, 214, 232
Tobin, V.A. 186, 188
Torcello 187
Toth, N. 138
Tournay, R. 15
Towers, J.R. 51
Trigger, B.G. 33
Tromp, N.J. 53, 94, 100, 212, 234
Tropper, J. 229
Troy 216
Tsumura, D.T. 52, 91, 101
Tucker, G.M. 5
Tur-Sinai, H. 35, 84, 85, 90
Tutankhamun 81
Tvaṣṭṛ 29
Typhaon 121
Typhaonion 108
Typhoeus 113, 121
Typhon 99, 101, 107, 108, 113, 121, 149
Tyrannike 108
Tyre 81, 119, 197

Ubar-Tutu 231
Ubara-Tutu 206
Uehlinger, C. 180
Ullendorf, E. 127
United States 186
Uroboros 231
Utnapishtim 206, 214-17

Vanir 36
Varuṇa 30, 31
de Vaux, R. 11, 59, 60, 87, 89, 91
te Velde, H. 33
Venus 44, 45
Vermeylen, J. 89
Vesuvius 213
Virgil 213
Virolleaud, C. 35, 233
Viṣṇu 106
Vita, J.P. 226
Vlaardingbroek, J. 233
Volcano 213
de Vries, S.J. 89
Vṛtra 29-31, 34, 37, 106, 107

Wakeman, M.K. 25, 36, 37, 228
Walcot, P. 121, 231
Ward, W.H. 15
Watson, W.G.E. 28, 33, 34, 36, 51, 52, 128, 147, 149, 229
Weber, M. 54
Weippert, M. 89, 91
Weiser, A. 120
Wenham, G.J. 101
Wensinck, A.J. 196, 223, 229, 230, 236, 237
West, M.L. 194, 196, 201, 226, 227, 229, 230, 231
Westendorf, W. 254
Westergaard, G.C. 138
Westermann, C. 101, 181
Wheeler, M. 90
Whitelam, K. 179, 226
Whitley, C.F. 58
Widengren, G. 15, 17, 152, 179
Wifall, W. 51
Wilkinson, R.H. 130

Winnett, F.V. 5
Wirgin, W. 17
Wolff, H.W. 66, 90, 178
Woodward, M. 25, 32, 35, 36, 53
Wright, G.E. 154, 180
Wright, G.R.H. 51, 146
Würthwein, E. 89
Wyatt, N. 15, 33-37, 51-53, 61-64, 88-91, 100, 101, 121-23, 128, 130, 141, 147-49, 178, 180-182, 185-88, 199, 227-30, 232-37, 254

Xella, P. 132, 182, 230, 234
Xisuthros 206, 207

Yadin, Y. 89
Yahiru 42
Yahweh 2, 6, 7
Yam 18, 21, 22, 24-29, 31, 32, 35, 45, 54, 72, 99, 106-108, 111-14, 116, 121, 122, 126, 131, 223, 224, 228, 233, 236, 237
Yam-Nahar 197
Yasibu 45
Yggdrasill 230
Yon, M. 115, 123

Zamora, J.A. 226
Zandee, J. 33, 254
Zatelli, I. 182
Zebulun 231
Zeus 99, 107, 113, 208
van Zijl, P.J. 123
Zion 104, 120, 121, 210, 211
Zipporah 62
Ziusudra 206, 207, 217, 231, 232